Beyond Separate Spheres

Beyond Separate Spheres

Intellectual Roots of Modern Feminism

ROSALIND ROSENBERG

Yale University Press   New Haven and London

Grateful acknowledgment is made to the following for granting permission to quote from materials in their possession: American Philosophical Society Library for the Franz Boas and Elsie Clews Parsons Papers; The Bancroft Library, University of California, Berkeley, for the Dane Coolidge and Robert Lowie Papers and for selections from Mary Roberts Coolidge, "How I Came to Write *Why Women Are So,*" "A Man's Job," "Facts for Young Men," and "The Social Value of Coeducation"; The Department of Special Collections, The University of Chicago Library, for the Marion Talbot, Presidents', and George Herbert Mead Papers; Stanford University Archives for the Clelia Duel Mosher Papers; Houghton Mifflin Company for reuse of parts of my article "The Academic Prism" in Carol Ruth Berkin and Mary Beth Norton, eds., *Women of America: A History* (1979); Franziska Boas for allowing me to cite from her reminiscences in the Columbia University Oral History Collection; The Schlesinger Library, Radcliffe College, for the Ethel Sturges Dummer Papers; Sterling Memorial Library, Yale University, for the James R. Angell and the Robert M. Yerkes Papers; The Columbia Oral History Collection for allowing me to cite from "The Reminiscences of Mrs. John D. Kennedy," copyright by The Trustees of Columbia University in the City of New York, 1975; *Feminist Studies* for reuse of parts of my article "The Search for Woman's Nature, 1850– 1930," vol. 3 (Fall 1975); and The Trustees of Columbia University for allowing me to cite from the Central University Files.

Published with assistance from the foundation established in memory of Philip Hamilton McMillan of the class of 1894, Yale College.

Designed by Nancy Ovedovitz and set in VIP Baskerville type.
Printed in the United States of America by Halliday Lithograph, West Hanover, Mass.

Library of Congress Cataloging in Publication Data

Rosenberg, Rosalind, 1946–
   Beyond separate spheres.

   Bibliography: p.
   Includes index.
   1. Feminism—United States—Philosophy.
2. Women social scientists—United States—Attitudes
—History.   3. Women college graduates—United
States—Attitudes—History.   I. Title.
HQ1410.R67 1982   305.4'2'0973   81–15967
ISBNs 0–300–02695–1   AACR2
      0–300–03092–4 (pbk.)

14   13   12   11   10   9   8   7   6   5   4

For Gerry, Clifford, and Nicholas

Contents

Illustrations

Acknowledgments

I am indebted to many individuals and institutions for their advice and assistance. Barton Bernstein and David Kennedy helped me define the topic of this study in its first incarnation as a doctoral dissertation, and they both worked tirelessly to help me clarify my ideas and improve my writing. Dorothy Ross, Linda Kerber, Barbara Harris, Loren Graham, Jack Garraty, and Peter Onuf gave me valuable suggestions about how to set my original interest in changing ideas about womanhood into a broader historical context. Thomas Haskell, David Hollinger, Carl Degler, Nancy Cott, Margaret Rossiter, Regina Morantz, Elizabeth Capelle, Susan Leon, William Leach, and Eric McKitrick read the entire manuscript, and each suggested important changes. Peter Hare saved me from several errors in chapter 6, as did Rhoda Metraux in chapter 8, and Walter Metzger improved my understanding of the educational changes discussed in chapter 2.

I have profited greatly from the friendship of several people in particular who talked to me about their work and shared with me their research. Barbara Solomon and Patricia Graham gave me a broader understanding of the history of women's education. Margaret Rossiter helped me see the women discussed here as part of the larger history of women scientists. Gina Morantz and Jim Reed were helpful throughout, giving encouragement and the benefit of their research in the histories of medicine and psychology. Elizabeth Capelle talked with me about most of the issues in this book, and her own work on Elsie Clews Parsons helped me to understand Parsons far better than I had.

Madeleine Rouxel gave me long periods of peace and quiet in which to work. Alison Hirsch and Rodrigo Sampere offered me valuable research assistance. And Miriam Levy, who typed my dissertation, continued to give me the benefit of her considerable editing skills as she typed the various versions of this manuscript. Chuck Grench far exceeded his duties as an editor in dispensing well-timed encouragement as well as firm criticism, and Barbara Folsom sharpened and clarified my prose as she copyedited the manuscript.

I am grateful to the Council for Research in the Social Sciences for financial assistance, which made my archival research possible; to the Columbia Center for the Social Sciences, where I discussed some of my work at a preliminary stage and where I benefited from the questions and comments of Jonathan Cole and Cynthia Epstein; and to the research staffs of the Stanford University Archives, the Bancroft Library, the University of Chicago Library, the American Philosophical Society Library, the Columbia University Library, and the New York Public Library, whose advice and assistance greatly enriched this study. I also want to thank Eleanor Woolley Fowler for sharing with me her memories of her mother, Helen Thompson Woolley.

My greatest debts, however, are to my family: to my husband, Gerry Rosenberg, for his domestic skills, his editorial judgment, and his steadfast support; and to my children, Clifford and Nicholas, for their cheerful independence.

Introduction

This book tells the story of those women who launched the modern study of sex differences. With the exception of the youngest, none of them was ever famous, and all are now forgotten. But their ideas have endured. Trained as social scientists in the new research universities of the late nineteenth and early twentieth centuries, these women formulated theories about intelligence, personality development, and sex roles that not only altered American thinking about the nature of women and men, but also affected the whole course of American social science.

I learned of these women indirectly, when research on the breakup of the woman's movement in the 1920s led me to *Equal Rights*, the journal of the National Woman's Party (NWP). The NWP intrigued me, as it does many feminists today, because of its uncompromising belief in sexual equality. At a time when most feminists believed in women's superior ethical insight and nurturant qualities, the NWP derided any reference to feminine distinctiveness, and in fact worried that such ideas would inhibit women's political advancement. The specific issue that most clearly divided the NWP from the rest of the woman's movement was protective labor legislation for women. To most feminists such legislation represented the natural culmination of women's long battle for political power. But to members of the NWP, any legislation that was limited to one sex violated the principle of equality for which all feminists should be fighting. They preferred having no protective labor legislation at all to having legislation for women only.

Many historians have lamented the internecine battles of the twenties that led to feminism's demise, and have chided the participants for their failure to compromise on the issue of protective legislation. But my own reading of the feminist debates of these years suggests that compromise was impossible. The disagreement over protective legislation was, at bottom, much more than a disagreement over political strategy; it was a disagreement over how women perceived themselves. To understand the breakup of feminism, I concluded, I would have to understand the fundamental shift that took place in the way women viewed themselves and their place in society.

Equal Rights itself did not explain this shifting view; it simply took sexual equality as a given and applied that conviction in political terms. But occasionally one of its articles would cite some psychologist or sociologist as an authority for rejecting conventional claims of female distinctiveness. As I read the works cited, I grew to know of the women studied here, a group of social scientists whose principal concern was not political strategy but, rather, the understanding of human nature. These scholars seemed important to me, not because of their political influence, which was slight, but because they epitomized the hope and the dilemma of the increasing number of women who went to college and joined the professions in the early twentieth century. Their writings revealed, as no article in *Equal Rights* did, how the very basis of women's understanding of themselves was changing. In studying their lives and work, one can see why the view of womanhood within which feminism first came of age could no longer accommodate the aspirations of a new generation of feminists.

The women studied here were caught between two worlds—the Victorian world of domesticity with its restrictive view of femininity, and the rapidly expanding commercial world of the late nineteenth and early twentieth centuries with its beckoning opportunities. Through much of the nineteenth century, restless women strained at the ideological bonds of domesticity, but until alternatives presented themselves, they could not break free. Higher education gave women their most important opportunity. With it came a dramatically altered perspective on the Victorian understanding of sex differences. A few women began to ask whether the biological differences between men and women were so great as commonly thought. But dissident women did not stop there. Once the seed of doubt was planted, it germinated in all directions. From questioning the extent of biological differences, women proceeded to challenge the universally accepted belief that men's and women's social roles were rooted in biology. Before they were through, they had challenged every tenet of the Victorian faith in sexual polarity—from the doctrine that women are by nature emotional and passive, to the dogma that men are by nature rational and assertive. Their insistence that the vast majority of observable sex differences could be traced to cultural conditioning violated Victorian science's bedrock belief in the primacy of biology over culture. But that insistence has become a fundamental assumption of modern social science, affecting the American understanding not just of sex but of human nature in general.

The story begins in Boston in the 1870s with Marion Talbot, one of the few girls at the college preparatory Chauncey Hall School. In the early seventies Talbot's mother was among those women who were trying to persuade Harvard to open its doors to women students. Emily Talbot and her friends met with unyielding resistance, expecially from Harvard overseer and former medical school professor Dr. Edward Clarke, who warned that college would destroy women's health and reproductive ability.

The idea that woman's mind was limited by her body was as old as antiquity. But at no time was that idea ever more fervently held or more highly elaborated than it was in America after the Civil War. In those years many, perhaps most, Americans feared that changes taking place in the traditional division of sex roles posed a serious threat to a social fabric already weakened by war. Rapid commercial expansion was luring farmers' daughters to work outside the home. Female benevolent societies were introducing middle-class women to urban squalor. A woman's movement, spawned by abolitionism, was urging women to demand greater autonomy. And, most alarming to male educational leaders, the need for women teachers was now spurring a movement to open higher education to females. Because the home no longer defined the limits of female activity and women were joining the men in the outside world, however marginally, many Americans believed that the need to draw a clear line between appropriately male and female activities had become acute.

No one drew that line more clearly than Dr. Clarke, whose views embodied Victorian America's increasingly restrictive conception of women's nature and capacity. Clarke accepted the Spencerian idea that the human body forms a closed-energy system in which any undue demand put on one part of the system inevitably depletes some other part, and he used that idea to prove that the mental strain of college would adversely affect the development of a young woman's reproductive organs. Clarke also accepted Herbert Spencer's idea that with higher civilization came increasing specialization, and that the divergence of male and female roles exemplified this civilized specialization in the realm of sex. The specificity with which Clarke described women's natural limits, and the scientific authority with which he supported that description, presented serious obstacles to feminists seeking wider opportunities. No one could easily dismiss arguments so deeply rooted in the principal intellectual assumptions of the day. And no woman in the 1870s or 1880s rejected the doctor's argument out of hand. But Clarke's very emphasis upon specificity provided women with an opportunity they had not had before, when claims of female inferiority had been the unconscious products of popular prejudice. Clarke's claims, at least, could be tested—and women did test them.

Though concerned by Clarke's dire warnings, Marion Talbot finished the Chauncey Hall School. Unable to go on to Harvard, she attended Boston University, and after graduation she organized a survey of female college graduates to determine what effect college had in fact had on their health. The survey did not challenge the fundamental hereditarian and evolutionary assumptions that informed Clarke's charges, but it did question Clarke's conclusion that college would destroy female health. The survey demonstrated that the excess energy thought to be necessary for the mental activity of college did not seem to have depleted the energy needed for the normal development of women's reproductive system. College women were just as fertile as their noncollege-educated sisters. With the publication of this survey, early college-educated feminists began to turn science to women's advantage.

The story of the attack on Victorian conceptions of femininity might have ended there. Feminists were an isolated group in those years; their resources and training were too limited to enable them to carry on extensive social scientific research. Furthermore, strategic considerations encouraged most feminists to believe in women's superior ethical insight and nurturant abilities. The difficulties of maintaining a political movement in the face of vigorous opposition put a premium on stressing the special qualities that united the participants. The woman's movement helped open higher education to women, and until 1920 it provided an important source of inspiration for those who criticized conventional attitudes; but after 1890 political feminism and the feminism of the women featured in this book diverged, and the seeds were sown for the fatal battles of the 1920s.

By the turn of the century the critical study of woman's nature had moved to the new research universities. Thwarted at the door of the established men's colleges, women enjoyed greater success in winning admission to the rapidly expanding universities at the end of the nineteenth century. In half a dozen schools across the country, women comprised fully half the student enrollment by 1900, a fact that rekindled the bitter debates of the 1870s over women's proper place in American higher education. Many faculty members objected to the influx of female students and resurrected Dr. Clarke's old arguments in support of their position. But other, usually younger, faculty members supported the new women students and actively encouraged them when they began to challenge Victorian assumptions about woman's nature. Marion Talbot, who became dean of women and assistant professor of sociology at the University of Chicago when it opened in 1892, fought relentlessly for the right of women students to an equal education, and it is no accident that so much of the research on sex differences took place at Chicago while she was there. But Talbot's support was not enough. It took encouragement from male faculty members for social science research on sex differences to thrive.

Three factors, in particular, prompted some of the younger men to offer this encouragement. First of all, men like John Dewey, James Rowland Angell, George Herbert Mead, and Henry Hollingworth, who worked with and encouraged women students, had all been educated at coeducational colleges and universities and were already used to working with women in an academic setting. Furthermore, they were all married to college-educated women and saw no conflict between womanhood and higher education.

Second, these men all found Victorian prescriptions for masculinity personally offensive. Reared in the years between the Civil War and the end of the nineteenth century, they rejected the rugged, aggressive individualism that was so important an ingredient of Victorian manhood, blaming it for the waste, the pollution, and the human cost of America's capitalistic expansion. The growing complexity and interdependence of modern society made the possibility of individual self-sufficiency seem increasingly less possible. They were drawn, instead, to the ideals of cooperation and social concern then thought to be particularly congenial to the female temperament. In another epoch such poor socialization as these men displayed would have resulted in nothing more than personal unhappiness, but the emergence in the late nineteenth century of the modern university enabled them to confer with similarly disenchanted women on reasonably frank terms. In this novel institutional setting, these would-be misfits found it possible to reconsider the theoretical significance of their peculiar view of themselves and their society.

Third, these men were part of a major transformation in American intellectual life at the end of the nineteenth and the beginning of the twentieth centuries, which stressed skepticism and scientific rigor in the face of the abstract theorizing of the nineteenth century. In economics Thorstein Veblen was debunking the laws of classical economics; in law Oliver Wendell Holmes, Jr., was deriding the orthodox faith in eternal legal verities; and in psychology John Dewey was questioning the mechanical conception of mental activity. In each of these fields and throughout American social thought, scholars faulted traditional theory for failing to explain social realities. Seeking to find workable solutions to the complex social problems produced by their industrializing society, they insisted on rooting the study of human nature and social structure in empirical investigations of the social conditions of the time.

Contrary to the conventional view of social development as the inevitable unfolding of either natural or ideological forces, these intellectual pioneers saw it as the unpredictable product of adaptive individuals interacting with a shaping society. They dismissed the Spencerian's use of the organic analogy, with its assumption that social change mirrors biological growth. They believed, instead, that humans could reform their society; and they assumed that, as women entered universities in large numbers, both the universities and society would change. What they could not see, in the beginning, was that women's entering the universities would alter not just social science's understanding of society but also its understanding of human nature.

These men were environmentalists to the extent that they believed, for instance, that poverty was more a function of social and economic conditions than of moral depravity. But they assumed that biology set fairly strict limits on how much the environment could modify individual differences. Nature, they believed, not nurture, exerted the controlling force in defining individuals—in distinguishing civilized man from primitive man, intelligent man from feebleminded man, and, especially, man from woman. In fact, sex differences seemed, at first, to be the subject least amenable to environmental analysis. Did not males and females, even when reared in identical environments, develop very different mental abilities, personality traits, and social functions? This was the question, more than any other, that preoccupied women graduate students in the social sciences who first undertook the study of sex differences.

That study took place at a variety of research centers across the country, but most intensively at the University of Chicago and Columbia University, which had the largest female enrollments in the social sciences and granted the bulk of the Ph.D.s after 1900. At these schools, in particular, women students' unique perspective on Victorian assumptions about womanhood combined with the skepticism of the infant fields of psychology, sociology, and anthropology to form a new understanding of sex differences. The effort to forge this new understanding began in psychology with Chicago graduate student Helen Thompson, whose pioneering intelligence tests of Chicago undergraduates demonstrated that men students differed only slightly, and in no consistent way, from women students. A few years later, at Columbia, psychology graduate student Leta Hollingworth tested the effect of menstruation on women's mental performance and investigated the Darwinian assumption that men are more variable in intellectual ability than women. Her conclusions confirmed Thompson's contention that the difference between male and female mental abilities had been grossly exaggerated. By World War I, Thompson and Hollingworth had persuaded leaders of the early mental testing movement that sex should be dropped as a separate category in testing individuals' intelligence. They had also raised serious doubts in some testers' minds about the legitimacy of other categories, such as race.

Of course, using college undergraduates as subjects in these early experiments loaded the experimental deck. The men, and especially the women, differed markedly from their contemporaries outside academe. To some social scientists, however, this fact made Thompson's and Hollingworth's findings all the more important. If a common educational experience could produce such surprising uniformity in intellectual performance, could other differences between the sexes be attributed to differences in women's and men's social histories? Between 1900 and 1920 a growing number of social scientists, including John Dewey, George Herbert Mead, W. I. Thomas, Henry Hollingworth, and Franz Boas, to name a few, concluded that the answer must be yes.

Sociologist W. I. Thomas responded most dramatically to the early psychological work on sex differences. In 1896 he wrote a doctoral thesis in which he insisted on the physiological basis of *all* sex differences. Within a decade he was citing Helen Thompson to support his revised view that, insofar as women differed from men in intelligence and temperament, they did so, not because of their peculiar physiology, but because society sheltered women from the "wide experience in life" necessary for independence and full intellectual development. Whereas Thomas began his career believing that the individual, with his or her physiological needs and drives, shapes society, his work with students like Thompson persuaded him that society must shape the individual. In no other way could he explain the amazing malleability of women when exposed to academic life.

Chicago graduate student Jessie Taft carried the idea of society's formation of the individual even further. Working under the supervision of George Herbert Mead, Taft wrote a philosophy dissertation in 1913 explaining the woman's movement as a consequence of women being forced to live in two worlds: the world of women, of esthetics, of nurturance; and, as a consequence of their increasing education, in the world of men, of rationalism, of personal achievement. Parents made women of their female children without even realizing they were doing so, by reacting approvingly to behavior that fit socially accepted feminine norms and disapprovingly to behavior that did not. But parents were never wholly successful in their goal of socialization. For even if women lived primarily in a subculture of women, they could readily observe the dominant culture of men, especially if they studied or worked in that culture.

In trying to conform to both worlds, women "found conflicts so serious and apparently irreconcilable that satisfactory adjustment was often quite impossible." But women were coming to believe, Taft argued, that precisely because they felt those conflicts some adjustment must be made. While many reformers of her generation sought to avoid conflict, Taft thought that conflict was essential to real social progress. Educated women in particular, she believed, who more than any other group were immersed in the separate cultures of femininity and masculinity, were uniquely suited to transcend the conflicts of their time, "to comprehend the conditions, the unsatisfied, conflicting impulses, upon the harmonization and fulfillment of which any solution that has the right to the name must be based." A decade later, sociologists at Chicago would be talking about the "marginal man," the black, the Jew, or other social outsider who lived in two cultures and who was impelled by that conflict in his situation to try to transcend it. No one ever mentioned that the "marginal man" began as a woman.

The woman social scientist who went furthest in challenging her culture's view of sex differences was sociologist/anthropologist Elsie Clews Parsons. After leaving her position in sociology at Barnard in 1906 to follow her husband to Washington, D.C., when he was elected to Congress, Parsons became an amateur anthropologist and commentator on the sexual mores of American culture. In her many books on women and the family, she challenged the widespread belief that Western society had reached a pinnacle of social development. The protocol of Washington society, Parsons declared, was in no significant way different from the rituals of primitive cultures. Men might think that Western civilization's technological accomplishments provided ample proof of its cultural superiority. But women could see, with the special clarity born of their social subordination, the primitive side of this civilized culture. A decade later, when American anthropologists became cultural relativists, Parsons's point gained wider currency.

Women social scientists broke with most aspects of Victorian theory about sex differences with little difficulty. For most of those differences represented liabilities for women within the academic world, and researchers like Thompson, Hollingworth, Taft, and Parsons wanted to demonstrate women's capacity to contribute equally with men to modern science. One aspect of womanhood that they found very difficult to question, however, was sexuality. For women intellectuals sex was a disturbing issue. It reminded them of their reproductive side—the side that was used so often to bar their intellectual progress. Yet early women social scientists had such boundless faith in the power of science to improve society that they did not fear to inquire into sex. Knowledge was always to be preferred to ignorance. Especially given the discoveries in the area of venereal disease at the turn of the century, women wanted to control sexuality; to do so they had to study it.

As those who lived a generation later in the shadow of Heisenberg's "uncertainty principle" could have anticipated, however, studying sexuality inevitably altered it. Sociologist Mary Roberts Coolidge and physician Clelia Mosher devoted two decades to studying sex. In the beginning they accepted the Victorian belief in sexual polarity. By the end they concluded that the blurring of gender lines would lead to better marriages. Their studies revealed that a whole range of sexual activities were far more common than the Victorians had thought, and that the sexual inhibitions felt by most women harmed their marriages. When society no longer viewed women's sexual function as their "only really useful contribution," Coolidge argued, women would be able to accept sexuality more easily. When society no longer exerted so much pressure on men to dominate their social and economic surroundings, men would lose some of their fascination with displays of sexual prowess, including both sexual abstinence and sexual athleticism.

This book is an investigation of the ideas developed by women in their study of sex differences. But it is also a story, along the way, of the lives of these exceptional women, of the frustration felt by those whose work was celebrated in graduate school but who could find no academic position in which to carry on their research; of the regret felt by those for whom sexual expression and intellectual achievement proved irreconcilable; and of the strain felt by those who clung to an image of themselves as committed reformers even while they were trying to prove themselves as objective, detached scientists. It is a story, in many ways, of failure—of women restricted by simple prejudice to the periphery of academe, who never had access to the professorial chairs of the major universities, who never commanded the funds to direct large-scale research, who never trained the graduate students who might have spread their influence, and who, by the 1920s, no longer had the galvanizing support of a woman's movement to give political effect to their ideas.

But these early women researchers were not without influence. If they themselves did not achieve fame, many of the men with whom they worked did. Mentors and colleagues like W. I. Thomas in sociology, Robert Lowie in anthropology, and John Dewey in psychology—among others—acknowledged the influence of one or another of the women discussed here. Not that the ideas expressed in the early dissident writing on sex differences lived on only in the writings of sympathetic men. Without question, the most important link between this first generation of researchers and contemporary social scientists interested in sex differences was a woman, Margaret Mead, whose early work is discussed in my concluding chapter.

The daughter of social scientists trained at the University of Chicago when work on sex differences was just beginning, Mead popularized the ideas of her parents' dissident contemporaries through her books and articles on primitive peoples. Journeying to the South Pacific, she found men and women whose attitudes, behavior, and social roles differed in every conceivable way from what someone brought up in Western society expected of men and women. This variety persuaded her that "many, if not all, of the personality traits which we have called masculine or feminine are as lightly linked to sex as are the clothing, the manners and the form of head-dress that a society at a given period assigns to either sex." Mead's claim, and the claim of her parents' generation of dissidents, that culture is the dominant force which determines personality and sexual roles, by no means commands universal acceptance today. But it has gathered such momentum that its effects may be detected not only in contemporary thinking about sex but also in modern reflections on human nature in general.

As early as the 1920s, the ideas growing out of the work discussed here appealed more strongly to the new generation of women than did the feminist ideology of the suffrage era. The university in its early period of rapid growth created possibilities for women and altered women's expectations in important ways—ways that broadened freedom for women, especially in giving them a more open-ended sense of their own capacities. But at the same time, the new university's scientific credo eroded the social ties that had formerly bound women together and given them a shared sense of purpose. No longer believing that they were uniquely moral, women trained in the scientific skepticism and relativism of the university rejected organized reform (whether on behalf of protective labor legislation for women or of the Equal Rights Amendment) as at best quixotic and at worst subversive of the dispassionate search for truth. Without a political base, their vision of a social order free from sexual polarization enjoyed only a limited and increasingly embattled acceptance. Not until the 1960s, when the civil rights and antiwar movements gave new legitimacy to politics among young scholars and the expansion of the universities opened the way to a new influx of women, did the insights of the pioneers discussed here achieve a social impact commensurate with their intellectual importance.

1 *In the Shadow of Dr. Clarke*

The friends who gathered at Boston's South Station on September 19, 1892, believed that Marion Talbot was making a serious mistake in moving to Chicago. A city swamped by a burgeoning immigrant population and dominated by corrupt politicians, Chicago had none of the genteel refinement that characterized Beacon Hill. The unfinished towers of the new university, where Talbot had been offered a position as dean, rose eerily from the mudflats south of the city, embodying the uncertain and tentative nature of both the frontier city and its newest educational enterprise. Financed by John D. Rockefeller and billed as a major research center, the "gas trust" university was just the sort of venture Bostonians might expect from the West, both grandiose and scornful of tradition. Grandiosity and scorn might suit the builder of an oil-refining empire, but they did not become an academic institution. As Talbot boarded the train for the journey westward, one concerned friend pressed a small carved box into her hand. "It contains," the friend whispered solemnly, "a piece of Plymouth Rock."[1]

Whereas Chicago's frontier quality horrified most Bostonians, it appealed to Talbot's pioneer spirit. One of the few young women her age to have attended college, she had cut herself off from the social life of her peers. "No 'Junior League' or 'Sewing Circle' or 'Vincent Club' of those days wanted as a member a young woman whose aims were so different from their own and whose time was absorbed by what seemed to them a hopeless tangle of tormenting questions whose solution got one nowhere socially when it was all over." Talbot's roots reached deep into New England soil through both her mother's and her father's families, and she grew up in an atmosphere of comfort and security, but at thirty-four she was an alien in her native community, having overstepped the conven-

1. Marion Talbot, *More Than Lore* (Chicago: University of Chicago Press, 1936), pp. 6 – 7.

tional bounds of feminine delicacy and refinement. To her, Chicago promised an escape from the restrictive conception of feminine capacity and purpose that had plagued her youth.[2]

The Crucible of New England Reform

The eldest of six children, Marion Talbot grew up in the years following the Civil War among the reform-minded intellectuals of Boston—the Howes, the Alcotts, the Higginsons, the Phillips, the Blackwells, and the Garrisons—men and women struggling to salvage their antebellum faith in radical individualism and human perfectibility in the face of the social dislocation created by war, industrialization, and immigration.[3]

Her father, Dr. Israel Talbot, was a graduate of Harvard and a homeopath, one of those irregulars who harassed the medical establishment of his day by denouncing the heroic purging and bloodletting so popular among orthodox physicians and by championing instead the curative power of nature. Homeopathy enjoyed wide popularity among Boston reformers, especially the women, because of its support of dress reform, temperance, and gymnastics, as well as its acknowledgment of women's nurturant talents. Lack of funds and the anti-institutional bias of the antebellum years made homeopaths slow to establish schools, but the medical problems produced by rapid urbanization persuaded them of the need for a more scientific and better organized attack on disease than informal training allowed. From the early days of his practice Talbot played a leading role in organizing doctors, and he became the first dean of Boston University's coeducational medical school when it opened its doors in 1873.[4]

Emily Talbot shared her husband's enthusiasm for health reform and helped him in his organizing activities, but her own experiences focused her attention on the issue of women's education. Reared in the Jacksonian era, when rapid commercial expansion absorbed scarce capital, leaving

2. Marion Talbot and Lois Rosenberry, *The History of the American Association of University Women, 1881–1931* (Boston: Houghton Mifflin Co., 1931), p. 405.

3. Richard J. Storr, "Marion Talbot," in Edward T. James, ed., *Notable American Women, 1607–1950*, 3 vols. (Cambridge, Mass.: Harvard University Press, Belknap Press, 1971), 3:423–24.

4. Unpublished biography of Israel Talbot in Boston University Medical School Archives, Boston, Mass.; *Dictionary of American Biography*, s.v. "Israel Tisdale Talbot"; Joseph Kett, *The Formation of the American Medical Profession: The Role of Institutions, 1780–1860* (New Haven: Yale University Press, 1968), pp. 132–55; William G. Rothstein, *American Physicians in the Nineteenth Century: From Sects to Science* (Baltimore: Johns Hopkins University Press, 1972), pp. 230–48, 278; Mary Roth Walsh, *"Doctors Wanted: No Women Need Apply": Sexual Barriers in the Medical Profession, 1835–1975* (New Haven: Yale University Press, 1977), p. 195.

communities with scant funds for schools and a limited supply of male teachers, she joined the growing number of young schoolmarms who struggled to keep order in unruly schools and to impart what little learning they had acquired from their own common school attendance. Frustrated by the reluctance of her students and the limits of her own schooling, Talbot wanted her daughters to have a richer intellectual life than she had had.[5]

Unfortunately, the same economic forces that offered women like Emily Talbot an opening wedge to the world of learning created enormous obstacles to further widening that wedge. The tremendous speed of commercial development in the antebellum period was eroding the provincial isolation of American communities and undermining the power of class, genealogy, and tradition to determine social position. Though most Americans applauded the decline of these traditional forms of social organization, they clung to sexual classification as the last remaining insurance against social disorder. Tied to the home as wives and mothers, women found themselves further bound by the anxiety born of rapid economic and social change. This anxiety set strict limits to the educational opportunities women could hope to achieve.[6]

Mid-century Boston provided its sons with the finest college and preparatory schooling available, but it restricted its daughters to those schools catering to boys with more modest educational ambitions. The private female academies that served the daughters of the affluent were little better. As Margaret Fuller complained of these schools, girls "run over superficially even more studies [than boys] without being really taught anything." Academy students studied sewing, literature, history, geography, and the Bible, but they were not expected to tackle such difficult subjects as Greek, Latin, or mathematics.[7]

For those who looked on women as pious guardians of the hearth and the young, the schooling available to Boston's girls seemed adequate, but Emily Talbot's teaching experience, combined with her exposure to Bos-

---

5. *Dictionary of American Biography*, s.v. "Emily Talbot"; Richard M. Bernard and Maris A. Vinovskis, "Beyond Catherine Beecher: Female Education in the Antebellum Period," *Signs* 3 (Summer 1978): 868.

6. *Dictionary of American Biography*, s.v. "Emily Talbot"; Nancy Cott, *The Bonds of Womanhood: "Woman's Sphere" in New England, 1780–1835* (New Haven: Yale University Press, 1977), pp. 98 and 101–25. See also John Higham, *From Boundlessness to Consolidation: The Transformation of American Culture, 1848–1860* (Ann Arbor; Mich.: William Clements Library, 1969), pp. 5–15.

7. Ann Douglas, *The Feminization of American Culture* (New York: Knopf, 1977), pp. 58–59; Kathryn Kish Sklar, *Catherine Beecher: A Study in American Domesticity* (New Haven: Yale University Press, 1973), pp. 59–77; Mary F. Eastman, "The Education of Woman in the Eastern States," in Annie Nathan Meyer, ed., *Woman's Work in America* (New York: Holt, 1891), p. 27.

ton's scientifically minded reform community, dimmed her faith in the power of piety and superficial study to provide either personal fulfillment or social improvement. In the increasingly interdependent society of industrial America, where depressions brought suffering to all regardless of personal merit, she believed that women could no longer rely on their roles as wives and mothers to cushion the harsh realities of commercial growth; nor did she think that they could depend on the casual schooling provided for young girls if they expected their daughters to deal with the complex social problems of an industrializing society.[8]

Convinced that higher education provided the key to both female fulfillment and social reform, Emily Talbot joined with other Boston women to agitate for greater educational opportunities for her daughters. With proper education, she believed, women would be able to do more than teach the young and comfort the sick and poor; they would be able to discover the social laws that would enable them to remedy the ills of industrialization. For reformers like Israel and Emily Talbot, the disillusionment created by industrialization's attendant social ills bridged the gap between the female world of piety and the masculine world of commerce and established the basis for a new partnership. To them higher education provided a necessary foundation for merging women's nurturant qualities with men's scientific talents. Only through such a merger, they believed, could the modern reformer hope to restructure society along more cooperative and harmonious lines.[9]

After the Civil War the growing demand for women teachers and the dissatisfaction with the superficiality of most schooling for young women prompted a movement to provide them with more sophisticated training. In 1865 Vassar opened, promising its students an education as rigorous as that given in the men's colleges, and other women's colleges threatened to follow. The Talbots, and especially Emily, played an active role in this educational campaign, which in Boston led to the demand that Harvard admit women. No act could have mobilized more effectively those who feared the masculinization of women and the abolition of sexual spheres than did this assault on Harvard's doors. Efforts to give a more precise definition to sex differences, which had been advanced sporadically for

8. For an interesting discussion of the tension inherent in the Puritan conception of womanhood, see Phillida Bunkle, "Sentimental Womanhood and Domestic Education, 1830– 1870," *History of Education Quarterly* 14 (Spring 1974): 13– 48.

9. For the origins of the social sciences in America, see Thomas L. Haskell, *The Emergence of Professional Social Science: The American Social Science Association and the Nineteenth Century Crisis of Authority* (Urbana: University of Illinois Press, 1977), pp. 24– 47 and passim, and Mary O. Furner, *Advocacy and Objectivity: A Crisis in the Professionalization of American Social Science, 1865 – 1905* (Lexington: The University Press of Kentucky, 1975), pp. 1– 34 and passim.

many years, suddenly crystallized into a clear exposition of women's physical limitations.[10]

Edward Clarke's Warning

In 1872 Emily Talbot's close friend Julia Ward Howe invited Dr. Edward Clarke, a member of Harvard's Board of Overseers and a former member of its medical faculty, to speak before the New England Woman's Club of Boston on the subject of higher education for women. Boston women considered Clarke a friend. Three years earlier he had denounced male medical students in Philadelphia for driving their female classmates out of the classroom with tobacco quids and tinfoil. Women, he stated, had "the same right to every function and opportunity which our planet offers that a man has." If women were capable of training themselves to be physicians, they should be permitted to do so. What Clarke did not stress at the time but made clear in his address to the Boston Woman's Club was that he did not believe women had the capacity to succeed in medicine in particular or in higher education in general. To the consternation of his listeners, he warned of the grave danger that higher education posed for the female sex. Women's unique physiology, he explained, limited their educational capacity. To expose them to the rigorous intellectual exercise of a Harvard education would seriously threaten their future reproductive capacity. The discussion that followed Clarke's talk was heated. Woman's Club members were accustomed to impassioned defenses of the sanctity of the all-male educational environment, but they were not prepared for so systematic a critique of women's innate aptitude for education. A little surprised by the hostility with which his women listeners responded to his talk, Clarke decided to explain his position more fully in a book entitled *Sex in Education; or, a Fair Chance for the Girls*.[11]

Clarke was not the first doctor to assert that women's unique physiology limited her social role. The conviction that women's subordinate position was biologically ordained had roots in antiquity, and it was a commonplace in nineteenth-century medical discussion to note that the womb exerted a supremely powerful force from which men were free. As one

10. For the history of the movement to open higher education to women, see Mabel Newcomer, *A Century of Higher Education for Women* (New York: Harper, 1959), pp. 5–51, and Thomas Woody, *A History of Women's Education in the United States*, 2 vols. (New York: Science Press, 1929), 2: 136–223.

11. Clarke's defense of women medical students against tobacco-quid throwing is discussed in Mary Roth Walsh, "*Doctors Wanted: No Women Need Apply*," pp. 120–21. *The Woman's Journal*, of which Julia Ward Howe was an editor, reported the Clarke speech on December 21, 1872, and covered the ensuing debate in the months that followed. See May 17, 1873, for a report of the debate over women's education at a meeting of the American Social Science Association, in which Emily Talbot was active.

physician explained, it was as though the "Almighty, in creating the female sex, had taken the uterus and built a woman around it."[12]

The womb, doctors emphasized, dominated a woman's mental as well as physical life, producing a weak, submissive, uncreative, emotional, intuitive, and generally inferior personalilty. "Think of that great power," exclaimed Professor Charles Meigs to his gynecological students at Jefferson Medical College in 1847, "and ask your own judgments whether such an organ can be of little influence on the constitution and how much."[13]

Most physicians acknowledged the womb's disturbing power, but before the middle of the nineteenth century they credited the uterus with only limited control over women's lives, assuming that personal and divine will exercise at least as much influence over physical and mental health. Early nineteenth-century medical authorities urged pregnant women to think sweet thoughts and adopt a pious manner to insure that they would remain healthy and that their unborn children would develop well. By the latter half of the century, however, doctors were minimizing the power of free will to affect physical development. Conscious desire, they concluded, could have little influence over innate biological conditions in preserving maternal health or in creating healthy children. This significant change in thinking, shifting medical and hereditarian responsibility from human and divine actors to impersonal and largely uncontrollable biological forces, reflected the growing appreciation among doctors, as well as all intellectuals, of how remote could be the determinants of individual behavior. At the same time, this growing emphasis on the power of biology revealed anxiety over the increasing instability of sex roles. As the volatile nature of commercial expansion provided opportunities for women that threatened the traditional concept of sexual segregation, careless assemblages of prejudice, casual references to women's spiritual qualities, and vague remarks about the womb's great influence no longer served to delineate sexual responsibilities.[14]

By the time Clarke wrote *Sex in Education* and its sequel, *The Building of a Brain,* the work of natural and physical scientists provided a necessary foundation to any medical argument, and Clarke had resolutely consulted the scientific writings of Charles Darwin, Herbert Spencer, Alexander Bain, Henry Maudsley, and Hermann von Helmholtz in an effort to

12. Quoted in Carrol Smith-Rosenberg and Charles Rosenberg, "The Female Animal: Medical and Biological Views of Women," in Charles Rosenberg, *No Other Gods: On Science and American Social Thought* (Baltimore: The Johns Hopkins University Press, 1976), p. 56.

13. Charles D. Meigs, *Lecture on Some of the Distinctive Characteristics of the Female. Delivered before the Class of the Jefferson Medical College, January 5, 1847* (Philadelphia: Collins, 1847), p. 18.

14. Charles Rosenberg, "The Bitter Fruit: Heredity, Disease, and Social Thought," in his *No Other Gods,* p. 39.

identify women's unique nature. Underscoring the importance of biology in defining social roles, he noted:

> The problem of woman's sphere, to use the modern phrase, is not to be solved by applying to it abstract principles of right and wrong. Its solution must be obtained from physiology, not from ethics or metaphysics. . . . Without denying the self-evident proposition, that whatever a woman can do, she has a right to do, the question arises, What can she do?

Though Clark bowed to the feminist convictions of those who campaigned for higher education for women, conceding that "Man is not superior to woman, nor woman to man," he added, "By this it is not intended to say that the sexes are the same. They are different, widely different from each other."[15]

Charles Darwin had just given renewed authority to this ancient belief in the *Descent of Man* (1871), where he provided a portrait of growing sexual divergence as an integral part of the evolutionary process. Males, endowed with a higher metabolic rate than females, had a greater tendency to vary, he argued. They grew stronger and more intelligent because they faced the forces of natural selection with a greater wealth of attributes than females could produce. Motherhood compounded the female's metabolic disadvantage by forcing her into dependence on the male. Standing at one remove from the full force of natural selection, she was in small part immune from its progressive tendencies. Over generations of natural selection, the female gradually fell behind the male.[16]

Elaborating on Darwin's theory of divergence, Clarke warned that to subject women to an education developed for men would expose them to mental stimulus that their relatively undeveloped brains could not tolerate. "The organs whose normal growth and evolution lead up to the brain are not the same in men and women," Clarke explained, "consequently their brains, though alike in microscopic structure, have infused in them different though excellent qualities." As Clarke's contemporary,

15. Edward Clarke, *Sex in Education; or, A Fair Chance for the Girls* (Boston: Osgood and Co., 1873), pp. 12–13.

16. Charles Darwin, *The Descent of Man and Selection in Relation to Sex*, 2 vols. (London: John Murray, 1871), 1:278–79, 2:368–75, 1:111, 1:273–74, 2:326–27. See also Conway Zirkle, "The Knowledge of Heredity before 1900," in L. C. Dunn, ed., *Genetics in the Twentieth Century* (New York: Macmillan, 1951), pp. 35–57. Darwin was ambivalent about Lamarckianism, and emphasized it more heavily in the 1870s than he had in the first edition of *The Origin of Species* (1859). See Loren Eiseley, *Darwin's Century: Evolution and the Men Who Discovered It* (1958; reprint ed., New York: Doubleday, Anchor Books, 1961), p. 131. Though Darwin is better known for his belief that characteristics could be acquired spontaneously through what is now called mutation, he also believed that characteristics could be acquired through the body's interaction with the environment. See Charles Darwin, "Inheritance," *Popular Science Monthly* 19 (September 1881): 663–65.

neurologist George Beard, observed, since civilized women had evolved to the point at which she "uses her brain but little and in trivial matters, and her muscles scarcely at all," it was not surprising that "the brain of woman is about one tenth less in weight than that of man; and the amount of brain work of the more severe kind, is incomparably less than that which man performs." Women were therefore less able to meet the demands of intellectual exertion. "Why," asked another physician, "should we spoil a good mother by making an ordinary grammarian?"[17]

For several decades phrenologists and physical anthropologists had been systematically measuring facial angles, cranial capacities, and brain weights to demonstrate just how widely the mental capacity of the sexes differed. The more civilized the skulls and brains, the more marked was the sexual difference they discovered. Alexander Bain, on whose work Clarke relied, reported in his book *Mind and Body* that the average European brain weighed 49½ ounces while the average female brain weighed only 44 ounces.[18]

The steady divergence of brain weight resulted, scientists believed, from the process of evolution described by Darwin. Through variation, natural selection, and environmental stimulus, the brain had evolved from a simple organ producing instinctive, involuntary, automatic, reflex behavior to a more complicated organ capable of complex reasoning and voluntary action. In a fully developed human brain highly organized mental channels had evolved which permitted abstract reasoning and a high sense of justice while inhibiting instinctive reactions. What eighteenth-century philosophers had attributed to advanced culture, Darwin attributed to cranial capacity.

Darwin postulated a hierarchy of mental functions ranging in descending order from reason, to imagination, to intuition, to emotion, and finally down to instinct. The more highly evolved male brain performed most efficiently at the higher range of mental functions, while the simpler female brain was adapted to the lower range. "It is generally admitted," Darwin reported, "that with women the powers of intuition, of rapid perception, and perhaps of imitation are more strongly marked than in

17. Edward Clarke, *The Building of a Brain* (Boston: Osgood and Co., 1874), p. 20; George Beard, *Eating and Drinking, A Popular Manual of Food and Diet in Health and Disease* (New York: G. P. Putnam, 1871), p. 103; T. S. Clouston, "Woman from a Medical Point of View," *Popular Science Monthly* 24 (December 1883):224.

18. Alexander Bain, *Mind and Body: The Theories of Their Relation* (London: King and Co., 1873), pp. 19–20; J. W. Redfield, "Measures of Mental Capacity," *Popular Science Monthly* 5 (May 1874): 72–76. For excellent reviews of the anthropometric literature, see John Haller and Robin Haller, *The Physician and Sexuality in Victorian America* (Urbana: University of Illinois Press, 1974), pp. 48–61, and Elizabeth Fee, "Science and the 'Woman Question,' 1860–1920: A Study of English Scientific Periodicals" (Ph.D. diss., Princeton University, 1978), pp. 71–102.

man." Having a simpler brain, women had sharper reflexes, were more irritable, and experienced greater difficulty than did men in inhibiting instinctive reactions.[19]

Anthropometry, in league with Darwinian theory, confirmed popular doubts about feminine intelligence. Woman's place on the evolutionary scale was anchored on the one side by her inferior brain weight, which prevented her from achieving intellectual equality with men, and on the other side by her stronger instincts and greater emotionality, which demonstrated her affinity for lower forms of life. The female, even more than the male, proved that "there is no fundamental difference between men and the higher mammals in their mental faculties." Having been sheltered from the cultural stimulus that had developed the male mentality, woman remained closer to the animal form. Far from regretting the mental divergence of the sexes, Clarke applauded it as a sign of civilization. "Differentiation is Nature's method of ascent. We should cultivate the difference of the sexes, not try to hide or abolish it."[20]

To impede sexual divergence by educating women in the same way as men would not only threaten progress and impose an undue strain on women's minds, it would do irreparable damage to women's bodies, Clarke believed. Doctors had often asserted that any affliction of the uterus could affect a woman's mental attitude, but with the aid of recent work in physics, neurophysiology, and technology, Clarke explicitly linked the physiological demands of an academic education to the reproductive impairment of the nation's future mothers. The work of Hermann von Helmholtz in thermodynamics and Herbert Spencer in sociology suggested that all physical systems, including the body, were subject to the principle of conservation of energy, and that force expended in one function would not be available to any other. Quoting Spencer, Clarke noted with alarm "that antagonism between body and brain which we see in those, who, pushing brain activity to an extreme, enfeeble their bodies." In the female the finite amount of energy available had to be carefully husbanded for her nutritive purpose.[21]

19. Darwin, *The Descent of Man,* 1:35– 38, 2:326– 29. The American neurologist John Hughlings Jackson described the hierarchy of mental functions in "The Evolution and Dissolution of the Nervous System," *Popular Science Monthly* 25 (June 1884): 171– 80. For further background on nineteenth-century ideas about the brain and how it functioned, see Robert M. Young, *Mind, Brain, and Adaption in the Nineteenth Century* (Oxford: Clarendon Press, 1970), pp. 101– 223.

20. Darwin, *The Descent of Man,* 1:35– 36; Clarke, *The Building of a Brain,* p. 53. For further amplification of the argument that women remain closer to the animal form, see the work of one of America's foremost zoologists, William K. Brooks, "The Condition of Women from a Zoological Point of View," *Popular Science Monthly* 15 (June 1879): 145– 55, 347– 56.

21. Clarke, *Sex in Education,* p. 133; Herbert Spencer, *The Study of Sociology* (New York: Appleton, 1874), pp. 315, 373– 83. See also Richard Hofstadter, *Social Darwinism in Ameri-*

"The system," Clarke explained, "never does two things well at the same time. The muscles and the brain cannot functionate in the best way at the same moment." To subject a girl at puberty to the intellectual demands traditionally placed on boys of that age was to court physiological disaster. "A girl upon whom Nature, for a limited period and for a definite purpose, imposes so great a physiological task, will not have as much power left for the tasks of school, as the boy of whom Nature requires less at the corresponding epoch." Those women who ignored this basic fact of physiology risked nervous collapse and sterility.[22]

To illustrate the dangers of female education Clarke discussed the cases of seven young women whose health had been wrecked by strenuous brain work. Miss D——, for example, entered Vassar College at the age of fourteen and left four years later an invalid. Through relentless study and physical exercise, even during menstruation when she should have taken particular care to rest, "the stream of vital and constructive force evolved within her was turned steadily to the brain, and away from the ovaries and their accessories." Ignoring the danger sign of painful menstruation, Miss D—— persisted in her strenuous study until her breasts and reproductive organs ceased to develop. By the time she was referred to Dr. Clarke, she had become "neuralgic and hysterical." To avoid the fate of Miss D—— and others like her, Clarke advised, young women should study one-third less than young men and not at all during menstruation.[23]

Clarke was not alone among doctors in urging rest. The prominent gynecologist Thomas A. Emmet went even further.

> To reach the highest point of physical development the young girl in the better classes of society should pass the year before puberty and some two years afterwards free from all exciting influences. She should be kept a child as long as possible, and made to associate with children. . . . Her mind should be occupied by a very moderate amount of study, with frequent intervals of a few moments each, passed when possible in the recumbent position, until her system becomes accustomed to the new order of life.

Neurologist S. Weir Mitchell put patients to bed for months at a time to

---

can Thought (1944; reprint ed., New York: Beacon Press, 1955), pp. 31–50; Elizabeth Fee, "The Sexual Politics of Victorian Anthropology," Feminist Studies 1 (Winter–Spring 1973): 23–39, and "Science and the Woman Problem: Historical Perspectives," in Michael S. Teitelbaum, ed., Sex Differences: Social and Biological Perspectives (New York: Anchor Press, 1976), pp. 175–223.

22. Clarke, Sex in Education, pp. 40, 54. Given Clarke's interest in the relationship of education to female health, it is perhaps worth noting that Clarke had to drop out of Harvard in his junior year due to "an attack of hemorrhage from the lungs." This same weak health hindered his studies for a number of years thereafter. See National Cyclopedia of American Biography, s.v. "Edward Hammond Clarke," 8: 213.

23. Clarke, Sex in Education, pp. 79–84.

cure what he believed to be uterine-based emotional disorders. Like Clarke, Mitchell condemned those who would subject young women to an educational regimen intended for men. Study during puberty inevitably brings injury to young women, he maintained, for "during these years, they are undergoing such organic development as renders them remarkably sensitive."[24]

Given women's special mental and physical qualities, Clarke charged that the campaign to open higher education to women could only have a destructive effect on American society. As the pressure of education destroyed the reproductive capacity of female students, the native American middle class would fail to reproduce itself and would soon be outnumbered by uneducated and fecund immigrants. Boston's rapidly growing and fertile Irish population was already generating widespread alarm that the political and social dominance of native Americans might soon be ended. Within two generations, Clarke predicted, "the wives who are to be mothers in our republic must be drawn from trans-Atlantic homes."[25]

Added to the threat of race suicide was the danger that schooling would undermine the separation of male and female spheres by masculinizing female students. To make of women lesser men, educators risked no less than the destruction of society's most essential stabilizing force, sexual division. Quoting the English physician Henry Maudsley, Clarke wrote:

> While woman preserves her sex, she will necessarily be feebler than man, and, having her special bodily and mental characters, will have, to a certain extent, her own sphere of activity; where she has become thoroughly masculine in nature, or hermaphrodite in mind,—when, in fact, she has pretty well divested herself of her sex,—then she may take his ground, and do his work, but she will have lost her feminine attractions, and probably also her chief feminine functions.

Having raised the specters of race suicide and masculinization, Clarke concluded, the "identical education of the two sexes is a crime before God

---

24. Thomas Emmet, *Principles and Practices of Gynaecology* (Philadelphia: Lea, 1879), p. 21; S. Weir Mitchell, quoted in Clarke, *Sex in Education*, p. 111. See also S. Weir Mitchell, *Lectures on Diseases of the Nervous System* (London: Churchhill, 1881), pp. 217–33, for a description of his rest cure, and Nathan Hale, *Freud and The Americans: The Beginnings of Psychoanalysis in the United States, 1876–1917* (New York: Oxford, 1971), pp. 47–70, for a discussion of female nervousness in the late nineteenth century. Not all male doctors assumed that females inevitably suffered a physiological crisis at puberty. See, for example, Ely Van de Warker, "The Genesis of Woman," *Popular Science Monthly* 5 (July 1874): 269–81.

25. Clarke, *Sex in Education*, p. 63. For an analysis of the nascent fear of race suicide, see James B. Reed, *From Private Vice to Public Virtue: The Birth Control Movement and American Society since 1830* (New York: Basic Books, 1978), pp. 197–203.

and humanity that physiology protests against and that experience weeps over."[26]

The Feminist Response

When she first read Clarke's dire warning in 1873, Marion Talbot was a fifteen-year-old student at the predominantly male Chauncey Hall School. With the Boston Latin School closed to girls and female academies unequipped to prepare their students in the classics, the Talbots decided to send Marion to Chauncey Hall simply because of its willingness, albeit reluctant, to include a few girls each year among the boys it was preparing for Harvard. Fifty-two years later Talbot still remembered her concern over Clarke's charge that "physiology protests against" the higher education of women. As her friend M. Carey Thomas recalled, "We did not know when we began whether women's health could stand the strain of education. We were haunted in those days by the clanging chains of that gloomy specter, Dr. Edward Clarke's *Sex in Education*." At the University of Michigan where women had been studying for only three years, it was reported that everyone was reading Clarke's book and that two hundred copies had been sold in one day. At the University of Wisconsin where women had studied since the Civil War but opposition to coeducation remained intense, the regents of the University explained in 1877 that "Every physiologist is well aware that at stated times, nature makes a great demand upon the energies of early womanhood. . . . It is better that the future matrons of the state should be without university training than that it should be produced at the fearful expense of ruined health." One can well imagine that Clarke's description of female students plagued with "dysmenorrhea, chronic and acute ovaritis, prolapsus uteri, hysteria, neuralgia, and the like" must have shaken even the most resolute of adolescent girls.[27]

Reading *Sex in Education* upset young Marion, but it did not dissuade

26. Clarke, *Sex in Education*, pp. 114–15, 127. See also Henry Maudsley, "Sex in Mind and in Education," *Popular Science Monthly* 5 (June 1874): 198–215. For a further review of the scientific literature opposing women's education, see Janice Trecker, "Sex, Science, and Education," *American Quarterly* 26 (October 1974): 352–66; and Flavia Alaya, "Victorian Science and the 'Genius' of Woman," *Journal of the History of Ideas* 38 (April–June 1977): 261–80.

27. Marion Talbot, "The Challenge of a Retrospect," *University Record* (Chicago) 11 (April 1925): 87; M. Carey Thomas, "Present Tendencies in Women's College and University Education," *Educational Review* 24 (1908): 68, quoted in an excellent discussion of the debate over Clarke's book in Mary Roth Walsh, *"Doctors Wanted: No Women Need Apply,"* pp. 119–32; Dorothy Gies McGuigan, *A Dangerous Experiment: One Hundred Years of Women at the University of Michigan* (Ann Arbor: University of Michigan Press, 1970), p. 56; Smith-Rosenberg and Rosenberg, "The Female Animal," p. 61; Clarke, *Sex in Education*, p. 23.

her from preparing for college at Chauncey Hall. Her mother had accustomed her to uncompromising educational demands for too many years for her to turn back now. From earliest childhood she had been expected to spend part of each day writing, even if she was away from home, and her work was subjected to strict editing. One letter home, written when she was only seven, prompted the following correction. "You say, 'I take my pen in hand to write.' Now that was a waste of time and strength," her mother scolded, "because of course I knew, without your telling me that you had your pen in hand, else how could you write?" Emily Talbot was no less thorough about her daughter's education in feminism. Marion read the *Woman's Journal* religiously and was writing letters to the editor when she was only twelve. The outcry from *Woman's Journal* readers against Dr. Clarke's book must have helped reassure her that her parents were not the only people who thought that a rigorous education was appropriate for girls.[28]

In the *Woman's Journal* and elsewhere proponents of higher education for women denounced Clarke's book as a polemic, which rested on scant and, in at least one case, faulty evidence. Graduates of Vassar and of several western colleges testified to their own good health; Julia Ward Howe charged that the stress of constant partying far exceeded the stress of study; and yet, Clarke's critics took his book seriously. Products of the same industrializing society, influenced by the same scientific trends, bred in the same culture of sexual segregation, proponents of higher education for women subscribed to the same evolutionary, hereditarian, and anthropometric theories that shaped Clarke's views. "I expected to find premises from which I should dissent," wrote the feminist Caroline Dall in her critique of Clarke, "but, with the exception of that upon which the book is based [that higher education would destroy female health] I did not find any." Those who supported women's education assumed, with Clarke, that evolution had produced a profound divergence in the physical and mental characteristics of the sexes and that women were weaker both physically and intellectually than men, but they maintained that women's special qualities justified their higher education and that their constitutions were sufficiently hardy to withstand the rigors of intellectual exercise.[29]

28. Emily Talbot to "My dear little daughter," July 9, 1865, Marion Talbot Papers, University of Chicago Archives; Marion Talbot to *Woman's Journal,* February 28, 1871, Talbot Papers.

29. A number of articles critical of Clarke were collected in Julia Ward Howe, ed., *Sex and Education: A Reply to Dr. Clarke's "Sex in Education"* (Cambridge, Mass.: Roberts Bros., 1874): see especially the comments of Howe, pp. 1 – 31; Thomas Wentworth Higginson on Clarke's misuse of evidence, pp. 35 – 40; reports of good health from Vassar, Antioch, Michigan, Lombard, and Oberlin, pp. 191 – 203; and Dall's comments, pp. 87 – 108. See also Anna C. Brackett, *The Education of American Girls* (New York: n.p., 1874), passim, and Eliza Bisbee

Darwinism has often been described as an ideology in defense of the status quo. To those like Clarke, who feared the social disruption posed by changing socioeconomic conditions and by the nascent woman's movement, Darwinism offered a defense of existing institutions and roles. But Darwinism provided reassurance as well to the feminist advocates of social change at the end of the nineteenth century, providing an anchor of certainty in a time of social flux—an anchor that could protect them not only from critics' hostility but, just as importantly, from their own uncertainty. Paradoxically, Darwinism provided the biological affirmation of female uniqueness that antifeminists needed to oppose change and that feminists relied on to defuse the threat of change.[30]

For a generation Darwinism proved to be all things to all people, principally because neither feminists nor antifeminists were yet willing to challenge the ancient belief in feminine uniqueness. Indeed, this uniqueness was so much at the core of the idea of American womanhood that liberation could only be conceived in terms of it. Those who sought to expand woman's role did so while defending the traditional conception of her nature. They debated where the division between sex roles should be made, but not whether there should be a division in the first place.[31]

There were a few feminists, like Elizabeth Cady Stanton, who could scoff at the idea of female separateness and rely on philosophical principle alone in supporting women's desire for personal autonomy and a fulfilling social role. In drafting the "Declaration of Sentiments" at the 1848 women's rights convention at Seneca Falls, New York, Stanton paraphrased the Declaration of Independence line for line and appealed to the Enlightenment belief in the psychical unity of mankind as a justification for abolishing discrimination against women. Reason was the same in all people, she believed, and equally possessed by all. The inequality that existed between the sexes in American society could only

Duffey, *No Sex in Education: Or, An Equal Chance for Both Girls and Boys* (Philadelphia: Stoddart and Co., 1874), passim.

30. Hofstadter, *Social Darwinism in America,* pp. 31–50. For another perspective on Darwinism and American concern for social order, see Robert C. Bannister, *Social Darwinism: Science and Myth in Anglo-American Social Thought* (Philadelphia: Temple University Press, 1979), pp. 3–13. For a more extended discussion of Darwinism's importance to feminist theorists, see Rosalind Rosenberg, "In Search of Woman's Nature, 1850–1920," *Feminist Studies* 3 (Fall 1975): 140–46. Many historians see greater opposition than I do between the views of woman's nature held by physicians like Clarke and feminists who supported higher education for women. See, for example, Ann Douglas Wood, " 'The Fashionable Diseases': Women's Complaints and Their Treatment in Nineteenth-Century America," in Mary Hartman and Lois Banner, eds., *Clio's Consciousness Raised* (New York: Harper & Row, 1974), pp. 1–22.

31. Jill Conway, "Stereotypes of Femininity in a Theory of Sexual Evolution," in Martha Vicinus, ed., *Suffer and Be Still: Women in the Victorian Age* (Bloomington: Indiana University Press, 1973), pp. 140–54.

have resulted from the willful perversion of natural law. Stanton conceded that the organs of procreation distinguished women from men, but in a day when the belief in the mind's independence from the body was still widely accepted, it was possible to argue that intellectual activity was not correlated with sexual organs.[32]

Stanton was a maverick, however, even among early feminists, an Enlightenment figure in a post-Enlightenment age. By the 1870s intellectual and social changes made Stanton's natural rights rhetoric appear even more dated that it had in the 1840s. To ignore the growing tendency to see humanity as an integral part of nature, and the mind as inextricably linked to the body, was to absent oneself from the main currents of intellectual debate. After the work of Darwin and Spencer and all of the natural and physical scientists on whom they relied, few felt that they could challenge women's domestic confinement without using the language of evolution.[33]

Women doctors, in particular, who struggled in mid-century for recognition from the orthodox, and increasingly scientific, medical establishment, often took special pains to acknowledge the contributions of Darwin and Spencer, fully conscious as they did so that they were reinforcing the popular belief in sexual polarity. Frances Emily White, professor of physiology at Woman's Medical College of Philadelphia, called attention to the implications of evolution for understanding women's nature in an 1875 issue of the *Popular Science Monthly*. In Darwin's *Descent of Man*, she observed, "we have gathered an accumulation of facts from vast fields of observation by many of the foremost naturalists of the age; and his deductive interpretations of these facts seem to have been accepted by a majority of the leading naturalists and physicists of the day. Such being the case, we are warranted in making this work the basis of our inquiry [into women's nature]." White readily conceded that evolution had led to sexual divergence. Men's struggle for existence as hunters and warriors had resulted in the "development of more robust intellects," she reported, while women's subjection "to the discipline of family life" had produced qualities of "tenderness and love . . . and devotional sentiment." White admitted that when men and women had struggled for existence in barbarous times, and animal courage had been highly prized, women's position had been "naturally a subordinate one," but she insisted that

32. Aileen Kraditor, *The Ideas of the Woman Suffrage Movement, 1890 – 1920* (1965; reprint ed., New York: Anchor, 1971), pp. 1 – 2, 38 – 43; Ellen Carol DuBois, *Feminism and Suffrage: The Emergence of an Independent Women's Movement in America, 1848 – 1869* (Ithaca, N.Y.: Cornell University Press, 1978), pp. 31 – 52.

33. The shifting arguments about the mind's relation to the body are discussed in George W. Stocking, Jr., *Race, Culture, and Evolution: Essays in the History of Anthropology* (New York: Macmillan, Free Press, 1968), pp. 112 – 32.

sexual divergence did not dictate female subordination under modern social conditions. With advancing civilization, "those qualities regarded as preeminently feminine, have risen in common estimation, and mere muscular superiority, and even intellectual power, are now put to the test of comparison with the higher moral qualities. Further civilization would depend, she concluded, in contrast to antifeminists like Clarke, on the further development of women's moral qualities.[34]

Antoinette Brown Blackwell, an early graduate of Oberlin, a minister, and an abolitionist, as well as a student of Spencer and Darwin's work, agreed with White that women held the key to society's continued progress. Condemning *Sex in Education* in the *Woman's Journal*, she argued that mental strength was not simply a function of cranial capacity or brain weight, as so many phrenologists and anthropologists insisted, but rather a product of the body's entire nervous system. "How incredibly singular, blind and perverse, then is the dogmatism which has insisted that man's larger brain, measured by inches in the cranium, must necessarily prove his mental superiority to Woman," Blackwell fumed. "First let Dr. Brown-Sequard or some other learned professor of the rapidly growing science of the nervous system, demonstrate the significance of the unique feminine plexus of nerves in the mammary glands, as related to the emotional, intuitional, and moral nature of womanhood." Woman were not inferior creatures, Blackwell insisted; their mental strength simply lay in different areas. "Women's thoughts are impelled by their feelings. Hence the sharp sightedness, the direct insight, the quick perceptions. Hence also their warmer prejudices and more unbalanced judgments, and their infrequent use of the masculine methods of ratiocination." To deny women the same educational opportunities afforded men risked disrupting society's natural balance by encouraging the development of men's cold calculation without also developing women's penetrating insight.[35]

34. Frances Emily White, "Woman's Place in Nature," *Popular Science Monthly* 6 (January 1875): 293, 295, 297, 300–01; Alfreda Worthington, "Frances Emily White," in Howard A. Kelley and Walter L. Burrage, eds., *Dictionary of American Medical Biography* (Boston: Milford House, 1928), p. 1290. My understanding of women physicians has been greatly influenced by conversations with Regina Morantz. See her articles, "The Lady and Her Physician," in Hartman and Banner, eds., *Clio's Consciousness Raised*, pp. 38–53, and (with Sue Zschoche) "Professionalism, Feminism, and Gender Roles: A Comparative Study of Nineteenth-Century Medical Therapeutics," *Journal of American History* 67 (December 1980): 568–88.

35. Antoinette Brown Blackwell, "Sex and Work," *Woman's Journal*, April 18, 1874; Blackwell, *The Sexes throughout Nature* (New York: Putnam 1875), pp. 131–32. Blackwell's preoccupation with Darwinism is revealed in her unpublished autobiography, "Antoinette Brown Blackwell, the First Woman Minister, as told to Mrs. Claude U. Gilson," 1909, Blackwell Family Papers, The Schlesinger Library, Radcliffe College, Cambridge, Mass.

Clarke's critics insisted that the theory of evolutionary divergence supported the value of higher education for women rather than negated it, but they took seriously his Spencerian warning that energy was finite and must be carefully husbanded to insure women's proper reproductive development. Vassar prohibited its students from participating in physical exercise during the first two days of their menstrual periods and attempted to regulate the study of each student so that "the end of no day shall find her overtaxed, even if that day has borne the added periodic burden." The physician Mary Putnam Jacobi sought to relax the concern over the energy issue by suggesting that because girls underwent less muscular development than boys, they matured earlier and had energy to spare during adolescence for the development of both their nervous and their reproductive systems. Even Jacobi, however, conceded that women did not have the energy to maintain by themselves the "robust, massive intellectual enterprises, which, in the highest places, are now carried on by masculine strength and energy." She urged the training of women doctors not because their strength and intelligence equaled men's but because

> the special capacities of women as a class for dealing with sick persons are so great, that in virtue of them alone hundreds have succeeded in medical practice, though most insufficiently endowed with intellectual or educational qualifications. When these are added, when the tact, acuteness, and sympathetic insight natural to women become properly infused with the strength more often found among men, success may be said to be assured.[36]

Accepting the evolutionists' belief in sexual divergence and the uniqueness of men and women's psychology as an accurate reflection of social conditions in industrial America, feminists condemned women's domestic confinement as a dangerous restriction of feminine influence. It was men, and not women, feminists believed, who threatened the natural harmony of sexual divergence by restricting female education and who risked social upheaval by encouraging the unbridled expression of male aggression, individualism, rationalism, and competition. But while feminists argued that women's energy, though limited, was nevertheless equal to the demands of both reproductive development and higher education, they could do no more in the 1870s than match Clarke's anecdotes of invalidism with anecdotes of blooming good health. No one could prove what effect college education would have on women until significant numbers of women defied prejudice by attending college and the results of their daring were known.

36. Howe, *Sex and Education,* pp. 192 – 94; Mary Putnam Jacobi, *The Question of Rest during Menstruation* (New York: Putnam, 1876), pp. 168– 69; Jacobi, "Women in Medicine," in Meyer, ed., *Woman's Work in America,* p. 177.

Marion Talbot (1892)

The Association of Collegiate Alumnae

In 1881, newly graduated from Boston University, Marion Talbot felt the isolation and alienation so common among early women graduates. Fired by her mother's intellectual fervor, she had breached the accepted limits of feminine refinement in gaining a college education only to find that there were "few ways outside the home in which such equipment might to advantage be utilized." Driven by the burning sense of social obligation that was the secularized remnant of her Puritan heritage, Marion Talbot longed to justify her struggle and to discover a calling.[37]

Since the Civil War a number of western state universities had begun accepting women students and several women's colleges had opened in the East, but the number of women graduates remained few and the opportunities available to them were limited almost exclusively to teaching. Emily Talbot encouraged her daughter to try to organize these

37. Talbot and Rosenberry, *History of the American Association of University Women*, p. 17.

women into an association that would provide them all with a new sense of feminine community and that would create opportunities commensurate with their education and social commitment. She envisioned the organization of "increasing numbers of young women with similar training and congenial tastes, drawn together in a great body for the advancement of human folk." Contacting college alumnae throughout the country, the Talbots created the Association of Collegiate Alumnae (ACA) and dedicated it to the twofold purpose of offering encouragement to young women wanting to go to college and expanding the opportunities for women graduates.[38]

Offering encouragement meant first, and most importantly, doing battle with Dr. Clarke. As Marion Talbot later recalled,

> The obstacles which the young women who composed the first group of members of the A.CA. had met in their insistence upon a college education had been many, but none was more serious than the opinion prevalent well-nigh universally, that young women could not, except at a price physically not worth while, undergo the intellectual strain which their brothers seemed to find no strain at all.

In an effort to prove that the "regular life and engrossing interest of college work tended to give greater rather than less physical vigor," the women of the association resolved to canvas their membership and to question them about their health. Throughout the 1870s the debate over women's nature had oscillated between metaphysical speculations and anecdotal claims. The ACA's attempt to examine empirically Clarke's claim of feminine frailty represented the most important development in the discussion of women's nature in ten years.[39]

Emily Talbot had been introduced to the reform possibilities of statistics in her work as secretary of the education department of the American Social Science Association (ASSA), and she helped pattern the study of alumnae health on earlier ASSA surveys. The ASSA was formed in Boston in 1865 by reformers disillusioned by the obvious failure of moral exhortation to remedy the social ills of industrialization. In an era that honored science as the preeminent source of wisdom and progress, they dedicated themselves to the discovery of scientific solutions to the problems of poverty, crime, and vice. Like most intellectuals, members of the ASSA believed in evolution, but they objected to Herbert Spencer's bleakly deterministic view of it. They were, on the whole, in greater sympathy with the idealist tradition in nineteenth-century thought than

38. Ibid., pp. 8 – 9; Woody, *A History of Women's Education in the United States*, 2:179– 92, 239 – 52.
39. Talbot and Rosenberry, p. 116.

with the positivistic tradition. To them science was an instrument of reform, and human beings were its creative agents.[40]

Empiricism is more often the tool of the positivist than the idealist, and it can lead to conservative conclusions as easily as reformist ones, but at a time of rapid social change the disjunction between popular assumption and fact can be large, as it was in the 1870s and 1880s when women started defying convention in large numbers by going to college. Under these conditions the empirical approach championed by the ASSA served as an important foundation for reform.

The personal experience of each of the early members of the ACA convinced them that physiology could be transcended, and they wanted to prove it. With the help of a group of doctors and teachers, they composed a questionnaire, which they sent to the 1,290 graduates belonging to the association in 1882. Carroll Wright, a friend of the Talbots, president of the ASSA, and chief of the Massachusetts Bureau of Statistics of Labor, offered to analyze the 705 returns and publish the results. He found that 78 percent of the respondents enjoyed good health, 5 percent were in fair health, and 17 percent suffered from bad health.[41]

Very little statistical work had been done by the mid-eighties that would allow the ACA to evaluate the significance of its findings. Mary Putnam Jacobi's 1877 study of menstruation, covering 286 women in the general population, reported that 56 percent of them claimed good health. The Massachusetts Bureau of Labor Statistics study of 1,032 "working girls of Boston" done in 1884 reported that 92.2 percent enjoyed good health upon commencing work, but that only 76.2 percent reported good health at the time of the investigation. The limited information available seemed to indicate that college was as healthy a place as any for young women. In fact, while 19.58 percent of the alumnae respondents complained of a deterioration in their health while in college, 21.13 percent reported improvement, possibly due to the emphasis placed on physical education at some colleges.[42]

40. Furner, *Advocacy and Objectivity*, pp. 14 – 16; Haskell, *The Emergence of Professional Social Science*, p. 142.

41. Annie Howes, *Health Statistics of Women College Graduates: Report of a Special Committee of the Association of Collegiate Alumnae* (Boston: Massachusetts Bureau of Statistics of Labor, 1885), p. 9; Talbot and Rosenberry, pp. 116 – 24.

42. Figures from Jacobi, *The Question of Rest*, and from the Massachusetts Bureau of Labor Statistics study of "Working Girls of Boston," are quoted with data from the ACA health survey in Howes, *Health Statistics of Women College Graduates*, p. 10. See also Dr. Edward Hitchcock, "Athletic Education," *Journal of Social Science* 20 (June 1885): 27 – 44, for a report on male student health at Amherst College, where Hitchcock found 25 percent of the students lacking in good health; and Louis Marvel, "How Does College Life Affect the Health of Women?" *Education* 3 (1883): 501, in which Marvel reports that mortality rates for women are lower than those for college men.

On the whole, the alumnae statisticians were relieved, but they could not deny that a significant number of college women suffered from poor health and well over half of them reported some physiological disorder. The respondents attributed their health problems to a variety of factors, including overwork, poor sanitary conditions, and physical accidents, but the ACA research group focused particularly on the reports of "constitutional weakness" and "emotional strain" in explaining the existence of poor health.[43]

Alumnae complained of "constitutional weakness" twice as often as they complained of any other factor when asked to explain poor health. Demonstrating how deeply ingrained were the hereditarian assumptions of the 1880s, even among the most fervent environmentalists, the authors of the ACA report argued that women owed their constitutional weakness to the uneducated "older New England dames," whose lives had been spent "with very limited knowledge of the many laws of sanitary science which guard our own" and who had passed poor physiques down to their descendents. The study implied that when women learned the laws of sanitary science, when they reformed their dress and their diets as well as their surroundings, they would raise daughters with sounder constitutions whose daughters, in turn, would profit genetically from their physiological improvement.[44]

Added to the burden of their defective physiological heritage, women complained of emotional strain, which the ACA attributed to the pious culture that absorbed so much of the leisure time of middle-class women. The influence of Puritanism, with its "introspective, self-accusing spirit," its "morbid sense of justice," and the "worriment and consequent dissatisfaction with life it produces," created a drain of "much vital energy" and produced "more than one-half of those nervous diseases to which American Women are specially prone." Where the cloistering of students at the women's colleges reinforced this highly emotional attitude, complaints of strain outnumbered similar complaints from coeducational schools by about one-third. The ACA report agreed with Dr. Edward Clarke that college women suffered ill health and nervous disorders, though not to the extent that he claimed and not from the effects of study. It was not women's nature that limited female students, but rather the ignorance of their antecedents and the inhibiting force of cultural expectations.[45]

43. Howes, *Health Statistics of Women College Graduates*, pp. 6– 8.

44. Ibid., p. 6.

45. Ibid., pp. 6– 8. For further evidence of the emotionally intense atmosphere of women's colleges in particular, see Nancy Sahli, "Changing Patterns of Sexuality and Female Interaction in Late Nineteenth-Century America" (paper delivered at the Third Berkshire Conference on Women's History, Bryn Mawr, Pa., June 11, 1976), passim. Concern over the danger posed to young women by excessive emotional excitement pervaded the Victorian

Published by the Massachusetts Bureau of Statistics of Labor in 1885, the "Health Statistics of Women College Graduates" reached few readers; but the following year a young instructor in philosophy at the University of Michigan, John Dewey, brought the report to a far wider audience when he reviewed its findings at length in the *Popular Science Monthly*. For two reasons Dewey was predisposed in favor of the ACA's study. First, he was a friend and admirer of William Torrey Harris, Emily Talbot's immediate superior in the ASSA's education department and the country's foremost proponent of philosophical idealism. Dewey shared with Harris the belief that science was an essential instrument of reform and that men and women were its guiding agents. Second, Dewey was engaged to Alice Chipman, a Michigan graduate and a member of the ACA.

Dewey began his review by praising the ACA report for finally rescuing the discussion of women's health and education "from the *a priori* realm of theory on the one hand, and the haphazard estimate of the college instructor on the other." But he faulted the study for its vagueness in defining good health and the conditions producing it, as well as for focusing the study so narrowly on the question of health.

> The number of hours studied should be given, instead of the vague terms "moderate", etc. Instead of indefinite inquiries as to whether the student went into society much or little, exact inquiries into the various modes of spending the hours of social recreation should be made. These and many similar points, which would suggest themselves at once, may be considered trivial; but, if we accept the general conclusion of the report that the pursuit of collegiate education is not in itself harmful, the importance of studying the entire environment, physical and social of the young student at once appears.[46]

Though Dewey did not condemn the higher education of women, he implied that college undermined women's ability to serve as wives and mothers. He reported with alarm that only 26 percent of the ACA respondents had married and that, of these, only 63 percent had borne any children. Among the children born, 12 percent had died, and 25 percent of these deaths were associated with childbirth. Dewey made no mention of Clarke's warning that education would inevitably impair women's

---

medical literature. See, for instance, Mary T. Bissell, M.D., "Emotions vs. Health in Women," *Popular Science Monthly* 32 (February 1888): 504– 10. Unlike many physicians, however, Dr. Bissell recommended the "discipline and opportunity" of higher education as "the best remedy for any tendency to excessive emotional disturbance," p. 510.

46. John Dewey, "Health and Sex in Higher Education," *Popular Science Monthly* 28 (March 1886): 606, 609. According to Carroll Wright, 4,000 copies of the statistical report were published, and newspapers were notified of the results. Carroll Wright to Annie Howes, May 12, 1884, Marion Talbot Papers. By comparison, the *Popular Science Monthly* reached about 11,000 readers a month. Hofstadter, *Social Darwinism*, p. 22.

ability to bear healthy children, but he suggested grimly that "these figures . . . speak for themselves."[47]

The figures, of course, did not speak for themselves, and Dewey would have been a little less alarmed if he had taken into account the relative youth of the respondents and if he had known the marriage, birth, and mortality rates in the country at large. Despite the widespread concern over the effect of study on female reproductive organs and on the children those organs produced, the offspring of college-educated mothers suffered a much lower mortality rate (one-half to one-third less) than did the offspring of less educated women, perhaps because college graduates knew more about sanitation than did most mothers. Though college-educated women had reasonably healthy children, they definitely had fewer of them, just as Dewey feared. While 92 percent of all married women bore three to four children each, only 68 percent of married college graduates bore any children, and most of them bore only one or two. College education alone, however, can not explain the ACA respondents' lower rate of parenting, for only about one-half to two-thirds of the upper-middle-class married women of the time became mothers, and, like their college-educated sisters, they bore only one or two children each.[48]

The one figure that really set college graduates apart from most women, and even most well-to-do women, was their rate of marriage. Even if one corrects the ACA report figure of 26 percent upward to 57 percent to include the graduates who eventually married, the graduates fell far below the national average of 95 percent and significantly below the upper-middle-class rate of about 68 percent. These early women graduates were a highly motivated and idealistic group, who worked hard while in college and strove after graduation to find ways of repaying society for the privilege that had been granted them. Marion Talbot, for example, discouraged young suitors at Boston University by her single-minded devotion to her studies. One particularly determined young man

47. Dewey, "Health and Sex in Higher Education," p. 610.
48. Mary Van Kleeck, "A Census of College Women," *Journal of the Association of Collegiate Alumnae* 11 (May 1918): 557–87. (Infant mortality statistics quoted in Van Kleeck are from the United States Department of Labor, Children's Bureau, *Infant Mortality Series*, nos. 3, 4, and 6 [1915–17]); Wilson H. Grabhill et al., "A Long View," in Michael Gordon, ed., *The American Family in Social-Historical Perspective* (New York: St. Martin's Press, 1973), pp. 374–96; Richard Jensen, "Family, Career, and Reform: Women Leaders of the Progressive Era," also in *The American Family in Social-Historical Perspective*, pp. 267–80. For an analysis of the upper-middle-class background of early college graduates, see Roberta Frankfurt, *Collegiate Women: Domesticity and Career in Turn-of-the-Century America* (New York: New York University Press, 1977), p. 38. John Dewey was not alone in his ignorance of the demographic trends of his day. A year after he published his review of the ACA survey, the *Popular Science Monthly* published an article which claimed, "The largest families of the present generation belong to the most highly educated women." Lucy M. Hall, "Higher Education of Women and the Family," *Popular Science Monthly* 30 (March 1887): 614.

tried to break through her reserve with a note that promised not to
"intrude upon your examination" if only she would allow him to call on
her. After graduation Talbot spent a season visiting friends, three
hundred in all, between Boston and Washington. Her diary reports many
social engagements, but it also records her distress over the benighted
views expressed by her male companions. It was difficult for a woman who
refused to defer to find common social ground with men who expected
deference. In the end, Talbot found the company of her educated women
friends far more satisfying than the company of her male contemporaries.[49]

Added to college graduates' unwillingness or inability to marry, Dewey
found their enthusiasm for teaching alarming, and he wrote, "It can
hardly be thought desirable that 60 percent of all the young women of our
country, who ought to have collegiate training, should have it only as a
preparation for one of the professions or for teaching." Dewey believed
that before colleges could develop a curriculum that would suit the needs
of women, much more would have to be known about women's needs and
capacities. Dewey recommended going "far beyond the questions of
bodily health" to questions about what women found to be helpful and
hindering in their schooling. In short, future studies should both study
women's physiology more exactly and then proceed to a fuller exploration
of women's psychology and social roles.[50]

The ACA never had funds to support sustained social scientific research, although that was one of its primary goals. Even if it could have
claimed greater financial resources, however, the impact of its work would
have been vitiated, because the ACA worked alone. No iconoclastic perspective on women's nature and role could flourish in the hostile intellectual climate of the late nineteenth century without greater institutional
support than the ACA was able to give. Only the disciplined community of
the research university could provide the kind of authority that would
support an altered view of women's capacity. As Dewey put it: "Discussion
on partisan lines is absolutely valueless and a priori discussion will effect
nothing. The unbiased study by educational experts of the fruits actually
borne by experience is invaluable, and the generalizations based upon
such data will show the lines upon which reform must work itself out."[51]

49. Van Kleeck, "A Census of College Women," p. 578; Grabhill et al., "A Long View,"
p. 393; T. A. Turner to Marion Talbot, March 12, 1880, Talbot Papers; Diary of Marion
Talbot, 1880–81, names listed at end, Marion Talbot Papers.

50. Dewey, "Health and Sex in Higher Education," pp. 610, 614.

51. Ibid., p. 613. My interpretation of the difficulty experienced by the ACA in its effort
to alter thinking about women has been influenced by Haskell, *The Emergence of Professional
Social Science,* p. 143. The importance that the ACA attached to long-term statistical research

Unwilling to wait for the reform of education that Dewey expected would follow a fuller understanding of women's nature, Talbot blazed her own path, and, as with the founding of the ACA, her mother provided inspiration. For Emily Talbot the fight for women's education and the defense of women's physical capacities were merely preconditions to a larger objective—that of creating socially useful work for college-educated women, both those who married as well as those who, for want of opportunity or because of a distaste for the confinement of Victorian domestic life, did not. As secretary to the education department of the ASSA, Emily Talbot promoted the development of social science, urging colleges and universities throughout the country to add courses in the "Punishment and Reform of Criminals," "Prevention of Vice," "Public and Private Charities," and "Sanitation of Cities and Private Dwellings" to the courses in government and political economy that most of them already offered in the 1880s. Though the established professions were closed to most women, Emily Talbot believed that women would be able to make a place for themselves in the yet unestablished area of social science, especially in "Sanitary Science," which she believed should put science at the service of both homemaker and the civic reformer.[52]

Marion Talbot worked to develop her mother's vision by studying at M.I.T. with Ellen Richards, who was then doing pioneer work in the application of chemistry to the problems of nutrition and sanitation, and she persuaded the administration at Wellesley College to allow her to teach a course in domestic economy. Talbot enjoyed her work but felt limited by it. And she objected to New England's conservative attitude toward women and education. President Charles Eliot of Harvard persisted in his opposition to coeducation, although he relented to the extent of endorsing the establishment of Radcliffe College as a separate school for women. Alarmed by the decline in Harvard's influence in an increasingly commercial age, he initiated an elective system, added courses in the natural sciences, and decreased Harvard's emphasis on Greek and Latin. His interest in educational reform, however, did not extend to the new

was noted by ACA member M. Carey Thomas in "The ACA in its Relation to Women's Education," *Publications of the Association of Collegiate Alumnae* 1 (December 1898): 44.
    52. Emily Talbot, "Methodical Education in the Social Sciences," *Journal of Social Science* 21 (September 1886): 13–21, 23–24; ibid. 22 (June 1887): 7–1, 12–27; and "Social Science Instruction in Colleges, 1886," *Journal of Social Science* 21 (September 1886): 34 – 49. See also Emily Talbot Box in Marion Talbot Papers. Women played an active role in the work of the ASSA departments of health, education, and social economy, where they comprised between 20 and 30 percent of the membership. American Social Science Association, "Constitution, List of Officers, and Members, 1884– 5," *Journal of Social Science* 20 (December 1885): 181– 86. The feminist dimension of the ASSA is superbly depicted in William Leach, *True Love and Perfect Union: The Feminist Reform of Sex and Society* (New York: Basic Books, 1980), pp. 292– 346.

area of social science, which he did not consider a serious area of study.[53]

Wellesley adhered to an even more conservative educational philosophy than did Harvard, and was neither financially able nor sufficiently interested to support the development of sanitary science in the scientific direction Talbot envisioned. Wellesley had been founded after the Civil War at about the same time as the other women's colleges, when the demand for teachers and the dissatisfaction with the superficiality of the schools available to young women prompted the movement to offer women the same classical training given to men. Resolutely, the women's colleges struggled to make good on their claim to provide young women with the same education available in the men's schools. This effort contained an irony, however. At Harvard College, President Eliot initiated his elective system at the very time that administrators and faculty at Vassar, Smith, and Wellesley were trying to pattern their schools on the traditional forms. Some educators, like Vassar's president John Raymond, appreciated the incongruity of the effort but explained,

> My own faith on this subject is briefly this: that while the education for men has outgrown the old college system, and is demanding room for expansion and free development in various directions, that for women has but just grown up to it, and needs for a season the bracing support of its somewhat narrow forms. And I think we shall commit a serious, if not fatal, mistake in our policy for the College if we overlook this important distinction.

So, ironically, the very effort of educators like Raymond to emulate the male pattern of education ended in New England women's being trained differently from men. In adopting a narrowly classical program, the women's colleges stifled the creative activity that was just then beginning to characterize some of the men's schools.[54]

When Marion Talbot received the offer to teach and act as dean at the new University of Chicago, she accepted. The opportunity to overcome the restrictive conception of women's physical and mental capabilities that had dominated the debates of her youth, and the possibility of creating careers for women beyond the home, appeared to be much greater at a major research university than at a small women's college. She had visited Chicago with her mother the summer before her senior year in college, "a

53. Laurence Veysey, *The Emergence of the American University* (Chicago: University of Chicago Press, 1965), pp. 86–98. Harvard did not establish a department of sociology until 1931. Marion Talbot recalled her feeling of stultification in her article, "The Challenge of a Retrospect," *University Record* (Chicago) 11 (April 1927): 87–88. On Eliot's opposition to coeducation, see Hugh Hawkins, *Between Harvard and America: The Educational Leadership of Charles W. Eliot* (New York: Oxford, 1972), pp. 193–96.

54. Mabel Newcomer, *A Century of Higher Education for Women*, p. 82. For evidence that Wellesley failed to raise the funds to pay Talbot, see Helen Shafer to Marion Talbot, July 14, 1891, Marion Talbot Papers.

rather unusual experience in those days for a Bostonian," and both mother and daughter had been greatly impressed with the city's raw, frontier spirit. Now, a dozen years later, the older woman urged the younger to return. "She was convinced," Marion later recalled, "that I should cast in my lot with the new University and the growing city." So, "though it cost her many a heart pang, she encouraged me to accept" the new position.[55]

In going to a major university, in trying to make a place for women in a man's world, Marion fulfilled her mother's most ambitious fantasies of what an educated woman could do, but there was a sizable personal cost involved. Marion had to say good-by not just to her parents but to the prospect of having her own family. At thirty-four she was already a spinster. Accepting the job at Chicago confirmed that state, though her friends preferred to view her choice as a kind of marriage and provided her with silverware, dishes, and linen as going-away presents. In 1892, women who challenged conventional views of feminine capacity usually found they had to do so alone.[56]

55. Diary of Marion Talbot, 1879–80, entry for June 13, 1879, Marion Talbot Papers; Marion Talbot, *More Than Lore*, p. 3. Talbot's association of the frontier and the city is interesting in light of a point once made by David Potter. "The wilderness," Potter wrote, "may have been the frontier for American men, and the cabin in the clearing the symbol of their independence, but the city was the frontier for American women and the business office was what gave them economic independence and the opportunity to follow a course of their own." Potter might have added that the city became a frontier for women not simply by providing clerical jobs but also by offering opportunities for social reform that the wilderness could not. David Potter, "American Women and the American Character," in Don E. Fehrenbacher, ed., *History and American Society: Essays of David M. Potter* (New York: Oxford, 1973), pp. 284, 277–304.

56. Marion Talbot, *More Than Lore*, p. 6.

2 *The Feminization of Academe*

The University of Chicago's first president, thirty-four-year-old William Rainey Harper, hardly presented the image of an educational revolutionary. Trained at Yale in the intensely clerical atmosphere of the 1870s, Harper subscribed to the conventional belief that moral philosophy and the classics provided the essential foundation for a sound education. Harper's interests, however, were more scholarly than they were religious. In common with many young men his age, he found greater inspiration in the work emanating from European research centers than from the sermons delivered from American pulpits. Furthermore, Harper appreciated the special problems plaguing American higher education at the end of the century. Universities faced intense competition in those years, both from each other and from the alternative attractions provided by the rapidly expanding business world. Any new educational venture risked the kind of financial uncertainty that troubled new companies trying to break into America's cutthroat rail, steel, or oil industries. To follow tradition was to risk failure at the outset.[1]

For American higher education to succeed, Harper believed it would have to transcend the traditional college education, develop research universities modeled on the German system, and attract the young with its ability to outstrip Europe in scholarly research and scientific development. Harvard's Charles Eliot might succeed in attracting students with his vision of the liberally educated gentleman but, in Harper's view, fundamental research should be the primary commitment of the educational reformer, especially when that reformer was engaged not simply in protecting an established institution like Harvard but in forging a new institution like Chicago. "It is only a man who has made investigation who can teach others to investigate," the young president declared, and so long

1. Richard J. Storr, *Harper's University: The Beginnings* (Chicago: University of Chicago Press, 1966), pp. 18– 20; Laurence Veysey, *The Emergence of the American University*, pp. 1– 21 and 366– 80.

as he directed Chicago's affairs, he insisted that "promotion of younger men in the department" would "depend more largely upon the results of their work as investigators than upon the efficiency of their teaching," although the latter would "by no means be overlooked."[2]

A specialist in Hebrew, Harper wanted particularly to build strong departments in Semitics, classics, and philosophy, and he focused his initial recruiting in these areas, hoping to hire the most established and respected scholars in these fields. Even when he offered salaries of $7,000 to senior professors then earning $4,000, however, he met with rejection from those who were suspicious of the university's newness, its Baptist origins, and its location in a notoriously corrupt and uncivilized city. Harper's initial failure prompted him to alter his course, and in the end he assembled a very different faculty from the one he had originally intended to attract—one weighted toward science and social science rather than toward classics and philosophy. He had to settle for relative unknowns in many cases, but these unknowns ultimately made Chicago's reputation as a major center for research.[3]

When Harper failed to persuade Harvard's George Herbert Palmer to head the department of philosophy, he turned instead to young John Dewey of Michigan to fill the post. Dewey brought with him George Herbert Mead and a number of others who were interested not only in philosophy but also in the nascent field of psychology. When he learned of financial problems at newly established Clark University and the widespread dissatisfaction there with President G. Stanley Hall's autocratic manner, Harper talked a number of the faculty members into coming to Chicago, promising freedom to work as they wished and ample resources to establish independent departments and laboratories. Albert Michaelson, the pioneer of experimental work in relativity, and six other scientists from Clark formed the core of Chicago's faculty in the physical sciences. From Cornell, Harper acquired the eccentric and iconoclastic Thorstein Veblen to edit the *Journal of Political Economy;* and from Colby College he attracted President Albion Small, who saw more excitement in the prospect of establishing the country's first department of sociology and creat-

2. William Rainey Harper, "First Annual Report of the President," President's Papers, 1889–1925, University of Chicago Archives, pp. 148–49. For an explanation of Eliot's relative lack of sympathy for scientific research, see Veysey, *Emergence of the American University*, pp. 95–96.

3. Darnell Rucker, *The Chicago Pragmatists* (Minneapolis: University of Minnesota Press, 1969), pp. 10–11; Storr, *Harper's University*, pp. 73–78. In the 1890s, $7,000 was "ample, in a time without income taxes, for a man to live in a big house, have two servants, go to the opera, and spend his summers traveling." Ray Ginger, *Altgeld's America: The Lincoln Ideal versus Changing Realities* (1958; reprint ed., New York: Franklin Watts, New Viewpoints, 1973), p. 308.

ing *The American Journal of Sociology* than in administering a small college.[4]

Though Harper accepted the need for innovation in education, he would have preferred to cling to tradition by restricting Chicago's faculty and student body to men, but the circumstances surrounding the development of higher education in the West made that impossible. More recently established and often without secure endowments, western colleges and universities were far more vulnerable to the pressure to admit women than were the older and more securely funded schools of the East. Eastern administrators managed to resist coeducation partly because of the success of their curricular reforms in attracting male students, and partly because of the alternative provided to women students by female colleges. In the West, however, curricular reform alone proved an inadequate guarantee of financial security, and wealthy benefactors proved too scarce to satisfy female demands.[5]

The staffing problems of the West's rapidly expanding public-school system added to the financial pressures that encouraged coeducation. Plagued by labor scarcity and indebtedness, most western communities found it difficult to recruit teachers. In their search for cheap labor they hired women and brought pressure to bear on state legislatures to provide them with adequate training. The University of Wisconsin began training women as teachers in its normal school during the Civil War, when male enrollment plummeted; and the University of Michigan adopted coeducation in 1870, when the legislature forced a reluctant administration to accept women rather than undertake the extra expense of building a separate school.[6]

Though the pressure to adopt a coeducational policy was especially strong where schools depended on public support, even private colleges suffered the kind of financial strain that made coeducation a necessary innovation. In Illinois, for instance, the old University of Chicago, estab-

4. Rucker, *Chicago Pragmatists,* pp. 10– 27; Alfred Raphelson, "The Pre-Chicago Association of the Early Functionalists," *Journal of the History of the Behavioral Sciences* 9 (April, 1973): 115– 21; Dorothy Ross, *G. Stanley Hall: The Psychologist as Prophet* (Chicago: University of Chicago Press, 1972), pp. 207– 30; Storr, *Harper's University,* pp. 74– 75.

5. The position of Harper and other principal figures involved in the founding of the University of Chicago on the issue of coeducation in 1890 was later recalled by Frederick Gates; see F. T. Gates to William R. Harper, October 16, 1902, Presidents' Papers, 1889– 1925, University of Chicago Archives, Chicago, Illinois. The most comprehensive treatment of the fiscal pressure for coeducation in the West can be found in Thomas Woody, *A History of Women's Education in the United States,* 2: 238– 60. See also Mabel Newcomer, *A Century of Higher Education for American Women,* pp. 5 – 51.

6. Patricia Albjerg Graham, "Expansion and Exclusion: A History of Women in American Higher Education," *Signs* 3 (Summer 1978): 759– 73; Thomas Woody, *A History of Women's Education,* 2:230– 47. For further details on Wisconsin, see Helen M. Olin, *Women of a State University* (New York: Putnam, 1909), pp. 22– 47. For further details on Michigan, see Dorothy Gies McGuigan, *A Dangerous Experiment,* pp. 15– 30.

lished at the time of the Civil War as a Baptist college for men, decided to admit women in the 1870s when presented with a petition from local women. The college had been prey to financial crisis since its inception, and with the depression of 1873 the school faced bankruptcy. Warning that "the financial resources of the university need to be enlarged in every particular," the trustees resolved to find some way to increase enrollments. The women's request for admission provided an obvious solution to the university's problems, and the trustees promptly resolved, "Young ladies coming to the University prepared to pursue with advantage the studies of the college classes shall be allowed opportunity to do so, upon condition of the payment of the same tuition fees." In the West it helped to be able to pay one's own way.[7]

Even Charles Eliot, a vocal foe of coeducation at Harvard, conceded that coeducation in some circumstances might be necessary. Though men and women are not "best educated in intimate association," he declared, coeducation "may nevertheless be justifiable in a community which cannot afford anything better. . . . Coeducation has the advantage of economy. Numbers increase pecuniary cheapness. Many of the colleges of the West were established for both men and women because the churches or the people could not afford two colleges in a single commonwealth."[8]

The admission of women did not insure a school's solvency, however; in fact, the old University of Chicago closed in 1886 despite female tuition fees. But by 1890 coeducation represented a well-established feature of western education, a necessary if not sufficient condition of financial stability as well as an accepted means of filling the West's need for teachers. When the new University of Chicago was founded in that year, its articles of incorporation directed Harper to extend "opportunities from all departments of higher education to persons of both sexes on equal terms."[9]

Believing that he should have at least a few women in the administration and on the faculty to supervise the female students, but reluctant to relax his academic standards, Harper searched for women who would be willing to be scholars as well as surrogate mothers. So few women had been able to pursue advanced study by 1890, however, that Harper found it difficult to recruit the kind of women he wanted. George Herbert Palmer's refusal to join the philosophy department added to Harper's

7. "University of Chicago Records, Minutes of the Meetings of the Board of Trustees," February 19, 1873, Old University of Chicago Papers, University of Chicago Archives. For the history of the old University of Chicago, see The Joseph Regenstein Library, *One in Spirit* (Chicago: University of Chicago Press, 1973), pp. 1–14.

8. Quoted in Woody, *A History of Women's Education*, 2:257.

9. See Articles of Incorporation in "An Historical Sketch," *President's Report*, 1892–1902, pp. 503–05.

difficulties, because Palmer was married to Harper's first choice as dean of women, Alice Freeman Palmer. Much to Harper's surprise and relief, however, the Michigan-trained historian and former Wellesley president did not let her husband's reservations about Chicago influence her own view. She found the opportunity promised to women at Chicago so appealing that she agreed to serve as assistant professor of history and dean on the condition that she only be required to be in residence twelve weeks a year. Realizing that she would need help if she were to succeed in splitting her time between her home in Boston and her job in Chicago, Palmer persuaded Harper to hire her young friend Marion Talbot as assistant dean and assistant professor of sociology. Palmer and Talbot comprised the core of the female faculty, a group that included Julia Bulkley in pedagogy, Martha Footé Crow in English, and Alice B. Foster in physical culture.[10]

Having met initial frustration in trying to hire the country's most esteemed scholars, Harper wisely turned to those who saw the city of Chicago's promise rather than its desolation. Such people proved to be disproportionately reform-minded and female. Commenting on the lure that Chicago held for them, Chairman of Sociology Albion Small reported: "The city of Chicago is one of the most complete social laboratories in the world. . . . The most serious problems of modern society are presented by the great cities, and must be studied as they are encountered in concrete form in large populations." In the English department, novelist Robert Herrick captured the flavor of that special laboratory in *The Web of Life* (1900). Portraying a physician who had decided to give up a lucrative practice to work in the slums, Herrick wrote: "From the decorous boulevard, with its clean asphalt pavement and pleasant trees, he turned at once into the dirty cross street. . . . India, the Spanish-American countries, might show something fouler . . . but nothing so incomparably mean and long." What attracted the new social scientists to Chicago was not simply Harper's munificent salaries and his promises of freedom from traditional administrative interference but the challenge provided by the city's incomparable meanness. In Chicago men who might, in less secular times, have been attracted to the ministry and

10.   American institutions began awarding doctorates in the 1870s. In 1888 universities awarded more than a hundred Ph.D.'s for the first time; only one of those degrees went to a woman. See Emilie Hutchinson, *Women and the PhD*. (Greensboro: North Carolina College for Women, 1929), p. 22. Barbara Miller Solomon, "Alice Freeman Palmer," in James, ed., *Notable American Women,* 3:4–8. William R. Harper to Marion Talbot, August 1, 1892, Marion Talbot Papers, University of Chicago Archives; Marion Talbot, "The Women of the University," *President's Report,* 1897–98, p. 111.

women who might have gone to China as missionaries found a common purpose in the slums. Revolted by the comfortable smugness of Victorian society, alarmed by the social cost of industrial progress but drawn to the excitement of urban life, these aliens from middle-class society sought to reform the city.[11]

For women this impulse toward reform had a special meaning. As Jane Addams of Hull House (founded 1889) put it, the work in the slums was important not so much for the slum dwellers as for the women college graduates who worked there whose education had cut them off so completely from conventional Victorian culture. Hull House provided both a sanctuary and a purpose for many women—a sanctuary from the "family claim" that so many of them found suffocating, and a purpose that satisfied their desire for independence and accomplishment without undermining their sense of womanhood. The Chicago settlement offered a halfway house between domestic tradition and the political world from which women had long been excluded.[12]

Most of the Chicago social scientists participated in some way in the work of Hull House, leading seminars, giving lectures, or just having dinner with the exciting group of people who always gathered there; and Jane Addams became a virtual adjunct professor in sociology at Chicago. John Dewey, who visited Hull House before deciding to accept Harper's offer to head the philosophy department, usually came on Sunday afternoons to lead uneducated immigrants in sessions about Greek philosophy, and he so admired the democratic spirit of the settlement that he named his daughter after its founder. Hull House became a laboratory for sociologists, psychologists, and economists, who helped to transform it from a home for the moral uplifting of impoverished immigrants to a

11. Quoted from the *Annual Register*, 1893–94, in *One in Spirit*, p. 29; quoted from Robert Herrick, *The Web of Life*, in ibid., p. 32. For an excellent discussion of the alienation of young intellectuals from middle-class Victorian culture, see Christopher Lasch, *The New Radicalism in America, 1889–1963: The New Intellectual as a Social Type* (New York: Knopf, Vintage, 1965), pp. 3–68. See also Allen Davis, *Spearheads for Reform: The Social Settlements and the Progressive Movement, 1890–1914* (New York: Oxford, 1967), pp. 26–39, and Roy Lubove, *The Professional Altruist: The Emergence of Social Work as a Career, 1880–1930* (1965; reprint ed., New York: Atheneum, 1973), pp. 1–54.

12. Jane Addams, *Democracy and Social Ethics* (New York: Macmillan Co., 1902), pp. 77–101. Allen Davis, *American Heroine: The Legend and Life of Jane Addams* (New York: Oxford University Press, 1973), pp. 53–57. For more on how women college graduates responded to the family claim, see Joyce Antler, "The Educated Woman and Professionalization: The Struggle for a New Feminine Identity, 1890–1920" (Ph. D. diss., State University of New York at Stony Brook, 1977), pp. 136–201. On educational background of women reformers, see Barbara Kuhn Campbell, *The "Liberated" Woman of 1914: Prominent Women of the Progressive Era* (Ann Arbor: UMI Research Press, 1979), pp. 25–46.

center for systematic social investigation and an agency of political and economic reform.[13]

For all of its male supporters and increasingly scientific approach, however, Hull House was and remained primarily a women's institution. It was always more peripheral in the lives of the men who were interested in it than in the lives of the women, many of whom made settlement work the center of their careers and considered it uniquely women's work. For Dewey, Hull House was a laboratory and an example of what he was trying to accomplish in education. For many women, Hull House was their life.

Marion Talbot directed a number of women students there to work, and through her the women of the university and the women of the Chicago reform movements maintained close contact, especially after 1895, when Palmer relinquished her deanship to Talbot. Reformers like Jane Addams, Julia Lathrop, and Florence Kelly worked in the local chapter of the Association of Collegiate Alumnae to encourage young women to attend college, while the university produced young women committed to social change who filled the ranks of reform organizations. Chicago graduate students Katherine Bement Davis, Sophinisba Breckenridge, Grace and Edith Abbott, Frances Kellor, Mary Belle Harris, and Annie Marion MacLean, among others, worked in the city for better sanitation, public health, labor legislation, prison and criminal court reform, building codes, and better schools.[14]

Talbot became a pivotal figure in this community of activists and scholars, a kind of chief of employment for Chicago's women students and academic dean for Chicago reformers. When Josephine Shaw Lowell inquired through the Association of Collegiate Alumnae for recommendations to fill the position of head of the Bedford Hills Reformatory, Talbot saw to it that graduate student Katherine Bement Davis got the job. When Harper granted her the money for an assistant, she hired Sophinisba Breckenridge and then argued with Harper for several years that Breckenridge was not being paid enough. When Small commenced publication of the *American Journal of Sociology* in 1895, Talbot served on the editorial board.[15]

13. Allen Davis, *American Heroine*, pp. 96—102. For more on women reformers and their relationship to the university, see Steven Diner, *A City and Its Universities: Public Policy in Chicago, 1892 – 1919* (Chapel Hill: University of North Carolina Press, 1980), pp. 52 – 75.

14. Solomon, "Alice Freeman Palmer," in James, ed., *Notable American Women*, p. 7; Marion Talbot and Lois Rosenberry, *The History of the American Association of University Women*, pp. 107 – 09. For reform work of Chicago graduate students, see individual entries in *Notable American Women*, and Marion Talbot's reports on "The Women of the University," in *President's Report*, 1892 – 1925.

15. Josephine Shaw Lowell to Marion Talbot, March 7, 1900, Marion Talbot Papers; William R. Harper to Marion Talbot, February 16, 1901, Marion Talbot Papers.

In the decade that followed Chicago's opening, women came in increasing numbers to the university, to the social sciences, and to reform work. The social turmoil in the city during these years, fed by the depression of 1893 and the violence surrounding the Pullman Strike of 1894, created a receptiveness to new ideas and new speakers among a public anxious for answers to the pressing problems of poverty and labor unrest. The chief beneficiaries of this receptivity were the women students and reformers who in less turbulent times would have had less opportunity to speak out.

Although these women believed that, as women, they were especially suited to social activism, they did not view reform as an exclusively feminine undertaking. Marion Talbot, in particular, believed that nothing better demonstrated the need to transcend Victorian society's separation of male and female spheres than did the disease and pollution of the modern city. While women confined their concern for the quality of life to their homes, and while men confined their technological expertise to industrial expansion, public life deteriorated for want of attention from either group. It was time to recognize, Talbot argued, that science could provide an important foundation for reform.

Talbot urged President Harper to allow her to establish a department of public health to train both men and women to deal with the problems of urban planning, sanitation, and consumer protection. She envisioned a program that would include courses in chemistry, physics, physiology, political economy, and modern languages—a program that would lead to the alleviation of urban problems at the same time that it discredited the dangerously stark line Victorian society had drawn between male and female abilities. Talbot asked Harper for money for laboratories and an assistant to launch this new venture—and she suggested that she should be made an associate professor, in keeping with her dual responsibilities as both department head and dean. Because he had overcommitted his funds, Harper promptly denied these requests, urging Talbot to work for her goals within the department of sociology.[16]

In the beginning, sociology proved a sympathetic home for Talbot and her plans. Though the men in the department considered themselves principally scholars, they assumed that there was an intimate connection between scientific study and social activism. When Albion Small started the *American Journal of Sociology*, he wrote, in "Scholarship and Social Agitation," that neither thought nor action could operate independently of one another, and that the scholar had much to learn from the reformer.

16. Marion Talbot to William R. Harper, August 13, 1892, Marion Talbot Papers; William R. Harper to Marion Talbot, August 22, 1892, Marion Talbot Papers. For Talbot's views on the interdependence of science and reform, see Marion Talbot, "Sanitation and Sociology," *American Journal of Sociology* 2 (July 1896): 74–81.

The most impressive lesson which I have learned in the vast sociological laboratory which the city of Chicago constitutes is that action, not speculation, is
the supreme teacher. If men will be the most productive scholars in any department of the social sciences, let them gain time and material by cooperating
in the social work of their community.[17]

The Gynecocentric Ideal

The common purpose that united men and women in the slums of
Chicago called into question both conventional assumptions about the
nature of social change and deeply entrenched ideas about woman's place
and identity. In the 1870s, during the first wave of Herbert Spencer's
popularity, the American Social Science Association worked alone in
championing organized social reform. By the 1890s, the growing concern
over the social costs that attended industrialization prompted wider support for an organized response to social problems, especially in major
urban centers; in fact, the increased complexity of urban problems fostered greater acceptance of organized activity than had been possible
among earlier reformers schooled in antebellum transcendentalism. In
the 1870s, feminists like Emily Talbot enjoyed little support in insisting
that women had both the capacities to play an active role in public life and
the special qualities needed to reform American society. By the 1890s,
women's far greater public activity gave wider currency to this feminist
assertion, and men's growing ambivalence about entrepreneurial individualism prompted an increasing number of men to work with women
and to endorse what they regarded as "feminine" values.[18]

Like others who made up the first generation of academics in social
science, reformers at Chicago began their education with Herbert
Spencer. Spencer's argument that all social systems progress ineluctably
from incoherent homogeneity to coherent heterogeneity seemed perfectly reasonable to those whose parents and grandparents had grown up
in the ethnically homogeneous and relatively unstratified society of the
Jacksonian era, but who themselves lived in a racially diverse and class-
ridden society. "I imagine that nearly all of us who took up sociology
between 1870, say, and 1890 did so at the instigation of Spencer," wrote
one sociologist. By the 1890s, however, disillusionment over crime, class
conflict, financial panics, and other economic and social problems, made
serious social thinkers suspicious of Spencer's faith that evolution pro-

17. Albion Small, "Scholarship and Social Agitation," *American Journal of Sociology* 1
(March 1896): 581– 82. For more on Small, see Vernon K. Dibble, *The Legacy of Albion Small*
(Chicago: University of Chicago Press, 1975), pp. 1– 149.
18. See Thomas Haskell, *The Emergence of Professional Social Science*, p. 206, for the lonely
battling of the ASSA in the 1870s.

ceeds efficiently. At Chicago, in particular, social thinkers rejected Spencer's laissez-faire attitude and insisted on the need for human intervention in the evolutionary process in order to protect men and women from the destructive impact of the competitive struggle.[19]

Disenchanted with Spencer, Chicago social scientists in the 1890s found inspiration in the work of Spencer's principal American critic, Lester Frank Ward, chief paleontologist of the United States Geological Survey and the author in 1883 of *Dynamic Sociology*. Albion Small called Ward a "Gulliver among the Lilliputians" in sociology and worked hard to make his theories more widely known among academics, publishing large parts of Ward's work in the early volumes of the *American Journal of Sociology*. Ward denounced Spencer's view of evolution as an inherently efficient process, arguing that "there is no true economy in the operation of the law of nature. It is a sort of trial and error process and involves enormous waste." For every sheaf of wheat growing in nature, thousands of seeds must be sown, but under the intelligent control of man, who "destroys competition, removes enemies, and creates conditions favorable to the highest development," wheat has evolved far more rapidly than it could ever have evolved under natural conditions. Without rational control, modern society is prey to the similarly destructive forces of cutthroat competition, financial panics, widespread poverty, epidemics, and warfare.[20]

Purposeless and destructive of human welfare, natural evolution, Ward believed, compounded social ills through an irrational differentiation of the sexes that inhibited women's mental and physical development and thereby undermined their stabilizing influence on society. Ward argued that the human race had begun with the female and that the male constituted a subsequent variation, an accidental addition, which nature provided as a means for improving on parthenogenic reproduction. Males had grown stronger and more courageous than females, not because of innate superiority, but because females had tended to select the stronger, more courageous males as their mates. Once strong enough to dominate the female and the process of sexual selection, the male proceeded to select his mates not on the basis of their strength or intelligence but rather on the basis of their ornamental value. It was time, Ward

19. Charles H. Cooley, "Reflections upon the Sociology of Herbert Spencer," *American Journal of Sociology* 26 (1920): 129, quoted in Richard Hofstadter, *Social Darwinism in American Thought*, p. 33.

20. Bernhard J. Stern, ed., "The Letters of Albion Small to Lester F. Ward," *Social Forces* 12 (1933): 313, quoted in Hofstadter, *Social Darwinism*, p. 84; Lester Ward, "Individual Telesis," *American Journal of Sociology* 2 (March 1897): 712, 710. Small published twelve articles by Ward in the *American Journal of Sociology* between 1895 and 1897.

thought, for men to recognize the social cost of this unfortunate practice and to begin working to rebuild female power and influence.[21]

Charlotte Perkins Gilman, an advocate of economic independence for women, a Hull House visitor, and a fellow contributor to the *American Journal of Sociology*, developed Ward's belief in the "gynecocentric" origins of human society in her own work. The mother of early time, she argued, had been loving, passive, efficient, industrious, conservative, and uncreative; while the father had been belligerent, passionate, selfish, lazy, and competitive. These differences had provided the impetus for evolutionary development, but they had also led to a society in which masculine competitiveness and love of adventure had completely overwhelmed feminine nurturance and stabilizing power. Like Ward, Gilman believed that men had stunted women's physical and mental development through their benighted approach to sexual selection; but unlike Ward, Gilman believed that men's failure to share in the development of what had come to be regarded as female qualities was as much to be regretted as women's failure to share equally with men in the development of men's much vaunted reason.[22]

Gilman illustrated what she believed to be the social cost of sexual divergence most clearly in a story of a mythical country she called "Herland," where women, descended by parthenogenesis from an aboriginal virgin mother and isolated from the rest of the world by treacherous cliffs, had built a civilization reflecting the special talents of women free of male domination. In Herland maternity shaped society. Carefully, the citizens laid out their collective fields and cultivated them to produce the most nutritious food for the community; they built towns with spacious gardens and parks to encourage a love of beauty and to permit athletic development; and they grouped houses to balance a sense of community with a sense of privacy, alloting two rooms and a bath to each adult and central nurseries for the feeding and nurturing of the infants and children. This was a peaceful civilization, tranquil, lovely, and carefully managed; but it was also, Gilman conceded, a fairly dull place, without competitive sports, without dramatic literature, and without great science. Herland illus-

21. Lester Ward, "Our Better Halves," *Forum* 6 (November 1888): 275, and "Genius and Woman's Intuition," *Forum* 9 (June 1890): 401 – 08, written in reply to Grant Allen, "Woman's Place in Nature," *Forum* 7 (May 1889): 258 – 63, which had, in turn, been an attack on "Our Better Halves." See also Ward, *Pure Sociology* (New York: Macmillan, 1903), pp. 290 – 377.

22. Charlotte Perkins Gilman, *The Man-Made World; Or, Our Androcentric Culture* (New York: Charlton Co., 1911), pp. 269, 39, 45, 132,156; Gilman, *Women and Economics: The Economic Factor between Men and Women as a Factor in Evolution*, ed. Carl Degler (1898; reprint ed., New York: Harper & Row, 1966), pp. 229, 239; idem, *The Man-Made World*, pp. 27, 260; ibid., pp. 260 – 62. Gilman believed that "Art, in the extreme sense, will perhaps always belong most to men" (ibid., p. 260).

trated women's special gifts, but it also revealed women's unique weaknesses, their lesser variability (and therefore want of genius), and their lack of ambition. For civilization to realize its highest potential, Gilman concluded, it must be able to draw on the full range of human talent. High civilization required one whole humanity, not two halves.[23]

A tension between nurturance and adventure, tranquility and excitement permeated the writings of the urban reformers and feminists, reflecting both their polarized view of sexual identity and their ambivalence about industrial progress. Even those not principally interested in the problem of sexual nature often revealed in their work a preoccupation with sexual themes. Thorstein Veblen, the young Chicago economist whose debunking attitude toward capitalism made him a favorite teacher of student reformers, argued that modern-day business enterprise owed its existence to the victory of one side of human nature over the other.[24]

Veblen believed that humans were governed by two conflicting impulses: the instincts of workmanship and predacity. In the early stage of social development, before the invention of tools, the instinct of workmanship prevailed in men as in women. But as tools made hunting possible, the predatory instinct developed among men who did the hunting, and these men enslaved those who were weaker. When successful hunting and further technological development created a surplus, women came to be valued by men, not for their ability as workers, but for their symbolic importance as trophies. With greater development came an accentuation of the predatory instinct in men and a further suppression of the instinct of workmanship. Veblen agreed with Gilman and Ward that women's subordinate status in modern society illustrated not the rational, coherent heterogeneity of Spencer's system but the irrational, and ultimately destructive, by-product of men's baser instincts.[25]

Veblen advocated the resurrection of the instinct of workmanship, long suppressed by the predatory side of man's nature, to correct the irrational and inequitable distribution of economic resources in America. The growing strength of the woman's movement struck him as an encouraging sign. Women's condemnation of conventional, paternalistic "ownership-marriage" represented, in his view, women's "reassertion of ancient habits of thought," and he dared to hope that these same ancient habits might "be expected also to work a disintegration of the correlative institution of private property."[26]

23. Charlotte Perkins Gilman, "Herland," *Forerunner* 6 (1915): 12– 17, 38– 44, 65– 72, 94– 100, 123– 29, 150– 55, 181– 87, 207– 13, 237– 43, 265– 70, 287– 93, and 319– 25.
24. Thorstein Veblen, "The Barbarian Status of Women," *American Journal of Sociology* 4 (January 1899): 514.
25. Ibid.
26. Ibid.

Ward, Gilman, and Veblen all believed in acquired characteristics, and their conviction that women's status could be changed rested on the assumption that their personalities could be modified, if not fundamentally transformed, through the purposive and adaptive power of the mind together with sexual selection and altered social conditions. The genetic studies of the 1880s and 1890s, however, made it increasingly difficult to support such a belief. August Weismann, in particular, who demonstrated that rats with their tails cut off persistently produced offspring with tails, cast doubt on the Lamarckian faith that basic physical structures were subject to heritable modification from environmental changes. If the genetic researchers were right and characteristics could not be acquired, then sexual differences must either be traceable to innate physiological conditions or they must be the product of each person's social history. Those who felt compelled to make this choice in the 1890s invariably chose to believe that most sex differences, from primary characteristics to complex social attitudes, were innate.[27]

One of Small's graduate students in sociology, William Isaac Thomas, developed this theory of female uniqueness in his doctoral dissertation, "On a Difference in the Metabolism of the Sexes," in 1897. Relying heavily on the work of the Scottish biologist Patrick Geddes, whose own work was an attempt to address Weismann's discoveries, Thomas reduced sexual differences to a basic difference in the cell metabolism of males and females. At the cellular level maleness was manifested in the expending of energy while femaleness was characterized by conserving of energy. From this simple biological division all social development followed. "Food and sex," he insisted, "are the irreducible factors of social life."[28]

Thomas combined Ward's gynecocentric theory of the feminine origins of human society with Geddes's theory of sexual metabolism and claimed that all life evolved from an energy-storing, or anabolic, stage to an energy-consuming, or katabolic, stage. "The katabolic animal form, through its rapid destruction of energy, has been carried developmentally away from the anabolic plant form," he explained, "and of the two sexes the male has been carried developmentally farther than the female from the plant process."[29]

The principal expression of woman's anabolism, Thomas argued, was

27. A. M. Winchester, *Heredity: An Introduction to Genetics*, 2d ed. (New York: Barnes and Noble, 1966), pp. 19–20; Loren Eiseley, *Darwin's Century*, pp. 217–21; George W. Stocking, Jr., *Race, Culture, and Evolution*, pp. 238–69. Neither Ward nor Gilman ever abandoned his or her Lamarckian beliefs despite familiarity with Weismann's work.

28. William I. Thomas, "On a Difference in the Metabolism of the Sexes," *American Journal of Sociology* 3 (July 1897): 31; idem, "The Scope and Method of Folk-Psychology," *American Journal of Sociology* 1 (January 1896): 445. See also Patrick Geddes and J. Arthur Thomson, *The Evolution of Sex* (London: Scott, 1889), passim.

29. Thomas, "On a Difference in the Metabolism of the Sexes," p. 31.

her reproductive system. "The superior physiological irritability of woman, whether we call it sensibility, feeling, emotionality or affectability, is due to the fact of the large development of her abdominal zone, and the activity of the physiological changes located there in connection with the process of reproduction. . . . Both social feeling and social organization are thus primarily feminine in origin—functions of the anabolism of woman."[30]

Although Thomas echoed the popular evolutionary belief that women occupied a lower point on the evolutionary ladder than men, he argued that evolutionary development had achieved such complexity that man's katabolic destructiveness, militarism, and competitiveness were posing a serious social danger. Society had reached a stage at which women's social proclivities could be appreciated and utilized to bring about reform. "It is now beginning to be true that the energies of women may find expression in forms of activity appropriate to their nature," he wrote, "and this will doubtless, in the long run, favor constructive, as over against destructive, modes of social interaction."[31]

Jane Addams, a friend of both Thomas and Geddes, gave popular expression to their physiological analyses in *Democracy and Social Ethics,* arguing that social progress depended on the moral insights of women. Addams dismissed those who argued that women's desire for public activity represented the wish for a career or selfish fulfillment. It was instead, she insisted, the natural expression of women's fundamental nature in the changed circumstances of the industrialized world where society no longer centered on the family. "The social claim is a demand upon the emotions as well as upon the intellect, and in ignoring it woman represses not only her conviction but lowers her springs of vitality."[32]

Genetic research prompted many social theorists, like Thomas and Addams, to dissent from the Lamarckian faith in sexual convergence shared by Ward, Gilman, and Veblen. But their technical disagreement on the issue of acquired characteristics did not, in itself, make them any less supportive of the woman's movement than the Lamarckians were. If anything, their belief in the innate and unalterable nature of sex differences made them believe more strongly in the need for greater female power.

Not all social scientists shared this sanguine assessment of the feminization of American society. Though the turbulent conditions of the late nineteenth century encouraged a growing number of reformers to champion

30. Ibid., p. 61.

31. William I. Thomas, "Sex in Primitive Morality," *American Journal of Sociology* 4 (May 1899): 787.

32. Jane Addams, *Democracy and Social Ethics,* p. 87. See also Jill Conway, "Stereotypes of Femininity in a Theory of Sexual Evolution," in Vicinus, ed., *Suffer and Be Still,* pp. 151– 52.

feminine values and to advocate a broader sphere for women, those same conditions fostered among many others an almost hysterical devotion to traditional roles. Psychologist G. Stanley Hall insisted with renewed fervor at the turn of the century that Edward Clarke had been right in opposing the education of women, for education tended to undermine the natural tendency toward sexual divergence and evolutionary progress. Coeducation, in particular, Hall believed, entailed the danger of thwarting social evolution. "Coeducation harms girls by assimilating them to boys' ways and work and robbing them of their sense of feminine character," Hall charged. "It harms boys by feminizing them when they need to be working off their brute animal element. Boys are eager for specialized knowledge, while girls are not suited to it."[33]

A product of his culture's limited conception of sex roles, and a man who struggled for many years to achieve professional acceptance as a psychologist, Hall occasionally expressed regret at the narrowness of the Victorian view of masculinity to which he subscribed, and he devoted a major part of his professional life to the study of adolescence, the age he considered the most feminine for both sexes. Adolescence, he wrote, was the "culminating stage of life with its all-sized interests, its convertability of emotions, its enthusiasms, and zest for all that is good, beautiful, true, and heroic." Hall's romanticization of femininity and adolescence, however, was more than offset by his concern over the danger they posed to the security of a mature, masculine identity, and many Victorians shared Hall's concern.[34]

In the 1870s those who were most worried about feminist agitation had dwelt on the danger of women's masculinization. Clarke and others decried the education of women because they feared it would endanger both motherhood and, by implication, the home, which men valued as a refuge from the competitive world. By the turn of the century, however, the concern over sexual identity was more often expressed as a fear of feminization. As women assumed increasingly public roles, especially as teachers and reformers, and challenged men's control of the public world, as men

33. G. Stanley Hall, *Adolescence: Its Psychology and Its Relations to Physiology, Anthropology, Sociology, Sex, Crime, Religion, and Education,* 2 vols. (New York: Appleton, 1904), 2:569, 602. Hall's remarks on coeducation appeared originally in his "Coeducation in the High School," *Proceedings of the National Educational Association,* 1903, pp. 446–60. Hall continued to argue against coeducation in "Feminization in School and Home," *World's Work* 16 (May 1908): 10237–44; "The Awkward Age," *Appleton's Magazine* 12 (August 1908): 248–54; and "The Budding Girl," *Appleton's Magazine* 13 (January 1909): 47–54.

34. Hall, *Adolescence,* 2:637. For Hall's ambivalence toward femininity and its roots in his troubled life, see Ross, *G. Stanley Hall,* pp. 336–40. The widespread belief in the great psychological differences between the sexes among early students of child development is discussed in Stephen Kern, "Freud and the Emergence of Child Psychology, 1880–1910" (Ph.D. diss., Columbia University, 1970), pp. 100–10.

gravitated increasingly to the white-collar and service-oriented work of the corporate world, the worry that women would lose their identity gave way increasingly to the concern that men would lose theirs. While reformers like Ward, Thomas, Gilman, Addams, and Veblen applauded women's growing power and intellectual fulfillment, many others stubbornly decried it, especially in the new universities where women were gravitating in ever greater numbers, threatening not just to balance male power but actually to overwhelm it.[35]

William Rainey Harper (1903)

The Fight over Coeducation

When the University of Chicago opened in 1892, women comprised about 40 percent of the undergraduate student body. By 1902 the enrollment of

35. Men's fear of feminization is thoughtfully treated in Peter Gabriel Filene, *Him/Her/Self: Sex Roles in Modern America* (1974; reprint ed., New York: Mentor, 1976), pp. 72–77.

women had outstripped that of men, and many feared that within a few years, if nothing was done to prevent it, the university would become a women's school. Chicago was not alone. Stanford University, which had opened at the same time as Chicago, had experienced the same surge in female enrollment. The founder's widow, Jane Stanford, so feared that the university, dedicated to the memory of her son, would become a female seminary, that she froze female enrollment permanently at five hundred. At Wisconsin the increase in female enrollment to about half the student body also produced a crisis and a reaction against coeducation. By the turn of the century, women nearly equaled or actually outnumbered men at California, Illinois, Iowa, Kansas, Michigan, Minnesota, Missouri, Nebraska, Ohio, Texas, Washington, and Wisconsin. If the great fear among educators in the post–Civil War years was of declining enrollments and bankruptcy, the great fear of the 1900s was that the universities might become female academies. Schools that had welcomed women when they represented economic salvation now worried that American universities had only been saved from the fate of insolvency to be subjected to the much worse fate of feminization.[36]

To most young men in 1900, business still presented a more attractive opportunity than higher education, especially in the Midwest and West, where the ideal of gentlemanly refinement held less appeal than it did in the East. It was still not clear that an engineering degree or a law degree could contribute in any significant way to business success. To women from the middle class, however, the business world remained closed, and the university represented the one institution open to them that led to respectable employment—teaching.[37]

Fearful that the University of Chicago was verging on the sexual tipping point, in danger of becoming a women's college, President Harper took decisive action. He proposed to segregate the younger men and women by using the funds recently donated by a generous benefactor to build a separate junior college for women. Only segregation, Harper believed, could stem the tide of feminization.[38]

Those who favored Harper's scheme emphasized that coeducation had its origins in economic necessity. "It was reluctantly accepted as simply a lesser evil than exclusion of women from college privileges altogether,"

36. Storr, *Harper's University*, p. 325; C. W. Elliot, *Stanford University: The First Twenty-five Years* (Stanford: Stanford University Press, 1937), pp. 132– 36; Woody, *A History of Women's Education*, 2:280– 95. See also F. E. Chadwick, "The Woman Peril in American Education," *Educational Review* 47 (February 1914): 109– 19.

37. The difficulty that educators encountered in trying to persuade a business-oriented public of the advantages of college training is discussed in David Nobel, *America by Design: Science, Technology, and the Rise of Corporate Capitalism* (New York: Knopf, 1977), pp. 20– 32.

38. Storr, *Harper's University*, p. 325.

recalled Albion Small in a letter supporting segregation. Though many professors believed in women's education and applauded their work in social reform, they thought that women's unique nature developed best under separate instruction, tailored to their special needs. Had women students "been allowed to follow their own instincts and preferences in all respects," wrote another faculty member, "I have no doubt that they would have chosen from the beginning separate instruction . . . but economic considerations have hitherto prevented this development." [39]

Many of the prosegregation writers argued that coeducation at the University of Chicago discouraged men from coming there. In other parts of the country, one professor wrote, "The strongest colleges for men admit men only. These colleges most strongly attract prospective college men who are wholly at liberty to choose. There is a growing disinclination on the part of such prospective college men to seek a coeducational college. . . . The steady increase in the proportion of girls enrolled operates more and more to divert from coeducational colleges a large number of the best class of college men." Having cast their lot with a new university, and often with a new discipline as well—as in the case of the sciences and social sciences—many faculty members and administrators at Chicago worried that the growing number of women there would destroy their efforts to create a prestigious research center. Relying at times on the prevailing scientific and popular assumptions of women's constitutional uniqueness, and at others on arguments about the danger posed to the university's reputation by having too many women, opponents of coeducation at Chicago urged the segregation of the sexes. [40]

Although a majority of Chicago's senior faculty and administrators endorsed segregation, a significant minority opposed it. One of those opponents was John Dewey. Sixteen years earlier, in his review of the Association of Collegiate Alumnae's "Health Statistics of College Women," he had been ambivalent about whether women should be educated in single-sex or in coeducational schools. Women's colleges seemed to have the advantage of paying greater attention to female health, yet coeducational institutions provided freer and more natural social relations. Now, in 1902, with sixteen years of teaching in coeducational universities behind him, more than a decade of work with women in Chicago reform movements, and sixteen years of marriage to a woman educated at Michigan and active as both a teacher and a mother, Dewey

39. Albion Small to the Recorder (Harper asked that faculty address their remarks to the Senate recorder), June 30, 1902, Presidents' Papers; Edward Capps to the Recorder, July 21, 1902, Presidents' Papers.

40. Nathaniel Butler to the Recorder, July 1902, Presidents' Papers.

had decided that coeducation was better for both men and women than single-sex education.[41]

Dewey wrote to Harper at length, justifying his opposition. "The argument that the separation will give opportunity for the growth of a more distinctively feminine and more distinctively masculine life," he wrote, "implies, in my judgement, the most profound, because the most subtle, of the attacks upon the coeducational principle." The policy of separation, he suggested, would produce feelings of difference that had not existed before. "The scheme is sure to accomplish what it is supposed to obviate—the fixing of attention upon sex matters."

> It at once draws the attention of the students coming to the university to the matter of sex as a fundamental consideration in determining the instruction they are to receive. . . . There is no point upon which public sentiment is so deeply and extensively sensitive as upon the question of sex.

If the university wanted to attract male students, it should direct its attention to improving itself, Dewey advised, not to creating segregated conditions. "The kind of man that will be kept from the University simply because he will have to associate upon equal terms with his equals is not the kind the University wants or needs," Dewey concluded.[42]

The idealized view of womanly uniqueness, to which Dewey and his colleagues had all been bred in sexually segregated Victorian society, and which many of them had used to champion women's widening sphere, was beginning to break down in the face of simple quotidian experience. Though many of the older faculty clung to traditional images of femininity and masculinity and were alarmed by the easy familiarity between men and women students, a growing number of younger faculty and students found that men and women differed far less than the laws of anabolism and katabolism dictated. As William I. Thomas conceded just two years after writing his dissertation, in an important shift of emphasis from his initial assertion that "all sociological manifestations proceed from physiological conditions," "I do not wish to imply that this [sexual] difference is altogether inherent in the male and female disposition; it is, in fact, partly a matter of habit and attention."[43]

41. John Dewey, "Health and Sex in Higher Education," pp. 612– 13. For Alice Dewey's influence on her husband, John, see Jane M. Dewey, ed., "Biography of John Dewey," in Paul A. Schilpp, ed., *The Philosophy of John Dewey* (Evanston, Ill.: Northwestern University Press, 1939), p. 21.

42. John Dewey to the Recorder, July 25,1902, Presidents' Papers; John Dewey to William R. Harper, January 9, 1902, Presidents' Papers.

43. William I. Thomas, "Sex in Primitive Morality," p. 787. Concern over the familiarity shown between men and women students is reflected in the correspondence from some of the faculty on the segregation issue. See, for example, Edward Capps to the Recorder, July 21, 1902. Presidents' Papers.

Of all the younger sociologists and psychologists who opposed segregation, the most vigorous was Marion Talbot, who mounted a campaign to defeat Harper's proposal. Though much of her life was led in a woman's world, participating in women's work with women who believed in women's special nature and mission, Talbot devoted the major part of her career to breaking down artificial sex divisions by fighting for equal rights for female students and faculty. Her life provided a bridge, linking an older view of feminine uniqueness to a more modern view of women's uncharted potential. When Harper started the practice of issuing a president's report, Talbot insisted that she be given space to report on the condition of women in the university. To the charge that women made acceptable undergraduates but had no interest in graduate study, Talbot replied that 12 percent of the male undergraduates and 14 percent of the women went on to graduate study. Of those with fellowships, 41 percent of the men and 36 percent of the women completed doctorates. To the charge that women had no talent for mathematics she wrote:

Men and women are doing more nearly the same amount of mathematical and natural sciences than is popularly supposed. At the University of Chicago 24% of the men graduates and 16% of the women graduates chose Mathematics after having completed their required Mathematics, but of the Bachelors of Science 47% of the women as against 39% of the men, chose Mathematics —a fact which is in startling contrast to the current statement that women have no aptitude for Mathematics.

Though she acknowledged that women predominated in literary subjects, she attributed this imbalance to the greater job opportunities available to women as teachers of literature and to the fact that, on occasion, "a girl is at the same time so old-fashioned in her views as to choose womanly subjects, and so radical as to be led by the assumed fitness of the subject for her sex as a whole rather than for herself as a member of it."[44]

In the *President's Report,* in private correspondence, and in person, Talbot insisted that women's education should differ in no way from men's, and she criticized the administration for not providing women with adequate fellowship assistance, for not naming women in adequate numbers to the faculty, for not paying women as much as the men were paid, and for not promoting women as rapidly as the men were promoted. As a dean, Talbot was a thorn in the side of the administration, keeping it uncomfortably aware of the fact that, despite its charter provisions, education at Chicago was not provided on equal terms to women and men. Talbot met frequent reverses in her struggle for equal treatment of

44. Marion Talbot, "The Women of the University," *President's Report,* 1901– 1902, pp. 145 and 122– 45.

women at Chicago, but the women for whom she fought proved to be a singularly determined lot; in 1900, when the national average of women earning doctorates was 6 percent, it was 20 percent at Chicago. During the fight over coeducation, Talbot wrote, "If the trustees could know how eager girls and women are to study as thinking beings and not as females, they would hesitate in justice to women to adopt this measure."[45]

Despite the arguments of Dewey, Talbot, and others both inside and outside the university, the prosegregation forces won the fight over coeducation and succeeded in building a separate junior college for women. The segregation of Chicago's younger men and women students, however, was only the first, and perhaps the least important, chapter in the story of academic segregation. The complex interplay of academic concerns at the turn of the century, especially in the social sciences, reinforced the trend toward sexual segregation signaled by the junior college fight.[46]

In the early 1890s the relatively limited resources of the new university caused a number of disciplines, now considered independent, to be organized under one department. Sociology combined with sanitary science and offered extension courses in working-class neighborhoods, while the department of philosophy included within it the fields of psychology and pedagogy. For over a decade disciplinary boundaries remained ill defined, philosophers published articles in psychological journals and collaborated with sociologists on anthropological essays; but as Chicago expanded, professional ambition, combined with the belief that specialization was necessary to scientific advance, led to the breakup of the interdisciplinary departments of the university's beginnings and facilitated the task of those who would segregate the sexes within the university.

Chicago economist J. Laurence Laughlin recognized the tendency of specialization, and especially of professionalization, to counteract the trend toward feminization at the turn of the century, and during the fight over coeducation he wrote:

> The congestion of numbers [of women students] is now largely due to the fact that the undergraduate courses are practically used by women as an advanced normal school to prepare for teaching. Just so soon as proper support and

45. Marion Talbot to William R. Harper, January 16, 1902, Marion Talbot Papers. Resentment over Chicago's treatment of women culminated in 1924, when Talbot joined with other faculty women to protest in a letter to the president and the trustees (Edith Flint, Marion Talbot, and Elizabeth Wallace to the President of the University and the Board of Trustees of the University of Chicago, December 1924, Marion Talbot Papers). For figures on women doctorates granted at Chicago, see "Women of the University," *President's Report,* 1902–04, p. 110. For national figures on women doctorates, see Jessie Bernard, *Academic Women* (1964; reprint ed., New York: Meridian, 1966), p. 70.

46. Storr, *Harper's University*, p. 326.

endowments are given to the work which offers training for careers in engineering, railways, banking, trade and industry, law and medicine, etc. the disproportion of men will doubtless remedy itself.

So Laughlin considered much of the liberal arts curriculum, as well as education and social work, doomed to feminization, but he believed that once the university succeeded in establishing its professional schools and in identifying the professional utility of departments like economics and sociology, it would be able to secure its reputation as a distinctively male institution training men for identifiably male work.[47]

In 1902 Marion Talbot abandoned her initial hope that either sanitary science or public health could become the central focus of the social and physical sciences in the reform of urban society and began asking Harper to put her in charge of a department devoted to the "household." Two years later Harper eliminated the field of sanitary science within sociology and established a separate department, called household administration, under Talbot's direction. Although Talbot had gained the independence she had been soliciting from him for over a decade, the very title of the department Harper finally bestowed upon her eliminated the androgynous tone of the field she had first sought to create. Because sanitary science comprised, as Talbot herself argued, a wide variety of scientific and political disciplines in which she had done no scholarly work, she could not defend her competence to administer such a broad field in a period of increasing specialization. As a woman, on the other hand, she was viewed as the embodiment of the qualities that fitted her for the position as head of household administration. The steady stream of letters she received from state universities asking for recommendations for teachers of home economics reinforced her belief that she should stake her claim to academic expertise in that area. Thus the trend toward specialization merged with traditional assumptions regarding sex roles to limit women's influence within the university, although Talbot continued to insist, somewhat lamely, that household administration dealt with the same far-flung concerns that she had intended sanitary science to cover. Despite her best efforts, Marion Talbot fell victim to the very process of academic sexual segregation that she was trying to fight.[48]

47. J. Laurence Laughlin to the Recorder, July 25, 1902, Presidents' Papers. For the reluctance of early sociologists to specialize, see Henrika Kuklick, "Boundary Maintenance in American Sociology: Limitations to Academic 'Professionalization,' " *Journal of the History of the Behavioral Sciences* 16 (July 1980): 201– 19, and Dorothy Ross, "The Development of the Social Sciences," in Alexandra Oleson and John Voss, eds., *The Organization of Knowledge in Modern America, 1860–1920* (Baltimore: The Johns Hopkins University Press, 1979), pp. 125– 26.

48. Marion Talbot's draft of a proposal to set up a separate department of "household technology," February 1902, Presidents' Papers; William R. Harper to Marion Talbot, March 28, 1904, Presidents' Papers; Marion Talbot to William R. Harper, February 18, 1904, Presidents' Papers.

At the same time that Harper separated household affairs from sociology, he also segregated reform activities, establishing an independent school of social work. The school of social work represented an important step for women in providing several women graduate students, including Sophinisba Breckenridge and Edith Abbott, with academic positions; but its founding also drove a wedge between women reformers and their academic supporters in the social sciences by establishing an institutional distinction between sociology's more masculine, theoretical side and its more feminine, practical side.[49]

Harper's desire to demonstrate the university's utility to a business-minded public, and his fear that the reformist activities of his social scientists would lead to the identification of sociology with socialism, fueled the trend toward sexual segregation—illustrated by the founding of the department of household administration and the school of social work. Harper's concern over the university's political involvement dated from the Pullman Strike in 1894, when economist Edward Bemis, a believer in the socialization of essential municipal services and a defender of labor, publicly questioned the justice of the railroad's case against the strikers. The university's public involvement in a politically charged issue brought widespread condemnation, and Harper instructed Bemis to temper his remarks while he remained at the university. Bemis did not remain long. Whether or not his dismissal resulted from his opinions, as he insisted, or from his lack of success as a lecturer in his extension courses, as Harper maintained, historians generally agree that "a quiet, conservative Bemis would have kept his post."[50]

Bemis's immediate academic superior, Albion Small, acted equivocally in this matter. On the one hand, he defended Bemis's reformist views and teaching ability; on the other hand, he disapproved of Bemis's public engagement in a politically controversial issue. Bemis reported that Small told him,

> I do not say that your conclusions are wrong, but in these days a man is not considered scientific, who claims to speak on more than one small corner of a subject. Then, too, there is so much misapprehension of Sociology as a science of reform that although I hope to take up reform movements years hence, I am now going off in my lectures into transcendental philosophy so as to be as far as

49. *One in Spirit,* pp. 77–79. For interesting insights into the process of sexual segregation within academics, see Margaret Rossiter, " 'Women's Work' in Science, 1880–1910," *ISIS* 71 (September 1980): 381–98, and Barbara Elizabeth Brand, "The Influence of Higher Education on Sex-Typing in Three Professions, 1870–1920: Librarianship, Social Work, and Public Health" (Ph.D. diss., University of Washington, 1978), pp. 79–449.

50. Storr, *Harper's University,* p. 84. For a fuller account of the Bemis case, see Richard Hofstadter and Walter Metzger, *The Development of Academic Freedom in the United States* (New York: Columbia University Press, 1955), pp. 425–36, and Mary O. Furner, *Advocacy and Objectivity,* pp. 165–98.

possible from these reform movements and thus establish the scientific character of my department.

Small later remarked that he had used "transcendental philosophy" figuratively in his conversation with Bemis, but he did not deny the substance of his remarks. Though Small often made eloquent appeals for the cooperation of reformers and scholars, he was reluctant to take sides on a controversial issue when doing so would endanger the prestige of the university. Because many women, both inside and outside the university, tended to be more outspoken on political issues than either Small or Harper thought proper, prompting the identification of socialism not just with sociologists but with feminist sociologists in particular, sexual segregation seemed all the more crucial to those who would protect the university's reputation as a bastion of authority and respectability.[51]

Although sexual segregation was sometimes imposed by administrators like Harper who feared feminization, it was also often chosen by women who rejected the narrow vision implicit in the increasingly specialized nature of university research. Women graduate students tended to be more interested in social work than in theoretical sociology, for social work paralleled in the public sphere the kind of work they had been reared to perform in the home. Even when women admitted the importance of scientific expertise, it often remained for them just a tool to be used in trying to soften the strident individualism and class antagonism of male-dominated public life rather than an ultimate goal, as it became for increasing numbers of men at the university and in the Progressive movement.

The Unanticipated Impact of Feminization

Fears of feminization tended to inspire efforts to impose sexual divisions within the university, but those efforts succeeded only partially. Women could be segregated within the university, but the time had passed when they could be denied a university education. Like it or not, women were there to stay, and their presence had ramifications for the American understanding of sexual identity that no one could anticipate. Resistant though people might be to changing ideas on so fundamental a subject as sex, the university provided the unique conditions for just such a change.

In undertaking education reform, and especially in sponsoring graduate research, the University of Chicago fostered a heretical spirit in many

51. Small's remarks to Bemis are quoted in Furner, *Advocacy and Objectivity*, p. 177– 78. Furner writes that Bemis claimed he took notes on his conversation with Small and reported them in a letter to Richard T. Ely (October 23, 1895, Richard Ely Papers, Wisconsin Historical Society). For a discussion of the public's tendency to identify feminism with socialism, see Allen Davis, *Spearheads for Reform*, p. 111.

of its faculty and students. If specialization carried with it the danger, as John Dewey warned, of encouraging "preoccupation with a comparatively remote field in relatively minute detail," it inspired, as well, a critical attitude toward conventional beliefs. Because Chicago had so many women students, not just in the traditionally female area of literature but also in the newly founded social sciences where sexual segregation had not yet become clearly established, the issues of women's nature and place in society generated great interest. Many women preferred reform work to scientific research, but others found in science the means for transcending the cultural bonds that limited their freedom. Even in the university's earliest years there were women, as well as men, who responded to the crisis of feminization at Chicago by rejecting conventional assumptions about sex differences rather than by trying to protect them. For these deviant scholars, academic disciplines became a prism through which men's and women's natures could never again be seen in quite the same way they had been seen before.[52]

For a number of years the Chicago situation remained unique. Most universities with graduate schools refused women admission, or admitted them only as auditors, and thus provided no incentive for developing new ways to think about sex. At schools where there was interest in the issue of sex differences—as at Clark University, where Hall supervised work on sexual identity, and at universities where Hall's students taught, such as Wisconsin and Iowa—antifeminist attitudes insured the perpetuation of conventional beliefs about sex differences. Having struggled against great prejudice to be accepted as scholars, most women who found a solitary place in a major research center strove to prove themselves within the accepted confines of their disciplines and did not risk questioning the prevailing views about women's psychology and sex roles. Even the newly established women's colleges showed little interest in the issue of women's psychology. Determined to establish the legitimacy of their fledgling institutions, leaders of the women's colleges sought to emulate the hallowed traditions of the male colleges just as the men's colleges were beginning to abandon their classical emphasis in favor of scientific research.

For new thinking to take place about sex it was necessary to have both a creative atmosphere and significant numbers of women. In addition, to provide dissident scholars with a sense of support in the face of the prevailing hostility to change in such a sensitive area, a university needed

52. John Dewey, "Academic Freedom," *Educational Review* 23 (January 1902): 9– 13, quoted in Storr, *Harper's University*, p. 340. In 1900, women outnumbered men in the departments of philosophy (which included psychology), pedagogy, history, sociology, Greek, Latin, the modern languages, and English. Men predominated in political science, political economy, and the natural and physical sciences (*President's Report*, 1901, p. 142).

to have at least a few figures in positions of power who thought of themselves as advocates of the woman's movement. Few schools could lay claim to the rare mixture of conditions needed to create an atmosphere conducive to initiating a challenge to conventional ideas about men's and women's natures. Several schools at the turn of the century could claim one or two of these conditions—coeducation, innovative research, or committed feminists—but only the University of Chicago could claim them all. And it was there, despite Harper's effort to segregate women and J. Laurence Laughlin's confident prediction that women posed no threat to conventional educational patterns, that the most dramatic alteration in American social thought in general, and thought about women in particular, took place.

Marion Talbot grew up and worked among women who conceived of feminism, in part, as an effort to right the balance between male individualism and female social concern. Some of her associates, like Antoinette Brown Blackwell in her mother's generation and Jane Addams in her own, believed that the surest way to achieve such a balance was to give women greater power. Others, like Charlotte Perkins Gilman and Talbot herself, believed that achieving this balance required, in addition to power, a broader conception of personality, one that conceded to both men and women feelings and abilities conventionally associated with the opposite sex. Neither Talbot nor Gilman did more than suggest the possibility that social behavior might transcend biological structure, for both women remained strongly tied to the Victorian belief in feminine uniqueness, and work in genetics around 1900 reinforced, at first, the belief in the unalterable nature of femininity and masculinity. But their example, and the example of their sympathetic male colleagues, inspired others to greater iconoclasm. Writers like Ward, Veblen, Thomas, and Addams, who celebrated feminine attributes and denigrated male achievements in the 1890s, laid the foundation for a new generation of scholars to think of feminine and masculine traits as alternative human characteristics rather than as badges of inferiority or superiority. These younger scholars could begin to wonder whether sex differences were so great as had previously been thought, and, more radically, whether most so-called sexual characteristics might not be innate at all.

3 The New Psychology and the New Woman

In the 1890s American magazine writers discovered the New Woman. Her distinguishing characteristics were her independent spirit and athletic zeal. She rode a bicycle, played tennis or golf, showed six inches of stocking beneath her skirts, and loosened her corsets. She expected to marry and have children, but she wanted a life beyond her home— perhaps even a career. Rheta Childe Dorr, a newspaperwoman and later a member of the National Woman's party, described the New Woman as one who wanted "to belong to the human race, not to the ladies' aid society to the human race."[1]

Marion Talbot's women students exemplified this irreverent figure. They disliked household duties, objected to having chaperones, and intended to meet men on a "ground of perfect fellowship" and "to converse freely on every topic." For want of a better alternative, most of them came to the University of Chicago with the goal of becoming teachers. Many who took classes in Chicago's department of pedagogy, however, developed an interest in psychology; for John Dewey, the young professor who supervised the teaching in both education and psychology, made it seem particularly relevant to their concerns. Dewey championed the New Psychology, which was divorced from religion and metaphysics and devoted to the empirical study of the mind; and he won over a number of women students to his cause because he and his colleagues were the first social scientists willing to ask the question which in 1900 seemed most

1. Rheta Childe Dorr, *A Woman of Fifty*, 2d ed. (New York: Funk and Wagnalls, 1924), p. 101. The New Woman first appeared on the stage and in magazines in the mid-1890s. Early examples include Sydney Grundy's 1894 play, "The New Woman," and Sarah Grand, "The New Aspect of the Woman Question," *North American Review* 158 (March 1894): 270–76. The clearest depiction of the New Woman is in Caroline Ticknor, "The Steel Engraving Lady and the Gibson Girl," *Atlantic Monthly* 88 (July 1901): 105–08. For more on the subject, see John Higham, "The Reorientation of American Culture in the 1890s," in his *Writing American History: Essays in Modern Scholarship* (Bloomington: Indiana University Press, 1970), pp. 73–102, and Peter Gabriel Filene, *Him/Her/Self*, pp. 5–25.

pressing to Chicago's women: were the mental traits of males and females as different as most researchers believed them to be?[2]

Helen Bradford Thompson

The student who first took advantage of the willingness to ask that question was Helen Bradford Thompson, one of the young women who came to Chicago to train for a teaching career. Her parents, Isabella and David, both grew up in midwestern farm families before the Civil War but fled the grinding toil of rural life after their marriage, joining the wave of discontented farmers who flooded Chicago in the postwar years. They built a home on the south side of the city and reared three daughters, of whom Helen was the second. David Thompson became a shoe manufacturer and an inventor, but the prosperity he sought eluded him. If his business or his inventions had been more successful, the Thompsons might have frowned on their daughter's teaching aspirations, for in 1890 most families with middle-class pretensions still wanted to support their daughters at home until they married. But as they lived in only modest comfort in a city home with little to occupy a grown daughter, they offered scant resistance to Helen's ambition; in fact, in different ways, each parent fostered her desire to break free from conventional domesticity and to join the growing number of self-confident New Women who wanted to exercise greater control over their lives than their mothers had been able to do.[3]

A conservative and devout Presbyterian who ruled her home with an iron will and forbade games or even reading on Sunday, Isabella Thompson instilled a firm sense of purpose in her middle child. David Thompson, by contrast, called himself a free thinker and fostered his daughter's desire for independence. Removed by an urban upbringing from her mother's pious, rural origins, and influenced by her father's skeptical example, Helen rebelled against her mother's religious regime when she was twelve and declared herself an agnostic. Many girls in her generation lost the religious faith that had given direction to their mothers' lives, but most went on to find fulfillment in social and domestic activities. Helen Thompson, however, saw little attraction in domesticity.

2. Ticknor, "The Steel Engraving Lady," p. 106.
3. Helen Thompson [Woolley] left no personal papers. I am indebted to her daughter, Eleanor Woolley Fowler, for responding to my inquiries about her mother's personal life with a detailed biographical memoir (Eleanor Fowler to author, July 20, 1976). For a discussion of middle-class families' reluctance to encourage daughters to work in 1890, see Robert Smuts, *Women and Work in America* (1959; reprint ed., New York: Schocken, 1971), pp. 19–20, 38–39. See also Margarite Zapoleon and Lois Stolz, "Helen Bradford Thompson Woolley," in Edward James, ed., *Notable American Women, 1607–1950*, 1:657–60.

Her mother's dislike of both cooking and feminine refinement discouraged her from pursuing these secular alternatives to the religious ideas she rejected. She decided instead to become a teacher, in the hope that the profession would provide a respectable release from both religion and housekeeping.[4]

The University of Chicago stood, only half built, in the swamp along Lake Michigan when Helen finished Englewood High School in 1893 at the head of her class; but it was already accepting students, and a disproportionate number of the young men and women who flocked to the new university from the surrounding area came from the families of small businessmen like David Thompson. President Harper observed that the student body did "not perhaps equal in outward polish that of one of the larger institutions of the East"; but what they lacked in polish, he hastened to add, they more than made up for with their "readiness to make sacrifices for the sake of intellectual advancement." Reassured by the proximity and the serious atmosphere of the new university, the Thompsons enrolled their daughter in the freshman class.[5]

The training of teachers at Chicago went far beyond instruction in pedagogical technique, for the chairman of the department of pedagogy, John Dewey, also chaired the department of philosophy and psychology, and he conceived of teacher education in unusually broad terms. Dewey had developed an interest in elementary and high-school education when, while teaching philosophy and psychology at the University of Michigan, he had been appointed a university investigator charged with certifying the instructional quality of the Michigan schools. The inadequacy of much of the public school education he surveyed persuaded Dewey that universities must take an active role in studying and reforming the education of young students. The University of Michigan offered him little support for doing this, and he left for Chicago in 1894, both because interest in educational reform was already firmly established in that city, and because Harper promised him the chance to direct graduate research in pedagogy as well as in philosophy and psychology.[6]

Dewey brought with him to Chicago his closest friend and colleague at Michigan, George Herbert Mead, who shared his wide-ranging interests. From the University of Minnesota, Dewey summoned his former student, James R. Angell, to supervise the department's work in experimental psychology. James Tufts, a former Michigan philosopher already at

4. Eleanor Woolley Fowler to author, July 20, 1976.

5. William Rainey Harper, *President's Report* (Chicago), 1892– 1902, p. xxxiii. The social and economic background of the Chicago student body is discussed in James H. Tufts, "The Senior Colleges," *President's Report,* 1892– 1902, pp. 83– 84.

6. George Dykhuizen, *The Life and Mind of John Dewey* (Carbondale: Southern Illinois Press, 1973), pp. 50– 51, 74.

Chicago, completed the department. Theirs was an exceptionally young group—Dewey was thirty-five, Tufts thirty-two, Mead thirty-one, and Angell only twenty-five—and their youth must have been an important factor in the iconoclastic approach they took to psychology. Over the course of the next decade these scholars, along with the students they taught, created a distinctively American brand of psychology. Because they shared an interest in pedagogy, they attracted a number of women students, like Helen Thompson, who came to Chicago originally to train as teachers but were attracted to the new work being done in psychology and decided to do graduate work in that field instead.[7]

The Origins of the New Psychology

Those who launched psychology at Chicago were all reared in the intensely religious environment of mid-nineteenth-century America. John Dewey grew up in Burlington, Vermont, under the pious supervision of a mother always anxious to know whether he was "right with Jesus." Dewey's father, a well-liked and reasonably successful grocer twenty years his wife's senior, was neither so religious nor so close to his son as she, and he exercised little influence over his son's upbringing. He clearly represented, however, an important model of manhood. Until at least the age of thirty, Dewey devoted an important part of his intellectual life to mediating between the feminine piety he had absorbed from his mother and the masculine example of secular business life that his father provided. His mature dissatisfaction with Victorian society's polarized view of sexual identity stemmed, in part, from his having incorporated both sides of that polarity into his own personality.[8]

To James R. Angell, George Herbert Mead, and James Tufts, the tension between piety and secularism never seemed so troubling as it did to Dewey. Their fathers were ministers and professors—men of piety, intellectuality, and importance in the community—that is, men who had combined both the feminine virtue of religion with public, masculine achievement. James B. Angell, a friend of the Dewey family, was for many years president of the University of Vermont at a time when "reverence," and often ordination, were essential qualifications for the office. Tufts's and Mead's fathers were both Congregational ministers, and Mead's father was also a professor of homiletics (the art of preaching) at the

7. Ibid., pp. 76–80. The significance of the Chicago contribution to psychology is discussed in William James, "The Chicago School," *Psychological Bulletin* 1 (January 1904): 1–5.

8. Neil Coughlan, *Young John Dewey* (Chicago: University of Chicago Press, 1975), pp. 3–5. I have profited greatly from Coughlan's discussion of Dewey's youthful intellectual struggles.

Theological Seminary at Oberlin College. So Angell, Tufts, and Mead all accepted religious feeling as an important part of manhood.[9]

All of these men developed an interest in philosophy while at college, where their clinically trained professors were struggling to reconcile their religious principles with the ideas of modern science. American professors of philosophy were still reeling from the stunning blow to their faith that David Hume had dealt a century before when he dismissed the intuitionist belief in innate ideas as simple mysticism and declared that thoughts are the product of experience, nothing more. The mind, Hume had argued, arranges the data provided by the senses in various ways, but it can produce no independent concepts itself. American philosophy professors accepted the value of empiricism for understanding the material world; but they disputed Hume's contention that the mind was a machine, passively receiving the impressions of the outside world. They argued instead that the mind knows because it is endowed with the basic capacity to see order in the world, to distinguish good from bad, and to know God.[10]

Although clerically trained professors resisted the idea of the mind as a passive machine, a growing number of philosophers trained in Germany seemed ready to embrace it. For Dewey, who sustained his religious faith throughout college in Vermont, the critical moment of doubt came when he entered graduate school at the Johns Hopkins University in 1882 to study philosophy and was introduced, in G. Stanley Hall's seminar, to the ideas emerging from German psychology laboratories. Hall was the first of the Americans to be driven to Germany for advanced training in physiology and psychology because of absence of opportunity at home. In Germany philosophers, physiologists, and physicists interested in mental activity were no longer willing to speculate about the nature and capacity of the human mind. They wanted to move the philosophical debates about mental activity off dead center by examining the mind empirically. Rather than arguing about the extent of innate abilities, they proposed to examine and measure what the mind actually did. This "New Psychology" first emerged from the laboratory of Wilhelm Wundt, whose early training had been in physiology, and who developed the mechanical apparatus

9. Ibid., pp. 6, 114; Dykhuizen, *Life and Mind of John Dewey*, pp. 3, 64. Besides having fathers whose careers transcended the conventional limits of masculine respectability, these men had strong mothers. George Herbert Mead's mother, for instance, became president of Mount Holyoke College in 1890.

10. David Hume, *An Inquiry concerning Human Understanding* (1748: reprint ed., New York: Library of Liberal Arts, 1955), pp. 15–68 and passim; Coughlan, *Young John Dewey*, pp. 11–14; Frank M. Albrecht, "A Reappraisal of Faculty Psychology," *Journal of the History of the Behavioral Sciences* 6 (January 1970): 36–40; Albrecht, "The New Psychology in America, 1880–1895," (Ph.D. diss., Johns Hopkins University, 1960), passim.

John Dewey (ca. 1895)

for measuring sensation, perception, reaction times, attention, and feeling. Drawing heavily on Hume and on English psychology, Wundt directed much of the work in his laboratory toward examining how ideas come to be associated. Hall transported these interests and techniques back to America, where his students patiently tested each other's vision, reflexes, and mental connections.[11]

In the company of his scientifically minded and skeptical peers, who included such future leaders of psychology as James McKeen Cattell and Joseph Jastrow, Dewey found it impossible to sustain his belief in intuition as the basis of knowledge and understanding; yet he was still deeply troubled by the idea that he was the victim of his subjective impressions,

11. Coughlan, *Young John Dewey*, pp. 33–36. Dorothy Ross, *G. Stanley Hall*, pp. 31–170; Edwin G. Boring, *A History of Experimental Psychology*, 2d ed. (New York: Appleton-Century-Crofts, 1950), pp. 316–43, 517–23.

forever divorced from the world beyond his senses. He was drawn to the
new psychology lab at Hopkins, but he could not abandon his conviction
that reason or spirit provided the center and organic unity of human
experience.[12]

Unlike the German experimentalists, Dewey could never see the mind
as a physiological mechanism responding automatically to environmental
stimuli. He believed that the mind was a shaping organ even as it was being
shaped, and that it created reality even as it was being influenced by it. He
was greatly influenced by Hegel in arguing that the material and spiritual
worlds cannot be separated, that subject and environment are one—
continuously shaping and being shaped in the process of their interaction.
But gradually he came to believe that his view of the mind as at one with its
environment did not need the vocabulary or metaphysics of Hegel to find
expression—that as a philosophical analysis of development it could
stand on its own.[13]

What made this possible was Darwinism. Darwin's analysis of humans as
part of nature, rather than above nature, satisfied Dewey's preoccupation
with organic unity without his having to rely on theistic principles. Dewey
read Darwin, Spencer, and Huxley in college and began to doubt the
theory of divine creation, the value of a priori reasoning, and the abstract,
intricate arguments about the nature of the soul. The more interested he
became in psychology, the more important Darwin's theory seemed to
him.[14]

Darwinism, however, inspired Dewey in a very different way from the
way in which it had inspired Dewey's mentor, G. Stanley Hall. In understanding sex differences, for instance, Darwinism provided Hall with a
system for justifying the steady divergence of sex roles with advancing
civilization. To Dewey, on the other hand, Darwinism provided no such
justification, but rather a method by which thinkers could free themselves
from old, metaphysical ways of thinking to see men and women as part of
the natural order, striving to adapt to changing circumstances in ways no
one could predict. During the 1909 commemoration of Darwin's fifty

12. Coughlan, *Young John Dewey*, pp. 33– 36; Boring, *History of Experimental Psychology*,
p. 520.

13. John Dewey, "The New Psychology," *Andover Review*, vol. 2 (1884), reprinted in Jo
Ann Boydston, ed., *The Early Works of John Dewey, 1882 – 1898*, 5 vols. (Carbondale: Southern Illinois University Press, 1967– 72), 1:60; Coughlan, *Young John Dewey*, pp. 18– 33,
37– 41; Dykhuizen, *Life and Mind of John Dewey*, pp. 28– 43.

14. John Dewey, "From Absolutism to Experimentalism," in George P. Adams and
William P. Montague, eds., *Contemporary American Philosophy*, 2 vols. (New York: Macmillan,
(1930), 2:13; Lewis Feuer, "John Dewey's Reading at College," *Journal of the History of Ideas*
19 (June 1958): 415– 21. See also Hamilton Cravens and John C. Burnham, "Psychology
and Evolutionary Naturalism in American Thought, 1890– 1940," *American Quarterly* 23
(December 1971): 634– 57.

years of influence, Dewey reflected on the different ways in which Darwinism had been used.

No one can fairly deny that at present there are two effects of the Darwinian mode of thinking. On the one hand, there are [those] making many sincere and vital efforts to revise our traditional philosophic conceptions in accordance with its demands. On the other hand, there is definitely a recrudescence of absolutist philosophies; an assertion of a type of philosophic knowing distinct from that of science.

The thought of both Hall and Dewey grew out of the Darwinian tradition of developmental biology and the German tradition of physiological research which had given America an experimental psychology; but Hall took the conservative path in both areas, while Dewey rejected the absolutist strain in Darwinist theory and the mechanism of German psychology in favor of what he called a functionalist approach.[15]

Evolutionism, Hegelianism, and the empirical investigations of the New Psychology thus worked in Dewey to free him from his earlier religious attitudes without requiring that he abandon his belief in individual autonomy and purpose. By the time Dewey left Michigan, he had abandoned the Congregational church and was ready to advance his own brand of the New Psychology. Those whom he encouraged at Michigan joined him in that commitment. George Herbert Mead, James Tufts, and James R. Angell all studied psychology in Germany, and each contributed to Dewey's move toward empiricism, while they all reinforced each other's basic impulse to see the world in organic terms. Only when the mind is studied in its social context, they believed, can mental activity be fully understood. It was time to relinquish the old dualism between sensation and idea, between body and mind. The mind is neither a mechanical instrument nor an ethereal soul, but an organ both shaped by and capable of shaping its environment.[16]

His critique of experimentalism notwithstanding, Dewey encouraged experimental work at Chicago. With the latest German laboratory equipment, which James Angell managed to commandeer from the 1893 Chicago World's Fair, Chicago boasted the most up-to-date psychology

15. John Dewey, *The Influence of Darwin on Philosophy* (New York: Henry Holt, 1910), p. 18. For an excellent analysis of Hall's conservative attitude toward sex roles, see Ross, *G. Stanley Hall*, pp. 261–66.

16. Dykhuizen, *Life and Mind of John Dewey*, p. 74; Alfred Raphelson, "The Pre-Chicago Association of the Early Functionalists," pp. 115–22. The convergence of the disparate intellectual forces that shaped the scholarly lives of Dewey and the young men he brought from Michigan can be most clearly seen in John Dewey, "The Reflex-Arc Concept in Psychology," *Psychological Review* 3 (July 1896): 357–59. See also Richard Lowry, "The Reflex Model in Psychology: Origins and Evolution," *Journal of the History of the Behavioral Sciences* 6 (January 1970): 64–69, and, more generally, David A. Hollinger, "The Problem of Pragmatism in American History," *Journal of American History* 67 (June 1980): 88–107.

lab in the country. The theory under which these devices were used, however, differed in important ways from the New Psychology that was being taught in Germany. Unlike their German mentors, Dewey and his associates did not conceive of the mind in universal terms—as a fixed structure to be explored and mapped. Members of a polyglot society, where individuality was honored as an ideal and diversity displayed as a social fact, the Chicago psychologists were much more interested in the individual mind than in the universal mind. They drew heavily, therefore, on Darwinian theory, for in Darwinism they found reflected their interest in the process of individual development and adaptation.

On this part-German, part-English base, the Chicago psychologists proceeded to build a new theory of the mind which, within the next decade, transcended both of these initial influences. The liberating potential in this German-English fusion for groups that had been traditionally relegated to one of the lower classificatory levels, either in religion's great chain of being or, more recently, on the evolutionary scale, was significant. The withering skepticism of the German experimentalists combined with the vision of interdependence and adaptation of the Darwinists provided ammunition, in the hands of those inclined to use it, for criticizing the social context in which minds developed, as well as for supporting the belief that minds are capable of rising above their social context.[17]

One of those who saw the possibilities in this German-English fusion was Helen Thompson. While still an undergraduate, she attracted the attention of her teachers in the departments of philosophy and psychology and of pedagogy. Slightly built, very pretty, and brilliant, she was everyone's favorite student. And everyone thought she should do graduate work in psychology.[18]

Women and Psychology at Chicago

The Michigan background of the entire philosophy department may explain, in part, the receptivity toward women at the University of Chicago. James Angell's father, as president of the University of Michigan, had been an outspoken advocate for coeducation from the beginning. When Edward Clarke first issued his dire warning about the dangerous consequences implicit in women's education, President Angell retorted that in Michigan's three years of experience with coeducation the female students "held their own with the young men in languages, as well as mathematics," "that they maintained good health and they lost no

17. John Dewey, "Psychology and Social Practice," *Psychological Review* 7 (March 1900): 119; "James R. Angell," autobiographical essay in Carl Murchison, ed., *A History of Psychology in Autobiography*, 3 vols. (Worcester, Mass.: Clark University Press, 1936), 3:27– 30; Angell, "The Province of Functional Psychology," *Psychological Review* 14 (March 1907): 61– 91.

18. "James R. Angell," pp. 30– 33.

charm." Eight years later Angell added, "I think that the solicitude concerning the health of the women has not proved well-founded. On the contrary, I am convinced that a young woman, coming here in fair health . . . is quite as likely to be in good health at the time of her graduation as she would have been if she had remained home." As to the quality of the women's work at Michigan, he reported, "There is no branch of study pursued in any of our schools in which some women have not done superior work. It was soon found that in those studies which are thought to make the most strenuous demand of the intellect, some of the women took equal rank with the men. They have desired and have received no favors."[19]

James R. Angell

19. James B. Angell, "Our Young Women," *Woman's Journal*, August 23, 1873, p. 267; J. B. Angell, "Co-education at Michigan University," *Pennsylvania School Journal* 29 (January 1881): 281. See also James B. Angell, "Co-education in Relation to Other Types of College Education for Women," *Proceedings of the National Education Association*, 1904, pp. 548– 49.

James R. Angell came to share his father's respect for scholarly women. After a year of graduate study in Germany, he married fellow University of Michigan graduate Marion Watrous. During the year he was in Germany, Angell received a steady stream of letters from Watrous, many of them peppered with feminist remarks and observations. She challenged him for complaining about the women in his German seminars and wondered whether Germany could be so different from Ann Arbor, "if the women don't show some work quite on a par with the men." She condemned a pamphlet she had read by "your friend Herbert Spencer" for advising against higher education for young ladies. And she praised another article by Alice Freeman Palmer supporting coeducation on the grounds that nothing would "take the foolishness and romantic notions out of a girl so quick as to work with young men," for then "she will find out how little they know."[20]

Angell later remembered with pride that after his marriage and move to Chicago, his wife not only cared for their two young children but also "won a place of importance for herself in the community, identifying herself with many significant social enterprises." Angell admired his wife for belonging to that class of "new women" who had transcended the "beaten path of the domestic treadmill with its everlasting insistence upon the incident of sex," and had entered "fields where social service is gauged by other standards than those of child-bearing, housekeeping and adorning pink teas."[21]

For the younger women who were his students at Chicago he foresaw even broader possibilities. Throughout the debate over coeducation at Chicago in 1902, Angell insisted on maintaining absolute equality of opportunity for women. He scorned those "men who insist that women will never become investigators of any consequence," who concede only that women have "capacities for assimilation," and who reluctantly teach women on the theory that, "as there must under existing conditions be some women teachers in both schools and colleges, it is desirable that they should receive the most thorough possible discipline." Angell predicted that when women were given encouragement in graduate study and when they no longer felt obliged to "conform their collegiate work to immediate bread and butter issues [i.e., becoming high-school teachers]," they would demonstrate broader interests and greater talents than they had been able to display up to that time.[22]

20. Marion Watrous to James R. Angell, November 1, 1893; November 5, 1893; November 5, 1893 (second letter of the day), James R. Angell Papers, Yale University Library, New Haven, Conn.

21. "James R. Angell," in Murchison, ed., *History of Psychology in Autobiography*, pp. 2, 12– 13; James R. Angell, "Some Reflections upon the Reaction from Coeducation," *Popular Science Monthly* 62 (November 1902): 20.

22. Angell, "Some Reflections," pp. 14– 15, 24, 13.

John Dewey shared Angell's attitude toward women and, like Angell, married a Michigan graduate. Dewey met his wife, Alice Chipman, at the University of Michigan boardinghouse where they both took their meals. Having taught for several years before entering college, she was the same age as Dewey (twenty-five) and had already developed a strong interest in philosophy. They married when she graduated from college in 1886. In addition to having six children, Alice Dewey shared actively in Dewey's work, helping to found and then directing the Chicago Laboratory School. She was widely admired as an exceptionally intelligent woman who had an important liberalizing influence on her husband. As her daughter later recalled:

> Her influence on a young man from conservative Burlington was stimulating and exciting. . . . She had a brilliant mind which cut through sham and pretense to the essence of the situation; a sensitive nature combined with indomitable courage and energy. . . . Above all, things which had previously been matters of theory acquired through his contact with her a vital and direct human significance.

Alice Dewey had a powerful influence on other women as well. An active member of the Association of Collegiate Alumnae, she fought for women's education and suffrage and encouraged her friends to do likewise. George Herbert Mead's sister-in-law once reported:

> Last night Mrs. Dewey and I sat before the open fire two hours discussing vital issues, and among other things she gave me a talk on Zola—his scope his scheme, his success. . . . My admiration for her is unbounded . . . I believe that Mrs. Dewey does look at things frankly, with the utmost honesty, the utmost reason and understanding I have yet seen in a woman—of men I say nothing. I enjoy Mrs. Dewey, and she helps me to think of life, real activities, more than the subjectivities of my own communings with self.[23]

George Herbert Mead's wife, Helen Castle Mead, was another unusual woman. Her father had gone to Hawaii before the Civil War to administer the financial affairs of the Calvinist missions there and had become a wealthy sugar planter. He sent both his son Henry and his daughter Helen to Oberlin College in the late 1870s, and it was there they met Mead. Both Henry and Helen made important contributions to Mead's thinking. Having grown up in a racially diverse but socially integrated culture, the Castles had an egalitarian attitude toward race relations that was still unusual in the United States. Jane Addams remembered Helen Mead after her death as the "absolute democrat," one who fully accepted

23. Jane M. Dewey, ed., "Biography of John Dewey," in Paul A. Schilpp, ed., *The Philosophy of John Dewey*, p. 21; Mabel Castle to Henry Northrup Castle, December 31, 1893, Henry Northrup Castle Papers, University of Chicago Library, quoted in Coughlan, *Young John Dewey*, p. 92. See also Judy Suratt, "Alice Chipman Dewey," in James, ed., *Notable American Women, 1607 – 1950*, 1:466 – 68.

Chicago's ethnic diversity and was not in the least disturbed when blacks started moving into Chicago's South Side.[24]

Mead and the Castles all grew skeptical of Calvinist orthodoxy while in college, and their postgraduate study in Germany reinforced their doubts. Though Henry Castle appears to have been the most important intellectual influence on George's young life, Helen clearly affected his attitude toward women by her cosmopolitan outlook, her independence, and her intellectual seriousness.

Married to exceptionally well-educated women who were all involved in the community activities of their day, these young philosopher-psychologists tended to accept and encourage talent among their women students to a degree unusual for that time. Besides, their field was still small, with only a handful of students each year and without, as yet, the prestige it was later to attain; in such circumstances it was prudent to encourage the best students they could find.[25]

Much of the work the women did simply helped the professors in their own research. Thompson, for instance, wrote a paper with James Tufts on "The Individual and His Relation to Society," and with James Angell on "A Study of the Relations between Certain Organic Processes and Consciousness." But the women saw personal relevance in the new psychology, and with the advice and support of their professors they used it to reexamine conventional views of sex differences.[26]

24. "Helen Castle Mead," a memorial, December 27, 1929, Widener Library, Harvard University, quoted in Helen Swick Perry (ed.), introduction to Harry Stack Sullivan, *The Fusion of Psychiatry and the Social Sciences* (1964; reprint ed., New York: W. W. Norton, 1971), pp. xxxi– xxxii. For further information on the Mead and Castle families, see Mary Castle, ed., *Henry Northrup Castle: Letters* (London: Sands and Co., 1902 [privately printed]; in the University of Chicago Archives); David Wallace, "Reflections on the Education of George Herbert Mead," *American Journal of Sociology* 72 (January 1967): 396– 408.

25. In 1897– 98, approximately 3 percent of the men and 2.5 percent of the women (both undergraduate and graduate) were taking courses in philosophy, psychology, and pedagogy, whereas 20 percent of the women and 8 percent of the men were taking courses in the university's most popular department, English (Marion Talbot, "The Women of the University," *President's Report,* 1897– 98, pp. 120, 125– 26). Until 1908 the University of Chicago produced one Ph.D. a year, while Clark University, the country's leading producer of psychologists, was producing three a year. After 1910, Chicago rarely fell below four a year, and in some years produced as many as ten (Robert Harper, "Tables of American Doctorates in Psychology," *American Journal of Psychology* 62 [October 1949]: 581). Among women doing graduate work in the late 1890s were Amy Tanner, Kate Gordon, Helen Thompson, Frances Kellor, and Harriet Penfield.

26. James Tufts and Helen B. Thompson, *The Individual and His Relation to Society* (Chicago: University of Chicago Press, 1898); James R. Angell and Helen B. Thompson, "The Relation between Certain Organic Processes and Consciousness," *Psychological Review* 6 (January 1899): 32– 69. For examples of women other than Thompson who published research about women, see Amy Tanner, "The Community of Ideas of Men and Women," *Psychological Review* 3 (September 1896): 548– 50, and Frances Kellor, "A Psychological and

In most other psychology laboratories in the 1890s, it was difficult for women graduate students to work on the topic of sex differences. The earliest women to make names for themselves in psychology found little opportunity for graduate training, and even less support for criticizing accepted beliefs about men's and women's natures. Christine Ladd-Franklin, an active feminist throughout her life and famous for her contributions to logic and the theory of vision, persuaded Johns Hopkins to let her take courses between 1879 and 1882; but though she completed the requirements for a Ph.D. the university refused to grant a woman a degree. Mary Whiton Calkins, who did early work in personality theory, completed the requirements for the Ph.D. in philosophy and psychology at Harvard under William James's direction but, despite the unanimous support of her department, was denied a degree by Harvard because she was a female.

Calkins conducted a pioneering experiment on women and the association of ideas at Wellesley after she became a professor there, which proved important in stimulating later work; but she did not pursue other work on sex differences. It was far from easy in a small, women's college laboratory, without the stimulation of a faculty and student body devoted principally to research, to conduct advanced research, especially on the topic of sex differences. Margaret Floy Washburn would have been a logical person to work in this area. She tried to study at Columbia in the early 1890s when James McKeen Cattell was building his lab and encouraging students to do studies of individual differences. Cattell held strictly traditional views about women, however, and Columbia refused to grant women students full academic standing until 1900—so Washburn left after one year.[27]

The two universities most open to women in psychology in 1892 were Cornell and Clark, but in different ways each limited the kind of research women felt free to do. When Washburn left Columbia in 1892, she went to

Environmental Study of Women Criminals," *American Journal of Sociology* 5 (July 1899– May 1900): 527– 43, 671– 82.

27. Dorothea Hurvich, "Christine Ladd-Franklin," in James, ed., *Notable American Women*, 2:354– 56; Hugh Hawkins, *Pioneer: A History of the Johns Hopkins University, 1874 – 1889* (Ithaca, N.Y.: Cornell University Press, 1960), pp. 259– 67. For a sympathetic account by Ladd-Franklin of another woman's difficulty in achieving intellectual recognition, see Christine Ladd-Franklin, "Sophie Germain, An Unknown Mathematician," *Century* 48 (October 1894): 946– 49. For the difficulties women faced at Harvard, see "Mary Whiton Calkins," autobiographical essay in Murchison, ed., *History of Psychology in Autobiography*, 1:31– 62; Laurel Furumoto, "Mary Whiton Calkins (1863– 1930): Fourteenth President of the American Psychological Association," *Journal of the History of the Behavioral Sciences* 15 (October 1979): 346– 56; Hugo Munsterberg, "The American Woman," *International Monthly* 3 (June 1901): 607– 33. For Washburn's difficulties at Columbia, see "Margaret Floy Washburn" in Murchison, ed., *History of Psychology in Autobiography*, 2:333– 58.

Cornell to work with Edward Titchener, who had just come from Wundt's laboratory. From Titchener she learned the orthodox German approach to psychology called structuralism. Structuralists confined their experiments to trying to identify and to analyze, through introspection, the elements of mental activity. They conceived of the mind in universal terms and considered a preoccupation with individual differences a distraction from the "real" purpose of psychology: understanding the mind in general. After graduating from Cornell, Washburn taught at Vassar, where she and her students carried out experiments on the structuralist model.[28]

Women who studied at Clark University worked in the shadow of G. Stanley Hall's hostility to any criticism of traditional views of sex differences, and none of them broached the topic in their research—although a few men, following Hall's approach, did write about sex differences. For the most part, the work of women psychologists followed the pattern established by their mentors. At Chicago, however, women students were encouraged to challenge some of the most widely accepted beliefs about sex differences. Those who did so contributed in important ways to the developing theory of the mind and personality at Chicago.[29]

The Mental Traits of Sex

In 1898, Helen Thompson finished her course work and began casting about for a dissertation topic. She knew that she wanted to work in the laboratory with Angell and to continue in some way the experimental work she had been doing with him on changes in mental states under varying conditions. The problem that interested her most was that of mental differences between men and women, and Angell agreed that it was time to try to make some sense out of the welter of popular and scientific testimony on this sensitive issue.[30]

28. Before 1920, the top producers of women Ph.D.'s in psychology were the University of Chicago (15), Cornell (10), Columbia (9), and Clark (4). For further figures, see Margaret Rossiter, "Women Scientists in America before 1920," *American Scientist* 62 (May– June 1974): 312– 23. For a summary of Titchener's approach to psychology, see Boring, *History of Experimental Psychology,* pp. 410– 20. One important exception to the lack of interest in individual differences at Cornell can be seen in the work of one of Titchener's women students, Stella Sharp, "Individual Psychology: A Study in Psychological Method," *American Journal of Psychology* 10 (April 1899): 329– 91. Sharp did not discuss sex differences.

29. Ross, *G. Stanley Hall,* p. 416. Examples of work done on sex differences by Hall's male students are Lewis M. Terman, "A Study of Precocity and Prematuration," *American Journal of Psychology* 16 (April 1905): 145– 83, and Arnold Gesell, "Accuracy in Handwriting, As Related to School Intelligence and Sex," *American Journal of Psychology* 17 (July 1906): 394– 405.

30. "James R. Angell," in Murchison, ed., *History of Psychology in Autobiography,* 3:30– 31.

Helen Thompson [Woolley]

As Thompson surveyed the literature on sexual differences that accumulated during the previous twenty-five years, she was able to identify four basic assumptions about human nature in general and woman's nature in particular:

1. At the turn of the century, scientific and popular writers agreed that human physiology mirrored, in its basic structure, the physiology of lower animals.

2. Human psychology was believed to be a product of human physiology, and differences in physiology were believed to correlate with differences in mental capacity.

3. Men, writers agreed, possessed a highly active metabolism that had, from the beginning of evolution, led to a broader spectrum of variability in males (more geniuses and more idiots) and in general to a more analytical mind. Women, on the other hand, were believed to possess a more quiescent metabolism, which produced less variation, a tendency

toward mediocrity, and, in general, an emotional and irrational mind.

4. These varying psychologies suited men and women to different roles within society. Men were particularly well adapted to lives of science and commerce, while women were best fitted to lives of family care and social activity. Popular writers and academicians, feminists and anti-feminists, all appeared to agree that women were metabolically less active than men and therefore psychologically less active as well.[31]

Beyond this general agreement about the nature of sex differences confusion prevailed. Most analyses, Thompson concluded, owed nothing to the new experimentalism; they were formalistic, rigid, deductive—and so inconsistent that many arguments failed to support the prejudices their writers sought to vindicate. For example, Thompson wrote:

> Women are said to represent concentration, patience, and stability in emotional life. One might logically conclude that prolonged concentration of attention and unbiased generalization would be their intellectual characteristics. But these are the very characteristics assigned to men. Women, though more stable in their emotions, are more influenced by them, and, although they represent patience and concentration, they are incapable of prolonged efforts of attention.

The popular use of the generative cells to illustrate the far-reaching nature of sex differences typified the confusion inherent in the prevailing biological view: the large immobile egg represented women's anabolic nature, while the small, agile sperm represented man's katabolism. Yet, given many of the conventional prejudices about women, Thompson observed, the evolutionists would have been far better served if the nature of the generative cells had been reversed.

> In that case, the female cell, smaller and more agile than the male, would represent woman with her smaller size, her excitable nervous system, and her incapacity for sustained effort of attention; while the male cell, large, calm, and self-contained, would image the size and strength, the impartial reason, and the easy concentration of men.

"The biological theory of psychological differences of sex," concluded Thompson, "is not in a condition to compel assent."[32]

---

31. Helen Bradford Thompson [Woolley], *The Mental Traits of Sex: An Experimental Investigation of the Normal Mind in Men and Women* (Chicago: University of Chicago Press, 1903), pp. 169–82. For an early effort to place Thompson's work in historical perspective, see Viola Klein, *The Feminine Character: History of an Ideology* (1946; reprint ed., Urbana: University of Illinois Press, 1971), pp. 91–103.

32. Ibid., pp. 173, 174, 176. Thompson faulted, in particular, the work of Geddes and Thomson, G. T. W. Patrick, W. K. Brooks, and Havelock Ellis, both for their extravagant claims of sexual divergence as well as for the inconsistencies in the analysis they advanced to support those claims. See Patrick Geddes and J. Arthur Thomson, *The Evolution of Sex;*

If Thompson achieved nothing else in her thesis, she demonstrated in her review of the current literature the inconsistencies and contradictions that characterized conventional wisdom about sex differences. Though belief in masculine and feminine uniqueness had never been so marked as it was in 1900, Thompson's assemblage of current writings demonstrated the inability of those most knowledgeable about the subject to reach any consensus on what those differences actually were. Only a careful, experimental investigation of men's and women's psychologies, Thompson believed, could resolve the disputes over sex differences. The experimental study of mental traits was still a novelty in 1900; laboratory techniques were primitive and I.Q. tests as yet undeveloped. The little experimental work that had taken account of sex differences had been in the form of isolated experiments on some single sense or intellectual process. Thompson wanted to "obtain a complete and systematic statement of the psychological likenesses and differences of the sexes by the experimental method."[33]

For her research Thompson chose fifty Chicago undergraduates, half women and half men, of the same age and background; and, in the best tradition of German experimentation, she devoted the major portion of her study to an examination of their motor skills and sensory abilities. She measured auditory and visual reaction times, rapidity of finger movement, ability to strike a target, pain threshold, and the ability to discriminate between heat and cold. Unlike German experimentalists, however, Thompson looked not for evidence of universal mental processes but rather for indications of individual, and especially sexual, differences.

She found wide variation in individual performance but only random patterns of sex differences. In her motor tests, for instance, the men demonstrated greater speed and endurance in the tapping test and greater accuracy in striking a target, as might have been expected, but the women prevailed in sorting different colored cards into piles and in producing spontaneous motor movements. The tests of perception and sensation proved similarly inconclusive. Though some of the results confirmed popular belief in women's greater sensitivity, others did not. The women generally demonstrated a lower threshold in recognizing touch, pain, sweetness, sourness, smell, and color, but the men showed a finer ability to discriminate between different tastes, weights, and colors. Some of the tests favored the men, others favored the women, but what most impressed Thompson was how slight the differences were.[34]

G. T. W. Patrick, "The Psychology of Woman," *Popular Science Monthly* 47 (June 1895): 209–25; W. K. Brooks, "Woman from the Standpoint of Naturalist," *Forum* 22 (November 1896): 286–96; Havelock Ellis, *Man and Woman: A Study of Human Secondary Characteristics* (London: Walter Scott, 1895).

33. Thompson [Woolley], *Mental Traits of Sex*, pp. 1, 3–6.
34. Ibid., pp. 8–92.

Thompson's emphasis on the similarities displayed by her subjects depended in part on her method of evaluating her data. Most students of sex differences averaged the results of their tests, but Thompson graphed them. Following the example of the English psychologist and statistician Francis Galton, she contended that it was more important to know the distribution of the measurements within a group than to know the simple average of those measurements. Though the average performance of the women she tested often differed from the average performance of the men, the distribution curve of any particular trait over the sample of women studied overlapped almost completely with the distribution curve of the trait for men. Given this marked overlapping of simple mental traits, Thompson doubted that they could be used as fundamental indices to either male or female intelligence.[35]

Statistical work by the young anthropologist and psychologist Clark Wissler, who was then working in James McKeen Cattell's Columbia laboratory, lent support to Thompson's skepticism. Wissler employed not only Galton's graphing techniques but his method of calculating correlation as well. When Galton displayed data concerning specific physical attributes (such as height or length of limb) on a graph, he was able to show that, for any physical trait belonging to a single person, the ratio between the measure of that trait and the average of the group remained constant. In other words, Galton's studies showed that long-legged people tended to be long-armed as well; moreover, long-legged and long-armed people tended to have large cranial capacities. Through correlating physical measurements, Galton believed he could measure mental ability, for if physical measurements could be correlated, then correlative studies of cranial capacity and simple mental abilities might yield a mathematical measure of less accessible qualities of intelligence.[36]

Though Cattell shared Galton's belief that tests of simple motor abilities and perception would provide an index to higher mental ability, Wissler concluded that the effort to infer general mental ability from reaction times and sensory tests was misguided. In the past, he explained— thinking, no doubt, of Cattell and Galton—"The measuring psychologist set down reaction time, perception time, accuracy of movement, etc. . . . as characteristics common to all acts." Exaggerating for the sake of clearness,

35. Ibid., pp. 6 – 7. For a discussion of Galton's contribution to the application of statistics to anthropometric data, see Boring, *History of Experimental Psychology*, pp. 478– 88, 499– 501. It should be noted that Galton believed his statistical analysis of sex differences demonstrated women's inferiority to men in all their capacities. Francis Galton, *Hereditary Genius* (London: Macmillan, 1869), pp. 326– 31.

36. Clark Wissler, "The Correlation of Mental and Physical Tests," *Monograph Supplement to the Psychological Review* 3, no. 16 (June 1901): 1– 60. For Galton's formulation of correlation, see R. G. Swinburne, "Galton's Law— Formulation and Development," *Annals of Science* 21 (March 1965): 21.

"he was tempted to hope that from a few figures in his laboratory notebook he could estimate the general worth of the man; in other words, assign him a place in some general scheme, such, for example, as a classification according to good, medium, poor."[37]

Wissler could find no justification for such classificatory ambitions in the data accumulated in the Columbia lab. Using college grades to indicate general intelligence along with standard tests of motor ability and perception to quantify elementary abilities, he found that, "while the marks of students correlate with each other to a considerable degree, they show little tendency to do so with the mental tests of the psychologists." The laboratory tests of which the experimental psychologists were so proud, he remarked, "tell us nothing as to the general individual worth of college students or of adults. Indeed, they lead us to doubt the existence of such a thing as general ability."[38]

Though Wissler included Barnard women in his experiments and recorded his results according to sex, he noted that sex differences were "incidental" to his research. He suggested, however, that the tests then in use among psychologists would provide no better guide to sex differences in intelligence.[39]

If minds differed in any regular way because of sex, Wissler suggested, and Thompson agreed, those mental differences must be due to qualities peculiar to the higher mental processes. Though psychologists had developed elaborate tests of motor skills and perception by 1900, they had been singularly unsuccessful in studying more complicated mental abilities. Thompson had to improvise her own tests. The simplest of these

37. Wissler, "Correlation of Mental and Physical Tests," p. 56. For evidence of Cattell's faith that tests of simple motor abilities would provide measures of intelligence, see J. McKeen Cattell and Livingston Farrand, "Physical and Mental Measurements of the Students of Columbia University," *Psychological Review* 3 (November 1896): 620, 648; Cattell, "Mental Tests and Measurements," *Mind* 15 (July 1890): 373–81. See also Edward L. Thorndike, "Professor Cattell's Relation to the Study of Individual Differences," in Robert S. Woodworth, ed., *The Psychological Researches of James McKeen Cattell,* Archives of Psychology, no. 13 (April 1914), pp. 92 – 101.

38. Wissler, "Correlation of Mental and Physical Tests," pp. 47, 55. Further support for Wissler and Thompson's doubts that simple mental tests could provide measures of general ability was provided by Stella Sharp, "Individual Psychology," pp. 388– 91.

39. Wissler, "Correlation of Mental and Physical Tests," p. 51. For further evidence that intelligence does not correlate with physical measurements, Wissler cited the research of Alice Lee, an assistant to Karl Pearson in London, who had compared the skulls of 60 men and 30 women with estimates made of their intelligence. "It would be impossible to assert any marked degree of correlation between the skull capacities of these individuals and the current appreciation of their intellectual capacities," Lee wrote. "One of the most distinguished of continental anthropologists has less skull capacity than 50 percent of the women students at Bedford College; one of our leading English anatomists [less] than 25 percent of the same students." Alice Lee, "A Study of the Human Skull," *Science* 12 (December 1900): 949.

tests originated in work that Mary Calkins had done in "association" at Wellesley College after her informal graduate work at Harvard. In Calkins's test the experimenter placed herself out of the subject's view and showed him or her a series of numbers paired with colors. Later the subject was shown a color and asked to "associate" it with a number. In her method of paired associates, Calkins sought to undermine the belief that learning depended on the mind's capacity to perceive relationships. Learning, she argued, in common with Hume and English associationists, proceeded simply by the random juxtaposition of images and ideas. Calkins believed she had found ammunition in her experiments for attacking the belief in women's intellectual inferiority and argued that women's thought patterns differed from men's only to the extent that their experiences differed.[40]

She demonstrated her theory of association as it related to sex by asking a group of Wellesley students to write one hundred words as rapidly as possible. The test was made as part of a debate between Calkins and Joseph Jastrow of Wisconsin conducted in the pages of the *Psychological Review* in 1895– 96. Jastrow gave the hundred-word association test to men and women students at Wisconsin, and when the two researchers compared data, they both observed a greater tendency among the women subjects to use words associated with interior furnishings and food. In this fact Jastrow found evidence of a "strong preference of the feminine mind for certain concrete and familiar classes of words." But Calkins argued that such associations were produced by habit and did not derive from innate predisposition: women's interest in domestic objects was neither innate nor evidence of a concrete mentality but, rather, due to cultivated interests.[41]

Jastrow and Calkins never resolved their debate, for as Amy Tanner, a Chicago graduate student, noted in a critique of their exchange, each psychologist was arguing from different assumptions about the mind. Jastrow accepted the Darwinian argument that the tendency to make particular associations is an innate, sex-differentiated trait, which has gradually evolved, while Calkins believed that associations are not themselves inherited, but are formed by each mind according to individual experience.[42]

40. Mary W. Calkins, "Community of Ideas of Men and Women," *Psychological Review* 3 (July 1896): 426. For a general history of association as it developed in the nineteenth century, see Robert M. Young, *Mind, Brain, and Adaptation in the Nineteenth Century,* passim, and Robert Woodworth, *Contemporary Schools of Psychology* (New York: Ronald Press, 1942), pp. 37– 67.

41. Joseph Jastrow, "Community of Ideas of Men and Women," *Psychological Review* 3 (September 1896): 548– 50.

42. Amy Tanner, "The Community of Ideas of Men and Women," pp. 548– 50.

Thompson believed, with Calkins, that learning proceeds by association, but she found the technical problems of convincing the Jastrow doubters insurmountable. Even though she had purposely chosen subjects of similar background, something that neither Jastrow nor Calkins had attempted to do, she found it impossible to derive satisfactory results from the Calkins-Jastrow test. "Until there is more unanimity in the psychological world about the best classification of associations, and the evaluation of the classified results, it seems useless to employ the test for a comparative study." Thompson's problem was more than technical; without general agreement on the nature of the mind or the importance of social attitudes in human development, there could be no consensus on the meaning of the tests' results.[43]

Using a simplified version of the association test, Thompson tried to reduce the difficulty of interpretation. She asked her subjects to list one hundred words beginning with a sex-neutral term like *flunk*, an immediately recognized concept in university experience, and she noted the speed of association and the number of general topics touched on. The women, she found, made associations more quickly and covered a greater number of topics. With some hesitation, however, she concluded that the test furnished no ground for any statement about comparative intellectual ability. "There are two factors which seem to be of equal importance in logical processes," she suggested: "one is the ability to concentrate the attention on one topic, and the other is the presence of a large number and great variety of associations. . . . The association test indicates that men have the advantage in one of these factors and women in the other."[44]

Thompson tried a more direct examination of intellectual ability with puzzles to test ingenuity and with general information exams. She found sex differences far more pronounced in the puzzle tests than they had been in the tests of either perception or association, but she believed that the men's superior performance could be traced to the emphasis placed on mechanical training among boys and therefore discounted the significance of this finding. In evaluating the results of her general information exams, she found no difference at all between the men and the women "who had taken the same course of education." Where she found differences in general knowledge, she also found differences in the selection of courses.

Many of the women were preparing to be teachers, and had, therefore, from practical considerations, devoted themselves primarily to those subjects in which the openings for women are most numerous, viz. literary subjects.

43. Thompson [Woolley], *Mental Traits of Sex*, p. 100.
44. Ibid., p. 109.

Compared with the intelligence tests later developed by Alfred Binet in France and Lewis Terman in America, Thompson's puzzles and information exams are strikingly crude; but despite their primitive quality they raised serious doubts about the existence of distinctively male and female types.[45]

If the examination of intelligence proved troublesome and sometimes inconclusive, Helen Thompson's desire to study emotion as well brought even greater difficulty. In the popular imagination, emotional differences seemed undeniably pronounced; indeed, the general conception of emotion as a visceral impulse would have dissuaded some students from considering it as a mental trait. The functionalists, however, had been trying to analyze the affective processes for many years. Dewey and Angell both believed that emotion is a variety of mental action, subject to the same forms of analysis used for other mental processes. Emotion, they argued, facilitates the resolution of mental conflict; a cry or a laugh relieves mental tension. To the functionalist, emotion is one of a range of mental traits enabling people to adapt to their environment. Different experience makes possible different adaptations.[46]

By her own admission, the methods Thompson used to examine the affective processes were even cruder than those she had used to evaluate intelligence. Besides measuring circulation and respiratory changes under different conditions, she asked each subject for an introspective account of his or her emotional processes and personality. Her dependence on the self-analysis of each individual troubled her, for, as she conceded, "many individuals will not be, or cannot be, perfectly honest in answering questions on personality." Despite this grave limitation on her research, she offered a few tentative conclusions.

> The physiological expression of affective processes, as shown in the experiments on circulation and respiration, is more intense in men than in women. As to the character of the affective processes themselves, the most striking thing revealed by the above questions on personality is their close coincidence in both sexes.

While those who believed that there were important psychological differences of sex had always pointed to emotion as the most telling example, Thompson found "a series of men and a series of women reacting

45. Ibid., pp. 135, 109–35.
46. John Dewey, "The Theory of Emotion," *Psychological Review* 1 (November 1894): 553–69, and ibid. 2 (January 1895): 13–32; James R. Angell, "The Influence of Darwin on Psychology," *Psychological Review* 16 (May 1909): 152–69. See also Helen T. Woolley, "Sensory Affection and Emotion," *Psychological Review* 14 (November 1907): 329–44.

towards questions about the life of feeling in wonderfully similar ways."[47]

The similarities Thompson observed between men and women extended to "the strength of the emotional nature, the form of its expression, and the degree of impulsiveness in action." The only differences she discovered related to inhibition.

> Women seem to have a greater tendency to inhibit the expression of emotion and to act from reason rather than from impulse. . . . Men are more frank than women and women are more easily embarrassed.

The frankness and daring of the New Woman were more fancied than real. Thompson understood this only too well. Defiant with respect to parental authority, outspoken in intellectual debate, she was nevertheless incapable of frank discussion of personal, especially sexual, needs. For her, intellectual liberation and professional fulfillment could not accommodate too close an examination of sexual feeling. While writing her thesis, she became engaged to medical student Paul Gerhardt Woolley. At first, the demands of professional training delayed their marriage, then Woolley began to doubt that theirs could ever be an intimate relationship. He wanted to break off the engagement, but his parents persuaded him not to, and after a five-year betrothal Thompson and Woolley married, without having resolved the unspoken differences between them.[48]

Thompson chose not to dwell on the issues of frankness and embarrassment that still divided men from women in her doctoral study, preferring instead to emphasize the marked similarity that seemed to exist in most mental abilities. Given the strength of society's belief in sexual polarity, her findings of similarity in mental traits were, indeed, her most important contribution. They undermined conventional beliefs at the same time that they illustrated the destructive effect, increasingly felt among psychologists, of careful experimentation on the Victorian preoccupation with unifying principles. As Dewey put it, the evidence from experimental work was "too great in mass and too varied in style to fit into existing pigeon holes, and the cabinets [were breaking] of their own dead weight." In no area of psychology was the material greater in mass or more varied in style than in the area of sex differences. Thompson's systematic investigation of mental traits simply revealed that great variety more starkly than anyone else had ever done, and therefore called into sharper doubt conventional ideas about sexual classification. The methods she used heightened the differences between her findings and those of other writers. Whereas most researchers

---

47. Thompson [Woolley], *Mental Traits of Sex*, pp. 138, 167–68.
48. Ibid., p. 168; Eleanor Woolley Fowler to author, July 20, 1976.

selected subjects at random, Thompson carefully matched her subjects according to social, economic, and educational background. While most researchers averaged the results of their tests and emphasized the differences in the averages between the male and female groups, Thompson graphed her results and emphasized the high degree of overlap in all of the tests.[49]

More than technique, however, set Thompson's work apart. The young men and women who volunteered to be tested differed fundamentally from those who had been examined in the past simply because of their peculiar educational experience. While most of their peers remained under the supervision of their families or in single-sex schools, they were pioneering on the frontier of social change. Female university students represented the newest manifestation of the New Woman. They were women who insisted on greater freedom in the way they dressed, in their choice of friends, and in their selection of lifetime work. And though popular discourse recognized no "new man" as a counterpart to the much discussed "new woman," male students at the new universities nevertheless represented a masculine model that differed in important respects from the conventional type. By virtue of their having to work with women on roughly equal terms, male students were forced to reconsider conventional assumptions about sex roles and both male and female nature.

Much of the concern over coeducation at the University of Chicago derived from the fear that young people, away from home and thrown into close, daily contact with the opposite sex would abandon the codes of conduct that governed civilized relations between the sexes. Men might become less manly and women less womanly if they spent so much time together at such an impressionable age. As one member of the Chicago faculty put it,

> [E]xperience has shown that, where men and women share the same quadrangle, sit side by side in the class-room, jostle each other in the halls and on the walks, cultivate interest in the same sports, form as far as possible a solid community, each sex loses something. . . . This opinion is based on the belief that there are certain virtues, traits, matters of deportment, and the like, more or less distinct for either sex, which should be cultivated in an educational institution during the formative years.

The opponents of coeducation agreed in one important respect with Thompson's conclusions: men and women at Chicago resembled one another more in their behavior than either scientists or popular writers had ever thought possible. Even though frankness, as Thompson ob-

49. John Dewey, "The Reflex-Arc Concept," p. 357.

served, still seemed a typically male attribute in 1900, students at Chicago already enjoyed the economic security and the freedom from parental control that was to spur a sexual revolution among American youth within a decade. With the coming of this revolution, frankness would increasingly dominate the relations of both sexes, and differences between male and female behavior would diminish even further.[50]

Repeatedly, Thompson emphasized the similarities between her men and women, but she had to admit that differences persisted despite all her novel techniques and the coeducational background of her subjects; indeed, some of her findings, especially on motor ability and puzzle solving, tended to confirm the theory of biological differences in male and female psychology. Though conceding these differences, she urged against jumping to hereditarian conclusions.

> In considering the question whether or not there is any other explanation for the facts in the case, it is important to remember that the make-up of any adult individual cannot be attributed entirely to inherited tendency. The old question of the relative importance of heredity and environment in the final outcome of the individual must be taken into consideration.[51]

Even where differences between the sexes seemed most marked—in men's superiority in motor skills and ingenuity—Thompson believed that training and social expectation, not physiology, were the causes. "The great strength of savage women and the rapid increase in strength in civilized women, wherever systematic physical training has been introduced," she argued, "show the importance of [training]," in developing motor ability. As for men's apparently superior ingenuity, "we find equally important differences in social surroundings which would tend to bring about this result. Boys are encouraged to individuality. They are trained to be independent in thought and action," while "girls are taught obedience, dependence, and deference."[52]

Little boys in a household of older sisters and no brothers, she pointed out, often wanted to play with dolls, while small girls with brothers wanted just as strongly to take part in boys' sports. "If it were really a fundamental difference of instincts and characteristics which determined the difference of training to which the sexes are subjected," she argued, "it would not be necessary to spend so much effort in making boys and girls follow the lines of conduct proper to their sex." For both Thompson and the men who encouraged her, Victorian society's polarized view of sexual

---

50. Edward Capps to the University Recorder, July 21, 1902, the Presidents' Papers, University of Chicago Archives.
51. Thompson [Woolley], *Mental Traits of Sex,* p. 176.
52. Ibid., p. 178.

identity and conduct had conflicted seriously with their personal experiences and aspirations. As children, none of them had fulfilled its prescriptions; as adults, they resented society's expectation that they should have done so.[53]

Faced with the raw data of her tests, Thompson looked for similarities. Faced with differences, she sought environmental causes for them. "The suggestion that the observed differences of sex may be due to differences in environment has often been met with derision," she admitted, "but it seems at least worthy of unbiased consideration." Indeed, what distinguished Thompson from previous researchers in the end was her egalitarian bias and corrosive skepticism combined with her functionalist training. Like her mentors, she tried to transcend the idealism that remained from her religious heritage and the materialism that emerged from her scientific training. Where sex differences did not give way to her careful observations or her statistical analysis, she applied the functionalist argument that the mind shaped experience even as it was being shaped, and that to study women at a specific point in history was to miss the transitional nature of their psychological development. While theology had confined women to a subordinate position, and Darwinism and Spencerianism had been widely used to confirm that subordination, functionalism combined elements of both traditions in such a way that, in the right hands, it could be used to question the assumption of women's innate inferiority.[54]

The Mental Traits of Sex provided a fresh view of sex differences, but as Thompson herself conceded, it was only a beginning. She had examined only fifty subjects. Her tests were crude and in some cases impressionistic. Her statistical analysis, though more advanced than that commonly in use, did not encompass the techniques of correlation already in use at Columbia, and she therefore failed to develop her argument as fully as she might have. Despite these deficiencies, however, her demonstration of the marked overlapping of men's and women's performances on her tests undermined the widespread belief that the female mind was a secondary sexual characteristic, while her analysis of the specific ways in which experience and social expectations shape particular abilities prompted many psychologists to look more critically at their hereditarian assumptions. In the study of sex differences in particular, and in the development of psychology in general, *The Mental Traits of Sex* raised important doubts about biological reductionism; and in the decade following its publication it inspired other women at institutions far less supportive of feminist

53. Ibid., p. 181.
54. Ibid., p. 177.

iconoclasm than Chicago to question the traditional faith in women's psychological uniqueness. Many years passed, however, before Thompson herself could further question this traditional faith in her own work.

Research, Feminism, and the Family Claim

When Helen Thompson completed her thesis in 1900, she was awarded the Ph.D. summa cum laude. Both Dewey and Angell thought her research was the best that had been done in the department, and sociologist William Isaac Thomas observed, "Her findings are probably the most important contribution to this field, and her general conclusions of differences of sex will, I think, hold also for differences of race." Fellow graduate student John B. Watson, later recalled Thompson's success:

> I received my degree Magna Cum Laude and was told almost immediately by Dewey and Angell that my exam was much inferior to that of Miss Helen Thompson, who had graduated two years before with a Summa Cum Laude. I wondered then if anybody could ever equal her record. That jealousy existed for years.

Watson's jealousy must have been tempered by his postgraduate success. He soon outdistanced his rival, winning faculty appointments first at Chicago and then at Johns Hopkins, and achieving notoriety when he declared his emancipation from functionalism in favor of a new approach to psychology he called behaviorism.[55]

At first Helen Thompson's prospects for professional advancement seemed bright. At the behest of Marion Talbot, the Association of Collegiate Alumnae awarded her a fellowship to travel and study in Europe for a year, and following that year Talbot offered to hire her as the head of one of Chicago's women's halls, a job that would have carried with it a position as instructor in psychology. But Thompson's advisor, James R. Angell, insisted that to accept this position would be a mistake because of the administration's tendency to apply a double standard in promoting instructors. Female instructors who headed the halls had to be good hostesses and surrogate mothers. "Scholarly equipment was desirable" in the head of a woman's hall, but "social quality . . . was essential." By contrast, the issue of "social quality" did not enter into the promotion decisions for any of the other instructors. Angell and others in the department believed that Thompson would be better off going elsewhere for her first job, and they recommended that she accept a position at Mount Holy-

55. W. I. Thomas, "The Mind of Woman and the Lower Races," *American Journal of Sociology* 12 (January 1907); 438, 446; "John Broadus Watson," in Murchison, ed., *History of Psychology in Autobiography*, 3: 274.

oke College. "Miss Thompson will do better now to go away for a year and teach outside anyway," observed George Herbert Mead to his wife. "The president [Harper] is favorably disposed toward her and she might be brought back later."[56]

Given the rarity with which major universities appointed women to their faculties, Mead's private speculation that Thompson might eventually find a regular faculty position at Chicago is remarkable. But personal events rendered those speculations moot. Torn between her professional aspirations and her desire for marriage, Thompson finally decided, after a year at Mount Holyoke, to marry Paul Woolley. For the next five years, the opportunities and demands of her husband's medical career precluded further psychological research. The Woolleys began their married life in the Philippines, where Paul Woolley had been offered a job as director of the Manila Serum Laboratory. For a year the new bride taught school, but when her husband received an appointment to act as medical advisor to the king of Siam, she left her job and moved again. In the next three years she moved three more times—back to Chicago, where the first of two daughters was born in 1907, then to Nebraska, and finally to Cincinnati, where Paul Woolley joined the University of Cincinnati medical school faculty. For most women the many moves and domestic responsibilities that burdened Helen Thompson Woolley would have killed all professional ambition. Blaming failure on either their own inadequacies or the unavoidable obligations of domestic life, they would have abandoned their youthful hopes of professional success. Woolley shared these feelings of inadequacy and fatalism about her domestic world and often felt isolated, but she was not defeated. Hoping that the move to Cincinnati would prove to be permanent, she began looking for work as a psychologist. Her husband did not actively support her ambitions, but neither did he stand in her way. As Woolley's daughter Eleanor later recalled:

> They lived quite separate lives. . . . He spent a lot of time in his lab and he had a study on the third floor of our house . . . where he spent long hours when he was at home. Summers he went off to Colorado to climb mountains while Mother took my sister and me to northern Wisconsin. . . . I remember endless games of croquet played by the adults—and Mother writing part of each day.[57]

56. George Herbert Mead to Helen Castle Mead, George Herbert Mead Papers, University of Chicago Archives. Marion Talbot, *History of the Chicago Association of Collegiate Alumnae, 1888 – 1917* (Chicago, 1920), p. 3.

57. Eleanor Woolley Fowler to author, July 20, 1976; Marguerite Zapoleon and Lois Stolz, "Helen Bradford Thompson Woolley," in James, ed., *Notable American Women,* 3: 657 – 60.

Woolley could not find academic work in psychology in Cincinnati, but with the help of women friends there, she made a new life for herself as a child development specialist, reformer, and suffrage leader. Cincinnati women reformers, concerned over the problem of child labor, hired Woolley to conduct a major study of working-class children that led to raising the age at which children could leave school in Ohio. In addition to directing this research, Woolley joined more directly in the reform work of the city, serving on the boards of the Cincinnati Community Chest, the Woman's City Club, and the Woman's Suffrage Committee of Greater Cincinnati. A frequent speaker at suffrage rallies, Woolley was usually asked to speak last, to provide a voice of well-informed reason as a counterweight to some of the other speakers' emotional militancy. Not that she shunned militancy when she found it called for: in 1921 she led an exodus from a professional meeting in a leading hotel when the admission of a black member was questioned.[58]

More than any of the women studied here, Helen Thompson Woolley succeeded in wedding her interest in science to a commitment to social reform. While other women social scientists, especially those who remained in academe, were beginning to retreat from the field of reform because they thought that its claims too often compromised the objectivity of science and woman's place within it, Woolley saw no reason why science should not guide reform nor why reform should not direct the use of science. After her marriage she lived almost exclusively in a world of women whose concerns and goals became her concerns and goals. Barred from academia by the claims of her family, Woolley nevertheless enjoyed rare professional success because of the organized effort of friends who saw in her skills a way of advancing their reform interests. The psychological research Woolley pursued as a consequence of this support contributed significantly to the understanding of working-class conditions and child development; but it was not the research she had envisioned in graduate school, when she embarked on her study of the mental traits of men and women. The study of sex differences did not inspire much interest from a woman's movement primarily concerned with issues of social welfare. Rather, it remained the special province of the research university and of the women graduate students who were trying to prove themselves there.

58. Ibid. For Woolley's study of working-class children, see Helen Thompson Woolley, *An Experimental Study of Children at Work and in School between the Ages of Fourteen and Eighteen Years* (New York: Macmillan, 1926).

4 *Toward a Sexless Intelligence*

The psychologist most influenced by the graduate work of Helen Thompson Woolley was Leta Stetter Hollingworth, who began graduate work in psychology at Columbia in 1911. At that time, Columbia's psychology department, under the direction of James McKeen Cattell, led the country in the study of individual differences and gave the best training available in statistics, testing, and experimental procedures. But Columbia was much slower than Chicago to welcome women graduate students, and Columbia's psychologists were singularly unsympathetic to feminist ideas. Leta Hollingworth might never have studied sex differences there had she not been married to Henry Hollingworth, a Cattell student teaching at Barnard, who, in contrast to his Columbia colleagues, was an outspoken defender of feminism. Henry's encouragement made it possible for Leta to raise questions to which the rest of the Columbia faculty was initially hostile.[1]

After Woolley's work, psychologists were less ready to emphasize the differences between male and female minds than they had been before, but especially among the builders of the new departments of psychology the firm conviction remained that at the upper ranges of intelligence and creativity women were less well represented because of their lesser variability. The leaders of psychology further believed that women are less reliable than men because of their periodic incapacity while menstruating, and less suited to the rigors of graduate training because of their instinctive preference for motherhood. These were the beliefs that Hollingworth devoted her early career in psychology to challenging.

---

1. For Columbia's importance in the development of American psychology, see Hamilton Cravens, *The Triumph of Evolution: American Scientists and the Heredity-Environment Controversy, 1900 – 1941* (Philadelphia: University of Pennsylvania Press, 1978), pp. 67 – 69; Edwin G. Boring, *A History of Experimental Psychology*, pp. 532 – 40, 548 – 49.

From Nebraska to New York

When the Hollingworths married in 1908, Henry had not yet finished his graduate training. The couple had met at the University of Nebraska two years earlier, and Leta had stayed behind to teach high school until Henry finished at Columbia. But they had tired of waiting and decided they could live on the income Leta could earn as a teacher in New York. What they did not realize, but soon discovered, was that New York barred married women from teaching! After four years of college preparation and two years of teaching experience, the new Mrs. Hollingworth found herself reduced to making a home in a small, dark New York apartment on the limited resources of some meager savings.[2]

In the time left over from housework, cooking, dressmaking, mending, washing, and ironing, Leta tried writing and took a few literature courses at Columbia; but her stories did not sell, and her classes, she declared, were full of "dry bones." Through her husband she developed an interest in psychology and applied for fellowships to pursue full-time graduate study—but with no success. Henry Hollingworth later recalled his young wife's sense of despair:

> Almost always she effectually stifled her own eager longing for intellectual activity like that of her husband. Day after day, and many long evenings, she led her solitary life in the meagerly furnished quarters, while he was away at regular duties or seizing on this and that opportunity to earn a few dollars on the side, by lectures, tutoring and assorted odd jobs. . . . There were occasional periods of discouragement; once in a while she would unexpectedly and for no apparent cause burst into tears. These slips from her customary determined and courageous procedure she could hardly explain then, even to herself. Later she was able to make it clear that it was because she could hardly bear, with her own good mind and professional training and experience, not to be able to contribute to the joint welfare more than the simple manual activities that occupied her.[3]

In 1909 Henry Hollingworth completed the work for his Ph.D. and received an appointment as instructor in psychology and logic at Barnard College. With his new income he decided to finance his wife's graduate work in educational psychology at Columbia and Teachers College. For

2. Henry L. Hollingworth, *Leta Stetter Hollingworth* (Lincoln: University of Nebraska Press, 1943), pp. 77–81, 97–99; Victoria Roemele, "Leta Anna Stetter Hollingworth," in Edward T. James, ed., *Notable American Women, 1607–1950*, 2: 206–08. Collections of Leta Hollingworth's published work are available at the University of Nebraska Archives in Lincoln, Nebraska, and the Archives of the History of American Psychology at the University of Akron, Akron, Ohio. Her private correspondence and journals appear to have been destroyed.

3. Hollingworth, *Leta Stetter Hollingworth*, pp. 98, 99–100.

most academic couples the commencement of a steady income signaled the start of childbearing, but the Hollingworths remained childless. Leta Hollingworth clearly enjoyed children and spent much of her career working with them; perhaps she would have liked to have some of her own but discovered she could not. On the other hand, her own frontier childhood had been a singularly miserable one—"There's no place like home—Thank God!" she once quipped, remembering her mother's early death in childbirth and her father's bitter wrangling with his second wife. Leta Hollingworth saw no romance in motherhood and publicly condemned the social pressures that forced most women to become mothers. Perhaps she chose to remain childless, believing that the financial and professional constraints on her life were too great to allow for motherhood.[4]

Women at Columbia

Few women had braved the struggle for a Columbia doctoral degree in psychology before Leta Stetter Hollingworth began graduate work in 1911. Twenty years before, in 1891, the Columbia trustees had modified their longtime opposition to female graduate education by delegating to the individual graduate faculties the power to enroll women as auditors. Even so slight a relaxation of traditional standards outraged the faculty of political science, which voted to exclude women from all of its classes. The faculty of philosophy, however, which offered work in psychology, took a more sanguine view of female visitors and agreed to extend auditing privileges to women with the consent of individual instructors. Under this provision Margaret Floy Washburn visited James McKeen Cattell's laboratory in 1891–92. Realizing that she would never be able to work for a degree, however, after a year she left for Cornell to pursue regular graduate study. Barnard, which opened as an undergraduate college in 1889, offered limited graduate work with the help of a few moonlighting Columbia professors; but not until 1898, when Teachers College became part of Columbia and began offering graduate work in educational psychology, and 1900, when Barnard surrendered all graduate instruction to Columbia, did women become regular students in Columbia's graduate degree programs.[5]

4. Curiously, Henry Hollingworth never mentioned the absence of children in his biography of his wife. For Leta Hollingworth's opposition to enforced motherhood, see Leta Hollingworth, "Social Devices for Impelling Women to Bear and Rear Children," *American Journal of Sociology* 22 (July 1916): 19–29.

5. Columbia University, "List of Theses Submitted by Candidates for the Degree of Doctor of Philosophy in Columbia University, 1872–1910," *Bulletin of Information*, 10th ser. 26 (January 10, 1910), passim; Columbia University, *Minutes of the Trustees* (December 7,

By 1906 women comprised half of the student body in the faculty of philosophy and one-third in all the other faculties, including pure science and political science, where women were still barred from some classes. This feminine enthusiasm for graduate education caused some concern among the faculty and administration. As dean of philosophy, Edward Perry noted in his annual report to the president: "The great increase in the number of women has naturally brought with it some problems of administration, the solution of which has not been easy. Certain subjects are almost entirely incapable of satisfactory treatment before a mixed audience." Though Dean Perry did not specify which courses posed this difficulty, he did explain that the problem had been solved by teaching the offending courses twice, once for women and again for men. Whatever the difficulties, he recognized that women were there to stay. "As has been often pointed out, the unusually large proportion of women graduate students at Columbia is due to our situation in a huge city, where women are in a large majority among the teachers in the schools. Many of these women have both the time and the ambition for self-improvement by attendance upon university courses."[6]

About 150 women a year were enrolling in advanced philosophy, psychology, and anthropology courses in 1906. Only two, however, had earned the Ph.D. Though many women could pay the $30–$45 per course on an occasional basis, few could devote themselves to full-time study at a cost of at least $600 a year for tuition and living expenses. Columbia offered twelve university fellowships each year, valued at $650, but none was open to women, and of the thirty-two scholarships offered to cover the $150 tuition, women could apply for only four.[7]

Added to the financial pressure faced by would-be women doctoral candidates was the more subtle, but equally powerful, weight of prejudice. Columbia's faculty and administration had little confidence in women's

1891); R. Gordon Hoxie et al., *A History of the Faculty of Political Science: Columbia University* (New York: Columbia University Press, 1957), pp. 64–67; "Margaret Floy Washburn," autobiography, in Carl Murchison, ed., *History of Psychology in Autobiography*, 2:338–39; Barnard College, *Dean's Annual Report*, 1896, pp. 8–10; Columbia University, Teachers College, *President's Report*, 1898, pp. 30–33; Columbia University, *Eleventh Annual Report of President Low to the Trustees* (October 1, 1900), pp. 5–6.

6. Columbia University, *Annual Reports of the President and Treasurer to the Trustees, 1906* (June 30, 1906), p. 132.

7. Ibid. Between 1899 and 1906, Columbia awarded Ph.D.'s to Elsie Clews Parsons (1899) and Naomi Norsworthy (1904) (Columbia University, Division of Philosophy, Psychology, and Anthropology, *Announcement*, 1908–10, pp. 26, 28). Information on fellowships and scholarships can be found in ibid., pp. 20–21. Chicago provided more generous assistance to women, but even so, in 1904 Marian Talbot criticized the university for the unequal distribution of graduate fellowships: ten to men and only three to women. Talbot, "Women of the University," *President's Report* (Chicago, 1904), p. 110.

James McKeen Cattell (ca. 1900)

scholarly abilities. "In most cases the women make good students, and some of the best we have had in the School of Philosophy have been women," Dean Perry conceded, "but on the whole, I think, a smaller proportion of them than of the men are capable, either by natural endowment or opportunity, of undertaking really advanced or original work, and the proportion of them who reach the doctorate is almost pathetically small." With the exception of Henry Hollingworth, the frontiersman from the coeducational University of Nebraska, members of the psychololgy faculty had had either few or no female classmates throughout their educational careers, and their wives filled very traditional roles, centered around rural homes from which their academic husbands made lengthy commutes to Columbia.[8]

Long after Edward Clarke raised the specter of race suicide, psychology chairman James McKeen Cattell was warning of its threat in the pages of

8. Columbia University, *Annual Reports, 1906*, p. 132. For personal background of Columbia faculty, see Michael Mark Sokal, "The Education and Psychological Career of James McKeen Cattell, 1860– 1904" (Ph.D. diss., Case Western Reserve University, 1972), pp. 280– 90, and Geraldine Joncich, *The Sane Positivist: A Biography of Edward L. Thorndike* (Middletown, Conn.: Wesleyan University Press, 1968), pp. 193– 212.

Edward Thorndike (1914)

the *Popular Science Monthly*. In 1909 Cattell observed: "Girls are injured more than boys by school life; they take it more seriously, and at certain times and at a certain age are far more subject to harm. It is probably not an exaggeration to say that to the average cost of each girl's education through high school must be added one unborn child." It was bad enough, Cattell believed, for women to be educated, but the great curse to modern society came from allowing them to be teachers.

> When spinsters can support themselves with more physical comforts and larger leisure than they would as wives; when married women may prefer the money they can earn and the excitement they can find in outside employment to the bearing and rearing of children; when they can conveniently leave their husbands should it so suit their fancy—the conditions are clearly unfavorable to marriage and the family. . . . There are in the United States about 400,000 women employed as teachers, and the numbers are continuously increasing. . . . This vast horde of female teachers in the United States tends to subvert both the school and the family.[9]

9. James McKeen Cattell, "The School and the Family," *Popular Science Monthly* 74 (January 1909): 91, 92. Cattell edited the *Popular Science Monthly*, which he bought in 1900 from William Jay Youmans, the brother of its founder (Sokal, "Career of James McKeen Cattell," p. 464).

The younger faculty tended to be somewhat more temperate in their views about the evils of educating women, but even they voiced doubts about female intellectual capacity. In his 1906 article, "Sex in Education," Edward Thorndike, a student of Cattell's and the man whom Cattell designated for an opening in educational psychology at Teachers College, recommended against the advanced training of women because of the well-established fact, known since Darwin, that women are less variable than men and therefore less likely to have the necessary ability to succeed in advanced work. "Not only the probability and the desirability of marriage and the training of children as an essential feature of women's careers, but also the restriction of women to the mediocre grades of ability and achievement should be reckoned with by our educational systems," he wrote; "postgraduate instruction, to which women are flocking in large numbers is, at least in the higher reaches, a far more remunerative investment in the case of men."[10]

Like Cattell, Thorndike thought it unwise to encourage women to pursue graduate work, but he saw a certain utility in having a few women working at the doctoral level. In 1902 he hired Naomi Norsworthy, Columbia's first woman graduate student in psychology, to assist him at Teachers College. As he informed his former Harvard professor, William James, "You will be glad to know that I have for next year and thereafter an instructor to take off a great deal of the burden of my work, so that I shall be able to give myself up almost entirely to graduate courses and the direction of research."[11]

The difference between Cattell's generation and Thorndike's was evident in Thorndike's clash with Cattell six years later when Thorndike wanted to make Norsworthy an assistant professor. Cattell adamantly opposed promoting a woman to a professorial rank, but Thorndike argued with him that Teachers College had special needs that could best be met by women.

> If you were in full acquaintance with our situation and with her work, I think you would include it in a wider point of view. Teachers College is in part a graduate school and in part a professional school. The most gifted people for training teachers in certain lines (e.g. elementary methods, kindergarten, domestic art) are at present and will for a long time be women. . . . Dr. Norsworthy is beyond any question enormously successful in training teachers. . . . I would be sacrificing the interests of Teachers College to do anything that helped withhold from her the promotion that a man equally competent would be sure to have had.

10. Edward Thorndike, "Sex in Education," *Bookman* 23 (April 1906): 213.
11. Joncich, *The Sane Positivist*, p. 221.

Thorndike won Norsworthy her promotion by persuading his superiors that the employment of a woman at Teachers College would not undermine the conventional view of womanhood to which most academics subscribed. But Norsworthy's example and the example of women who followed her modified this conventional view considerably.[12]

The Experimental Perspective

Though Columbia gave no more than grudging support to its women students and faculty, and adhered to a conservative view of women's potential, its psychological researchers manifested an aggressive skepticism in their experimental work which threatened that very conservatism. Thorndike, in particular, achieved notoriety for the enthusiasm with which he tore into established psychological doctrine. As psychologist Lewis Terman later recalled, "He seemed to me shockingly lacking in a decent respect for the opinions of mankind!"[13]

Between 1900 and 1910 Columbia became an important center for the growing attack on armchair, evolutionary thinking, as a new generation of psychologists completed their doctorates and began looking with a jaundiced eye at the current understanding of the human and animal minds. Less encumbered with the religious and philosophical baggage of the past than their mentors, Edward Thorndike, Robert Woodworth, Clark Wissler, and others practiced what their teachers had often only preached—a rigorous, experimental examination of human behavior. For all of their prejudices against women, they slowly put together the skeptical elements of a psychological system that could accommodate a very different view of feminine behavior from the one their own biases allowed.[14]

As they devised ever more carefully controlled experiments, these psychologists developed a special scorn for those fathers of modern science, like Lester Frank Ward and G. Stanley Hall, who indulged in romantic speculations about the origins of human society and intelligence. In 1898 Edward Thorndike articulated that scorn in his doctoral thesis on animal intelligence. Evolutionists believed that the mental likeness between animals and humans could be demonstrated by observing the reasoning powers displayed by animals and the instinctive behavior

12. E. L. Thorndike to J. M. Cattell, November 17, 1908, Cattell Papers, Library of Congress, Washington, D.C.

13. "Lewis M. Terman," autobiography, in Murchison, ed., *History of Psychology in Autobiography*, 2: 319.

14. Cravens, *The Triumph of Evolution*, pp. 193–201. I have found Cravens's discussion of this subject very helpful, though I would differ with him in his final assessment of evolution's triumph among social scientists. For a significant portion of American social scientists, evolution failed. See, for instance, George W. Stocking, Jr., *Race, Culture, and Evolution*, pp. 234–69.

exhibited by humans; but Thorndike argued that animals were neither so intelligent nor so instinctive in their behavior as most evolutionists assumed.[15]

Thorndike studied animal intelligence with the help of a slotted cage in which he built a door that opened by pulling a string. He placed a hungry dog, cat, or monkey in the cage and set some food outside as a reward for getting out. Leaving the animal to his own devices, he observed its behavior until it succeeded in opening the door. The animals Thorndike studied gave no sign of trying to reason their way out, nor did they show any instinctive understanding of how to open the door. Instead, they clawed all over the box until, by accident, they struck on the right technique. Gradually, through subsequent trials and much additional flailing, they reduced the time it took to get out. Blind trial and error, Thorndike concluded, not reasoning or instinct, explained their behavior.

Increasingly skeptical of both instinct and reasoning in animals, he began to look more critically at behavior assumed to be either instinctive or rational in humans. Much of the activity that psychologists casually labeled instinctive—for example, the "instinct of self-preservation"—could be better explained, he decided, as a simple reaction to a particular experience—for example, "eating to get rid of hunger." On the other hand, much of human learning, conventionally attributed to conscious reflection, stemmed, he believed, from the same kind of trial and error displayed by animals in his box. Neither animals nor humans, he concluded, relied as heavily on either instinct or ratiocination as most social theorists assumed.[16]

Thorndike's colleague, Clark Wissler, added fuel to the antievolutionary fire with his ill-fated attempt to correlate lower mental activity with intelligence in his 1901 doctoral thesis. Further work at Columbia confirmed Wissler's finding that no direct connection exists between morphology and ideas, and that Cattell's initial faith in the possibility of constructing tests of intelligence based on simple motor tests would have to be abandoned. By 1909 Thorndike could report that sensory discrimination had little to do with general intelligence.

> The present results [demonstrate] that the efficiency of a man's equipment for the specifically human task of managing ideas is only loosely correlated with the

15. Edward L. Thorndike, "Animal Intelligence: An Experimental Study of the Associative Processes in Animals," *Psychological Review, Monograph Supplement*, no. 8 (June 1898), 109 pp.; Joncich, *The Sane Positivist*, pp. 126–48; Robert Woodworth, *Contemporary Schools of Psychology*, pp. 48–56.

16. Thorndike, "Animal Intelligence," pp. 38–46, 105–09; idem, *Educational Psychology*, vol. 1: *The Original Nature of Man* (New York: Teachers College, 1913), p. 14.

efficiency of the simpler sensori-motor apparatus which he possesses in common with other species.[17]

Faith in the body's power to control the mind waned further as psychologists examined the problem of mental fatigue. One of the basic assumptions of Spencerian psychology, as well as the critical foundation of Edward Clarke's condemnation of advanced education for women, was the belief that the mind and body form a closed-energy system. When demands on that energy grew too heavy, psychologists and psychiatrists believed, the body broke down and nervous disease ensued. Trying to test this basic assumption, researchers conducted dozens of experiments on the mental effects of fatigue. As Columbia's Robert Woodworth told a group of psychiatrists in 1906, these experiments showed that the brain is not so susceptible to fatigue as had long been thought. The tiredness that overcame subjects engaged in prolonged mental labor was "a sensory or emotional affair, a feeling of fatigue not a true fatigue in the sense of incapacity." When experimenters urged subjects to resist the desire to stop work and to "determine to stick to it for a while longer," the subject usually found that his brain was "still in good working order, that the feeling of fatigue" had passed away. Very often, in fact, the subject found that his best work was "done after rather than before the time his feelings told him he was played out." Attitude, Woodworth and his colleagues came to believe, played a more important role in intellectual accomplishment than physical endurance. Along with the work being done on animal intelligence, human instinct, and the correlation of mental traits, studies of fatigue prompted a few male researchers to question the popular belief that a unique female physiology gave rise to a unique female intelligence.[18]

In 1906 the *New York Independent* sponsored a debate on the issue of female intelligence between members of the old guard and the new.

17. Edward L. Thorndike et al., "The Relation of Accuracy in Sensory Discrimination to General Intelligence," *American Journal of Psychology* 20 (July 1909): 367; Clark Wissler, "The Correlation of Mental and Physical Tests," pp. 1 – 60.

18. Robert Woodworth, "Psychiatry and Experimental Psychology" (1906), in *Psychological Issues: Selected Papers of Robert S. Woodworth* (New York: Columbia University Press, 1939), p. 170. The popular belief that the body was a closed-energy system came under increasing attack in the early 1900s. See also William James, "The Powers of Man," *American Magazine* 65 (November 1907): 56 – 65; Edward L. Thorndike, "Mental Fatigue," *Psychological Review* 7, no.1 (September 1900): 466 – 82, ibid., no.2 (November 1900): 547 – 79; Nathan Hale, *Freud and the Americans,* pp. 140 – 41. For evidence that the closed-energy system idea continued to enjoy widespread popularity, see F. B. Rosa, "The Human Body as a Machine," *Popular Science Monthly* 57 (September 1900): 491 – 99. Both Havelock Ellis and Sigmund Freud continued the popularization of the closed-energy system idea well into the twentieth century; see Paul Robinson, *The Modernization of Sex: Havelock Ellis, Alfred Kinsey, William Masters and Virginia Johnson* (New York: Harper & Row, 1976), pp. 15 – 16.

Lester Frank Ward, representing the liberal wing of the traditional evolutionary theorists, opened the discussion with a recapitulation of his theory of sexual divergence. This divergence, he argued, which had begun with the lowly protozoa and had steadily increased with evolutionary development, could be arrested, or even reversed, if only men would begin choosing their mates for qualities of intelligence and strength rather than for qualities of delicacy and vacuity, as they had in the past. G. Stanley Hall, representing the more conservative evolutionists, accepted Ward's evolutionary premise but ridiculed his Lamarckian faith that feminine characteristics had been acquired and thus could be eradicated. No such mortal interference in evolutionary development as Ward envisioned, Hall charged, could obviate the biological trend toward ever greater sexual differentiation.[19]

Edmund Wilson, a young Columbia cytologist who had just discovered the chromosomal basis of sex determination, and psychologist Clark Wissler, castigated Ward and Hall alike for their speculative evolutionism. Wilson objected particularly to Ward's anthropomorphic description of the origins of sexual differentiation, in which he assumed that lowly organisms discriminated among sexual contenders in the same way that human beings do. How could Ward seriously argue, Wilson wondered, that "males when no more than 'shapeless masses' or 'mere sperm-sacs' engage in a rivalry to be selected, and that females of animals at so low a stage of development had the wit to 'select the best and reject the inferior' from their misbegotten progeny"? While Wilson the cytologist questioned the anthropomorphic imposition of esthetic standards on physiological activity, Wissler the psychologist and ethnologist challenged the imposition of physiological laws onto human intelligence. "It is curious," Wissler wrote, "that it has always seemed necessary to carry the theory of evolution up through morphology into the psychic life of animals and men and finally into those human practices that are designated conventional. While there is doubtless some connection between the fundamental elements of psychic life and physiological function, the direct connection between the details of ideas and such function is not clear."[20]

Wilson and Wissler believed that their research cast doubt on some of

19. Lester F. Ward, "The Past and Future of the Sexes," *New York Independent*, March 8, 1906, pp. 541–45; G. Stanley Hall, "The Feminist in Science," ibid., March 22, 1906, pp. 661–62; Edmund B. Wilson, "The Origin of Sex," ibid., pp. 662–63; Clark Wissler, "Professor Ward and Ethnology," ibid., pp. 663–65.

20. Wilson, "The Origin of Sex," p. 663; Wissler, "Professor Ward and Ethnology," p. 664. In the early 1900s Edmund Wilson played an important role in genetic research on the determination of sex. In 1906 he codiscovered, with Nettie Stevens of Bryn Mawr, the chromosome that determines sex.

the popular beliefs about the nature of womanhood, but they did not pursue this doubt. Their chief interest lay in their research, not in public debates over its social implications. Not until scientists began training women as researchers did the revolutionary implications of some of these experiments for the understanding of woman's nature become evident.

Periodicity, Variation, and Maternal Instinct

Henry Hollingworth introduced his wife to experimental psychology by asking her to assist him on an experiment measuring the effects of caffeine on mental and motor abilities. One of the precautions he took in his "zeal to control all of the possible variables," as he later recalled, "was to have the women subjects record the occurrences of the menses, during the six weeks experimental period." When the results of the experiment were reported, Leta Hollingworth noticed that no mention was made of the influence of menstruation on the work of the women subjects. Out of curiosity she studied the data herself and found no evidence that the women's performances had varied with their menstrual periods as her husband had feared they might.[21]

Though Henry Hollingworth saw no special importance in this nonfinding, Leta Hollingworth found it highly significant. No dogma about women's nature enjoyed wider acceptance among doctors and psychologists, from Edward Clarke to Havelock Ellis, than the idea that women suffered periodic incapacity from menstruation. In fact, some did not limit their allegations of women's disability to the menstrual period itself. Ellis, for instance, believed: "Menstruation is not an isolated phenomenon. It is but the outward manifestation of the climax of a monthly physiological cycle, which influences throughout the month the whole of a woman's physical and psychical organism." Whatever one thought of women's mental abilities, one could still argue that the debilitating effect of the menses, and the deranging influence of the physiological cycle associated with it, justified the maintaining of separate male and female spheres of activity, and many argued just that.[22]

Incensed by charges of menstrual-related disability, Leta Hollingworth chose to study the effect of women's menstrual cycle on their motor and

21. Hollingworth, *Leta Stetter Hollingworth*, pp. 114–15. See also Stephanie Shields, "Ms. Pilgrim's Progress: The Contributions of Leta Stetter Hollingworth to the Psychology of Women," *American Psychologist* 30 (July 1975): 739–54, and Shields, "Functionalism, Darwinism and the Psychology of Women: A Study in Social Myth," *Amercian Psychologist* 30 (August 1975): 852–57.

22. Havelock Ellis, *Man and Woman*, rev. ed. (New York: Scribner's, 1909), p. 384, quoted in Leta Hollingworth, *Functional Periodicity: An Experimental Study of the Mental and Motor Abilities of Women during Menstruation* (New York: Teachers College, 1914), p. 1.

Leta Stetter Hollingworth (1910)

mental abilities for her doctoral research. From among the students at
Teachers College, where she was studying with Edward Thorndike, she
recruited twenty-three women and two men to serve as subjects for her
study. She told no one of the experiment's purpose but asked each subject
to give a daily report of any physical complaints or unusual events, and
asked the women to record the occurrences of their menses. The subjects
ranged in age from twenty to forty years and had worked or were working
in a variety of professional occupations (teaching, nursing, administration, and so on), in addition to studying at the college. Eight of the
volunteers took the battery of mental and motor tests daily for three
months, while the remaining seventeen were examined only every third
day for a month.[23]

23. Hollingworth, *Functional Periodicity,* pp. 11 – 14, 86 – 87. Though no one was told of
the purpose of the test, some figured it out for themselves (see pp. 12 – 13).

Henry Hollingworth (1913)

When she had tabulated data, Hollingworth looked in vain for evidence of a cyclical pattern in her subjects' test results. In two instances women suffered pain on the first day of menstruation, and these two women fell off in their performance on the "naming of opposites test," but in no other test could any cycle be observed in any of the tests administered. "The present study by no means covers all phases of the question of the mental and motor abilities of women during menstruation," she conceded, but on the other hand, nothing in the test results provided any evidence for the widespread belief that women suffer periodic incapacity in their physical and intellectual abilities.[24]

24. Ibid., pp. 57, 94, 92 – 95.

Hollingworth attributed the "striking disparity" between received wisdom on this subject and her empirical findings to the bias of most authorities. Prejuduce against the uterus, that ultimate and most compelling symbol of feminine divergence from the male type, and belief in its disturbing power, had simply been passed from author to author without critical analysis. Furthermore, she observed, the belief that the uterus incapacitates women from normal work in the male world had originated in reports from male physicians.

> It should be obvious to the least critical mind that normal women do not come under the care and observation of physicians. To investigate the matter experimentally has been somewhat difficult, because until recently all investigators were men, and the taboo put upon the phenomenon by men and women alike rendered it a more or less unapproachable subject for experiment by men who were not physicians.[25]

The only woman doctor to study menstruation systematically since Mary Putnam Jacobi had examined Clarke's charge that menstruating women needed rest was Clelia Duel Mosher, whose results, published in 1911, added support to Hollingworth's conclusions. Mosher began her study of menstruation as a graduate student in physiology at Stanford in 1894 and continued it, first at Johns Hopkins Medical School, and then back at Stanford, where she became the physician for the women students. In the course of her experiments Mosher examined the menstrual periods of four hundred women over the course of 3,350 menstrual cycles. Like Hollingworth, she faulted earlier studies, observing that they had been unsystematic and based on single interviews with a limited number of women. Even Jacobi's study had been flawed by its reliance on a mailed questionnaire. Most studies suffered further by being conducted by men, with whom women could not be frank. Mosher, by contrast, conducted a longitudinal survey. Each woman kept a diary throughout each month, while Mosher conducted frequent interviews and had "an intimate knowledge of the conditions under which the women were living and working." Throughout the study she kept records of respiration, blood count, and blood pressure. When patients reported physical complaints, she tried to determine whether the symptoms were caused by the menstrual function or simply associated with it, as she believed was usually the case.[26]

---

25. Ibid., p. 95. Curiously, Havelock Ellis was particularly careful to distinguish between healthy and unhealthy men in his discussion of male homosexuality in *Sexual Inversion* (1915), pp. 91 – 92, 264, 301; see Paul Robinson, *The Modernization of Sex*, p. 9.

26. Clelia Duel Mosher, "Functional Periodicity in Women and Some Modifying Factors," *California Journal of Medicine* (January – February 1911): 1, 4, 6; Mary Roberts Coolidge,

Mosher attributed most complaints to constricting dress, inactivity, poor diet, constipation, and the standard assumption that discomfort, if not pain, was inevitable.

> The effect upon the mind of constantly anticipated misery can scarcely be measured. Imagine what would be the effect on the function of digestion if every child were taught to refer to it as a sick time!. After each meal every sensation would be exaggerated and nervous dread would presently result in a real condition of nervous indigestion, a functional disturbance.

A climate of opinion rooted in superstition, together with poor diet and dress, produced most menstrual disability, Mosher believed.[27]

Mosher's finding that periodic incapacity was not the inevitable by-product of womanhood but rather the remediable effect of poor habits and a morbid attitude reinforced Hollingworth's own conclusions. The general good health and confidence of her Teachers College subjects and their steady performances on her battery of psychological tests suggested that the idea of periodic incapacity had been grossly overstated. As Thorndike, Woodworth, and others were finding in their studies of fatigue, the mind enjoys a certain independence from the body. A person's attitude appeared to be at least as important in determining mental performance as his or her supply of nervous energy. Neither Hollingworth nor any other contemporary researcher advocated returning to Descartes's mind-body dualism; they all accepted the post-Darwinian belief that the mind is rooted in physical structure and physiological forces. They increasingly doubted, however, that the link between the body and the mind was as simple and predictable as Darwin's early followers had thought. Clearly the mind was far more complicated and far more susceptible to outside forces than had been suspected.

While Hollingworth was completing her course work and research, she learned of a temporary, part-time job as a mental tester at the Clearing House for Mental Defectives, run by the City of New York. Few testers had been trained by 1913, and Hollingworth saw this part-time job as an opening wedge to a full-time professional career. Indeed, the temporary, part-time job quickly became a full-time job as the work of mental testing expanded in the next two years, and in 1914 Hollingworth filled New York's first civil service position in psychology. By 1916, when she com-

---

"Clelia Duel Mosher: The Scientific Feminist," in *Pioneer Women in Physical Education,* supplement to the *Research Quarterly of the American Physical Education Association* 12 (October 1941): 623–45.

27. Mosher, "Functional Periodicity," p. 10. Modern research on menstruation has tended to confirm Hollingworth's and Mosher's work. For a summary of modern research, see Barbara Sommer, "The Effect of Menstruation on Cognitive and Perceptual-Motor Behavior: A Review," *Psychosomatic Medicine* 35 (November–December 1973): 515–34.

pleted her Ph.D., she was offered the job as chief of psychology at Belle-vue Hospital.[28]

In its early days clinical psychology dealt predominantly with retarded children, and Hollingworth typically saw children referred to her by the courts, various charitable agencies, and school authorities. Most of these children were boys, as any psychologist at the time would have expected. Ever since Darwin, scientists had believed that men were more variable than women and that one should expect to find a disproportionate number of idiots among them. As Hollingworth's advisor, Edward Thorndike, reported in his 1914 treatise on experimental psychology, "It is well known that very marked intellectual weakness is commoner amongst men than amongst women. Two times as many men as women will be found in asylums for idiots and imbeciles."[29]

Hollingworth noticed something about the population at her clinic, however, that no one had ever observed before: the preponderance of retarded males in the clinic as a whole resulted from there being many more boys under sixteen years of age than there were girls of the same age. In speculating on the reason for this curious fact, she suggested that social influences might be responsible. First, she noted, "boys, because they are less restricted, come more often into conflict with the law than do girls, and are thus scrutinized and referred more often by the courts." Second, "the subjective notion as to what constitutes intelligent behavior is different in the case of girls from what it is in the case of boys."

A female with a mental age of six years has as good a chance to survive inconspicuously in the educational, social, and economic milieu of New York City as a male of a mental age of ten years.

By the time women were finally committed to mental institutions, it was usually because they had lost their dependent status through the death of a husband, for instance, or because of illness, if the woman was a prosti-tute. "There seems to be no occupation which supports feebleminded

28. Hollingworth, *Leta Stetter Hollingworth*, pp. 101– 04. For more on the growing enthusiasm over mental testing in the 1910s, see Cravens, *The Triumph of Evolution*, pp. 224– 68; Frank Freeman, *Mental Tests: Their History, Principles and Applications* (Boston: Houghton Mifflin, 1926), pp. 32– 163; and Mark Haller, *Eugenics: Hereditarian Attitudes in American Thought* (New Brunswick, N.J.: Rutgers University Press, 1963), pp. 95– 110.

29. Edward L. Thorndike, *Educational Psychology*, vol. 3: *Mental Work and Fatigue, and Individual Differences and Their Causes* (New York: Teachers College, 1914), p. 189. One of the most prominent exponents of this view was Havelock Ellis; see his "Variation in Man and Woman," *Popular Science Monthly* 62 (January 1903): 237– 53.

men as well as housework and prostitution support feebleminded women," Hollingworth ruefully observed.[30]

The apparent preponderance of male retardates provided evidence for only one side of the variability position, of course. The greater incidence of male genius contributed the most compelling evidence of greater male variability. As James McKeen Cattell wrote in his study of eminent men: "I have spoken throughout of eminent men as we lack in English words including both men and women, but as a matter of fact women do not have an important place on the list. They have in all 32 representatives in the thousand. . . . Women depart less from the normal than men—in fact that usually holds throughout the animals series." Edward Thorndike agreed, "Eminence in and leadership of the world's affairs of whatever sort will inevitably belong oftener to men. They will oftener deserve it."[31]

Cattell and Thorndike's statistics did not sway Hollingworth, however. If social factors could explain the underrepresentation of women among mental defectives, those same factors, she believed, could account for women's limited showing among those who had achieved eminence. Research she conducted at the New York Infirmary for Women and Children reinforced her belief that females are just as variable as males. Reviewing measurements made at birth on 20,000 infants, she concluded that the variation in the female measurements matched the variation in male measurements. Given the growing doubts about the correlation of physical measurements with intelligence, Hollingworth's study of neonatal measurements provided less than overwhelming evidence of women's potential for genius, but it certainly undercut the contrary claim that women are innately mediocre. Before psychologists explained women's lesser eminence by reference to their alleged lesser variability, Hollingworth advised, they should consider first "the established, obvious, inescapable fact that women bear and rear children, and that this has always meant and still means that nearly 100 percent of their energy is expended in the performance and supervision of domestic and allied tasks, a field where eminence is impossible." Only when psychologists had exhausted women's domestic responsibilities as an explanation for their

30. Leta Hollingworth, "Differential Action upon the Sexes of Forces Which Tend to Segregate the Feebleminded," *Journal of Abnormal Psychology and Social Psychology* 17 (April–June 1922): 44, 46, 53, 55. See also, idem, "The Frequency of Amentia as Related to Sex," *Medical Record*, October 25, 1914; and Leta Hollingworth and Max Schlapp, "An Economic and Social Study of Feeble-minded Women," *Medical Record*, June 6, 1914, pp. 1–15.

31. James McKeen Cattell, "A Statistical Study of Eminent Men," *Popular Science Monthly* 62 (February 1903): 375; Thorndike, *Educational Psychology*, 3:188. Thorndike examined the data reported by Helen Thompson and Clark Wissler in their studies of mental traits and found evidence of slightly greater male variability, but he conceded that his findings were ambiguous (ibid., pp. 186–96).

lesser eminence, she argued, should they "pass on to the question of comparative variability, or of differences in intellect or instinct."[32]

The typical psychologist's reference to "maternal instinct" always represented the last word in the argument over sex differences. Whatever women's physical strength or intellectual capacity, maternal instinct precluded them from achieving fulfillment. Curiously, Thorndike continued to believe in maternal instinct long after he had discarded as too vague and mentalistic such instincts as that of self-preservation. As he wrote in 1914, "The maternal instinct . . . is the chief source of woman's superiorities in the moral life. The virtues in which she excels are not so much due to either any general moral superiority or any set of special moral talents as to her original impulses to relieve, comfort and console." Hollingworth objected heatedly to this description of female character "in the absence of all scientific data" on the subject. Anyone who claimed to be a scientist should, at the very least, "guard against accepting as an established fact about human nature a doctrine that we might expect to find in use as a means of social control." Though Thorndike urged his students to "exhaust first the influence of the known physical differences and second the influence of instinct" before resorting to speculations about "the hypothetical cause of differences in purely intellectual caliber," Hollingworth insisted that physical differences and alleged instincts provided the least reliable measures of intellectual differences she could think of.[33]

Experimental psychologists resorted to a double standard of scientific proof, Hollingworth contended. In most of their work they condemned anthropomorphic thinking and the careless definition of instincts. In addition, they insisted that researchers should subject the assumptions that dominated psychological work to the most searching criticisms. When studying sex differences, however, they wore blinders, and when reporting their results they lapsed into conventional platitudes. The restricted vision of the male researchers who examined sex differences confirmed Hollingworth's conviction that women should train themselves for work in experimental psychology.

32. Leta Hollingworth and Helen Montague, "The Comparative Variability of the Sexes at Birth," *American Journal of Sociology* 20 (November 1914): 335– 70, 528. Henry Hollingworth raised doubts about the conventional view of women's lesser variability in his own work, "Judgments of Persuasiveness," *Psychological Review* 18 (July 1911): 234– 56. Both of the Hollingworths found support for their attack on the conventional wisdom regarding variability in the work of Karl Pearson. See Pearson, "Variation in Man and Woman," in his *Chances of Death* (London: E. Arnold, 1897), pp. 234– 56.

33. Edward L. Thorndike, *Educational Psychology: Briefer Course* (New York: Teachers College, 1914), p. 27; idem, *Educational Psychology*, 3: 203; Leta Hollingworth, "The Vocational Aptitudes of Women," in Henry L. Hollingworth, *Vocational Psychology* (New York: Appleton, 1916), pp. 238– 39; Leta Hollingworth, "Sex Differences in Mental Traits,"

Thus in time, may be written a psychology of women based on truth, not opinion; on precise not on anecdotal evidence; on accurate data rather than on remnants of magic. Thus may scientific light be cast upon the question so widely discussed at present and for several decades past,—whether women may at last contribute their best intellectual effort toward human progress, or, whether it will be expedient for them to remain in the future as they have in the past, the matrix from which proceed the dynamic agents of society.[34]

The Psychological Consensus by World War I

In the years after 1900, and especially after 1910, psychological research in the United States mushroomed. No one could hope to keep abreast of the work in different fields, and thus considerable influence fell to those specialists who summarized and reviewed for the general reader the work being done in specific fields. One journal in particular, *Psychological Bulletin,* specialized in such reviews, and beginning in 1910 it ran reviews of the literature on sex differences. During the next eight years Leta Hollingworth shared the work of. preparing these essays with Helen Thompson Woolley, who, though no longer conducting research on sex differences, was still regarded as the leading authority in the field. Though making no secret of their feminist convictions, Hollingworth and Woolley tried to provide a picture of the consensus that had emerged by the First World War on the issue of sex differences in mental traits. That consensus, they believed, underscored their conviction that intelligence should no longer be considered a secondary sex characteristic.[35]

Woolley and Hollingworth covered not only work in psychology but also work in genetics, anatomy, and physiology that bore on the issue of sex differences. Much of the fanciful speculating done at the end of the nineteenth century about the origins of sex differences derived from misguided notions about the nature of heredity. For all that biologists had learned about evolutionary development, no one before 1900 understood the mechanism that governs heredity. With the rediscovery of Mendel's work at the turn of the century and the discovery of the sex chromosome in 1906, however, most biologists could no longer accept either Hall's

---

Psychological Bulletin, 13 (October 1916): 377 – 85; idem, "Comparison of the Sexes in Mental Traits," *Psychological Bulletin* 25 (December 1918): 427 – 32.

34. Leta Hollingworth, *Functional Periodicity,* p. 99.

35. Helen Thompson Woolley, "A Review of Recent Literature on the Psychology of Sex," *Psychological Bulletin* 7 (October 1910): 335 – 42; idem, "The Psychology of Sex," ibid. 11 (October 1914): 353 – 79; Leta Hollingworth, "Sex Differences in Mental Traits" and "Comparison of the Sexes in Mental Traits."

notion of the divergence of the sexes or Ward's belief in acquired characteristics.[36]

As Woolley reported in 1914, Thomas Hunt Morgan and other geneticists believed that "the part played by sexual selection in evolution [is] very
small. There is little evidence that it takes place at all in animals. Even
when consciously practiced it is incapable of originating modifications of
species, or producing steady change in any direction." Geneticists argued
further, according to Woolley, "that it is impossible to find any single
secondary character which belongs exclusively to either sex throughout
the animal kingdom. For instance, superior size and brilliant plumage in
some species belong to the female, while even the instinct for incubating
eggs is assigned in some species to the male." In a separate article Hollingworth noted: "No mental trait has ever been proved to be sex-limited
in inheritance, or to exist as a secondary sex character. So far as we know,
daughters inherit mental traits from fathers as well as from mothers, and
sons inherit them from mothers as well as from fathers." By World War I,
work in genetics had generated widespread skepticism over the once
universally held belief that women were becoming steadily more differentiated from men through the process of heredity, sexual selection,
and acquired characteristics.[37]

Theoretically, as Woolley conceded, the brain and nervous system
might carry sex-linked factors, but increasingly work in anatomy and
physiology cast doubt upon that possibility. In 1909 Johns Hopkins
anatomist Dr. Franklin Mall appeared to have the final word on the issue
of the female brain. Mall reported that even with the most careful measuring techniques he could demonstrate no correlation between brain weight
and levels of intelligence. Nor could he find a correlation between brain
weight and either sex or race. Mall defied researchers, who typically
studied the brain of a known sex and looked for distinguishing characteristics, to sort unidentified brains according to sex.

> Each claim for specific differences fails when carefully tested, and the general
> claim that the brain of woman is foetal or of a simian type is largely an opinion
> without any scientific foundation. Until anatomists can point out specific dif-
> ferences which can be weighed or measured, or until they can assort a mixed
> collection of brains, their assertions regarding male and female types are of no
> scientific value.

36. Conway Zirkle, "The Knowledge of Heredity before 1900," pp. 35–58.
37. Woolley, "The Psychology of Sex," pp. 354–55; Leta Hollingworth, "Vocational
Aptitudes of Women," p. 241; Garland Allen, "Thomas Hunt Morgan and the Problem of
Sex Determination, 1903–1910," *Proceedings of the American Philosophical Society* 110 (Febru-
ary 1966): 48–57; Thomas H. Morgan, *Heredity and Sex* (New York: Columbia University
Press, 1913), passim.

Mall doubted that any such distinctions could ever be made. "For the present," he concluded, "the crudeness of our method will not permit us to determine anatomical characters due to race, sex or genius, and if they exist they are completely masked by a larger number of marked variations."[38]

As the latest anatomical evidence discredited traditional assumptions about sex differences in cranial capacity, the latest medical tests undermined popular belief in the immutable nature of the female physical form. Studies of menstruation by Hollingworth and Mosher suggested that environmental factors as well as attitude influence women's physiological functions, and studies in America and Denmark showed that just one generation of improved food and exercise made a significant difference in the physical development of girls. No longer could social theorists adhere to the view of clear-cut physical differentiation that had been popular a generation earlier, because physical differences appeared to be neither so great nor so permanent as had once been assumed.[39]

As researchers abandoned their belief in a fixed physical form, they also began to question their assumption of the existence of fixed male and female minds. Though most experimenters maintained their belief in the existence of general intelligence and insisted that it could be measured, they no longer believed, as Cattell once had, that it could be judged by reference to lower skills or physical traits, or that it could be correlated with sex differences. By 1918 references to sex differences in intelligence were beginning to go out of style in psychology. As Hollingworth remarked: "It was formerly a kind of convention to include in the summary or results of a study where both male and female subjects participated, a paragraph on 'sex differences.' There seems now to be a growing tendency among those who have studied individual differences most extensively to omit this customary paragraph."[40]

38. Franklin Mall, "On Several Anatomical Characters of the Brain Said to Vary According to Race and Sex, With Especial Reference to the Weight of the Frontal Lobe," *American Journal of Anatomy* 9 (1909): 27, 32.

39. Hollingworth, *Functional Periodicity*, pp. 1–101; Mosher, "Functional Periodicity," pp. 1–21; Woolley, "The Psychology of Sex," p. 355. Mosher kept records of female students' height from 1893 to 1923 and found that college freshmen had gained 1.5 inches in thirty years (Mosher, "Some of the Causal Factors in the Increased Height of College Women," *Journal of the American Medical Association* 81 [August 1923]: 528–35). The most extensive study of the environmental influence on growth conducted in America was carried out under the direction of the Franz Boas for the United States Immigration Commission in 1909. Boas found that daughters of immigrants were taller and matured earlier than their mothers had. Boas, *Changes in the Bodily Form of Descendents of Immigrants*, U.S., Congress, Senate, Document no. 208, 61st Cong., 2d sess., 1910, pp. 1–7.

40. Hollingworth, "Comparison of the Sexes in Mental Traits," p. 428. For further discussion of psychologists' views of general intelligence, see Boring, *History of Experimental Psychology*, pp. 570–78.

Even claims that eminence would always be restricted to men appeared less often. Lewis Terman, who achieved fame during World War I for helping to develop tests for the army, reported in his 1917 study of schoolchildren that his findings on patterns of male and female variability confirmed conclusions drawn by Leta Hollingworth in her work. "There is no evidence of any wider range of intelligence among boys, such as has been commonly supposed to exist," he wrote. "The difference, if any exists, seems to be in the other direction." Among the first- through eighth-grade children Terman tested, the girls performed consistently better than the boys and had the highest scores until the age of fourteen, in which year the boys did slightly better. The boys' sudden improvement, Terman cautioned, should not be seen as a reflection of a suddenly improved intelligence. Rather, the schools typically skipped their brightest students, who were disproportionately female, from the seventh grade into high school, leaving the fourteen-year-old eighth-graders without the same level of competition they had had in earlier years. "The evidence," he concluded, "seems to point to the existence of a small sex difference in intelligence, which, but for the influence of selection, would probably be in favor of the girls at all ages."[41]

Psychological fashion had clearly shifted by the end of World War I. Though psychologists could continue to point to an unending array of small differences in the performance of boys and girls on specific tests, the slight superiority demonstrated by girls overall persuaded testers that they should stop referring to sex in measuring intelligence. Commenting on the reaction to girls' slightly superior performance on standardized tests, Woolley noted with heavy irony, "So far as I know, no one has drawn the conclusion that girls have greater native ability than boys. One is tempted to indulge in idle speculation as to whether this admirable restraint from hasty generalization would have been equally marked had the sex findings been reversed!"[42]

---

41. Lewis Terman, *The Stanford Revision and Extension of the Binet-Simon Scale for Measuring Intelligence* (Baltimore: Warwick and York, 1917), p. 70.

42. Woolley, "Psychology of Sex," p. 365. Interest in sex differences in intelligence continued after 1920, but research more often focused on particular mental traits than on general intelligence. For general reviews, see C. N. Allen "Studies in Sex Differences," *Psychological Bulletin* 24 (April 1927): 294– 304; Florence Goodenough, "The Consistency of Sex Differences in Mental Traits at Various Ages," *Psychological Review* 34 (November 1927): 440– 62; Institute of Educational Research, Division of Psychology, Teachers College, "Sex Differences in Status and Gain in Intelligence Scores from Thirteen to Eighteen," *Pedagogical Seminary and Journal of Genetic Psychology* 33 (1926): 167– 81. The final step in eliminating sex from general I.Q. tests came with the 1937 revision of the Stanford-Binet test, from which questions favoring one or the other sex were eliminated. See Quinn McNemar, "Sex Differences," in his *The Revision of the Stanford-Binet Scale: An Analysis of the Standardization Data* (Boston: Houghton Mifflin, 1942), pp. 42– 54.

The Impact of Women on Psychology

By 1920 American psychologists had buried the doctrine of female uniqueness propounded by their Victorian mentors. No longer did researchers claim, as G. Stanley Hall had in 1906, "that with civilization the dimensions of the woman's body, her life and her psychic traits become more different from those of men rather than less so." Two decades of physical measurements had demonstrated a convergence of male and female form rather than the steady divergence which the first generation of psychologists, by reading Darwin, had been led to expect. Furthermore, years of mental testing suggested that the difference between male and female psychic traits had also been grossly overstated.[43]

That this rejection of Victorian orthodoxy took place in the years when coeducation through the collegiate level was becoming an accepted feature of American schooling and the first women were earning doctorates in psychology was no accident. Though the corrosive skepticism of the younger generation of male psychologists did much by itself to dissolve old dogmas about sexual identity, the critical faculties of these same men frequently lapsed when the issue of sex differences arose. Those generally suspicious of instincts still clung to their faith in innate maternal feeling; those typically skeptical of the wholesale implantation of evolutionary theory into psychology still accepted without question the evolutionary doctrine of greater male variability; those who questioned the Spencerian belief that the body forms a closed-energy system still accepted without comment the traditional belief in female periodicity in mental as well as physiological functioning. As Woolley ruefully observed of her male colleagues, "as to the nature of the psychological characteristics of sex," they were "convinced that they are inherent and are not to be explained by environmental influences during the life of the individual. . . . Differences which remain constant at different ages and in different countries must, they think, be inherent in sex itself. They do not seem to have considered whether or not there are factors in the social environment of sex which remain constant in all modern civilized countries." Had girls not been present in the schools to be tested along with their brothers, and had women psychologists not noticed and broadcast the egalitarian implications of the data being collected, it is hard to believe that psychology would have so readily rejected the traditional view of sex differences.[44]

Women made a mark on psychology, in part, because they forced male colleagues to live up to their critical ideals when dealing with the issue of sex differences; but they did more. In focusing on sex, they contributed in an important way to the trend toward environmentalism in American

43. G. Stanley Hall, "The Feminist in Science," p. 661.
44. Woolley, "The Psychology of Sex," p. 374.

psychology. For most psychologists, the female sex represented the limiting case in how seriously they could question biological determinism. To doubt the physiological basis of feminine psychological differences was considerably to loosen the keystone of the arch of biological determinism. If researchers were to discard their belief in maternal instinct, and if they were to agree that the assignment of people to separate groups solely on the basis of sex represented an arbitrary and generally unjustified system of classification, how could they go on believing in instincts at all, and how could they defend the validity of any group classification? The dramatic decline in the popularity of instinct doctrine and of racial classification in the 1920s and 1930s might well have taken place even if the issue of sex differences had never been raised; for psychology was beginning to open up to groups other than women who had not previously been welcome in American academic circles, and these new, religiously and ethnically diverse academics fostered a strong, democratic critique of the first generation's hierarchical ideas that bore no necessary relation to the debate over sex. The doubts raised by women critics, however, provided an important and early element in fostering a skeptical attitude among psychologists. A number of researchers commented that the lessons they had learned from studying women affected their attitude toward studying psychology in general. Thorndike and Terman, among others, first came to grips with the issue of group classification because of feminist challenges: only after they had abandoned sex classification did they confront and develop doubts about the question of race differences in their mental testing.[45]

For many women psychologists, the particular professional work experience available to them underscored their environmental leanings. Even in its early and unpopular days, academic psychology offered women little opportunity beyond the level of graduate training; but clinical psychology, which expanded dramatically after 1910 as an adjunct of reform and industrial personnel management, absorbed large numbers of women. The markedly different conditions under which experimentalists and

45. David Hollinger, "Ethnic Diversity, Cosmopolitanism and the Emergence of the American Liberal Intelligence," *American Quarterly* 27 (May 1975): 133–51; David Krantz and David Allen, "The Rise and Fall of McDougall's Instinct Doctrine," *Journal of the History of the Behavioral Sciences* 3 (October 1967): 326–38; John C. Burnham, "On the Origins of Behaviorism," ibid. 4 (April 1968): 143–51; Cravens, *The Triumph of Evolution*, pp. 69–71, 210–19; Samuel Fernberger, "The American Psychological Association," *Psychological Review* 50 (January 1943): 33–60. For evidence that psychologists abandoned race norms, see the 1926 discussion of "Norms for Sex, Race and for Social Groups," in Freeman, *Mental Tests*, pp. 296–97. As early as 1914, with the popularization of his three-volume *Educational Psychology*, in *Educational Psychology; the Briefer Course* Edward Thorndike eliminated all reference to greater male variability but included references to greater European white variability (as compared with Negroes), see pp. 340–53.

clinical psychologists saw people in the course of their work tended to influence their observations of mental functioning. The person who appeared in the experimental lab came as a subject for a narrowly defined research project. As Leta Hollingworth once characterized the researcher's approach: "It has become a fashion in educational research to rush forth hastily with a huge load of pencil and paper tests; to spend an hour or two on a hundred children; to rush hastily home to the adding machine, there to tabulate the performances of the children, not *one* of which has ever been perceived as an individual child."

The person who came to the clinical psychologists, on the other hand, arrived as an individual who needed help in dealing with a sometimes complex array of social and environmental forces. Given the nature of their clientele, clinical psychologists tended to emphasize factors other than intelligence in assessing abilities. Helen Woolley, for instance, in her postgraduate studies of working children, discovered that a variety of factors besides intelligence contributed to the success or failure of individual children. "The importance of general appearance, manner, style of dress, and such qualities as persistence, ambition, and social ease, is frequently impressed upon us," Woolley wrote. Another clinical psychologist, Augusta Bronner, who took her doctorate with Thorndike at the same time Hollingworth did, began to doubt whether mental tests should even be used. Working with delinquent children at the Juvenile Psychopathic Institute in Chicago, she found that children's performances on mental tests varied dramatically depending on their attitudes when she gave them the test. The longer Bronner worked with delinquents, the more convinced she became that her tests were measuring the effects of a troubled background rather than innate mental abilities.[46]

The Limits on Women's Achievement

Egalitarian bias, born of their own experiences with discrimination, and environmental bias, reinforced by clinical experience, made many of the early women psychologists critical of traditional thinking in psychology. For a variety of personal, institutional, and professional reasons, however, their criticisms and their influence fell far short of what one might have

46. Henry Hollingworth, *Leta Hollingworth*, p. 146; Helen Thompson Woolley, 'A New Scale of Mental and Physical Measurements for Adolescents, and Some of Its Uses," *Journal of Educational Psychology* 6 (November 1915): 534; Augusta Bronner, "Attitude as It Affects Performance of Tests," *Psychological Review* 23 (July 1916): 303– 31. Other women working with Bronner at Healy's Psychopathic Institute who contributed to the environmental attitude were Julia Lathrop, Edith Spaulding, Mary Hayes, and Jean Weidensall. Edward G. Boring, *History of Experimental Psychology*, pp. 570– 78; Cravens, *The Triumph of Evolution*, pp. 253– 364; Fernberger, "The American Psychological Association," pp. 33– 60.

anticipated, given the rapid incursion of women into graduate work at the turn of the century and the strikingly egalitarian and environmental bias of their early work.

Women found it extraordinarily difficult, for example, to pursue any professional work in psychology beyond the graduate level. Woolley's and Hollingworth's success in doing so represented telling exceptions in proof of the rule. Only the support of women reformers in Cincinnati enabled Helen Thompson Woolley to return to psychology in 1910, and only the untimely death of Naomi Norsworthy opened a place on the faculty at Teachers College for Leta Hollingworth in 1916. Between the two of them, Woolley and Hollingworth covered the academic and clinical subdivisions within psychology, but the difficulties they faced in pursuing their work illustrate both how unusual their success was and how hard it was to realize the full potential of that success.[47]

Woolley and Hollingworth bridged two worlds, one dying, the other struggling to be born. On the one hand, they lived in a world of women and devoted much of their life to reform activities, fighting for women's suffrage and a better life for children. But by 1920 the women's movement was dying, in part as a result of the forces in the professional world in which these two psychologists had been trained. The values of individualism, egalitarianism, scientific objectivity, and careerism that characterized the scholarly outlook in the emerging American university turned many women students away from the ideals of womanhood that had shaped their upbringing—ideals like selflessness, feminine purity, and social reform.

The most obvious manifestation of this fundamental conflict in values among women was the split in the women's movement following the passage of the Nineteenth Amendment, when the social reformers in such organizations as the League of Women Voters refused to support the Equal Rights Amendment proposed by the professional-minded members of the National Woman's party. After 1920 it became increasingly difficult to reconcile reform with science, and the polarization that resulted among women persisted for two generations. Psychologists like Woolley and Hollingworth were caught in the middle of this split. Much of their work was devoted to and made possible by the efforts of women reformers who were united by a common sense of purpose. Much of their

47. Fowler to author, July 20, 1976. Hollingworth, *Leta Stetter Hollingworth*, pp. 215–43. For work on the personal problems faced by academic women, see Margaret Rossiter, "Women Scientists in America before 1920," *American Scientist*, pp. 312–23; Alice Bryan and Edwin Boring, "Women in American Psychology: Statistics from the OPP Questionnaire," *American Psychologist* 1 (March 1946): 71–79; Jessie Bernard, *Academic Women*, pp. 215–41, and passim; Helen S. Astin, *The Woman Doctorate in America: Origins, Career and Family* (New York: Russell Sage Foundation, 1969), pp. 100–10; Emilie Hutchinson, *Women and the Ph.D.*, pp. 90–98, and passim.

work, however, was aimed at dissolving the body of Victorian assumptions that underlay that unifying purpose.

Psychologists Woolley and Hollingworth straddled these two worlds better than many of their contemporaries and better than most of the new generation of social scientists, who simply retreated from politics and reform into their professional careers. Both women were considered exemplars of the new woman professional, yet both thought of themselves as reformers. They believed that effective reform depended on the work of good researchers, and they realized that the kind of research in which they were most interested depended upon the success of reform activity.

But in the end they belonged more to the new world than the old. Hollingworth, especially, identified more strongly with science than with the feminism of her day. Too often, she lamented, feminists fell back on "erroneous reasoning" to advance their political goals. Two types of erroneous reasoning, in particular, offended her. First, most feminists claimed that women needed special protection because of their unique physical disabilities; but on the basis of the most recent experimental evidence, she did not believe that women had any better claim to protective labor legislation than did men. Second, many feminists believed that women were superior to men, that they had once ruled society and had lost power only as a consequence of men's brute force. But Hollingworth, writing with anthropologist Robert Lowie, argued that no anthropologist had yet discovered a culture ruled by women and that there was no evidence, apart from myth, that any culture had ever existed that had been ruled by women. "Feminist literature," Hollingworth observed, "has not been free from misrepresentation of the facts." To her, the new world of science provided a surer key to the improvement of women's social condition than did the sometimes overzealous world of politics.[48]

The new world of science, however, did not offer women the support that the old world of social reform had. As Henry Hollingworth recalled after his wife's death:

> For her actual work, at any designated responsibility, she was always rewarded with promotion and due compensation. But she was never successful, as many appear easily enough to be, in enlisting the aid of any of the social agencies, foundations, or institutions in any original enterprise of hers, however significant. No one will ever know what she might have accomplished for human

48. Robert Lowie and Leta Hollingworth, "Science and Feminism," *Scientific Monthly* 4 (September 1916): 278, 277, and 277–84; Fowler to author, July 20, 1976; Hollingworth, *Leta Stetter Hollingworth,* pp. 119–20. Leta Hollingworth, in particular, was admired by members of the National Woman's party. See, for instance, Rheta Childe Dorr, "Is Woman Biologically Barred from Success?" *New York Times Magazine,* September 19, 1915, p. 119. For a general discussion of the split in the women's movement after 1920, see William Chafe, *The American Woman: Her Changing Social, Economic and Political Role, 1920–1970* (New York: Oxford, 1972), pp. 112–32.

welfare, always her dominant motive, if some of the sponsorship freely poured out on many a scholarly dullard had been made available for her own projects.

Both Woolley and Hollingworth were unusually successful in providing work and direction to younger psychologists, but neither succeeded as well as many male contemporaries in marshalling the foundational support that was becoming increasingly important to the conducting of psychological work.[49]

While personal and institutional obstacles hampered women psychologists in their efforts to alter old-fashioned attitudes about women's capacities and social role, their commitment to science and their social class also set limits on what they felt justified in saying. Woolley and Hollingworth believed in the scientific validity of the tests they administered as part of their professional work. When their tests revealed the similarity of male and female abilities, they used that information to undermine antifeminist ideas. Where their tests revealed sex differences, however, they were forced either to accept those differences as accurate indications of innate sex differences, or they had to question the ability of those tests to determine basic psychological characteristics. Especially when their attention turned from sex to educational testing, they came increasingly to trust the tools of their trade. Woolley, who so laboriously provided alternate social and environmental explanations for each difference in mental ability among the men and women students at Chicago in 1900, much more willingly accepted the evidence of her intelligence tests twenty years later, when she studied schoolchildren and discovered that those who left school earlier tended to test less well than those who stayed. Rather than pointing to the predominantly working-class background of those with inferior tests scores, she explained the children's poor performance by their lower intelligence. Similarly, Hollingworth, though believing maternal feeling to be socially controlled, never looked beyond genetic factors to explain feeblemindedness.[50]

As differences persisted in the measurement of abilities, feminist psychologists found themselves caught between the Scylla of their feminist faith that differences were born of social discrimination and the Charybdis of their newly found scientific method, which relied on the

49. Hollingworth, *Leta Stetter Hollingworth*, p. 100; Cravens, *The Triumph of Evolution,* pp. 181 – 88. For careers for women in psychology in the 1930s, see Helen T. Woolley, "The Psychologist," in Catherine Filene, ed., *Careers for Women* (Boston: Houghton Mifflin, 1920), pp. 439 – 43.

50. Woolley, *An Experimental Study of Children,* pp. 721 – 23; Leta Hollingworth, "Differential Action upon the Sexes of Forces Which Tend to Segregate the Feebleminded," p. 57. Class bias was probably an important factor limiting their environmental analysis. Leta Hollingworth, in particular, stressed the biological basis of intellectual differences. See Nicholas Pastore, *The Nature-Nurture Controversy* (New York: King's Crown Press, 1949), pp. 101 – 06.

validity of their experimental findings. As scientists they relied on their
tests and avoided speculation, but the feminist within them persisted in
the belief that these tests could not plumb the depths of sexual division
nor explain all its causes. Increasingly, they deferred to other investigators, especially social psychologists, sociologists, and anthropologists,
for an understanding of the formation of feminine and masculine personality.[51]

51. On the final page of her last review of the literature in psychology on sex differences,
Helen Thompson Woolley turned to some of the work being done in social psychology and
sociology and wrote, "They all lay stress on the view that social conditions account for most of
the traits ordinarily considered feminine, and particularly for the limited accomplishment of
women in art and science" ("The Psychology of Sex," p. 375).

5 *The Social Roots of Personality*

Mental testers and experimentalists did much to weaken the Victorian belief in separate spheres by revealing unexpected similarities in male and female psychology. But the further weakening of that Victorian belief fell to others, especially those more intimately involved in the social laboratory of the modern city. Ultimately, the social scientists who studied the city's saloons and police courts proved more sensitive than the testers and experimenters to the ways in which rapidly changing social conditions were affecting traditional patterns of behavior. Not that those studying city life always linked their research to sex. Most researchers had little time and less inclination for speculating about the implications of their work for the understanding of sex differences. Indeed, the pressures of their work were such that these social scientists tended more often to view science as a means of creating order amid the chaos of urban life than as a means of challenging the validity of what little order traditional sexual relationships provided.

A few researchers, however, were sufficiently involved in the urban social laboratory to realize the new diversity in American society and yet sufficiently detached from it to be able to see the potential of that diversity for challenging traditional ideas about human nature and social change. Typically, these were scholars who conceived of the social scientific enterprise in unusually broad terms. They included people like George Herbert Mead and Jessie Taft, who were philosophers interested in psychology and sociology, and others like W. I. Thomas, who was a sociologist interested in anthropology and psychology. Working between 1900 and World War I, they were strongly influenced by the new functional psychology, and were therefore predisposed to think of the individual as part of a larger social context. Furthermore, they worked with and, significantly, felt drawn to the immigrants who flocked to the city in these years. And finally they combined, as few social scientists

114

before or since have done, a commitment to social change with an appreciation of the power of society to resist change.

The importance of these researchers lay in their capacity to conceive of the individual's relation to society differently from the way earlier social scientists had conceived of it. Whereas their predecessors had tried to explain how the individual, with his or her distinctive biological drives, shaped society, they tried, instead, to explain how society shaped the individual. Sex proved to be an important issue in this theoretical reversal, for most thinkers assumed that sex differences were the personal characteristics most resistant to social shaping, and that they would therefore provide an obvious limit to any trend toward environmentalism. Yet within the urban setting, social scientists were finding that men, and especially women, were failing to conform to traditional patterns of behavior. This failure pushed environmental thinking to new limits.

Jessie Taft

Until 1892, when the University of Chicago opened on a year-round basis, summer sessions were virtually unknown in America, and few administrators perceived any demand for them. This indifferent attitude notwithstanding, William Rainey Harper's inauguration of summer classes proved an instant and stunning success. With the close of the conventional school year each June, classes were opened to a hitherto untapped collegiate constituency: teachers from rural school districts, eager to escape their unruly and unresponsive charges and to bask, for a few short weeks, in the sun of academic debate.[1]

In 1908 two such refugees met at the University of Chicago and in the course of that summer began to see possibilities for themselves beyond the high-school classroom. Virginia Robinson, twenty-five, a teacher at Louisville Girls High School, and Jessie Taft, twenty-six, a teacher at West Des Moines High School, both boarded in the home of Professor James Tufts that summer. A common interest in philosophy drew them together, and their joint attendance in Professor William Isaac Thomas's course on primitive social control and Professor James R. Angell's course on the psychology of the educational process cemented their friendship.[2]

"The atmosphere here at Chicago is not that of the quiet dignity and repose produced by grey stone buildings covered with Ivy and students

1. Laurence Veysey, *The Emergence of the American University*, p. 340; Lawrence Cremin, et al., *A History of Teachers College, Columbia University* (New York: Columbia University Press, 1954), pp. 66–73.
2. Virginia Robinson, ed., *Jessie Taft: Therapist and Social Worker* (Philadelphia: University of Pennsylvania Press, 1962), pp. 28–30.

wearing gowns," Virginia Robinson wrote a former Bryn Mawr classmate. Instead, the feeling at the university was one of

> hurry and confusion resulting from too many buildings in too small a space and too many people thronging hither and thither—not distinctly students. It's a university in perfection—crowds and crowds of people of every type and nationality eager to grasp a little knowledge—school teachers from rural districts, country preachers intent on getting a modern idea or two.

Modernity, Robinson continued, infected the entire place. "Pragmatism is in the air and everybody starts with it as a basis. I do not know how I shall escape the influence." Listening to Thomas, Angell, and others, she reported, "I simply sit and gasp as one by one the old standbys—the arguments we staked our life on and accepted as truisms in philosophy at Bryn Mawr—are cast aside as so much dead wood."[3]

As Robinson and Taft sat in their classes, walked the Midway, rowed on the lagoon in Jackson Park, and explored the big city, they reveled in their newfound personal and intellectual freedom. Here was a setting in which they could escape the frustration of indifferent students, the loneliness of their lives as strong-minded, single women in small communities, and the oppressiveness of conventional thinking. They found in each other friendship and understanding neither had experienced before. Each had had other friends. Jessie Taft had known a man in college who had shared her philosophical interests, and she had been very close to an older woman, a doctor in Des Moines, who had encouraged her desire for life and experience. Virginia Robinson had developed several close friendships at Bryn Mawr. But never before had either met anyone who accepted so completely her intellectual enthusiasms and personal ambitions. The great difference in their backgrounds contributed to their friendship rather than detracting from it. Taft admired Robinson's refinement and her eastern sophistication, while Robinson marveled at Taft's straightforward frankness and western unselfconsciousness. "She's large and ungainly, and Western," Robinson wrote a friend about Taft, "but with the kindest eyes I've ever seen.

> There is no escaping the appeal of her good, straightforward common sense and understanding of things ... I've never met such frankness in mortal being. . . . She is so frank and sincere and free from conventionality that she compels you to a like frankness, and you find yourself telling her things in the most natural, matter-of-course manner.[4]

When the summer was over the two women returned to their respective teaching positions, but their weeks together had changed their perspec-

3. Ibid., p. 29.
4. Ibid., pp. 26, 29– 30.

tive on their lives. They wrote to each other often, comparing their discontent with teaching and affirming their intention to find new work and to be together. Neither one could inspire in her students the same passion for learning that she herself felt. Nor could either satisfy her restless desire for socially meaningful experience through high-school teaching. They agreed to return to Chicago if they could find the means to do so, but only Taft succeeded in winning a fellowship. For a time Robinson sought the "real experience" she could not afford in Chicago by augmenting her teaching with work in the suffrage movement in Kentucky. "How infinitely much better such a meeting is where each person really says something, than a tea or a reception where conversation is always scattered and marked by inanity only," she exclaimed after meeting with a group of women in a small town near Louisville. But meetings, even stimulating ones, still involved just talk. Robinson wanted "real work."[5]

The two friends' chance for exciting work together finally came in 1912 through a mutual friend who had taken charge of the New York State project for the investigation of criminal women. The project needed investigators to interview women who had been committed to the Bedford Hills Reformatory and institutions in New York City. They would be working under Katherine Bement Davis, superintendent at Bedford Hills, who had a Ph.D. from the University of Chicago. Though the job required Robinson's leaving school in the middle of the year and Taft's interrupting her doctoral work, the chance to be together, to work with "people," and to have a "chance for vital, gripping experience," persuaded them to go.[6]

"We began work," Robinson later recalled, "in New York on April 1, 1912, living in a furnished room at 7 West 16th Street,"

> setting out in the early mornings to catch a boat across the East River to Blackwell's Island where, in a cell converted into an office, we interviewed the drunks and prostitutes committed from Night Court. Evenings were spent observing the prostitutes soliciting on 14th Street or being brought into Night Court, and week ends in Bedford getting acquainted with that institution and talking with Miss Davis about our experiences . . . our choice was soon made to leave teaching and to stay in this field of work with people, a choice that included staying together and working together.[7]

5. Ibid., pp. 30–32.
6. Ibid., p. 32; W. David Lewis, "Katherine Bement Davis," in Edward T. James, ed., *Notable American Women,* 1:439–41; Katherine Bement Davis, "A Study of Prostitutes Committed from New York City to the State Reformatory for Women at Bedford Hills," in George J. Kneeland, *Commercialized Prostitution in New York City* (1913; rev. ed., New York: Century, 1917), pp. 173–282.
7. Robinson, ed., *Jessie Taft,* p. 33.

Taft's and Robinson's work for Davis represented the culmination of a decade of reform activity. In 1901 Marion Talbot had placed Davis at the Bedford Hills Reformatory through her old friend Josephine Shaw Lowell, and Davis, trained in sociology and economics by Thorstein Veblen and W. I. Thomas, had sought to apply some of the new techniques of social science to running the prison. Her principal goal, finally achieved in 1912, was to establish a program that would identify different types of offenders through psychological tests and individual interviews, and separate those criminals who might be reformable from those too mentally handicapped to warrant training. Taft and Robinson joined this program as two of the first interviewers.[8]

Davis found inspiration for her reforms, in part, from the work of one of her Chicago classmates, Frances Kellor. In 1900 Kellor published an extended critique of a book called *The Female Offender* written by the famed Italian criminal anthropologist Cesare Lombroso. Kellor visited reformatories, workhouses, and prisons one summer and took the standard anthropometric measurements of sixty-one female criminals, which she compared with those taken from fifty-five students. According to Lombroso, female criminals could be identified by their brachycephalic head form, but Kellor reported that she could find no correlation between any of her subjects' physical traits and their social behavior.[9]

In addition to taking anthropometric measurements, Kellor administered psychological tests, observed and interviewed a large number of prisoners, examined the records of the various institutions, and visited the areas from which the prisoners came. As she explored her subjects' impoverished neighborhoods and learned of their unsavory acquaintances, inadequate education, poor circumstances, and "inadequate moral training," she came to believe that social conditions more than head form shaped criminal behavior.[10]

Though Kellor insisted that the power of social forces to inspire crime had been underestimated, she remained persuaded by the conventional scientific wisdom of the time that those forces were limited in their effects

8. Josephine Shaw Lowell to Marion Talbot, March 7, 1900, Marion Talbot Papers, University of Chicago Archives, University of Chicago, Chicago, Illinois; Robinson, ed., *Jessie Taft,* p. 32. The women's prison reform movement is the subject of Estelle Freedman, *Their Sisters' Keepers: Women's Prison Reform in America, 1830 – 1930* (Ann Arbor: University of Michigan Press, 1981).

9. Frances Kellor, "Psychological and Environmental Study of Women Criminals, I and II," *American Journal of Sociology* 5 (July 1899– May 1900): 527– 43, 671– 82; Cesare Lombroso, *The Female Offender* (1895; reprint ed., New York: Appleton, 1900), pp. xv– xviii, 3, 21, 27. For another excellent and damaging review of *The Female Offender*, see Franz Boas, review in *Psychological Review* 4 (March 1897): 212– 13. A brachycephalic head is one that is short and broad.

10. Kellor, "Study of Women Criminals," pp. 528– 29, 672.

by each subject's physiological predisposition to particular patterns of behavior. Women, for instance, tended toward "feminine" crimes, she believed, while men tended toward "masculine" offenses. "Women's crimes are more closely associated with immorality," she explained, "because biologically she inclines to this rather than to crimes of force." When a woman did become involved in a violent crime such as a homicide, Kellor attributed her involvement to the fact that "the emotional conditions in woman, as contrasted with the motives of gain in man are often at work."[11]

Though Frances Kellor and Katherine Bement Davis contested the orthodox criminologist's claim that criminal behavior derived predominantly from cephalic abnormalities, they never doubted that physiological forces played an important part in criminality and that many women criminals were mentally deficient. The reform which they sought, and which Davis achieved, was the use of new techniques of psychology and sociology to separate the redeemable from the hopeless criminal. Those who showed intellectual promise were given special training, while those who performed below the intellectual level of the average twelve-year-old were labeled feebleminded, were given no training, and were cautioned against ever having any children. As Davis warned one "feebleminded" inmate:

Dr. Davis: Now, no matter how nice a young man comes along after you get out you will not be able to marry him.
Frances: I have found that out all right.
Dr. Davis: You will have to make your own living and support yourself, because you can't marry another man. Do you understand that?
Frances: Yes'm.[12]

To insure that her investigators would be effective in their work, Davis sent them to Dr. Charles Davenport's famed eugenics center in Cold Springs Harbor, Long Island. From Davenport, students learned to take family histories and to identify psychological and physical weaknesses that might be passed on to future generations. Taft and Robinson attended Davenport's classes for several weeks in the summer of 1912, and Taft later recalled with mixed feelings her "elaborate charts and mass of unanalyzed, unassimilated facts, gathered in the hills and backwoods of Dutchess County or some other spot where Jukes and Kallikaks

11. Ibid., pp. 529, 672.

12. Quoted from papers at Bedford Hills by William Isaac Thomas to Ethel Sturges Dummer, Thomas to Dummer, July 27, 1920, Dummer Papers, Schlesinger Library, Radcliffe College, Cambridge, Mass. For Kellor's later career, devoted largely to the campaign for immigration restriction, see John Higham, *Strangers in the Land: Patterns of American Nativism, 1860–1925* (1963; 2d ed., New York: Atheneum, 1973), pp. 239–49, 257–62.

abounded, at great risk of limb and loss of shoeleather."[13] That facts were needed Taft had no doubt; that mental tests were valuable she also believed. She wondered, however, as she hiked through rural New York in search of degenerate relatives of criminal women, whether those facts and tests really explained feeblemindedness. The tests at Bedford Hills seemed to indicate that at least a third of the inmates were feebleminded and therefore, presumably, unreformable. Yet Taft worried that she and her fellow interviewers and testers were giving way too easily to their classificatory impulses. She felt torn between her desire to learn and to apply the latest mental tests and interviewing techniques, and her nagging uncertainty over the ultimate value of these tests and techniques. At the end of their summer as social investigators and students of eugenics, Robinson stayed on, and Taft returned to complete her doctorate at Chicago, intending to work permanently in prison reform when she was done. But back at Chicago, Taft's doubts about her role as an investigator increased.[14]

While reformers like Katherine Bement Davis and Frances Kellor were fighting for the political and financial support to initiate new programs to sort criminals into manageable categories, the professors who had helped launch them in their careers as reformers were rethinking the social and psychological assumptions which underlay that strategy. By the time Jessie Taft reached the Chicago classroom a decade after Kellor and Davis, faith in classification had sharply diminished, and students intent on careers as reformers found themselves caught between the old teaching of the reformers in whose paths they sought to follow and the new teaching of the professors under whom they studied.

William Isaac Thomas: From Instinct to Habit

Jessie Taft's doubts about the Bedford Hills method of dealing with criminal women derived, in part, from her exposure to W. I. Thomas, the Chicago sociologist with whom she began graduate study. Thomas had spent his childhood "in the woods [of Tennessee] with a rifle, without a dog, shooting at a mark, and regretting the disappearance of large game and the passing of the Indian and pioneer life." He spent his adulthood trying to explain the social and psychological repercussions and readjustments prompted by the cultural passing he so regretted. At the University of Tennessee, a biology teacher had interested him in Darwinism a generation before Tennessee discovered the dangers inherent in teaching evolution. In the years following graduation, while supporting a

13. Robinson, ed., *Jessie Taft*, pp. 34, 57. For a fuller treatment of Davenport and his training program, see Charles Rosenberg, "Charles Benedict Davenport and the Irony of American Eugenics," in his *No Other Gods*, pp. 89–97; and Mark Haller, *Eugenics*, pp. 63–75.

14. Robinson, ed., *Jessie Taft*, p. 33.

William Isaac Thomas

young family by teaching classical and modérn languages, Thomas devoted his free time to reading reports from the American Bureau of
Ethnology and Spencer's *Principles of Sociology*. When he heard of
Chicago's new department of sociology in 1894, he seized the opportunity
to transform his amateur interest in sociology into a new career, and
moved his wife and children to the new university.[15]

  For Thomas, Chicago represented a new kind of frontier, and even
more than his professors Albion Small and Charles Henderson, he

15. Thomas left virtually no personal record, a curious fact about a man whose major
lifework, the five-volume *Polish Peasant in Europe and America* (1918– 21), relied heavily on
personal correspondence. Only the goading of sociologist Harry Elmer Barnes prompted
him to prepare the short memoir from which Barnes wrote "William Isaac Thomas: The
Fusion of Psychological and Cultural Sociology," in Harry Elmer Barnes, ed., *An Introduction
to the History of Sociology* (Chicago: University of Chicago Press, 1948; abridged ed., Phoenix
Books, 1966), pp. 436, 437, and passim.

enjoyed exploring Chicago's strange neighborhoods, with their exotic denizens and curious social practices. "I remember," Thomas later wrote, "that Professor Henderson, of sainted memory, once requested me to get him a bit of information from the saloons. He said that he had never himself entered a saloon or tasted beer." Thomas encouraged his wife Harriet to join in his adventures—she once almost tried smoking—but she found her time and interests consumed by the care of their young children, who were frequently ill. Though she participated in Chicago reform activities, she left the explorations of Chicago's back streets to her husband.[16]

From Albion Small, Thomas learned to view society and nature as interdependent. "Sociologists declare," Small taught his graduate students, "that the experience bounded by the reactions between men and physical nature, on the one hand, and the reactions of men with one another, on the other, is an interconnected experience, and that we shall have a science of it only in the proportion of our insight into the way and degree in which each item of this experience is affected by every other item of it." The dominant factors in that interdependence, Thomas concluded after taking courses with Jacques Loeb in physiology and Adolf Meyer in brain anatomy, were nature in general and human physiology in particular.[17]

Thomas's initial faith in the power of physiological forces shone forth from his 1897 doctoral thesis on the metabolic basis of sex differences. All social phenomena, he argued, have their origin in biological conditions, and the anabolic and katabolic factors, which originally produced sexual differentiation, created, at a later stage of evolution, the impetus for the industrial development of the present day. As he wrote in an article in 1896:

> [I]t is important to recognize that food and sex are the irreducible factors of social life; and that beginning with these, we may hope to understand the meaning of the different variables of society: ideas, institutions, beliefs, senti-

16. Ibid., p. 437. George Herbert Mead referred frequently to the Thomas family in his correspondence with members of his own family, and it was he who noted Harriet Thomas's failed effort to smoke during a dinner party with the Deweys one evening. George Herbert Mead to Helen Castle Mead, July 1, 1906, George Herbert Mead to Helen Castle Mead, July 1, 1906, George Herbert Mead Papers, University of Chicago Archives, University of Chicago, Chicago, Illinois.

17. Albion Small, *The Meaning of Sociology* (Chicago: University of Chicago Press, 1910), p. 61; Barnes, "William Isaac Thomas," in his *Introduction to the History of Sociology*, p. 437. For Small's approach to sociology, which he struggled earnestly to establish as the queen of the social sciences, see also Albion Small, "Fifty Years of Sociology in the United States," *American Journal of Sociology* 21 (May 1916): 721–864; Harry Elmer Barnes, "The Place of Albion Woodbury Small in Modern Sociology," *American Journal of Sociology* 32 (July 1926): 15–44; and Vernon K. Dibble, *The Legacy of Albion Small*, pp. 10–19.

ments, language, arts, literature — and to trace the red thread of consciousness through them.

In concert with a number of other liberal evolutionists in the 1890s, Thomas attributed the surge of reform activity at the turn of the century to a predictable readjustment of natural forces. The katabolic power that had produced modern industrialism had fostered aggressive competitiveness, 'with its ugly social consequences, as a necessary by-product. Social reform, and especially the woman's movement, represented the countervailing anabolic power of feminine social feeling, which should be accepted and even encouraged, for social equilibrium depended on maintaining a balance of male and female qualities.[18]

Despite the vigor with which Thomas asserted his faith in the physiological foundation of social development, he began to develop doubts about that faith almost as soon as he had articulated it. Several factors diminished his belief in the power of physiology, among them his developing friendships with psychologists John Dewey, James R. Angell, and George Herbert Mead, whose influence could be seen in Thomas's work as early as 1899. In "Sex in Primitive Morality" (May 1899), Thomas qualified the distinction he was drawing between male and female approaches to morality by adding, "I do not wish to imply that this difference is altogether inherent in the male and female disposition; it is, in fact, partly a matter of habit and attention."[19]

A few months later Thomas explained what he meant by "attention" and "habit" in "The Psychology of Modesty and Clothing" (September 1899). Dismissing the theory advanced by both William James and Havelock Ellis that modesty is rooted in instinct, and ignoring his own earlier suggestion that women are by their anabolic nature more concerned with "personal morality" than men, Thomas labeled modesty a habit, a practical aid to psychological equilibrium, rather than an instinct. All societies, Thomas argued, depend on habits to maintain social order. The nature of the habits does not much matter; in some societies nakedness is a habit, whereas in others the complete draping of the body is the rule. "Psychologically the important point is that when the habit is set up," Thomas explained, a person's "attention," that is, his ability to "take note of the outside world and manipulate it," is in "equilibrium." A person in

18. William I. Thomas, "The Scope and Method of Folk-Psychology,"p. 445; idem, "On a Difference in the Metabolism of the Sexes," pp. 31 – 63.

19. Thomas, "Sex in Primitive Morality," p. 787; Barnes "William Isaac Thomas," in his *Introduction to the History of Sociology,* p. 438; Morris Janowitz, introduction to Thomas, *W. I. Thomas on Social Organization and Social Personality* (Chicago: University of Chicago Press, 1966), pp. xix– xx; John W. Petras, "Changes of Emphasis in the Sociology of W. I. Thomas," *Journal of the History of the Behavioral Sciences* 6 (January 1970): 70 – 79.

psychic equilibrium can go about his routine affairs in a fairly automatic way. When his attention is disrupted, however, the person is "upset." "When once a habit is fixed," Thomas continued, "interference with its smooth running causes an emotion. The nature of the habit broken is of no importance. If it were habitual for *grandes dames* to go barefoot on our boulevards or to wear sleeveless dresses at high noon, the contrary would be embarrassing." The emotional upset caused by this surprise alters the attention, which then comes into play in an attempt to reestablish a new psychological balance, either by calling on reason to rationalize the reaction, explaining it, for instance, as a reasonable response to an inherently disgusting act, or, more rarely, by changing the subject's attitude about barefoot and sleeveless women.[20]

Thomas's newly functionalist perspective transformed modesty from a characteristically feminine instinct into a broadly human form of behavior. Modesty, he concluded, is simply one of many habits that enables people to maintain a state of psychological equilibrium. When some surprise interrupts the flow of habit and disturbs the attention, a person naturally tries to reestablish the lost equilibrium, either by rationalizing and reasserting the habit, or by changing it if necessary.

The same psychological mechanism which underlies feelings of modesty underlies racial prejudice, Thomas later concluded. Through habitual association with whites, the white man has developed a fixed conception of human color. When confronted by a black man his conception is disrupted, and he reacts hostilely. Reason enters only after habit is disturbed and fear is evoked — not to provide a rational assessment of the interloper, but to rationalize the fear. Instincts provide impulses for action and reason provides rationalizations, but neither reason nor instinct controls social organization as much as habits do, Thomas declared. In reducing reason in human affairs to the role of rationalizer, Thomas broke with liberal-Darwinist colleagues like Ward, who continued to believe in both mental evolution and the power of reason to direct that evolution.[21]

Throughout his career Thomas drew heavily on both sexual and racial examples to explain his points. An avid reader of ethnology since before his graduate training, Thomas was more thoroughly familiar with the

20. William I. Thomas, "The Psychology of Modesty and Clothing," *American Journal of Sociology* 5 (September 1899): 249–50. In discussing the functional basis of emotion, Thomas quoted extensively from James R. Angell and Helen B. Thompson, "A Study of the Relations between Certain Organic Processes and Consciousness," *Psychological Review* 6 (January 1899): 32-69. For an example of the instinct-analysis of modesty, see Havelock Ellis, "The Evolution of Modesty," *Psychological Review* 6 (March 1899): 134.

21. William I. Thomas, "The Psychology of Race Prejudice," *American Journal of Sociology* 9 (March 1904): 593– 611.

anthropological debates of the day than any other sociologist. In the beginning Thomas used this literature, and especially the part that dealt specifically with race and sex, to illustrate, in a perfectly conventional way, his evolutionary beliefs. Nothing seemed so stable as sex and race; nothing seemed so suited to illustrating life's hierarchical structure. Increasingly after the 1890s, however, Thomas used sexual and racial illustrations to buttress a very different analysis of society. From serving as examples of society's most stable categories, sex and race suddenly become examples of great instability.[22]

In part, this shift in Thomas's thinking simply reflected influence of his functionalist friends in psychology, who objected to the formalistic way in which he first approached his work. But his newly fashioned functionalist perspective was most decisively shaped by his firsthand experiences in Chicago with both sex and race. Half of Thomas's students were women, and though many of them fit conventional stereotypes of femininity with their diffident behavior in his large lecture classes, others proved startlingly different from what he expected women to be. Helen Thompson [Woolley], Frances Kellor, Katherine Bement Davis, among others he knew, challenged, in their lives as well as their work, his assumptions of feminine frailty and intellectual mediocrity. Suddenly, all the ethnological data he had accumulated on primitive women seemed to illustrate not different stages of development but different ways of dealing with society. As Thomas became more familiar with the immigrants of Chicago, in whose neighborhoods he spent most of his professional and much of his personal time, he was struck by the massive changes the fact of immigration had imposed on their lives, how far away their villages and social practices sometimes seemed in the new urban setting. In Chicago, both at the university and in the ghettoes, social and personal change were coming too quickly to be explained within the framework of leisurely evolutionary development.[23]

22. Thomas's wide reading in ethnology is discussed in George W. Stocking, Jr., *Race, Culture, and Evolution*, p. 264.

23. Thomas's new functionalist perspective and changing attitudes toward sex and race made him more sympathetic than he had originally been to dissident authors in fields other than psychology, especially to anthropologist Franz Boas, who declared as early as 1894 that "the probable effect of civilization upon an evolution of human faculty has been much overestimated" (Franz Boas, "Human Faculty as Determined by Race," *Proceedings of the American Association for the Advancement of Science* 43 [1894]: 301–27), and to Gabriel Tarde, the French sociologist, who argued that mental development takes place not through the evolution of the brain but through the imitation that takes place when one group comes in contact with another (Gabriel Tarde, *The Laws of Imitation*, trans. Elsie Clews Parsons [1890; 2d ed., New York: Holt, 1903]). Thomas acknowledged these intellectual influences in a letter to Boas in 1907; W. I. Thomas to Franz Boas, May 14, 1907, Franz Boas Papers, American Philosophical Library, Philadelphia.

From Dewey, Mead and Angell, Thomas learned to see the individual not so much as an instinctual being, directed by fixed patterns of behavior, but rather as a purposive agent trying to adjust to an ever-changing environment. His women students and the young women he observed in the immigrant neighborhoods persuaded him that this purposive impulse knew neither sexual nor racial boundaries. In an article he wrote in 1906, called "The Adventitious Character of Woman," Thomas focused on the extreme case of the female criminal, the woman whom physical anthropologists had labeled most clearly the victim of physiological dysfunction. He argued that her abnormal behavior resulted, not from defective instincts, but from the failure of the group in which she lived to satisfy the basic desires for activity and response that motivated all people, men and women alike. Taking pains to emphasize the absence of sex differentiation in these basic human wishes, Thomas insisted that the same social conditions which prompted the male to criminal activity also prompted the female.

> The gamester, the adventuress, and the criminal are not usually abnormal in a biological sense, but have failed through defective manipulation of their attention, to get interested in the right kind of problems.

Because of the limited number of "problems" which society permitted women to interest themselves in, the tendency to break with acceptable social behavior was somewhat more pronounced in females.

> The mere superinducing of passivity, as in the extreme cases of solitary confinement, is sufficient to produce insanity. . . . Modern woman is in a similar condition of constraint and unrest, which produces organic ravages for which no luxury can compensate. The general ill-health of girls of the better classes, and the equally general post-matrimonial breakdown, are probably due largely to the fact that the nervous organization demands more normal stimulations and reactions than are supplied. . . . It is a wonder that more of them do not lose their minds; and that more of them do not break with the system entirely is due solely to the inhibitive effects of early habit and suggestion.

Those inhibitions were often relaxed in the young girl who left the structure of the rural family, either in Poland or in rural Illinois, to work in the city, where she sought the stimulation that was denied women in society. In becoming a prostitute, she did nothing more than seek "what, from the psychological standpoint, may be called a normal life." Thomas believed that prostitution was both a normal and more frequent activity for young women than most people thought.

> To pass from a regular to an irregular life for a season and back again, before the fact has been noted, is a course much more usual than is ordinarily suspected. The theory which accounts for the shorter career of the fast woman on the score of an early death is well-nigh groundless. Society simply cannot keep track of these women.

Women did not become prostitutes because they were emotional, as Thomas's student Frances Kellor had suggested, and as he himself would have argued before 1900, nor because they were depraved or impoverished, as many believed, but because they had so few ways to express themselves.[24]

To argue that modesty is not instinctive in women and that prostitution is not a sign of psychological degeneracy was to call into serious question conventional ideas about women's mental uniqueness. Thomas's growing skepticism found further confirmation in Helen Thompson Woolley's doctoral research, which, he thought, undermined conventional thinking about both sex and race. From Thompson, Thomas learned that sex differences in mental traits were not so great as he had assumed. From his own reading, thinking, and personal observations of social customs, he was becoming convinced that mental traits are highly mutable. By 1907 Thomas was arguing that the mental processes of women differed from those of men only to the extent that women's attention was usually focused on a narrower range of activity than men's.

> The direction of attention and the simplicity or complexity of mental processes depend on the character of the external stituation which the mind has to manipulate. If the activities were nil, the mind would be nil. The mind is nothing but a means of manipulating the ouside world.

In other words, if mental differences could be observed in adulthood, the disparity should be sought in the individual's experience and relationship to the group in which he has developed rather than in his relationship to his own biological processes.[25]

The importance of experience to intellectual development was amply demonstrated by the difficulties female students encountered when they first attempted to compete with men in colleges. About forty years before Thomas focused on the female mind, the University of Zurich first opened its doors to women. One of the professors at that time wrote of his distress over the women students, whose mental processes appeared to be unequal to the opportunity afforded them. Thomas quoted him at length in "The Mind of Woman." The young women arrived early at lectures; they took copious notes; they 'crammed' for their exams; and they responded admirably to direct questioning. But, as soon as the questioning became abstract and indirect, as soon as an answer had to be reasoned out rather than answered from memory, the women were lost. At laboratory

24. William Thomas, "The Adventitious Character of Woman," *American Journal of Sociology* 12 (January 1906): 43, 41, 42, and 32–44. On the related issue of Thomas's treatment of attitude as a product of one's social situation, see Donald Fleming, "Attitude: The History of a Concept," *Perspectives in American History* 1 (1967): 322–31.

25. William I. Thomas, "The Mind of Woman and the Lower Races," pp. 438, 446.

work they were incredibly inept. Despite their delicate fingers, they left in their wake "fragments of glass, broken instruments, broken scalpels, and spoiled preparations." The professor concluded that he was dealing with a lower level of intellectual life, but Thomas thought otherwise.

> Without a wide experience of life, and without practice in constructive thinking, they naturally fell back on the memory to retain a hold on results in a field in which they were not sufficiently trained to operate independently. It is frequently alleged, and it is implied in Professor Vogt's report, that women are distinguished by good memories and poor powers of generalization. But this is to mistake the facts. A tenacious memory is characteristic of women and children, and of all persons unskilled in the manipulation of varied experiences in thought. . . . The awkwardness in manual manipulation shown by these girls was also surely due to lack of practice. The fastest typist in the world is today a woman.[26]

In another article Thomas suggested that what he was saying about women's analytical powers held for the human mind in general.

> Number, time, and space conceptions and systems become more complex and accurate not as the human mind grows in capacity, but as activities become more varied and call for more extended and accurate systems of notations and measurement.

Simple environments, Thomas maintained, foster simple habits and a simple mental life. He still believed in the superiority of Western culture, but he doubted that superior minds had produced it. Building on his earlier analysis of humanity's habitual tendency, he wrote that new ideas and new habits develop, not from the progress of man's developing reason, but rather as a result of the new needs produced by disruptions in habitual patterns of behavior and thought. A disruption in group life that interrupts the flow of habit gives rise "to changed conditions of consciousness and practice." Out of the "general sudden and catastrophic occurrences which are new or not adequately provided against" develop the inventions that promote evolution. Reason is invoked only after crisis has disclosed the inadequacy of the current habit. Even the power of reason is circumscribed by the cultural complexity within which it operates. Though Thomas still believed in progress, he no longer saw progress as evidence of intellectual superiority but rather as evidence that crises had broken comfortable habits and that contact with outside groups had been sufficient to provide a broad base for imitation and invention. Human beings are not very original, Thomas argued, but they are great imitators.[27]

26. Ibid., p. 467.
27. William I. Thomas, "Is the Human Brain Stationary?" *Forum* 36 (October 1904): 320.

In women, as in humanity generally, the ability to reason depends on experience. But it also depends on something else: overcoming inhibitions that have been instilled in women from childhood. Women had great difficulty in class discussion, Thomas believed, because direct conversation with men had almost the nature of an immodesty to them.

> Men and woman still form two distinct classes and are not in free communication with each other. Not only are women unable and unwilling to be communicated with directly, unconventionally and truly on many subjects, but men are unwilling to talk to them. I do not have in mind situations involving questions of propriety and delicacy alone, but a certain habit of restraint, originating doubtless in matters relating to sex, extends to all intercourse with women, with the result that they are not really admitted to the intellectual world of men; and there is not only a reluctance on the part of men to admit them, but a reluctance—or rather, a real inability—on their part to enter.

Of course, in the years since colleges and graduate schools had been open to women in America there had been examples of outstanding success; but "the trouble with these cases," wrote Thomas (undoubtedly reflecting on the case of the newly married Helen Thompson Woolley, who was then in the jungles of Southeast Asia), "is that they are either swept away and engulfed by the modern system of marriage, or find themselves excluded in some intangible way from association with men in the fullest sense, and no career open to their talents."[28]

The more Thomas thought about the social and psychological boundaries limiting the development of women's minds and personalities, the more he questioned his original assumptions about the uniqueness of the feminine mind and character. And the more he questioned the uniqueness of women's minds and characters, the more he wondered whether psychologists or sociologists could legitimately make any judgment about any *particular* person's mind or character with the tests then in use. Few psychologists or sociologists were willing to carry such questioning that far. Even Helen Thompson Woolley, who questioned whether it was correct to assume that men's and women's minds differed at a structural level on the basis of sex, still assumed that there was a wide range of psychometrically identifiable mental differences within the population at large. Thomas was not so sure. Of the great enthusiasm among many social scientists around 1910 for the eugenics movement and its effort to breed better brains, he wrote, "what has been true in the past will happen again in the future, that the group which by hook or by crook comes into possession of the best techniques and the best copies will make the best show of intelligence and march at the head of civilization." What had always worked for the group worked also, Thomas believed, for the

28. Thomas, "The Mind of Woman and the Lower Races," pp. 463, 468.

George Herbert Mead

individual. Each person's mind was limited in its development by the range of techniques it could imitate.[29]

While most sociologists and psychologists between 1900 and 1920 were struggling to achieve professional recognition through the development of tests and questionnaires that could classify and contribute to the control of social forces, Thomas was developing a progressively more inconoclastic stance. As the years passed, the one lesson which above all others he

29. Thomas, "Is the Human Brain Stationary?" p. 320. See also, William I. Thomas, "Eugenics: The Science of Breeding Men," *American Magazine* 68 (June 1909): 190–97. Scholars who have written about Thomas's work have dismissed the first decade of his career as unimportant. This may be due to the fact that his early articles are best known as chapters in Thomas, *Sex and Society: Studies in the Social Psychology of Sex* (Chicago: University of Chicago Press, 1907). Rather than noting the stunning intellectual transformation displayed in this collection, environmentalist-minded scholars have been put off by the biological reductionism of Thomas's opening salvo, "The Organic Differences in the Sexes," and have dismissed the book as a whole. See, for example, Ellsworth Faris, "W. I. Thomas (1863–1947)," *Sociology and Social Research* 34 (March–April 1948): 756; Julia Schwendinger and Herman Schwendinger, "Sociology's Founding Fathers: Sexists to a Man," *Journal of Marriage and the Family* 33 (November 1971): 783–99.

came to emphasize in his teaching was a skepticism toward doctrinal claims about the fixity of psychological types. "The upshot of a great deal of the lecture presentation," wrote one of Thomas's students, "was that primitive people are one of a kind with modern people. The graduate student was made to recognize even some of his own behavior as being akin to that of his ancient, unknown, and unlearned ancestors." To those students like Jessie Taft, who were embarking on clinical careers, this was an inspiring, but also disturbing, lesson.[30]

George Herbert Mead: The Social Self

From W. I. Thomas, Jessie Taft learned to look for the social roots of both male and female behavior. Though Thomas conceded that all human beings possess basic impulses for activity and response and that these impulses set limits on the power of society to control individual behavior, he nevertheless believed that men and women are creatures of habit, whose behavior is shaped less by instinctive urges than by their natural tendency to imitate prevailing custom. What Thomas did not explain, however, was how habits are instilled and why one person imitates another, or a particular category of others, in the first place. As a woman concerned with finding a place for herself in a male world, Taft wanted to understand personality formation more fully than Thomas's focus on ethnology and sociology allowed; and therefore, as she began work on her doctoral thesis, she decided to work with philosophy professor George Herbert Mead, whose interest in social psychology had led him to focus on personality formation. While Thomas offered his students range and vision, Mead gave them depth and precision.[31]

Unlike his colleagues in sociology and psychology, Mead published very little, only a small number of difficult philosophical articles outlining his position. His influence was realized through his friends and students. Painfully shy, Mead disliked the impersonality of the lecture hall. He never appeared until everyone had been seated for some minutes, one student later recalled:

30. Emory Bogardus, "The Sociology of W. I. Thomas," *Sociology and Social Research* 34 (September–October 1949): 36. See also Ernest Burgess, "William I. Thomas As a Teacher," *Sociology and Social Research* 32 (March–April 1948): 760–64.

31. The following are particularly useful for Mead's career at Chicago: David L. Miller, *George Herbert Mead: Self, Language, and the World* (Austin: University of Texas Press, 1973), xi–xxxvii; Charles W. Morris, introduction to George Herbert Mead, *Mind, Self, and Society: From the Standpoint of a Social Behaviorist* (Chicago: University of Chicago Press, 1934), pp. ix–xxxv; Anselm Strauss, introduction to Strauss, ed., *George Herbert Mead on Social Psychology* (Chicago: University of Chicago Press, 1964), pp. vii–xxv; Van Meter Ames, "George Herbert Mead: An Appreciation," *University of Chicago Magazine* 23 (June 1931): 370–73; and Darnell Rucker, *The Chicago Pragmatists*, pp. 20–22.

whereupon he would stride to the front of the room, sit down, take up a piece of chalk or other object, fix his eyes on a corner of the ceiling, and begin talking without any sign of awareness that there was anyone else present. He would cogitate aloud without interruption for the duration of the hour; then just before the time was up, without stopping his lecture, he would walk to the back of the room, stop talking at precisely the end of the hour, dart out the door, shutting it behind him. Before the most agile student could get out of the room, Mead was on his bicycle and off for home.

Though Mead seemed unapproachable in public, to students who knew him well he was a warm and devoted man who exercised a powerful influence on their intellectual development. Students seem to have appreciated him most in seminars and in private discussions in his home and at his office. As another student wrote:

> It is fitting that the influence of such a personality should have been highly personal. . . . Chiefly his writing was the only kind that Plato thought really serious—that which is done directly on the minds of men. Thesis after thesis was written under him by students who were fired to develop ideas of his.

Even students who found his lectures opaque, or who openly disagreed with his ideas, revered him. "I didn't understand him in the classroom," John Broadus Watson later admitted, "but for years Mead took a great interest in my animal experimentation, and many a Sunday he and I spent in the laboratory watching my rats and monkeys. On these comradely exhibitions and at his home I understood him. A kinder, finer man I never met."[32]

Mead worked and reworked his lectures, always delivered extemporaneously, but he delayed the formal writing and publishing of his ideas, for he never succeeded in satisfying his own exacting standards of precision. In 1915, after fifteen years of teaching social psychology, he complained to his son that he was dissatisfied with the inchoate quality of his lectures that year. That anything is known of his own ideas is due primarily to the devotion of his students. In the late 1920s, several students decided to transcribe the aging Mead's lectures. After his death in 1931, they printed the transcripts, which by themselves comprise the bulk of Mead's published work. Most scholars have focused on the social psychology Mead presented in these lectures; but Mead had developed the basic elements of his system by 1912, as can be seen from a set of

32. Rucker, *The Chicago Pragmatists*, p. 21; Ames, "George Herbert Mead," p. 370; "John Broadus Watson," autobiographical sketch, in Carl Murchison, ed., *A History of Psychology in Autobiography*, 3:274.

students' notes from that year that remain in manuscript form, as well as from the dissertation Taft was writing under Mead's direction.[33]

In his lectures and his few articles Mead emphasized the interpersonal origins of personality. Neither innate tendencies nor physical environment, he told his students, was capable alone of supplying the kind of stimulus needed to elicit a social reaction from a person. The principal force determining a personality is a person's *relationship* with other people. Mead believed that intelligence is neither innate, nor simply imposed from without, but rather is the result of reflexive activity within a social sphere.

Mead's social perspective derived in part from Charles H. Cooley, with whom he had taught at the University of Michigan. Like Cooley, Mead tried to distinguish social psychology from natural science by emphasizing the differences between social and natural functions. They both dismissed the Spencerian belief that the body is limited by a fixed supply of nervous energy, arguing that the analogy from thermodynamics had no place in psychology. As Cooley put it: "The physical law of persistence of energy in uniform quantity is a most illusive one to apply to human life. There is always a great deal more mental energy than is utilized, and the amount that is really productive depends chiefly on the urgency of the suggestions."[34]

Mead parted company with Cooley, however, in his explanation of the social basis of human life. When Cooley described the individual as a social being, he meant that the individual imposes a social attitude on the world in which he lives, that the individual is an innately social creature and thus acts in a social way. Cooley believed in innate sociability; whereas Mead, the more insistent of the two in separating psychology from nature, believed in acquired sociability. To his students Mead described " a social consciousness that is organized from the periphery toward the center. . . . This 'me' which arises in consciousness arises as an object in the same fashion that other selves have arisen. . . . The self is an object in just the

33. George Herbert Mead to Henry Castle Mead, January 21, 1915, George Herbert Mead Papers. The transcription of Mead's lectures from the late 1920s was published as *Mind, Self, and Society: From the Standpoint of a Social Behaviorist* (Chicago: University of Chicago, 1934), and *Movements of Thought in the Nineteenth Century* (Chicago: University of Chicago Press, 1936), both edited by Charles W. Morris. The unpublished transcript of Mead's 1912 lectures for Philosophy 321, "Social Psychology," can be found in the George Herbert Mead Papers.

34. Charles Horton Cooley, *Organization: A Study of the Larger Mind* (New York: Scribner's, 1909), p. 328. Mead's theory of the interpersonal origins of personality had a far-reaching impact on American psychiatry, especially through the work of Harry Stack Sullivan. See Bruce Kuklick, "Harry Stack Sullivan and American Intellectual Life," *Contemporary Psychoanalysis* 16 (July 1980): 307– 19.

same sense that the others are. Solipsism is an absurdity. That self has a reality only as the other selves have reality." "Cooley's contention," Mead noted, "is that other persons are made up out of our sentiments of those emotional and intellectual contents that answer to their gestures." Mead insisted in putting it the other way around. "Other selves come into existence first of all and later one becomes aware of himself." The self could only be understood, Mead insisted, as a part of the social environment, acting reflexively with other selves.[35]

Mead shared his contemporaries' belief in human purposiveness, but he added to that belief the view that even before the mind acts on the social world, the social world acts on the mind. His analysis of the reflexive quality of mental and social development was his distinctive contribution to American psychology. Like W. I. Thomas, Mead believed that children learn by imitating those around them, but he thought it important to explain why children imitate some patterns of behavior in their environment while ignoring others. The answer, Mead concluded, lies in the fact that children only imitate that which has meaning for them, and that meaning emerges in different ways for each child out of his or her gradually evolving experience of social stimulation and response. The baby cries, and the parent reacts to baby's crying. The response made by the parent affects the response made by the baby. If the parent smiles at the baby, the baby might smile back, but not by imitation, Mead argued. "The likeness of the actions is of minimal importance compared with the fact that the actions of one form have the implicit meaning of a certain response to another form." Two individuals may react differently to the same stimulus, not because of innate differences, but because they have had different histories of interaction. The child plays the role of the people in his environment; "to be aware of another self as a self implies that we have played his role."

Not that we assume the roles of others toward ourselves because we are subject to a mere imitative instinct, but because in responding to ourselves we are in the nature of the case taking the attitude of another than the self that is directly acting, and into this reaction there naturally flows the memory images of those responses of others which were in answer to like actions. Thus the child can

35. George Herbert Mead, transcript of lectures for Philosophy 321, "Social Psychology," (1912), George Herbert Mead Papers, pp. 53, 56. For Cooley's position, see Charles Horton Cooley, *Human Nature and the Social Order* (New York: Scribner's, 1902), pp. 139– 45, which was part of the assigned reading for Mead's course. For Mead's final judgment on Cooley, see George Herbert Mead, "Cooley's Contribution to American Social Thought," *American Journal of Sociology* 35 (March 1930): 693– 706.

think about his conduct as good or bad only as he reacts to his own acts in the remembered words of his parents.

Mead's idea of social interaction proved important to those searching for nonbiological sources of sex differences by suggesting that female infants enter a different social world at birth from the one their brothers enter. Without realizing it, parents react differently to the earliest expressions and activities of their female and male children and thus, in subtle and often unconscious ways, foster femininity in their daughters and masculinity in their sons.[36]

Mead called himself a behaviorist; but behaviorism for him meant something different from that made famous by his erstwhile student John B. Watson, who wanted to limit psychology to the study of observable actions. "John B. Watson's attitude was that of the Queen in Alice in Wonderland," Mead later recalled, "Off with their heads!—there were no such things. There was no imagery, and no consciousness." Though Mead agreed with Watson that "social psychology is behavioristic in the sense of starting off with an observable activity," he nevertheless insisted that social psychology " is not behavioristic in the sense of ignoring the inner experience of the individual. . . . On the contrary, it is particularly concerned with the rise of such experience within the process as a whole." Psychologists who analyzed the mind in terms of instincts and those who restricted themselves to observable behavior both erred, in Mead's view, in their onesidedness—the first in emphasizing instinct at the expense of external influences, and the second in emphasizing external influences at the expense of internal meaning. Of all those working in the field of psychology in 1912, Mead probably felt the strongest affinity for Sigmund Freud. Though Mead believed that too much of Freudian theory reduced to the sexual impulse and therefore violated his own effort to free himself from biological reductionism, he nevertheless admired and accepted Freud's attempts to understand the way in which the mind mediates

36. George Herbert Mead, "Social Psychology as a Counterpart to Physiological Psychology," *Psychological Bulletin* 6 (December 1909): 405, 406; idem, "The Social Self," *Journal of Philosophy* 10 (July 1913): 377. See also Mead, "What Social Objects Must Psychology Presuppose?" *Journal of Philosophy, Psychology, and Scientific Methods* 7 (March 1910): 174– 80. Good assessments of Mead's place in the history of social psychology can be found in: Don Martindale, "Symbolic Interactionism," in his *The Nature and Types of Sociological Theory* (Boston: Houghton Mifflin, 1960), pp. 339– 75; T. V. Smith, "The Social Philosophy of George Herbert Mead," *American Journal of Sociology* 37 (November 1931): 368– 85; and Gordon Allport, "The Historical Background of Modern Social Psychology," in Gardner Lindzey, ed., *Handbook of Social Psychology*, 2 vols. (Cambridge, Mass.: Addison Wesley, 1954), 1:3– 56, especially 2– 24.

between the urges of the body and the demands of the social situations into which the body is placed.[37]

Though Mead's concerns were deeply philosophical, they were never merely academic. He was always interested in the social concerns of his day: Hull House, the Chicago school system, labor problems, and, though few scholars have ever noted it, the woman's movement. Mead liked and admired women and encouraged all he knew well to pursue meaningful work. Within weeks after the birth of his first and only child, Mead reported that his wife was looking for work. Trained in languages, she wanted to work as a translator for a publishing house. Mead clearly loved his son and might well have wanted more children, but, as he had written his closest friend and future brother-in-law a decade earlier about his feelings concerning his own sister's long and difficult labor: "The poor girl was in horrible torture for eighteen hours. No rack or boot or thumbscrew could have been more terrible than that was. It put the whole matter in an entirely new light to me. I could never ask any woman to bear me children save it was the desire of her own heart." For Mead, children were tremendously important, but there was more to life than childbearing and childrearing, especially since so many of the functions associated with them were being taken from the home.[38]

Among his friends was his daughter-in-law, Irene Tufts Mead, daughter of his colleague James Tufts, a former student in his course in social psychology, and a valued critic of his work. In 1920 Irene Mead solicited her father-in-law's advice about whether or not she should go to medical school. She already had a young child, and most of her friends were arguing that since she did not particularly care to do research, but was concerned instead with public and mental health, she should work in a

---

37. John B. Watson, "Psychology as the Behaviorist Views It," *Psychological Review* 20 (March 1913): 158–77; David Bakan, "Behaviorism and American Urbanization," *Journal of the History of the Behavioral Sciences* 2 (January 1966): 5–28; John C. Burnham, "On the Origins of Behaviorism," *Journal of the History of the Behavioral Sciences* 4 (April 1968): 143–51; George Herbert Mead, "The Point of View of Social Behaviorism," in his *Mind, Self, and Society,* pp. 2–3, 7. Mead discussed Freud's significance in a letter to his son (George Herbert Mead to Henry Castle Mead, July 12, 1914, George Herbert Mead Papers). For a discussion of the similarity of Mead's and Freud's ideas, see William H. Desmonde, "G. H. Mead and Freud: American Social Psychology and Psychoanalysis," *Psychoanalysis* 4–5 (1957): 31–50.

38. Helen and George Mead to Castle parents, January 12, 1892, George Herbert Mead Papers; George Herbert Mead to Henry N. Castle, November 15, 1883, George Herbert Mead Papers. Mead's reform interests are discussed in George Herbert Mead, "The Working Hypothesis in Social Reform," *American Journal of Sociology* 5 (November 1899): 367–71; George Herbert Mead, review of Jane Addams, *The Newer Ideals of Peace,* in *American Journal of Sociology* 13 (July 1907): 121–28, and Rucker, *Chicago Pragmatists,* pp. 21–22. See also Mary Jo Deegan and John S. Burger, "George Herbert Mead and Social Reform: His Work and Writings," *Journal of the History of the Behavioral Sciences* 14 (October 1978): 362–73.

volunteer capacity for any of a variety of reform-minded groups. George Herbert Mead disagreed with his daughter-in-law's friends and asserted unequivocally that she should attend medical school. It would be very difficult, he conceded realistically, "but worthwhile things are always difficult." The Meads were financially secure, thanks largely to Helen Castle Mead's legacy from her family's sugar fortune, and Irene could well afford assistance in raising her child and running her household. Given this security, Mead saw no reason for his daughter-in-law to hesitate about further training. "For the most normal situation," Mead advised her, "a woman as well as a man should have the training for a social calling apart from the family life, this for the sake of the best family life but principally for the independence of the mind and self which everyone legitimately craves." It was true that Irene already had a young child and many would urge her to wait until he was older before continuing any education, but Mead urged her not to delay:

> The training cannot naturally be put off in the case of a woman any more than in that of a man beyond the years within which such professional training is normally given. On the other hand, these are the years within which you will naturally bear children, so that the training will have to be taken more slowly, but there is nothing in the family life nor in the training which detracts from either.

Arguing that sex role differentiation in modern society had been carried to an extreme that was positively injurious to intellectual as well as stable emotional life, Mead continued:

> The intellectual interest you will have in study will make you a finer woman and therefore a better mother and wife, and while the care of children will reduce the amount of time you can give to training, it will also give you a feeling for all the social values which give their meaning to professional activities. . . . If you have the will and the courage you can have both the social independence which comes with competence in some real social function, together with breadth of view and the capacity to criticize life and the living of it—what Thomas calls the man's intellectual world into which woman as yet so seldom enters—and as well, the family life which should be yours in these years.

Mead recognized that the intelligent women of his generation had, in general, been happy to acquire the cultural background provided by college and to participate in the myriad volunteer organizations that worked to soften some of the harsher aspects of modern industrial life, but he did not believe that the next generation of women would be satisfied with living as amateurs in an increasingly professionalized society. In response to the advice of friends who were trying to persuade his daughter-in-law to satisfy herself with volunteer work, Mead wrote:

You need the method and clinical training [of medical school] to raise you above the amateur, and to give you both the capacity and the standpoint that your interest demands. What [others recommend] for you is a sort of scientific culture, which would leave you in the class of those who appreciate but have no competent reaction nor independence of judgment. For the fullest normal development, an individual must be able to act competently—to have some social field. If he does, his conduct in this field, brings him into real relations with the rest of life.

In conclusion, Mead warned Irene against falling into the trap of intellectual dependence on her husband, a trap sanctioned by long tradition and contemporary custom.

Do not let the dependence on others which we all have for those whom we love carry with it intellectual dependence. [You] cannot have real intellectual independence, that which gives one the fundamental self-respect on which one builds, without competence in some field of society which is responsible for the very existence of ourselves. Cultural training never gives this—only training for a practical end.[39]

For Mead, professional training—be it medical, legal, business, or sociological—created a vehicle for transcending old social boundaries. With growing interdependence and "the increase in the number and extent of human relations," Mead believed that the petty tyranny of prejudice would govern less often—people would come to know each other more completely, to value each other more fully, and to see possibilities for their own lives they had never seen before. To Mead the new urban, industrial center, with its polyglot citizenry, represented not a threat to America's traditional community-centered order but, rather, a vital social laboratory which would permit the transcending of that order. From that social laboratory would emerge a richer society comprised of more fully developed individuals.[40]

Though Mead rejected his fellow reformers' tendency toward sanctimonious moralizing and their fear of diversity and conflict, he retained the typically Progressive faith that knowledge brings freedom—freedom from fear and freedom from hate. An individual could only be as complete as the breadth of his or her social and intellectual relations allowed. The broader a person's social relations and the

39. George Herbert Mead to Irene Tufts Mead, August 28, 1920, George Herbert Mead Papers. This letter has been published in Steven J. Diner, "George Herbert Mead's Ideas on Women and Careers: A Letter to His Daughter-in-Law, 1920," *Signs* 4 (Winter 1978): 407–09. It did not occur to Mead to suggest that his son Henry should assume greater responsibility for childcare or housework.

40. George Herbert Mead, transcript of lectures for Philosophy 321, "Social Psychology" (1912), p. 123, George Herbert Mead Papers.

more highly developed his or her critical skills, the more fully developed he or she would be as a human being. Where social relations were limited, social consciousness remained constricted, and society as a whole inevitably suffered, as Jessie Taft understood and explained in her thesis, *The Woman's Movement from the Point of View of Social Consciousness.* [41]

Jessie Taft: The Woman's Movement

After a lifetime of social work and psychiatric counseling, Jessie Taft looked back on her dissertation with some amusement, particularly at her presumption in writing about social conditions and women's psychology from within the confines of the university library. Yet, of all the efforts made at that time to describe the feminine character and the woman's movement, Taft's dissertation was particularly insightful. [42]

Drawing on the work of both Thomas and Mead, Taft argued that the uniqueness of feminine character derived neither from innate qualities nor from physical surroundings, but from the particular social attitudes assumed toward females from earliest infancy.

> Physical environment alone is incapable of supplying the kind of stimulus requisite for calling out the social reaction, and it is just through the social attitude that the human being finally becomes aware of himself.

Differences in physical environment might account for *class* differences in society, but they could not account for personality differences between men and women of the same class. These differences, Taft maintained, were due to social conditions. A girl has no attitude toward herself at birth: she develops one only as she observes those who deal with her and learns to anticipate their responses to her acts and to shape her acts accordingly.

> The earliest and most imperative demand for the child is that he shall adjust himself to social objects. His knowledge of himself is not nearly as important for him as his knowledge of the adults around him on whom he depends for survival. He must be able to put himself in their places, to take their attitudes, to play their parts, to get enough of an idea of them as persons that he may in a measure anticipate their responses to his own acts. All this necessarily precedes his discovery of himself and conditions it. [43]

The child's anticipation of social response includes every facet of behav-

---

41. Jessie Taft, *The Woman's Movement from the Point of View of Social Consciousness* (Chicago: University of Chicago Press, 1916). A briefer version of Taft's thesis appeared as "The Woman Movement and the Larger Social Situation," *International Journal of Ethics* 25 (April 1915): 328–45.

42. Robinson, ed., *Jessie Taft,* p. 37.

43. Taft, *The Woman's Movement,* p. 38.

ior, including emotion. Functionalists like Dewey, Angell, and Helen T. Woolley had provided a new perspective on emotion by elevating it from the status of an irrational instinct to the position of a functional aid to reason. They argued that emotion is not so much a paralyzing force as a warning to the body that reason is needed to resolve some conflict. Summarizing this position, Taft wrote:

> Emotion is a danger signal, the reporter of some kind of tension in what has been a smooth-going process. The sudden rush of feeling indicates the value to the self of the various imperiled ends, and measures the importance of making some kind of adjustment and the relative weight which is to be given to the conflicting impulses.

What distinguishes the sexes most sharply, Taft thought, is that women and men have learned to deal with emotional signals differently in order to satisfy the expectations of those around them, and to function most profitably within the constraints of the social system within which they live. As Thomas had observed, the little girl quickly learns that modesty is approved in her so she strives to be modest. Unfortunately, her modesty sets her apart from men, and it prevents her from becoming inquisitive enough to consider changing herself. Women develop narrow and subordinate personalities, both because such personalities are expected of them and because their social surroundings are relatively restrictive.

> The condition of attaining self-consciousness is therefore a social environment, and the degree of complexity or the completeness of self-consciousness attained will vary with the complexity of the social organization of which it is a part. A simple form of society with simple problems in which necessary social attitudes are comparatively few, unorganized, and simple, will build up undifferentiated narrow selves whose meanings and emotions are limited to a narrow range of objects and which are not highly conscious of those meanings as peculiarly a part of the self.[44]

Charlotte Perkins Gilman was right in arguing that women could not be expected to exhibit genius while restricted to the individual kitchen. But Taft did not believe that economic independence would emancipate women until the traditional ideals of womanhood were abandoned: it would not profit the woman to get out of the kitchen until she was surrounded from babyhood by people who did not expect her to be modest. Much less could one expect the granting of the vote or any other right or privilege to alter women's lives. The suffrage campaign, which was reaching a crescendo as Taft wrote, premised its demands on an older theory of personality, to the degree that it appealed to any theory at all. Suffragists argued either that women, being superior because of their

44. Ibid., pp. 15, 39–40.

maternal traits, were potentially better citizens than men and only needed the vote to prove it, or, harking back to Enlightenment thought, that they were the potential equals of men and only needed the vote to actualize that equality. Taft argued that emancipation was not simply an economic or a political problem; it was a psychological one as well. The very claim of maternal superiority in the suffrage campaign belied the claim of emancipation. No fundamental change in women's social position was likely until rationality was no longer regarded as a hallmark of masculinity and until "the maternal virtues" were no longer regarded as exclusively maternal.

To transcend this most basic of social divisions would not be easy, Taft conceded, for the world in which early twentieth-century man lives, she observed, is not only different from the world in which woman lives, "it is even hostile and antagonistic in many respects to the world of woman." For many women, and Taft included herself among them, the only possible personal solution to this painful social division was to seek companionship with another woman. "Everywhere we find the unmarried woman turning to other women," she wrote:

> building up with them a real home, finding in them the sympathy and understanding, the bond of similar standards and values, as well as the same aesthetic and intellectual interests, that are often difficult of realization in a husband, especially here in America where business crowds out culture. The man who comes within her circle of possibilities is too often a man who has no form of self expression beyond his business and who, therefore, fails to meet her ideal of companionship in marriage.

In Virginia Robinson, Taft found someone who would provide her with a home and loving companionship. Theirs was not, perhaps, a conventional solution to the problem of creating a satisfying home life. It meant giving up children, though they later offset that sacrifice through adoption. But the life they created together gave them both greater opportunities for personal fulfillment than either believed she could find with a man.[45]

Although Taft's personal life exemplified the separatist element in Victorian feminism, her professional and intellectual life bespoke a commitment to sexual integration. She lived, as she put it, in two worlds: the world of women, of aesthetics, of nurturance; and, as a consequence of her education, the world of men, of rationalism, and of personal achievement. Trying to conform to both worlds," she and others like her found "conflicts so serious and apparently irreconcilable that satisfactory adjustment is often quite impossible"; but they were coming to believe, precisely because of those conflicts, that some adjustment must be made.

45. Ibid., pp. 10–11.

Jessie Taft (1912 or 1913)

> All of this hopeless conflict among impulses which the woman feels she has a legitimate right, even a moral obligation, to express, all of the rebellion against stupid, meaningless sacrifice of powers that ought to be used by society, constitutes the force, conscious or unconscious, which motivates the woman movement and will continue to vitalize it until some adjustment is made.

The fundamental purpose of the woman's movement, as Taft saw it, was not the gaining of political power for women, though she believed women deserved it, but rather the freeing of *all* people to "feel within themselves as their own the impulses and points of view of all classes and both sexes." Though not a political activist, Taft believed that she and other social scientists like her had a special role to play in the woman's movement. If Thomas and Mead were right that progress derives principally from conflict in the social order, which creates the conditions for greater awareness and broadened perspective, then the educated woman, caught as she was between two hostile worlds, was better situated than anyone else could be "to comprehend the conditions, the unsatisfied, conflicting im-

Virginia Robinson (1910)

pulses, upon the harmonization and fulfillment of which any solution that has the right to the name must be based."[46]

Implicit in Taft's analysis of the educated woman's unique place in society were two ideas that developed more fully in the sociological theory of the 1920s through 1940s. The first was the idea of marginality evolved by Robert Park and his students at Chicago; the second, the idea of role strain developed by Talcott Parsons and Mirra Komarovsky.

Marginality, according to Park, is the distinguishing characteristic of the "marginal man," the person who lives in and yet apart from the dominant culture. Park, a contemporary and longtime friend of W. I. Thomas and George Herbert Mead, began teaching at Chicago in 1913, the year after Taft completed her dissertation. For several years before that he had worked as a publicist for Booker T. Washington at Tuskegee Institute, and he had written extensively on race relations. What Taft saw from her vantage point as a woman, Park saw from the perspective of a

46. Ibid., pp. 55, 57.

man fascinated by the exotic—that some people, notably American Negroes, live lives divided between two worlds. Both Park and Taft lamented
the anguish produced by the inevitable conflict such people feel—but at
the same time, they both celebrated the progressive potential of those who
are socially detached. Taft believed that the conflict women felt had
produced the woman's movement. Park argued, more broadly, that the
marginal man "inevitably becomes, relatively to his cultural milieu, the
individual with the wider horizon, the keener intelligence, the more
detached and rational viewpoint. The marginal man," he concluded, "is
always relatively the more civilized human being."

Closely related to the idea of marginality was the idea of role strain.
Talcott Parsons and Mirra Komarovsky, among others, used the idea of
role strain in the 1940s to explain the unhappiness felt by educated
women, reared to be wives and mothers but educated to be independent
thinkers. Parsons thought that the tension could be eased if women would
only accept the role of the "good companion" to their husbands, but
Komarovsky was not so sanguine. She saw the conflict between domestic
tradition and educational freedom as inevitably destructive of women's
interests and urged the abandonment of traditional expectations for
women as the only viable solution to this conflict. In contrast to Taft and
Park, however, neither Parsons nor Komarovsky suggested that the
conflict women experienced could have any socially progressive tendencies.[47]

Having identified the critical social issue of her day as the resolution of
sexual conflict, and having assigned to the social scientist the task of
achieving that resolution, Taft returned to the Bedford Hills Reformatory to put her social-psychological perspective to good use. Criminal
women held a particular fascination for her, as they did for many Progressive reformers. In part, the fascination lay in the spectacular way in which
these women had renounced Victorian standards of feminine propriety;
in part, it lay in their symbolization of the conflict inherent in all modern
women's lives. There was a bit of the prostitute in every woman who felt
torn between her natural wish for self-expression and the inhibiting
effects of social repression. The freedom of modern life, and especially

47. Robert E. Park, introduction to Everett V. Stonequis, *The Marginal Man: A Study in
Personality and Culture Conflict* (New York: Scribner's, 1973), pp. xvii–xviii; Talcott Parsons,
"Age and Sex in the Social Structure of the United States," *American Sociological Review* 7
(October 1942): 613; Mirra Komarovsky, "Cultural Contradictions of Sex Roles," *American
Journal of Sociology* 52 (November 1946): 184–89. Park introduced the idea of the marginal
man in his "Human Migration and the Marginal Man," *American Journal of Sociology* 33 (May
1928): 881–93. Park did not explicitly include women within his discussion of marginality,
but his students sometimes did (see Stonequist, *The Marginal Man*, pp. 6–7). On Park's use of
marginality, see Fred H. Matthews, *Quest for an American Sociology: Robert E. Park and the
Chicago School* (Montreal: McGill-Queen's University Press, 1977), pp. 136, 169–71, 187.

the breakdown of old community constraints, inevitably nurtured revolt. In explaining the behavior of one promiscuous young woman, Taft used words that could have applied to herself or any one of her women friends from graduate school. Taft attributed this woman's delinquency, not to any defect, but rather to "the blocking of [her] work and play interests and the complete quenching of her egoistic ambitions."[48]

Despite Jessie Taft's interest in criminality and strong commitment to prison reform, two problems bedeviled her efforts. The first was the fundamental split between older professionals like Katherine Bement Davis and younger workers like Taft over which of the inmates were redeemable and which were not. Davis referred to the 30 percent of the Bedford inmates who were committed for prostitution and who tested at or below the level of the average twelve-year-old, as "decidedly mentally defective," and added that this figure represented "an extremely conservative estimate." These women, she lamented, "are not as a class given to introspection or self-analysis. They are, as a rule, incapable of this even if they try." Jean Weidensall, one of Taft's contemporaries from Chicago who administered most of the tests, interpreted the test results very differently. She emphasized the women's working-class background, their lack of formal education, and she insisted that patience and proper training would "lessen the number of those who must be classified as feebleminded." Taft concurred in Weidensall's judgment and urged that feeblemindedness not be used as a blanket term that would pigeonhole people for life. As W. I. Thomas expressed this sentiment in his own study of the treatment of women criminals: " 'Feeblemindedness' is partly a classificatory term for those personalities whose behavior we have not been able to conform to the usual standards because of lack of knowledge and method. We shall not know what conditions to call feeble-minded until we have determined the limits of the social influences which we can apply."

The second problem that Taft encountered in her work at Bedford Hills was the enormous difficulty of helping women to change their lives within the confines of a prison. If she had learned anything from Thomas and Mead it was the importance of the social situation to the development of a personality. The prison situation was too artificial an environment for lasting personal change. If women were to change their lives, especially in adulthood, they would have to do so in the world to which they would return upon leaving prison. After two years, Taft left Bedford Hills in

48. Jessie Taft, "Some Problems in Delinquency—Where Do They Belong?" *Publications of the American Sociological Society* 16 (1922): 195; Jessie Taft, "Mental Hygiene Problems of Normal Adolescence," *Annals of the American Academy of Political and Social Science* 98 (November 1921): 61–67.

frustration and joined the mental health movement with the intention of working with women in a more natural setting.[49]

For Taft feminism and social science were synonymous, yet she did not become actively involved in the woman's movement, nor did social science have any direct impact on that movement. Taft believed that women's primary problem was not political but psychological, and that the psychological problem was extremely complex and required intense, long-term personal interaction to effect any significant change. This perception differed markedly from the conviction of a generation of reform-minded feminists that women's condition could best be improved through organized political activity directed toward social, economic, and political change. Many social workers after 1920, trained in the new social science disciplines and self-consciously professional about their work, began to emphasize their clients' inner psychological problems, some-times at the expense of coming to grips with the social circumstances which gave rise to the problems. Jessie Taft never went this far. Trained as a scientist, she found much reform activity superficial, sentimental, and unduly moralistic, but she never renounced political activism, nor did she ever argue that women should adjust to their situation. She believed that women's position should change, but she also believed that the most lasting changes would not come from legislative fiat but only much more slowly, through changes in attitudes and experimentation with new social roles.[50]

49. Katherine Bement Davis, "A Study of Prostitutes Committed from New York City to the State Reformatory for Women at Bedford Hills," pp. 198, 195; Jean Weidensall, *The Mentality of Criminal Women* (Baltimore: Warwick and York, 1916), pp. 283, 280–86; William I. Thomas, *The Unadjusted Girl: With Cases and Standpoint for Behavior Analysis* (1923; reprint ed., New York: Harper Torchbook, 1967), pp. 251–52; Jessie Taft, "Supervision of the Feeble-minded in the Community," *Mental Hygiene* 2 (July 1918): 434–42; Robinson, ed., *Jessie Taft*, pp. 43–55. For Taft's role in the mental health movement, see Barbara Sicherman, "The Quest for Mental Health in America, 1880–1917" (Ph.D. diss., Columbia University, 1967), pp. 428–29.

50. For an excellent account of the shift among social workers from a concern with political and economic reform to a more pointed interest in psychological adjustment, as well as a description of the dismayed reaction to this trend among older social activists, see Roy Lubove, *The Professional Altruist*, pp. 22–177.

6 *The Primitive Side of Civilized Culture*

American reformers have always been drawn to environmental explanations of social issues. Therefore they listened sympathetically during the Progressive years, when the first social psychologists argued that feminine traits were rooted in social expectation. They were not so sympathetic, however, to the assumption, implicit in the psychologists' argument, that reformers should actively try to alter social expectations in order to eliminate sex differences. In the view of virtually all Progressive era social theorists and reformers, Western society had evolved toward an advanced stage of social and technological achievement because of its extensive division of labor. Even after many social scientists began to doubt that male and female brains had diverged over the course of evolutionary history, they clung to the belief that the division of labor along sex lines was an essential condition of progress. To interfere with this sexual specialization, many feared, was to risk returning to a simpler and less highly evolved epoch by undercutting this most basic of social divisions.

Not until social scientists began to question the idea of cultural evolution and the American faith in progress was it possible to challenge directly the social need for women's subordination. The first social scientist to do so was Elsie Clews Parsons, a sociologist and anthropologist whose association with anthropologist Franz Boas made her look critically at evolutionary theory, and whose life as a woman made her skeptical of progress.

Of all the pioneering women who ventured into the nascent social sciences at the turn of the century, there was no more unlikely a candidate than Parsons. Most of the first generation of female psychologists, sociologists, and anthropologists came from small business or professional families in which the propriety of advanced education for women had come to be accepted, albeit in some cases reluctantly. Henry and Lucy Clews, however, viewed their daughter's academic ambitions with unalloyed dismay.

147

The Clewses' marriage had been a "business proposition," joining Henry Clews, an Englishman and founder of the Wall Street banking firm that bore his name, and the much younger Lucy Madison Worthington, a distant relation of President Madison and a southern belle, whose family had suffered serious financial reverses. Clews's money together with Worthington's social lineage secured the couple's place in New York society, and they expected their only daughter and eldest child Elsie to enter that society and to lead a life befitting a young lady of her social and economic station. But Elsie Worthington Clews proved singularly intractable, being more strongly motivated by her father's celebration of American individualism than her mother's nostalgia for southern social grace. Given the privilege of private tutoring and attendance at Miss Ruel's school in New York City, she demanded what to her parents was an altogether unnecessary, even objectionable, exposure to higher education at Barnard College. The Clewses belonged to a social circle "opposed to college-going for girls," and they despaired of the effect that college would have on a girl who already displayed a distressing indifference to clothes, domesticity, and society life. Henry Clews worried publicly over the extradomestic ambitions of "the modern woman," and in frequent speeches he reminded his audiences that woman "is endowed and equipped by nature for a higher and more important sphere of action, and her activities should centre in her home life." Only his pride in his daughter's keen intelligence and independent spirit enabled Elsie to win his grudging permission to enroll at Barnard.[1]

Education and Reform

Founded in 1889, Barnard maintained an uncertain relationship with Columbia throughout the 1890s. Though Columbia's newly appointed president, Seth Low, wanted to encourage a greater academic integration of the two institutions, a large and vociferous portion of the Columbia faculty insisted on keeping Barnard completely separate. Nowhere was

---

1. Elsie Parsons Kennedy, "The Reminiscences of Mrs. John D. Kennedy, 1966," Oral History Collection, Columbia University, pp. 8, 1–17; Elsie Clews Parsons, *The Old-Fashioned Woman: Primitive Fancies about the Sex* (New York: Putnam, 1913), p. 285; Henry Clews, "Woman in Politics, Nature, History, Business and the Home," in Henry Clews, *Financial, Economic, and Miscellaneous Speeches and Essays* (New York: Irving, 1910), p. 317; Paul S. Boyer, "Elsie Clews Parsons," in Edward T. James, ed., *Notable American Women, 1607–1950*, 3:20–22; A. L. Kroeber, "Elsie Clews Parsons," *American Anthropologist* 45 (April–June 1943): 252. The pre-1918 personal papers of Elsie Clews Parsons are in the possession of Peter Hare of the State University of New York at Buffalo, and are not yet available for general scholarly use.

this sentiment more strongly expressed than in the faculty of political science, where Dean John Burgess would not even permit the admission of women as auditors, though the board of trustees had given its approval. Low finally forced greater cooperation from Burgess by appealing to his entrepreneurial spirit and promising two new chairs in the faculty of political science in return for a commensurate number of staff hours devoted to separate courses at Barnard. Thus, in 1894, as Elsie Worthington Clews entered her junior year, Columbia created new chairs in history and sociology and offered instruction in those two disciplines to Barnard students for the first time. One of the junior faculty members assigned to Barnard to fulfill Burgess's part of the Low-Burgess accord, and the professor who introduced Elsie Clews to the infant social sciences, was sociologist Franklin Giddings. Up to that time, Giddings had been commuting to Columbia once a week from his regular post at Bryn Mawr to teach a course in sociology, but Low's maneuvering with Burgess finally created a full-time position for him at Columbia and formal academic recognition for his new discipline.[2]

Like many scholars of his generation, Giddings's interest in sociology had been inspired by the works of Herbert Spencer. For many years, however, sociology remained an avocation, an interest he pursued, in the hours he had free from his work as a journalist, by reading and attending scholarly meetings. At one such meeting in 1887, the thirty-two-year-old Giddings met Lester Frank Ward, who persuaded him to leave journalism for a career in the social sciences. Though sociology was not yet a recognized academic field, and employment not easy to find, Giddings found a job at Bryn Mawr teaching political science, and he supplemented his regular classes with a course in "Methods and Principles of Charity and Correction."[3]

Giddings accepted Spencer's portrayal of society as an organism in which development proceeded according to natural law from the homogeneous savage stage through barbarism to the heterogeneous pinnacle of civilized society. He dissented, however, from Spencer's glorification of unrestrained individualism. In common with most other social scientists in the 1890s, Giddings regarded the social and economic disloca-

2. R. Gordon Hoxie et al., *A History of the Faculty of Political Science*, pp. 64–67, 176–77, 286–89.

3. Leo Davids, "Franklin Henry Giddings: Overview of a Forgotten Pioneer," *Journal of the History of the Behavioral Sciences* 4 (January 1968): 62–73; John L. Gillin, "Franklin Henry Giddings," in Howard Odum, ed., *American Masters of Social Science* (New York: Holt, 1927), pp. 191–230; Clarence Northcott, "The Sociological Theories of Franklin Henry Giddings: Consciousness of Kind, Pluralistic Behavior and Statistical Method," in Harry Elmer Barnes, ed., *An Introduction to the History of Sociology*, pp. 180–204.

Franklin Giddings (1893)

tions of America's burgeoning urban centers with alarm, and he agreed
with Lester Ward that evolution had reached a stage at which men could
comprehend the laws of development and should try to correct the waste
and hardship that attended their workings. Rather than leave social
progress in the irresponsible hands of either the dissolute poor or the
avaricious captains of industry, Giddings advocated the conscious direction of social development by those best equipped to act as guides—that
is, white Anglo-Saxon Protestants, trained in both the theory and the
practice of social evolution.[4]

Philanthropists had long been trying to mitigate some of the harsher
aspects of industrial progress, Giddings observed, but amateur charitable
agents must inevitably fail, because they dealt with social problems at a
superficial level. Together with Albion Small, Giddings founded
academic sociology in the United States with the aim of remedying the

4. Franklin Henry Giddings, *Principles of Sociology: An Analysis of the Phenomena of Association and of Social Organization* (New York: Macmillan, 1905), pp. 1–20, 124–31, 352–53,
363–75.

hopelessly miscellaneous approach of contemporary philanthropy. As Giddings told the amateur reformers of the American Social Science Association in 1894, sociology "is not a study of one special group of social facts: it examines the relations of all groups to each other and to the whole. It is not a philanthropy: it is the scientific groundwork on which a true philanthropy must build."[5]

Giddings's courses attracted women students both because of his interest in philanthropy, a field in which women had played an important role for many years, and because of his innovative theoretical approach. Like Ward, Small, Dewey, Mead, and other liberal social scientists of the 1890s, Giddings was trying to transcend the sharp division between positivism and idealism that had characterized nineteenth-century thought. Society changed not simply as a consequence of either physical or rational forces, he argued, but because of the complex interaction between the two.

> Causation in society is not at one extreme a merely physical process; nor is it, at the other extreme, an outworking of some mysterious entity called free-will, that is in no wise conditioned by the external world. Like the activity of the individual mind, it is a psycho-physical process, in which physical stimuli, on the one hand, and motor reactions, accompanied by feeling and thought on the other hand, are inseparably associated."[6]

To those who, in their own lives, were trying to bridge the wide Victorian chasm of sexual division, the formula for intellectual transcendence offered by Giddings held a strong personal appeal. In emphasizing the interplay of physical and rational forces, Giddings denigrated Spencer's emphasis on man's bestial, competitive impulses in favor of what many young women found a more appealing emphasis on humanity's communal feeling. Society developed, he believed, because of man's ability to identify with other creatures. Giddings called this ability "consciousness of kind"—that is, "a state of consciousness in which any being, whether low or high in the scale of life, recognizes another conscious being as of like kind with itself."[7]

Giddings defined progress, not as the elimination of inferior social groups by their superiors, but rather as an "increasing intercourse, a multiplication of relationships, an advance in material well-being, a growth of population, an evolution of rational conduct." This progress

5. Giddings, "The Relation of Sociology to Other Scientific Studies," *Journal of Social Science* 32 (November 1894): 144–45. For an excellent discussion of the tension between practical and theoretical sociology, see Thomas L. Haskell, *The Emergence of Professional Social Science*, pp. 190–210.

6. Giddings, "A Theory of Social Causation," *Publications of the American Economic Association* 5 (1904): 144.

7. Giddings, *Principles of Sociology*, p. 17.

came as heterogeneous groups, coming into contact with one another, recognized the possibility "of an ideal and future unity of kind, to be realized through the gradual assimilation of heterogeneous elements by means of a common speech, a common civic interest and a common aspiration." Through "consciousness of kind," humanity was being led to an ever greater commitment to universal brotherhood; and Giddings believed that Christian philanthropic enterprises, under the guidance of greater sociological knowledge, were "rapidly outgrowing the esoteric sentimentalism of their youth, and devoting themselves to the diffusion of knowledge, to the improvement of conditions, and to the upbuilding of character," and, as a consequence, were "uniting the classes and the races of men in a spiritual humanity." The sociologist could contribute to this development, in Giddings's view, by discovering the process through which "consciousness of kind" transformed both the individual and his society and led to evolution's highest achievement: self-realization.[8]

Giddings's ideal of self-realization appealed strongly to his strong-minded women students, especially Elsie Clews, who saw in this concept a weapon against the constraints that middle-class Victorian society imposed on female achievement. Franklin Giddings, however, never intended his evolutionary scheme to support the woman's movement, and he must have been taken aback by those students, like Miss Clews, who read into his thought a strategy for winning women's emancipation. Insistent on the interdependent relationship of individual freedom and social cohesion, Giddings based the achievement of self-realization on the premise of a highly developed and stable social order in which each "individual must have a definite part in the division of labor, and in the common life of the nation, the local community and the family." Full realization, Giddings believed, could only be achieved by evolution's highest product—the mature, rational, Anglo-Saxon male—and only if he found support in a social order in which everyone else faithfully performed his or her own duties. Less sanguine about women's capacity than some of his colleagues in Chicago, Giddings believed that women's tendency to "subordinate judgment to emotion" must restrict them to private rather than public duties. But as he told the graduating seniors at Bryn Mawr in 1894, women had an important, though admittedly subordinate, role to play in evolutionary progress. Because women were not caught in "the rush and whirl of business" as were men, and because they could enjoy "abundant leisure," they could try "to make life . . . more of a poetry book than it is." If women could succeed in this poetic role, Giddings believed, they would indirectly "raise the whole tone of national

8. Ibid., pp. 359–60.

life, and give our civilization the fullness that it lacks, for if they raise themselves, they will infallibly raise the men with them."[9]

Elsie Clews preferred Giddings's ideals to his social prescriptions; she saw no reason why, as a woman, she should be restricted to a vicarious enjoyment of men's self-realization. If humanity progressed through ever greater "consciousness of kind" to final self-realization, then it was wrong, and even counterproductive, for women to be arbitrarily subordinated within this grand process. Having completed her undergraduate studies, Clews boldly declared her intention to enter graduate school, determined that she, for one, would not be confined to a secondary social role. Unused to female classmates, A. L. Kroeber and other Columbia doctoral students watched in astonishment "as her statuesque figure floated through the seminar alcoves of the Low Memorial Library on Morningside Heights." Her wealth, her chiseled features, her poise, and, of course, her sex, set her apart from her classmates and gave her an air of Olympian detachment. Learned Hand later wrote that her interest in anthropology must have come to her naturally, for "she was always disposed to look at folks from a little distance." Many found this distance unnerving, and Hand, for one, confessed that though he found her one of the most interesting people he had ever known, he was always a little afraid of her.

Much of Clews's graduate work was in the history of education and government, done under Nicholas Murray Butler of the philosophy department, and her dissertation and first book were entitled *The Educational Legislation and Administration of the Colonies.* But her M.A. thesis, "On Certain Phases of Poor-Relief in the City of New York," was done with Giddings, who must have accorded her at least grudging approval, for he accepted her as an assistant in his sociology course when she completed her Ph.D. in 1899. Her job was to give Barnard undergraduates "training in accurate habits of social observation as preparation for the technical study of advanced problems in sociology or for the active work of philanthropy and social reform."[10]

Determined though she was to play an active role in social betterment and intellectual development, Elsie Clews did not view family life as a necessary barrier to her ambitions, as did so many educated and ambitious women of her generation. That she could feel this way was due, in part, to

9. Ibid., p. 397; Giddings, *Democracy and Empire* (New York: Macmillan, 1901), p. 210; Giddings, "The Relation of Social Democracy to Higher Education," in ibid., pp. 227–28.

10. Over forty years later, fellow graduate student A. L. Kroeber described the "memorably astonishing sight" of Parsons's presence at Columbia in his memorial essay, "Elsie Clews Parsons," pp. 252, 255; Learned Hand to Elsie Clews Parsons, February 9, 1940, Parsons Papers, American Philosophical Society, Philadelphia; *Barnard College Catalogue,* 1899–1900 (New York: Columbia University, 1900). I am indebted to Elizabeth Capelle for bringing Hand's comments about Parsons to my attention.

the uncommon tolerance of Herbert Parsons, a lawyer six years her senior, whom she married in 1900. Educated at St. Paul's, Yale College, and Harvard Law School, Parsons played an active role in political reform circles and was one of the younger men selected by Theodore Roosevelt to carry on the fight against the New York bosses after T. R. left New York for the national arena. In addition to his law practice and a variety of civic activities, Parsons served as a New York City alderman, as a congressman (1905– 11), as a Republican committeeman, and as a member of Pershing's staff in World War I. He seems to have been a typically idealistic, Progressive reformer, who believed that the energies and intelligence of good men would eliminate the waste and corruption of American society. More than most of his fellow politicians, however, he believed that women should participate in this reform work, and his love and respect for his wife was strong enough that even when her views began to grow steadily more radical, diverging markedly from his Progressive outlook, their marriage survived.[11]

Elsie Clews Parsons's first unconventional act as a young wife was to return to her teaching position at Barnard, where she remained until her husband was elected to Congress in 1905. Few women at the turn of the century taught after marriage; virtually none did so after motherhood. But Parsons bore six children, four of whom survived childhood and two of whom arrived while she was teaching at Barnard. Her passion for sociology, together with her husband's tolerant attitude, did much to make this unusual combination of motherhood and teaching possible. Without her family's wealth, however, and the large homes and retinue of servants it could command, her unconventional achievement might never have been realized. Though reared according to the strictest rules of New York society life, Elsie Clews Parsons succeeded better than most other women of her generation in ignoring the social conventions of her time, simply because she could afford to do so.[12]

Although Parsons's combination of young motherhood with college teaching was highly unconventional, her approach to sociology in the early years of her career fell comfortably within contemporary reform strategy. She shared with Giddings a belief in the ineluctable power of evolutionary progress and regarded her teaching position as an opportunity to help smooth the way. Once students understood the process of social development, she believed, they would be better able to abandon the "purely charitable impulse" that governed most philanthropy and

11. Elsie Parsons Kennedy, "Reminiscences of Mrs. John D. Kennedy," pp. 17, 33– 45; *New York Times,* September 17, 1925; Boyer, "Elsie Clews Parsons," in James, ed., *Notable American Women,* 3:20.

12. Boyer, 3:20. Parsons's children were Elsie ("Lissa") born in 1901, John Edward (1903), Herbert (1909), and McIlvaine (1911).

Elsie Clews Parsons with her daughter Lissa (1900)

work for a more rational and efficient social order. Along with Giddings, she believed that the problems of the urban poor could be ameliorated only through a coordinated effort of state regulation, improved public services, and systematic education. She recommended attacking prostitution, for instance, through the passage of minimum wage laws, the municipal inspection of prostitutes' health, and the development among people of the "monogamous instinct." Because Parsons believed in progress and assumed that the class from which she sprang represented an advanced stage of development, she displayed a typically Progressive, class bias in her approach to reform. While teaching students enrolled in Giddings's "Principles of Sociology" how to collect data, she also encouraged them to help immigrant families develop habits of cleanliness and order, and to promote thrift among them by collecting money for the Penny Provident Fund.[13]

13. Elsie Clews Parsons, "The School Child, the School Nurse, and the Local School Board," *Charities* 14 (1905): 1102; Parsons, "Sex and Morality and the Taboo of Direct

Feminism and Family Life

Elsie Clews Parsons's fieldwork with immigrant families and her own experience as a young wife and mother prompted her to focus her research on the problem of the modern family and women's place within it. Giddings encouraged this interest, permitting her to teach her own class on "Family Organization," and he underscored the importance of the topic by arguing that the family was the fundamental element of society and that "the study of its organization and history is of the same importance for the sociologist that the study of cell structure and differentiation is for the biologist.[14]

Out of Parsons's teaching grew a number of articles and a book she called *The Family* (1906), which assembled the lectures she had developed to introduce college students to the history of the family and its current tendencies. In common with most writers on the subject, Parsons arranged her ethnological sources in the evolutionary sequence through which the family was presumed to have evolved—from primitive savagery through matriarchy and patriarchy, up to what Parsons dubbed "the modern simple family." Widely enough read not to insist on the absolute nature of this evolutionary framework, Parsons conceded that some anthropologists doubted whether matriarchy was a necessary antecedent to patriarchy, and that authorities were not altogether certain what constituted a matriarchy anyway. Some applied the term to what was, in effect, nothing more than a kinship system that marked descent through the mother, while others insisted that the matriarchate represented a fixed stage of evolutionary development during which women determined not only lineage but also economic and political relations as well. Many feminists with a cursory knowledge of ethnology perceived in studies of matriarchy evidence of a golden age that might one day be recaptured, but Parsons took a less sanguine view of the ethnological literature. Given the dearth of women ethnographers and what she viewed as the inept nature of most male reporting on female status in primitive cultures, she believed that little about the family's history or women's changing status within it could be accepted with certainty. Mindful of the pitfalls in sociological fieldwork, she warned her own students to take special care in observing the families they visited, noting the structure, division of labor, and relations among the various family members, so as to rectify any preconceived notions they might have about immigrant life. "The habit of evolutionary thought is almost too readily acquired by embryonic scien-

---

Reference," *Independent* 61 (August 1906): 391–92; Parsons, "Field Work in Teaching Sociology," *Educational Review* 20 (September 1900): 163.

14. Franklin Giddings as quoted in Frank Tolman, "The Teaching of Sociology in Institutions of Learning in the United States," *American Journal of Sociology* 7 (May 1902): 890.

tists," Parsons remarked of her students. *"Stages of development* are clamoured for and pursued. This is merely one of the innumerable expressions of the mind's classifying habit, a habit that may lead to nonscientific just as well as to scientific results."[15]

Despite her caveats about the snares of evolutionary thinking and the inadequacies of male ethnography, Parsons accepted the prevailing view that the modern family represented the most highly evolved form the family had ever known. Increased affluence had provided offspring with a prolonged childhood and a lengthy education; freedom of migration had tended to weaken kinship ties; advances in science had weakened the religious sanction of custom in general and family custom in particular; and the spirit of freedom for individual development and initiative had undermined marital and paternal privilege. The general economic and cultural advances of the nineteenth century had succeeded in "side-tracking most of the survivals of the patriarchal family"; however, Parsons added, the contemporary family still retained vestiges of the patriarchical family form, and in significant ways husbands still exercised proprietary control over wives and children. Parsons believed strongly that "if the golden rule of democracy, equal opportunity for all for the development of personality, is to become a more influential social ideal than it is now . . . the desirability of change in many social relations in and out of the family will have to be frankly faced, and, if necessary, new adaptations must be welcomed."[16]

That evolution could further improve upon the modern family was a novel suggestion and one not typically found in sociological writing; but, as Parsons observed, ethnography had traditionally been barred to women, and because most male social scientists were themselves convinced of female inferiority, they rarely noticed the many ways in which the lives of women remained bound by patriarchal forms. Parsons believed that women suffered in a variety of ways under the archaic survivals of past inequality. For instance, they were limited to inferior education, confined to the home, and encouraged in superstitious beliefs. Society bore the consequences. "Not just in so far as a woman's education is limited is she handicapped as an educator of her children," Parsons observed.

It is unfortunate that in the *emancipation of women* agitation of the past half-century the reformers failed to emphasize the social as adequately as the

15. Elsie Clews Parsons, *The Family: An Ethnological and Historical Outline* (New York: Putnam, 1906), pp. 64, 162. 198, vii. For Victorian anthropologists' debates over women's changing status in evolutionary development, see Elizabeth Fee, "The Sexual Politics of Victorian Anthropology," in Hartman and Banner, eds., *Clio's Consciousness Raised*, pp. 86– 102.

16. Parsons, *The Family*, pp. 354– 55, xi.

individualistic need of change. If women are to be fit wives and mothers they must have all, perhaps more, of the opportunities for personal development that men have.

Though Parsons maintained a careful academic distance between her sociological analysis and the woman's movement, being all too familiar with the scathing criticism accorded female political agitation by her mentor and other scholars, she clearly accepted the feminist position of the Progressive period that, as women became more active publicly, they would be better mothers and would soften the hard edges of political and industrial life. As soon as the "ethical necessity" of female education and work "is generally recognized the conditions of modern industry will become much better adapted to the needs of women workers than they are now." As a consequence, "the hygiene of workshop, factory and office will improve, and child bearing and rearing will no longer seem incompatible with productive activity." Parsons even foresaw the day when women's presence in industry would bring pressure for part-time work and flexible hours for all, though she conceded that "in the present temper of the community and under existing economic conditions it is likely to be a losing fight."[17]

If Parsons had limited her book to its dry, almost encyclopedic discussion of family organization and its high-minded "ethical" conclusion that women should more actively participate in communal affairs, *The Family* might have received a few appreciative reviews from feminists and some complimentary nods from knowledgeable sociologists as being informative but too detailed for general classroom use. But the suggestions she reserved for her final eight pages created a public scandal. Traditionalists and political opponents of Herbert Parsons, newly elected to Congress, denounced *The Family* from pulpits and newspapers as "barbarous" and as "a debasement of marriage" that would lead to the "tainting of the family and the corruption of civilization." It was one thing to defend the public utility of improved education and greater access to the public arena for women; it was quite another to advocate, as Parsons did, professional careers for all educated women, trial marriages, and sexual expressiveness for men and women alike.[18]

17. Ibid., pp. 346–47; Elsie Clews Parsons, "Higher Education of Women and the Family," *American Journal of Sociology* 14 (May 1909): 763. For an excellent discussion of Parsons's relationship to American feminism, see Elizabeth Capelle, "Elsie Clews Parsons: A New Woman" (Master's thesis, Columbia University, 1977).

18. "Dr. Dix on Trial Marriages: Rector of Trinity Says Mrs. Parsons' Views Are Barbarous," *New York Times*, November 18, 1906; "Dr. Dix Speaks Out to Save the Home: Rector of Trinity Protests against Loose Marital Relations: First Duty Is to the Child," *New York Times*, November 19, 1906; "Trial Marriage Idea Denounced in Churches: Dr. Parkhurst Calls It Merely Consecutive Polygamy: Disgusting, Says Dr. Wylie," *New York Times*, November 30, 1906; Parsons, *The Family*, pp. 347–55. For a more temperate review of *The Family* by a

Unlike most Progressive era feminists, Parsons did not think that a college education followed by marriage, motherhood, and/or social reform work would improve either the family or society very much beyond their current quasi-patriarchal stage of evolution. A generation before, when Marion Talbot had entered the campaign for higher education for women, college had seemed a potentially revolutionary institution, one that might bring an end to the family. By 1906, however, college was well accepted among all but the most socially elite families, and a college degree no longer seemed to be the liability in the marriage market it had two decades earlier. In fact, the typical college graduate now married, and "her round of occupations is very much like that of every other housewife," Parsons noted. "Her household may be run a little more systematically, but it is run in the traditional way." Attacking the argument, popular among many feminists, that women should become educated consumers, Parsons concurred with Veblen's judgment that such women would be nothing more than vicarious consumers of their husband's wealth and the foremost illustrations of his power for conspicuous waste.[19]

Parsons believed that encouraging the perpetuation of the social division between male producers and female consumers would ultimately destroy families rather than improve them, and she pointed to the rising divorce rate as a clear indication that the social emphasis on sex differences posed a grave threat.

> Does not the incompatibility between the overcultivated, leisure-class wife, self-cultivated because she has nothing to do, and the undercultivated and overworked husband, unresponsive to anything but 'business,' largely because of the elaborate scale of expenditure by the non-productive wife, does not this incompatibility express itself in the varied forms of the frictions that lead to divorce?[20]

If the family was to be saved from the divisive force of sex differentiation, higher education in America would have to abandon its belief in female uniqueness and reconsider its purpose with respect to women students. Rather than contenting itself with imparting general culture, the university must train women as well as men to see liberal arts as a first step toward a professional career. "There is no subject, however academic," Parsons insisted, "that cannot be taught in a way to make the student realize that self-culture is incomplete unless taking in is followed

social scientist, see Frederick Morgan Davenport, review of Elsie Clews Parsons, *The Family,* in *Political Science Quarterly* 22 (December 1907): 744– 47.

   19. Parsons, "Higher Education of Women and the Family," pp. 761– 62.
   20. Elsie Clews Parsons, "Sex and Morality and the Taboo of Direct Reference," p. 392.

by giving out, unless production follows consumption, unless the knowledge he acquires he in some way or another applies."[21]

Parsons shared Charlotte Perkins Gilman's belief that work is essential
to female dignity, but unlike Gilman, she argued that employment can
accomplish little without the independence of mind that comes with the
right kind of higher education. It was "on the fight of the professional
women to get back into the family that the future of the family will
depend," Parsons believed. While working on *The Family*, Parsons had
translated *The Laws of Imitation*, a book by the widely influential French
sociologist Gabriel Tarde. Tarde believed in a trickle-down theory of
progress whereby social influence could be seen to spread by imitation
from the better-educated upper classes to those less privileged. Parsons
employed this theory to buttress her argument for the professional training of women.

> The hard-driven tenement house-wife who supports her good-for-nothing or
> unemployed husband, the farmer's wife who works harder than even her
> hard-working husband, or the factory hand's wife who supplements his wages,
> are in spite of their labor thoroughly unemancipated women. Because in many
> ways a more primitive type of woman, they are perhaps even more subject to
> marital mastery than their leisure-class sisters. As Gabriel Tarde has pointed out
> to us, it is only people at the top of the scale who have enough social prestige to
> negotiate radical changes.[22]

To its benighted attitude toward women and work, Parsons charged,
the modern family added an equally archaic and highly destructive approach to sex. The Victorian condemnation of sexual desire originated,
she believed, in early Christianity's effort to exert social control over its
members. Though this negative attitude toward "sexuality tended no
doubt to regulate purely sexual relations to the advantage of women,"
Parsons conceded, sensitive as she was to the dangers women faced in
frequent pregnancies and the fear that sex therefore held for them, it
nevertheless "was and is a grave obstacle to the development of women's
personality."

> Women were stigmatized as the means of satisfying unworthy desire. As such
> they became objects of seclusion and repression. Absolute subordination to a
> master, to male relative or husband, was required of both unmarried and
> married, particularly married women.

If women could learn to feel more positive toward sex, Parsons argued,
then sex could not be used against them so effectively. To suggest that

21. Elsie Clews Parsons, "The Aim of Productive Efficiency in Education," *Educational
Review* 30 (December 1905): 502.

22. Parsons, "Higher Education of Women and the Family," p. 763; Gabriel Tarde, *The
Laws of Imitation*.

women could learn to view sex more positively implied that women had a greater capacity for sexual feeling than was popularly believed. But Parsons did not develop this implicit assumption, nor did she give more than glancing treatment to a second assumption, that contraception would soon become widely accepted in America. In 1906, a full decade before Margaret Sanger's birth-control movement gained notoriety, such an assumption seemed at best visionary, at worst, immoral.[23]

Despite her cursory treatment of the difficult social issues she had relegated to the final few pages of *The Family*, Parsons appreciated that the full modernization of the family would not be easily achieved. But, as she noted elsewhere, "much of the painful friction of transition that is one of the costs of progress is due to the attempt to suppress instead of to adapt to new social tendencies." The job of the sociologist was to perceive new tendencies and to learn how to minimize "painful friction" by devising means for adjusting to them. Rather than fight against the professional training of women and an acceptance of a more expressive sexuality, people should realize that ultimately the achievement of consciousness of kind and social unity depended on the further expansion of the democratic ideal of self-realization to all people, including women. Whatever adjustments were necessary to achieve this goal should be made. The adjustment that Parsons thought most sensible and that made her the subject of such vigorous attack was her suggestion of "trial marriage." Because young people mature sexually before they mature emotionally and before they can complete professional training, she believed that they should live together before marrying. She advocated "trial marriage" with the understanding that "the relationship would be entered into with a view to permanency, but with the privilege of breaking it if it proved unsuccessful and in the *absence of offspring* without suffering any great degree of public condemnation." Not only would the adjustment of trial marriage smooth the way for greater professionalism for women and a greater acceptance of sexuality, it would cut down on divorce by protecting young people from too hasty a marital decision.[24]

Most Progressives viewed divorce as the consequence of an excess of individualism, not, as Parsons suggested, as a result of too little personal freedom. Anticipating the attacks she would elicit for feeding an already marked tendency toward rampant selfishness, she asked rhetorically, "Is there not a growing realization that individualism and altruism are mutually dependent, that the state must develop through the individual, but that the individual must also develop through the state?" While the mainstream of the woman's movement was arguing that the future of

23. Parsons, *The Family*, pp. 334, 345, 347.
24. Elsie Clews Parsons, "Penalizing Marriage and Childbearing," *Independent* 60 (January 1906): 146; Parsons, *The Family*, pp. 347–50.

society depended on giving altruistic women the political power needed to balance the individualism of men, Parsons, along with a growing number of liberal social scientists, contended that altruism and individualism could and should be balanced within each individual.[25]

In the weeks following *The Family*'s publication, the editorial staff of the staid *New York Times* joined those who condemned the book for its subversive tendencies; but the editors tempered their attack on this "self-confident adventurer in speculation," with the observation that "in general, the mania of world-bettering by sudden and happy thoughts is curable." In Parsons's case this prediction proved quite wrong. Indeed, *The Family* reflected conventional social scientific thought about the family and woman's place within it far more closely than any of Parsons's later writings were to do. Though in a subsequent book she felt compelled to write under the pseudonym John Main to avoid further embarrassment to her husband, she certainly did not curb her views; rather she expressed her ideas on sex, woman's nature and role, trial marriage, and divorce far more fully and with more radical implications than she had within the short chapter she devoted to these topics in 1906.[26]

Ethnology Opens Your Eyes

When her husband was elected to Congress in 1905, Elsie Parsons dutifully left her position at Barnard College and moved her family to Washington, where they remained until 1911. These were difficult years. In New York, Parsons had been able to escape the vacuous society life in which she had been reared and, to some degree, continued to live, by commuting up to Morningside Heights, meeting with students, and conversing with professors. Not only did moving to Washington mean leaving the job she so loved, it meant leaving a cosmopolitan city for what was then nothing more than a village—a village which, to further her pain, observed the rules of social etiquette even more punctiliously than did members of New York's social register. In Washington, as in India, she later reported, "a wife assumes her husband's qualities," and "the wife, however young, of a senator or a cabinet officer precedes the wife, however old, of a representative or general. 'Les femmes n'ont pas de rang [Women have no rank].' " Though removed from an academic setting, Parsons did not abandon her interest in social science. A congressional junket to the Philippines in 1905, led by William Howard Taft, then secretary of war and a close political associate of her husband's, introduced her to the ethnological field trip. Back in Washington she began

25. Parsons, *The Family*, p. 355.
26. "Trial Marriage," *New York Times*, December 2, 1906; Elsie Clews Parsons [John Main], *Religious Chastity: An Ethnological Study* (New York: n.p., 1912).

reading widely in the ethnological literature. Transforming her feelings of alienation into an attitude of scholarly detachment, she contented herself for a time by carefully documenting the curious social practices of the natives into whose midst fortune had cast her. Life in Washington became a kind of extended ethnological field trip.[27]

Parsons had always been more interested in social observation than her mentor, whose views were too deeply rooted in the nineteenth-century speculative tradition of sociology to be seriously affected by his oft-voiced ambition to establish sociology as an empirical science. Significantly, Giddings divided the teaching in sociology at Barnard by assigning Parsons the fieldwork and reserving the teaching of theory for himself. Though always grateful to Giddings for his guidance, Parsons counseled students against too ready an acceptance of his evolutionary theory with its neatly defined stages, and she probably agreed with Albion Small when he described Giddings's *Principles of Sociology* as "a picturesque yoking together of the scientific ox and the speculative ass," in which "he deliberately chooses to cast his main argument and to mass his material in the mould of speculation and deduction, instead of organizing the material at his command so as to show its precise inductive value."[28]

Parsons found encouragement for her fieldwork in the writings of Columbia anthropologist Franz Boas, whose own fieldwork and rigorous empiricism were undermining anthropologists' commitment to evolutionary theory and biological determinism. At the beginning of the twentieth century, no one outside academia, and only a few within, bothered to distinguish between sociology and anthropology. Both relied heavily on ethnographic sources, and both shaped those sources into an evolutionary scheme; in most universities the two fields comprised a single department. The principal difference between them was that sociology focused on the higher end of the evolutionary scale, on the complexities of civilized culture, while anthropology focused on the lower end of that scale, on the more primitive and presumably simpler societies.

At Columbia, however, because of Boas, sociology and anthropology differed markedly from their beginnings in the mid-1890s. Whereas Giddings searched for the fundamental laws governing the development of advanced civilization, Boas devoted his efforts to what seemed to him the more pressing need of recording the particular customs of primitive societies. Reviewing Parsons's career after her death, Boas distinguished between the sociological and the anthropological approaches and explained anthropology's growing appeal for the young female scholar.

27. Elsie Clews Parsons, *The Old-Fashioned Woman*, p. 53; Elsie Parsons Kennedy, "Reminiscences of Mrs. John D. Kennedy," pp. 36–37.

28. Albion Small, review of Franklin Giddings, *Principles of Sociology*, in *American Journal of Sociology* 2 (September 1896): 296.

Franz Boas (1899)

Sociology, he wrote, "lays primary stress upon the complexities of our culture," while anthropology addresses the "wider inquiry, the question of the manner in which more primitive or alien societies have solved their problems—a necessary preliminary of the study of what is generally human and of what is historically determined. The position of women in society, the forms of the family, demanded inquiry from a wider point of view." Sociologists like Giddings studied ethnographic reports in their libraries and looked for vestiges of what human nature once had been, while Boas went to live with the Eskimos, the Bella Coolas, and the Kwakiutls, and discovered what is generally human in all cultures. Of the Eskimos, Boas wrote that "they enjoyed life, and a hard life, as we do; that nature is also beautiful to them; that feelings of friendship also root in the Eskimo heart; that although the character of their life is so rude as compared to civilized life, the Eskimo is a man as we are; that his feelings, his virtues and his shortcomings are based in human nature, like ours."[29]

Suspicious of the conventional belief that racial groups differ in their basic mental organization, Boas wrote as early as 1894, "There seems to be no doubt that the anatomical characters of the races have in all their main points remained constant. . . . It seems to me that the probable effect of civilization upon an evolution of human faculty has been much overestimated." Impressed by Gabriel Tarde's writings on imitation and the work of the new experimental psychologists on learning, Boas worked out a psychological approach to racial differences that emphasized the importance of experience and habit rather than of native ability. One of the "fundamental laws of psychology," he concluded, is "that the repetition of mental processes increases the facility with which these processes are performed, and decreases the degree of consciousness that accompanies them." Along with Thomas, Dewey, and Mead, Boas concluded that all human beings are capable of abstraction and that all societies subject human impulse to some form of social control. Progress he attributed, not so much to the inventive genius or superior moral sensitivity of any one group, but to the unconscious diffusion of customs and habits through migration and conquest.[30]

The massive study of immigrants to New York that Boas undertook between 1908 and 1909 confirmed his growing skepticism over physical anthropology's belief in fixed racial types. He discovered that the children of immigrants grew taller than their parents, and that daughters menstruated earlier than their mothers had. If more healthful surroundings could alter physical forms and processes, what, then, could education do for the mental faculty?[31]

A German Jew, Boas first came to America as a geographer with the intention to study the Arctic but ended up staying as an anthropologist more intrigued by the people than the land he was exploring. Reared in middle-class German comfort and schooled in the principles of the Revolution of 1848 as well as in physics and geography, Boas was more egalitarian than most of the founders of American social science, men who came predominantly from Anglo-Saxon Protestant families secure in their cultural superiority. Boas's commitment to egalitarian principles had been forged in his childhood by painful experiences with anti-

29. Franz Boas, "Elsie Clews Parsons, Late President of the American Anthropological Association," *Scientific Monthly* 54 (May 1942): 480; Melville Herskovits, *Franz Boas: The Science of Man in the Making* (New York: Scribner's, 1953), p. 1.

30. Franz Boas, "Human Faculty as Determined by Race," pp. 325, 322–23. For an excellent analysis of Boas's contribution to the understanding of human nature, see George W. Stocking, Jr., *Race, Culture, and Evolution*, pp. 195–233.

31. Franz Boas, *Changes in the Bodily Form of Descendents of Immigrants*, U.S., Congress, Senate document no. 208, 61st Cong. 2d sess.,1910, pp. 1–7; Stocking, *Race, Culture, and Evolution*, pp. 175–80.

Semitism, together with his great fondness for a sister who achieved unconventional success in classical studies. Though egalitarian in his outlook, even with respect to women, Boas was thoroughly conventional in his personal life, and he never actively encouraged women to participate in anthropology; in fact, his training of female anthropologists began only after the Columbia administration exiled him to Barnard during the First World War because of his dissident political views, and women began to come to him as they had to Giddings in the 1890s. If Boas did not actively recruit women, and even complained that he could not train a decent secretary because each promising candidate grew interested in anthropology and left him, he was too much an egalitarian to turn them away. Besides, by the time he began including women in anthropology he was old enough to be their father and not to feel so threatened by them as he might have as a younger man. To students who knew him well he was Papa Franz.[32]

Elsie Clews Parsons was the first woman Boas ever interested in anthropology, and she initiated the friendship. He seems to have regarded her as a well-educated amateur who might be of use to him in his chronically underfinanced projects. They knew one another as early as 1907, and in 1912 Boas helped Parsons arrange a trip to Yucatán and tried to further her interest in anthropology. Parsons found that Boas's empiricism appealed to "something fundamental in her nature" while promising greater insight into women's condition than Giddings's abstract theories had allowed. As she recalled many years later, "Sociology had its day. It dipped a little into the customs of primitive peoples for illustrations but like historians or political scientists, never seriously considered societies other than those related to or constituting our own civilization. Primitive cultures were merely background for our own."[33]

Convinced that ethnology could help women, Parsons also believed that women could aid ethnology, for "a woman student would have many opportunities for observing the life of women and children that male ethnographers have lacked." Trapped in Washington, Parsons did most of her fieldwork there, studying the customs and rituals of its inhabitants, and especially its women. "Ethnology," she observed, "opens your eyes to what is under your nose." In a curious way, Parsons complemented Boas's

32. Herskovits, *Franz Boas*, pp. 9–12; Franziska Boas, "The Reminiscences of Franziska Boas," Oral History Collection, Columbia University, pp. 2, 9, 10; Hamilton Cravens, *The Triumph of Evolution*, pp. 90–120; Stocking, *Race, Culture, and Evolution*, pp. 195–233.

33. Franz Boas to Elsie Clews Parsons, January 4, 1907, Franz Boas Papers, American Philosophical Society, Philadelphia: Boas to Parsons, December 14, 1912, Franz Boas Papers; Boas to Jorge Engerrand, December 14, 1912, Franz Boas Papers; Elsie Clews Parsons, "The World Changes," fragment in Elsie Clews Parsons Papers.

Elsie Clews Parsons in the Southwest (ca. 1920)

work among primitive peoples. Whereas Boas looked at the Eskimos and saw himself, Parsons looked at her friends and relations and saw a primitive people. Each observer buttressed the other's growing belief in the psychic unity of humanity.[34]

During the years before Wold War I, Parsons felt constrained by the youth of her children from undertaking extensive fieldwork. Nevertheless, she did travel to the Southwest in 1910, 1912, and 1913. By 1915 she was thoroughly addicted to ethnographic trips. Her husband tolerated these trips, for he too liked the outdoors, but the rest of the family was slightly appalled. "She would come back to New York after one of them," her oldest child Lissa recalled of her later trips, "looking, really, as my grandma said, perfectly dreadful, 'scandalous' my grandmother said."

---

34. Parsons, *The Family*, p. 198; Elsie Clews Parsons, "Seniority in the Nursery," *School and Society* 3 (January 1916); 15.

She wore khaki clothes and she had no felt hat and she was touching up her hair
and of course it hadn't been touched up while she'd been away, so she wore a
bandanna around it, and then these saddle bags full of manuscripts. 'Disreputable' was the word my grandmother would use, referring to the luggage. She
would say, 'Your mother is here, and that disreputable looking luggage in the
front marble hall belongs to her.'

Parsons won approval for her efforts not from her family but from
Columbia's younger anthropologists, especially A. L. Kroeber and Robert
Lowie. Lowie later recalled that her door was always open to impecunious
graduate students, whom she would feed and then transport to her box at
the Opera. In the beginning, she approached anthropology as an
amateur. She enjoyed selecting materials from other cultures to throw
light on her own. But the insights she mined from this material were
novel, even revolutionary. Kroeber described her quality of mind:

Intellectually, her outstanding quality was perhaps the faculty of making up her
own mind. She forged her own convictions, often slowly, sometimes painfully;
put them to the test; and did not lightly discard them. She did reforge them to
the end, as might seem needful. But their temper represented self-trial, experience, resolution, and tenacity against which contrary views were likely to shat-
ter, especially if based on shallow enthusiasm or alloyed with facile dexterity or
any ingredient of pretense. In this quality she was spiritually close kin to Boas.[35]

To the insights that life in Washington provided, and to the enthusiasm
for ethnology that she derived from Boas, Lowie, and Kroeber, Parsons
added the intellectual ferment of Greenwich Village upon her return to
New York in 1911. In Mable Dodge's Salon she met Walter Lippmann,
with whom she remained lifelong friends and with whom she helped
found the *New Republic*; Max Eastman, for whose frankly radical magazine the *Masses* she sometimes wrote; Margaret Sanger, whom she joined
in the fight for birth control; and Randolphe Bourne, with whom she
steadfastly opposed U.S. involvement in World War I. The talk revolved
around psychoanalysis, the tyranny of patriarchal rule, socialism,
Nietzsche, the sexual revolution, and the unconscious. Disillusioned with
modern society and even progress, precursors of the more extensive and
cynical revolt of the 1920s, these young intellectuals were less sure of
humanity's ability to reason its way to a better world, less convinced of the
importance of self-abnegation, than older social critics had been or con-

35. Kroeber, "Elsie Clews Parsons," p. 255; Elsie Parsons Kennedy, "Reminiscences of
Mrs. John D. Kennedy." For Parsons's generosity to graduate students, see Robert F.
Murphy, *Robert H. Lowie* (New York: Columbia University Press, 1972), p. 6. Parsons's trips
to the Southwest were reported to me by Professor Peter Hare, who is writing Parsons's
biography.

tinued to be. "We inherit freedom," Walter Lippmann wrote of his generation, "and have to use it."

> The sanctity of property, the patriarchal family, hereditary caste, the dogma of sin, obedience to authority,—the rock of ages, in brief, has been blasted from us. Those who are young to-day are born into a world in which the foundations of the older order survive only as habits or by default.

American social scientists had been chipping away at the "foundations of the older order" for almost a generation when Parsons returned to her writing in 1912, but no other scholar had her flair for popularizing the new ideas about the cultural and psychological roots of sexual identity. The very fact that Parsons stood somewhat removed from academe after leaving Barnard meant that she could write for a wider audience than could someone like Franz Boas, who was so concerned with establishing his discipline as a scientifically respectable field that none but his most devoted followers could ever understand what he was saying in his tortured discussions of kinship systems and linguistic diffusion.[36]

A Farewell to Evolution

One of the first works to grow out of Parsons's altered perspective was *The Old-Fashioned Woman,* a book that traced woman's life cycle from its beginning in infancy through childhood and adolescence to marriage, motherhood, and widowhood. Scrupulously "raking through the ethnographic data," she assembled examples of females at comparable stages of life from cultures throughout the world, and argued that wherever a woman might be born, however she might be reared, the stream of her life followed the same basic course. Everywhere she fell subject to restrictions and taboos. Of married women, for instance, she wrote:

> It is not "proper" for a Tartar to shake hands with her, for a Hindu to touch her dress or give her a present or call out to her or wink or smile at her, for a Beni-Mzab or a Leti, Moa or Lakor Islander to speak to her in the street or away from her husband, for a Ewe to pay her a compliment, for a Gilbert Islander to pass her on the road, for a Californian Indian to stroll with her in the woods, for a Creek to drink out of her pitcher, for an Anglo-Saxon American to take her to a play or a tropical island.

Stressing the primitive quality of American social rites of passage, Parsons

36. Walter Lippmann, *Drift and Mastery* (New York: Kinnerly, 1914), p. 16; Kennedy, "Reminiscences of Mrs. John D. Kennedy," pp. 31–33; Henry May, *The End of American Innocence: A Study of the First Years of Our Own Time, 1912–1917* (1959: reprinted ed., New York: Quadrangle 1964), pp. 311–12; Christopher Lasch, *The New Radicalism in America, 1889–1963,* pp. 104–40; David Kennedy, *Birth Control in America: The Career of Margaret Sanger* (New Haven: Yale University Press, 1970), pp. 9–10, 12, 14.

described the culture in which she herself had come of age—a culture of teas, debuts, formal dinners, calling cards, and elaborate dress—all leading to the wedding ring, that "token of inadequacy as well as of 'respectability.' "[37]

To Parsons's consternaton, her own daughter Lissa grew up adoring all of the social rites of passage against which she had rebelled. Closer to her society-minded grandmother than to her mother, Lissa found Elsie's primitive analogies neither amusing nor apt. She later complained that her mother was not so good an anthropologist in writing about her own social class as she was later to become in writing about primitive peoples. "She wouldn't look at [New York or Washington society] as anthropology," Lissa objected, "[whereas] she wasn't intolerant of the Indians or the Mexican people." But Elsie Parsons did not equate anthropology with tolerance, nor did she think that anthropologists had to be tolerant of a society to see it clearly. Furthermore, she saw no reason, in the years when she was writing about women, why she should not use her skills as an anthropologist to retaliate against the society that had tried to tie her down. For her, anthropology was a weapon, and she was ruthless in its use.[38]

Impressed by the constancy of sexual classification from one cultural group to the next, Parsons lost all faith in the utility of evolutionary theory as an aid to understanding human behavior. She fully appreciated, however, the power that evolutionism continued to exercise in American social thought.

> In ethnology as elsewhere evolutionary theory has been running amuck. Customs are described as if they were living species. Illustrations of their different phases are assembled from scattered societies and the composite is labeled a life history. Culture is treated as an independent growth.

Parsons saw little reason to hope that cultural change might be viewed more critically, for "the concept of social evolution is so unchallenged a pattern of American opinion that it seems as an armor against observations however massive or analysis however penetrating." The only way that ethnologists could ever avoid the "ethnological Frankensteins" that a slavish devotion to evolutionary theory had produced was "through realizing that similarities in culture point not to the existence of set cultural stages through which all societies must pass, but to the homogeneity of the human mind and its tendency to express itself, given like circumstances, in like ways. For example, the custom of widow segre-

37. Elsie Clews Parsons, review of J. A. Todd, *The Primitive Family as an Educational Agency,* in *Science* 39 (May 1914): 655; Elsie Clews Parsons, *The Old-Fashioned Woman,* pp. 121, 50.

38. Kennedy, "Reminiscences of Mrs. John D. Kennedy," p. 29.

gation does not always presuppose or inevitably lead to that of widow immolation."[39]

Disillusioned with evolutionary theory, Parsons made of herself a "*de facto* functionalist," according to one colleague, long before "functionalism was first put on our professional map." Like Tarde, Thomas, and Boas, Parsons argued that the principal motives of human behavior are unconscious, and that in this respect civilized peoples are no different from primitive peoples in their behavior. It was time, Parsons believed, to look at customs not as relics of the past but as important elements in the functioning of modern society.

> Study of existing institutions or customs should not be carried on, it seems to me, exclusively on the current scientific theory that they are merely rationalized relics of the past, but far more on the popular theory that human nature has changed little if at all and that characteristic feelings and ideas are for-ever finding re-expression.

To emphasize the primitive quality of civilized culture, as Parsons did, raised a troubling question: why did habit and custom hold such power in a culture that prided itself on its rationalism, as modern Western society did? This was the question Parsons posed for herself in her subsequent books and articles. Her answers varied, but one that she found particularly appealing was that human beings, by their very nature, fear change. At the same time, humanity is innately sociable. To be sociable, however, opens a person to the risk of association with those different from himself. From the very beginning, humanity's solution to this fundamental conflict has been to classify, in order to facilitate companionship while shielding people from those who are different.[40]

One of the oldest, and perhaps most faithfully observed classifications is sexual. In much the same way that W. I. Thomas explained racial prejudice, Parsons explained sexual antagonism. To men, maleness is normal; by contrast, females are anomalous and are "shunned, segregated, and disqualified." As creatures of habit, men fear that which is different and react to this fear by classifying and regulating the offending group. Women came to assume a subordinate position in all cultures, not so much because of actual inferiority (though as a group they were weaker than men), but because, on the basis of a few superficial characteristics, they were perceived as anomalous. Women were among society's first

39. Parsons [Main], *Religious Chastity*, p. vii; Elsie Clews Parsons, review of Arthur Calhoun, *A Social History of the American Family from Colonial Times to the Present*, in *Dial* 65 (September 1918): 160; Parsons [Main], *Religious Chastity*, p. vii.

40. Kroeber, "Elsie Clews Parsons," p. 254; Elsie Clews Parsons, *Fear and Conventionality* (New York: Putnam, 1914), p. xi.

anomalies, and around them in all cultures sprang up a series of rules and conventions regulating their behavior.[41]

Women's subjection was based on humanity's fear of the unlike, but it was intensified by men's and women's particular anxiety over sex. "To objectify psychological peril seems to be a natural human tendency," Parsons wrote. "Danger from without is so much easier to understand and meet—or dodge—than danger from within." Parsons illustrated the calming effect that classification and custom can exercise on people (and in so doing demonstrated her debt to the functional psychologists' study of emotion) by pointing out that "a woman takes a man's arm not out of fear of slipping," but rather because "by taking his arm I do raise up an imperceptible kind of barrier between us, a barrier covertly soothing to the sense of disquiet, extremely slight in this circumstance of course, the difference in sex arouses. As a gesture of sex, taking a man's arm is a kind of inoculation against sex."[42]

From the psychological perspective that Parsons adopted in explaining sexual division, marriage, that most powerful institution within the classificatory scheme pertaining to sex, maintains its control over women not so much because of man's economic leverage, as Charlotte Perkins Gilman had argued, but rather because both men and women fear change. Women cooperate in their own subjection, Parsons added, by trying "hard to live down to what is expected of them." Parsons did not believe that men would ever willingly think of women in other than sexual terms, and she doubted that women really wanted them to; for the order created by conventional sexual classification is as important to women as it is to men.

> To be declassified is very painful to most persons and so the charge of unwomanliness has ever been a kind of whip against the would-be woman rebel. Not until she fully understands how arbitrary it is will she cease to feel its crack. . . . The *new woman* means the woman not yet classified, perhaps not classifiable, the women *new* not only to men, but to herself.[43]

The impulse to classify helped explain sex segregation and male exclusivity, but Parsons came to feel that it did not fully explain the vehemence behind sexual antagonism. "In any study of the relations between personality and social classification," Parsons wrote, "the queries arise why the social categories are alike so compulsive to the conservative mind and so precious? . . . Do they serve only as measures against change,

41. Parsons, *Fear and Conventionality*, pp. x–xv; William I. Thomas, "The Psychology of Race Prejudice," *American Journal of Sociology* 9 (March 1904); 593–611.

42. Parsons, *Old-Fashioned Woman*, p. 272; Parsons, *Fear and Conventionality*, p. xiii.

43. Parsons, *Old-Fashioned Woman*, p. 210; Elsie Clews Parsons, *Social Rule: A Study of the Will to Power* (New York: Putnam, 1916), p. 55.

as safeguards of habit? This was the answer that Parsons had originally found most convincing, but now, though she conceded that the protection afforded by classification "is no trifling social function," the division of the sexes into separate groups performs a "positive as well as a negative service, . . . an unparalleled means of gratifying the will to power as it expresses itself in social relations."[44]

The idea that human beings are naturally possessed of a "will to power" was in the air before World War I, but it had a special appeal to Parsons, who valued control above all other personal qualities, "first in herself," according to her friend A. L. Kroeber, "and then in others." When her husband was killed in a freak motorcycle accident in 1925 and Walter Lippmann came to see her, "all prepared to do what he could," she sat through lunch with him without once referring to Herbert's death. "Emotions undid people," Elsie told her children.[45]

Much though Parsons valued personal control, she deplored what she called "social control," that is, the impulse to control others. This was the impulse, she believed, that the natural tendency to classify tended ultimately to serve. From having seen classification as a safeguard of habit, Parsons had come to see it as a tool of oppression. "The preeminent function of social classification," she concluded, "appears therefore to be social rule." Having identified this darker side of human nature, Parsons argued that "it is not hard to see why the classification of women according to sex has ever been so thorough and so rigid."

> As long as they are thought of in terms of sex, and that the weaker and more submissive, they are subject by hypothesis to control. Just as soon as women are considered not as creatures of sex, but as persons, sex regulations cease to apply. . . . Womanliness must never be out of mind, if masculine rule is to be kept intact.[46]

Like a growing number of contemporary European thinkers, Parsons was beginning to see the unconscious as a reservoir not just of automatic response, as the experimental psychologists were arguing, but also of more sinister and less easily controlled forces. The ideas of Freud and Nietzsche figured prominently in the debates among New York's avant-garde intellectuals, and Parsons contributed to the wider dissemination of these views in her dozens of articles and books after 1912. Writing for the

44. Parsons, *Social Rule*, pp. 1–2. Parsons cites Hobbes's description of man's "perpetual desire of power after power that ceaseth only with death," as the source for her new approach (*Social Rule*, p. 2), but Nietzsche's theory of man's "will to power" was widely discussed in America by this time and probably influenced her also.

45. Kroeber, "Elsie Clews Parsons," p. 255; Kennedy, "Reminiscences of Mrs. John D. Kennedy," p. 32.

46. Parsons, *Social Rule*, pp. 4–5, 54.

Psychoanalytic Review, she attributed the average Victorian's desire to control the sex life of others to "infantile psychosis," and in other writings she referred repeatedly to the power of irrational forces in the shaping of human behavior. Like virtually all American social theorists, however, Parsons insisted on using psychoanalytic theory on her own terms. She clearly believed that psychiatrists had more to learn from anthropologists than anthropologists had to learn from psychiatrists, and she often criticized the naivete of Freud and his followers about ethnology. The Freudians' gullible acceptance of such outdated evolutionary ideas as recapitulation, the theory that the history of the race can be seen recapitulated in the development of each child, attracted one of her most barbed reviews. "The psychologists have discovered ethnology," she observed derisively.

> There is Freud with his book on totemism and taboo and Dr. Otto Rank writing about the hero myth. And the other day in the hands of one of their American translators, a well-known alienist, I noted with surprise a volume of "The Golden Bough." At a later moment I was still more surprised to hear the theory of recapitulation issuing from his respectable lips. That alluring theory the Freudians, it seems, have resurrected to serve their turn. And for their theory of infantile psychosis it does nicely. How long it will satisfy them is another question. Meanwhile it is a means of directing their attention to the study of comparative culture.[47]

Given her growing emphasis on the deep-seated conservative tendencies of both males and females, Parsons grew discouraged over the prospects for reform in general and the woman's movement in particular.

> Men will cede to women only what by ceding gives them an assurance of power, like making an allowance to a wife or educating a daughter to citizenship, or they will cede only what they consider has ceased to give mastery—just as they are now ceding the vote or the ecclesiastical profession.

With men conceding so little and women unwilling to claim very much, Parsons warned feminists against expecting fundamental social changes from their struggle for economic equality. "Establish woman's right to a job and new forms of sex subjection may ensue," Parsons cautioned.

> Even the woman movement we have called feminism has not succeeded by and large in giving women any control over men. It has only changed the distribution of women along the two stated lines of control of men, removing vast numbers of women from the class supported by men to the class working for them.

47. Elsie Clews Parsons, "Marriage and the Will to Power," *Psychoanalytic Review* 2 (October 1915): 478; Elsie Clews Parsons, "Discomfiture and Evil Spirits," *Psychoanalytic Review* 3 (July 1916): 288. For more information on the intellectual currents in New York before World War I, and especially talk about Freud and Nietzsche, see Henry May, *The End of American Innocence,* pp. 206–10, 233–36.

And in their fight against the exclusiveness of men, women, motivated by the same unconscious forces that guide men, unwittingly perpetuate and even celebrate sex segregation.

> In regard to the exclusiveness of women the movement has as yet taken no destructive position, rather it has from time to time countenanced or even encouraged that invidious spirit, the very spirit most characteristic of the ardent woman hater. 'As women,' declares the Woman's Peace Party in a preamble of its platform, 'as women, we feel peculiar moral passion of revolt against both the cruelty and waste of war.' Seldom have men been more exclusive.[48]

Field Work as a Refuge

By the outbreak of the World War I, Parsons considered progress a foolish and even dangerous illusion. She had not yet adopted the egalitarian position of the cultural relativist, but she argued forcefully that Western culture was just as unworthy as any other, just as superstitious and burdened by prejudice. Even science, the inspiration of her youth, now seemed dangerous to her, especially in the hands of social reformers determined to better society through eugenics.

> Modern mechanisms of war might be but petty horrors compared to the undertakings of social reformers, rampant in attempts to control people scientifically, to control birth and death, to regulate mating, to control feeling and thought and will, personality itself. The tyranny of traditional morality might be insignificant compared with that of the morality of eugenics. With the will to power of the social reformer unrestrained, his zeal for scientific management untempered, many of the subject classes would be re-victimized—children, women, the defectives and the criminal, 'backward peoples.' Once a progressive god is imagined, he too will be enslaved to the determination to improve the race. For such a progressive deity theories of evolutionary culture have paved the way. Culture as a self-developing entity is an embryonic god.

Parsons was too much a product of the reform generation into which she had been born to renounce science entirely, but she trusted science more because of its dependence on critical thinking than because of its potential for social engineering. Like Freud, she admired the power of critical thought to plumb the unconscious, lay bare the demons that lurked there, and enable people to transcend those paralyzing forces.[49]

Real sexual equality depended on transcending unconscious forces so that men and women could view personality in a fundamentally new light. Woman would have to view herself not only as man's equal but in most ways as his mirror image, sharing his innate weaknesses along with his innate strengths. Convinced of the universality of unconscious fears and

48. Parsons, *Social Rule*, p. 56, 172, 53– 54; Elsie Clews Parsons, *Social Freedom: A Study of the Conflicts between Social Classifications and Personality* (New York: Putnam, 1915), p. 28.
49. Parsons, *Social Rule*, p. 47.

the will to power, Parsons doubted feminist claims of female uniqueness and moral superiority. Neither the vote advocated by suffragists nor the economic independence demanded by Charlotte Perkins Gilman would bring equality until "a subordination of sex to personality far more sweeping than we dream of today came to be," Parsons wrote. Feminists had to gain an "ethnological inkling of themselves" and their position, so that they could see the attacks on women's efforts at emancipation from sex-exclusiveness as the product of irrational forces. When people argue that women should not do certain things because they are women, the wise woman should not be irritated, she should be observant. Without an ethnological understanding, "she loses an opportunity for fieldwork, and wearies herself in the futile task of opposing concepts to mystical, prelogical representations."

So reason still has a role to play in making life better, but not if people expect it to unfold automatically, only if they appreciate that it must transcend the very powerful forces of repression that lurk within everyone—only if they come to detach personality from status.

> Once it ceases to be 'funny' for a man to thread a needle or shop or hold a baby, or for a woman to cast a ballot or sit on a jury or introduce a bill, domesticity and politics will become optional for both.

For such social freedom to be possible, men and women have to persuade themselves that they are essentially alike in their mental endowment and personal capacities and that the sexual categorization of contemporary society is both artificial and unnecessary.[50]

Whatever modest hope Parsons had for progress and reform was dashed by World War I. "The supreme horror of the war lay in its assault on our sense of progress," she lamented. Even after her husband went off to serve with Pershing, Parsons persisted in her pacifism, "refusing to shake hands with any member of the armed force," A. L. Kroeber recalled. "She had always disapproved the gesture as a dictation," Kroeber continued, "she was doubly annoyed by the hierarchical status implied in the uniform." Parsons helped found the New School as a sanctuary for dissident intellectuals who lost their jobs over opposition to the war, and she taught there a year herself, but that was as close as she came to reform activity after the war.[51]

At the war's end, Parsons made a final break with public life and her own brand of feminism and escaped into anthropological fieldwork. Her friend Kroeber later suggested that she burned out on reform and that

50. Ibid., p. 57; Parsons, *Old-Fashioned Woman*, p. v; Signe Toksvig, "Elsie Clews Parsons," *New Republic* 2 (November 1919): 17; Parsons, *Old-Fashioned Woman*, p. 148.

51. Elsie Clews Parsons, "The Teleological Delusion," *Journal of Philosophy, Psychology, and Scientific Method* 14 (August 1917): 467; Kroeber, "Elsie Clews Parsons," pp. 252–53.

her growing understanding of culture's power over the individual made her even less optimistic about individual action. For twenty years she devoted herself to painstaking research among the Indians of the Southwest, becoming one of anthropology's "most skilled ethnographers." Those who remembered her after her death all insisted that she never lost sight of her early social commitment to change; but that commitment was deeply suppressed after World War I. "She had never had too much faith in reason unarmed with fact," Kroeber remembered, "and she had less now." Science, once the promise of a new era, became simply a refuge for her, in which she sought greater understanding for its own sake, not for the sake of reform. Having seen the havoc that science in service to reform could wreak, she persuaded herself that science free of reform efforts would be less dangerous and better able to reveal truth. In the mid thirties, Boas gave Parsons a picture of himself on which he wrote, "Elsie Clews Parsons, fellow in the struggle for freedom from Prejudice." Parsons reflected on the meaning of the inscription in a letter to Robert Lowie, writing, "I began that way and he ends that way. I suppose somewhere our trails crossed."[52]

Like so many other women social scientists, Parsons found in science a vehicle for transcending the restrictions of her sex, but that vehicle set her apart from the world in which she had been bred—the world of womanhood, idealism, and social reform. Parsons's daughter later recalled that she "preferred men to women," and Parsons herself confided to Boas after World War I her "prejudices" against her own sex. In transcending Victorian womanhood, Parsons and scholars like her offered both men and women a new and less restrictive vision of sexual identity, but at the same time they lost the sense of shared purpose and identity that had given force to the woman's movement. Working in relative isolation, without the woman's movement's cohesive force, the impact of their thought was inevitably dissipated. However, their vision was not completely lost. Gradually, younger scholars began to adopt and to disseminate the egalitarian view of male and female potential which these early mavericks first developed, and gradually, through new generations of students, their influence spread. This was especially true in the field of anthropology at Columbia, where Parsons's generous support enabled a generation of graduate students to do fieldwork they could not otherwise have afforded to do.[53]

52. Kroeber, "Elsie Clews Parsons," pp. 242–53; Parsons to Lowie, January 6, 1938, Robert Lowie Papers, Bancroft Library, University of California, Berkeley.

53. Kennedy, "Reminiscences of Mrs. John D. Kennedy," p. 25; Parsons to Boas, April 24, 1920, Boas Papers.

7 The Reluctant Revolutionaries

Women social scientists broke with most aspects of Victorian theory about sex differences with little difficulty because most of those differences represented liabilities for women within the academic world, and researchers like Woolley, Hollingworth, Taft, and Parsons wanted to demonstrate women's capacity to contribute equally with men to modern science. The one aspect of woman's nature that they found very difficult to discuss, however, was sexuality. Quick to discard long-held ideas about the variability of male intelligence and the innateness of motherly feelings, they shrank from questioning Victorian attitudes toward sexuality. For a number of reasons, sex was a troubling issue to these researchers, and their attitudes about sex were, initially, as Victorian as those of their most conservative peers. Yet between 1890 and 1920 these same people shifted to an unprecedented openness and, in a few instances, even enthusiasm, about sex.

For years historians have searched for the roots of the freedom and enthusiasm that seem to mark modern sexual relations, but they have not been able to agree on their origins. Some believe the roots are quite recent. Others trace them back to the 1920s. Still others go back to the years immediately preceding World War I. And a few retreat to the late nineteenth century. Complicating the debate, some argue that no revolution was necessary, for Victorian Americans were not as different from contemporary Americans in their attitudes toward sex as has long been thought.[1] Historians' failure to agree stems in part from their failure to specify which groups and what changes in attitude they mean to include

1. William O'Neill, *Divorce in the Progressive Era* (New Haven: Yale University Press, 1967), pp. vii– viii; Frederick Lewis Allen, *Only Yesterday: An Informal History of the Nineteen-Twenties* (New York: Harper Bros., 1931), pp. 88– 122; James R. McGovern, "The American Woman's Pre– World War I Freedom in Manners and Morals," *Journal of American History* 55 (September 1968): 315– 33; Daniel Scott Smith, "The Dating of the American Sexual Revolution: Evidence and Interpretation," in Michael Gordon, ed., *The American Family in Social-Historical Perspective*, 2d ed. (New York: St. Martin's Press, 1978), pp. 432– 33; Carl Degler, "What Ought To Be and What Was," *American Historical Review* 79 (December 1974): 1467– 90.

within their analysis of sexual revolution. I intend to limit myself here to a discussion of American social scientists and the college-educated Americans they studied. Within this one group, I believe, a major change in attitude did take place, and it did so in the first two decades of this century. I want to explain, first, why social scientists—especially women social scientists—were reluctant to study sex; second, why, despite this reluctance, they studied sex anyway; and third, how studying the sexual behavior and attitudes of educated Americans altered their own thinking about sex.

Sex Research: The Early Years

In 1892, almost fifty years before Alfred Kinsey conducted his first interview, Mary Roberts Smith persuaded members of the Mothers Club of Madison, Wisconsin, to join in a scientific investigation of sex. Like Kinsey, Smith wanted to know more about the sex life of the normal person. Unlike Kinsey, she assumed that a systematic examination of sexual experience would reveal the need for greater sexual inhibition.[2]

A graduate of Cornell, Smith had worked with Marion Talbot in the early 1880s on the Association of Collegiate Alumnae's health survey of women college graduates, and from 1886 to 1890 she had taught history and economics at Wellesley College. Her marriage in 1890 to mechanical engineering professor Albert Smith had ended her teaching career and brought her first to Cornell and then to Wisconsin, where her interest in social research helped fill the void left by her retirement from academia.[3]

In the 1890s dozens of books circulated offering advice on how to conduct oneself within marriage, but none had ever attempted to describe what actually took place there. Persuading members of the Madison Mothers Club that any improvement in marriage depended on a more scientific approach to the "marital relation" than that taken by armchair

2. Smith's role in this pioneering effort in sex research has been pieced together from scattered sources, including Smith's private papers, deposited with the papers of her second husband, Dane Coolidge, at the Bancroft Library, University of California at Berkeley, Berkeley, California, and the private papers of Clelia Duel Mosher, deposited at the Stanford Library, Stanford University, Stanford, California. See especially, Clelia Duel Mosher, "Statistical Study of the Marriage of Forty-seven Women" (begun in 1892; hereafter cited as Mosher Survey), introduction, Mosher Papers; Mary Roberts [Smith] Coolidge, "Clelia Duel Mosher—The Questioner" (1932), pp. 1–5, Mosher Papers; Coolidge, "How I Came to Write Why Women Are So" (1915), pp. 1–2, Coolidge Papers. For Kinsey's investigative intentions, see Alfred C. Kinsey et al, Sexual Behavior in the Human Female (Philadelphia: Saunders, 1953), p. vii; and Regina Markell Morantz, "The Scientist as Sex Crusader: Alfred Kinsey and American Culture," American Quarterly 29 (Winter 1977): 519–46.

3. James McKeen Cattell, ed., Leaders in Education: A Biographical Dictionary (New York: Science Press, 1932), s.v. "Mary Roberts Coolidge"; and Cattell, ed., American Men of Science (New York: Science Press, 1906), s.v. "Albert William Smith."

theorists, Smith launched modern sex research. She enlisted one of her former students, Clelia Duel Mosher, to formulate a questionnaire that would elicit concrete data about women's private lives. Mosher, a biology major intent on a career in medicine, had been inspired by Smith at Wellesley to commit her life to the woman's movement and had followed her mentor first to Cornell and then to the University of Wisconsin. Smith's suggestion that she study the sexual behavior of normal wives and mothers appealed to the would-be doctor as a way of preparing herself to help future patients.[4]

Eleven of the twenty-five questions Mosher posed the Mothers Club members solicited conventional information about their health, as well as that of their grandparents, parents, husbands, and children; but the final fourteen questions asked the respondents to describe in detail their sexual practices and attitudes. In particular, Mosher wanted to know: what knowledge of sex the women had acquired before marriage; how often they had intercourse with their husbands; whether they experienced orgasm; what they believed "the true purpose of intercourse to be"; whether they used "any means to prevent conception"; and finally, what the women would consider an "ideal" habit in their sexual relations with their husbands.[5]

The Roots of Inhibition

Of the seven wives and mothers who completed Mosher's questionnaire in the spring of 1892, and of the forty-five women who completed it in the years that followed, Mary Roberts Smith provided the fullest answers. She began on a positive note, reporting that she found sex to be "agreeable" and that she generally experienced orgasm. For reasons she could not explain, however, happiness eluded her. She wanted to believe that sex could produce "complete harmony between two people," but she had to admit that her own sexual experience was filled with troubling dishar-mony. Intercourse with her husband took place about three times a month, a rate she found excessive. It left her with a backache and "often great nervousness," whether or not she had reached orgasm. During the first year of her marriage she had shared her husband's bed, but in the six months since had slept apart, for "sleeping on my guard made me nervous and irritable." Smith was not alone in her ambivalence toward sex. Though over 80 percent of the wives Mosher enlisted in her survey

4. Coolidge, "Clelia Duel Mosher," Mosher Papers, pp. 1 – 5; Mosher Survey, introduction. For an excellent survey of the marital-advice literature then in print, see Michael Gordon, "From Unfortunate Necessity to a Cult of Mutual Orgasm: Sex in Marital Education Literature, 1830– 1940," in James Henslin, ed., *Studies in the Sociology of Sex* (New York: Appleton-Century-Crofts, 1971), pp. 56– 67.

5. Mosher Survey, passim.

Clelia Duel Mosher (1896)

reported having experienced orgasm, most said they would be happier if
intercourse took place less often than it did.[6]

In part, the reluctance toward sex expressed by these women derived
from their fear of pregnancy, as the answers to Mosher's queries about
contraception reveal. Living in a commercial society, where children were
economic liabilities, these women refused to leave their reproductive fate
in the hands of nature. Though most late nineteenth-century medical

6. Ibid., case no. 2. The questionnaires were answered anonymously, but the biographical data in case no. 2 clearly identify the respondent as Mary Roberts Smith. For a different
interpretation of the Mosher survey results, see Carl Degler, "What Ought to Be and What
Was," pp. 1467– 90. Professor Degler, who first alerted historians to the existence of the
survey, argues that the high rate of reported orgasm indicates that Victorian women were
far more accepting of sexuality than either contemporary commentators thought possible or
later historians have believed. Though I would agree that Mosher's respondents had sexual
feelings and a remarkably open attitude toward sex, I would emphasize that among those
who responded to the questionnaire in the 1890s, sexual reluctance heavily outweighed
sexual enthusiasm.

authorities denounced contraception as "ineffective" and "immoral," the women Mosher studied confessed to the use of a variety of devices, all of them faulty, to prevent conception.[7]

A majority of the women relied on some form of douche and managed to limit themselves to about three children each. Because they never knew when douching would fail them, however, day-to-day anxiety made it difficult to feel confident in its power. Withdrawal, usually combined with what the respondents referred to as the "safe period," provided the next most popular means of birth control. But as several women made a special point of declaring, the safe period was "not infallible," a discovery one might well expect, given the massive confusion that existed over what period was safe. Some late nineteenth-century medical authorities argued that ovulation could take place in the middle of the menstrual cycle (as physiologists succeeded in proving by 1930), but many others believed that ovulation took place either during or near the monthly flow. Therefore, several women reported abstaining from intercourse during the weeks before and after menstruation, only to find themselves pregnant from coitus carefully confined to the one week in the middle of the monthly cycle. Regrettably, despite their contraceptive efforts, which included the added protection of a condom in three cases, all but one of the mothers reported accidental conceptions.[8]

One woman spoke for countless others when she said: "I most heartily wish there were no accidental conceptions. I believe the world would take a most gigantic stride toward high ethical conditions if every child brought into the world were the product of pure and conscious choice." By Mosher's respondents even more than by most middle-class women, this sentiment must have been deeply felt. In an era when less than 2 percent of American women graduated from college, 60 percent of Mosher's respondents held college degrees. For them, frequent and unanticipated pregnancies meant not only physical and emotional strain but also the destruction of the sense of personal effectiveness and autonomy that education had given them.[9]

7. For information on birth-control advice in the nineteenth century, see Gordon, "From Unfortunate Necessity," p. 59; and James Reed, *From Private Vice to Public Virtue*, pp. 3 – 18.

8. These conclusions are based on Mosher's cases from the 1890s: case nos. 1 – 6, 9 – 11, 13 – 16, 18 – 19, 21 – 22, 24 – 25, 28, 33 – 36. Three cases in the survey could not be dated and have been omitted from analysis. A discussion of the fertile period appears in Vern Bullough and Martha Vought, "Women, Menstruation, and Nineteenth-Century Medicine," *Bulletin of the History of Medicine* 47 (January – February 1973): 66 – 82.

9. Case no. 24. For a fuller discussion of Victorian women's desire to be able to choose when they would be mothers, see Linda Gordon, *Woman's Body, Woman's Right: A Social History of Birth Control in America* (New York: Grossman, 1976), pp. 95 – 115; and Daniel Scott Smith, "Family Limitation, Sexual Control, and Domestic Feminism in Victorian America," in Hartman and Banner, eds., *Clio's Consciousness Raised*, pp. 119 – 36.

Because of their desire to limit childbearing and the disappointing quality of their contraceptive aids, these women suffered from chronic anxiety over pregnancy. Indeed, where anxiety was greatest, it generated its own, last-ditch contraceptive protection by producing sexual inhibition strong enough to lead to abstinence. The desire to avoid frequent pregnancies, however, cannot fully account either for the exhortations against sexual excess that filled the late nineteenth-century prescriptive literature or for the intensity of many women's sexual inhibition. Smith, for instance, was protected by a condom in intercourse with her husband and had no children. She should have been less nervous than most women; and yet, if anything, she seemed more nervous than others in the survey. Something in the sexual relation itself, beyond the conscious fear of pregnancy, bothered educated, middle-class women. Smith gave no further hint in 1892 of the source of her feelings about sex; but twenty years later, looking back over the rearing of women of her generation, she wrote of the social conditions and attitudes that had led to the sexual ambivalence that she and others felt.[10]

The daughter of an academic father, Smith had aspired to be an intellectual; the daughter of a domestically minded mother, she had acquired the housewifely skills of a proper young woman. Of her dual heritage she reflected, "To be an intellectual is all right—to be domestic is all right—but to try to be both is hell!" Her problems began with her mother's unwillingness to talk to her about sexual matters and her own conclusions that sex must be a dangerous and even ugly matter. Everything in the social influences around girls of her generation "tended to produce repulsion, if not terror, for the only approved destiny" that society permitted them. This terror was mitigated to some extent for Smith by the books she began to find after she was sixteen. Alice Stockham's *Tokology* and T. R. Trall's *Sexual Physiology and Hygiene* both tried to counteract the influence of the more draconian Victorian literature and to leaven their recommendations of restraint with a positive attitude toward sexual feeling for its own sake. "Whatever may be the object of sexual intercourse," wrote Trall, "whether intended as a love embrace merely, or as a generative act, it is very clear that it should be as pleasurable as possible to both parties. . . . There must be mental harmony and congeniality between the parties." Smith's sense of foreboding was mitigated too by the "effeminate fiction of the day, whose chief note was love and lovers, with an happy ending in marriage."[11]

10. Coolidge, "How I Came to Write *Why Women Are So*," Coolidge Papers, pp. 1– 4; Mary Roberts Coolidge, *Why Women Are So* (New York: Holt, 1912), passim. Though *Why Women Are So* purports to be a discussion of American women in general, many of its references are clearly autobiographical.

11. Coolidge, *Why Women Are So*, pp. 235, 15– 16; R. T. Trall, M.D., *Sexual Physiology and*

But the facts of married life destroyed the calming effects of this romantic ideal. Husbands of her generation entered "upon marriage with slight illusions and with the natural impulses of a healthy animal," while wives, who had learned "to ignore the very idea of passion," found the reality of sex very different from the romantic ideal they had cultivated. Husbands did not understand their wives' sexual feelings, and wives found it difficult to respond to their husbands' demands. Regretfully, brides put away their girlish illusions along with the delicate trousseaux they had prepared for their marriage, replacing them with a franker understanding and a wardrobe of "plain, stout materials to be washed with their own hands."[12]

Neither submission to sexual reality nor the adoption of sensible clothes, however, could overcome Smith's disappointment with marriage. Once self-supporting, Smith found herself, upon her marriage, a dependent creature, keenly sympathetic with wives who "wept in secret humiliation" to have to ask for what they considered their due. Because she was childless, this humiliation hurt her even more, she believed, than it might if she had been a mother. "Instead of being compelled to do something necessary to the household and worthy of a human being," she found herself making work and then feeling dissatisfied with what she had done. Domesticity "manacled" her and prevented her from choosing what she would like or what she was "fitted to do." In the end, this social coercion "suppressed her initiative and originality to a degree beyond imagination." While memories of meaningful work receded, she had to confront "the pervasive belief" that her "sex functions" represented her "only really useful contribution to society." Without being fully conscious of the fact, Smith felt betrayed by the "sex functions" that symbolized her new, devalued status. Everytime she gave in to her sexual feelings, she felt she was further erasing her human (namely, intellectual) self.[13]

That Mosher's other respondents shared Smith's sexual inhibition can best be seen in their answers to the final question: "What, to you, would be an ideal habit?" Most responded simply that they would prefer to have less frequent intercourse with their husbands, but some elaborated further, stressing repeatedly the importance they attached to "temperance" and "moderation" in their sex lives. "I think to the man and woman married

Hygiene (New York: Fowler and Wells, 1866), pp. 291–92. Smith described her reading of sex literature in her answers to Mosher's questionnaire, case number 2. For a discussion of Victorian literature as related to sex, see Walter Houghton, *The Victorian Frame of Mind* (New Haven: Yale University Press, 1957), pp. 355–56; and William Wasserstrom, *Heiress of All the Ages: Sex and Sentiment in the Genteel Tradition* (Minneapolis: University of Minnesota Press, 1959), pp. 3–19.

12. Coolidge, *Why Women Are So*, pp. 31, 26.

13. Ibid., pp. 35, 79–81, 315.

from love," one woman wrote, "[intercourse] may be used temperately, as one of the highest manifestations of love, granted us by our Creator." Another woman sanctioned intercourse but pointedly added, "Oh but I believe in temperance in it." And yet another wrote, "I think the pleasure is sufficient to warrant it provided people are extremely moderate, and do not allow it to injure their health or degrade their best feelings toward each other." Some women extended their wish for temperance to the point of recommending that intercourse be confined to "reproduction only," and one older woman suggested, "after the change of life . . . not at all."[14]

Though the average rate of intercourse among respondents was about once a week, the average preferred rate was about once a month. In general, the wives believed that their husbands needed sex more than they did, and they regarded the frequency of intercourse as a compromise between what they would have liked and what their husbands wanted. Alfred Kinsey later reported that the frequency of intercourse among married couples declined steadily after the turn of the century, a trend he attributed to women's growing power within the family. That Mosher's respondents engaged in intercourse less often than the youngest, and presumably most assertive, of Kinsey's female interviewees suggests that highly educated women were already exercising significant power within their marriages, even in the days of Victorian patriarchy.[15]

Indirect evidence from Mosher's study, however, suggests that masculine inhibition was also at work. Though the husbands of the respondents were by no means so reticent as their wives, they appear to have shared many of the same anxieties and to have accepted a view, widely expressed in the advice literature, that abstinence could be an important factor in professional achievement. Alice Stockham explained this quasi-thermodynamic, quasi-economic conviction when she wrote in the *Tokology* that the "procreative element" when "retained . . . is taken up by the brain and may be coined into new thought—perhaps new inventions— grand conceptions of the true, the beautiful, the useful. . . . It is a procreation on the mental and spiritual planes instead of the physical." One woman in Mosher's survey reported that her husband considered continence an important element of business success; and many wives, including Mary Roberts Smith, noted that their husbands tried to control their sexual urges. The relative infrequency of reported intercourse (by post-Kinsey standards) and the scattered references to male restraint suggest

14. Case nos. 10, 13, 14, and 33. For an excellent discussion of the general phenomenon of sexual reluctance among Victorian women, see Nancy F. Cott, "Passionlessness: An Interpretation of Victorian Sexual Ideology 1790– 1850," *Signs* 4 (Winter 1978): 219– 36.
15. Kinsey et al., *Sexual Behavior in the Human Female,* pp. 359, 397.

that the husbands of the women studied by Mosher conspired with their wives to limit sexual relations.[16]

Sexuality troubled both men and women because it reminded them, more than any other part of their being, how deeply rooted they were in the natural order. They valued the cultural attainment of technology and symbols because these accomplishments allowed them to transcend nature and to dominate it. For women, whose bodies often doomed them to the mere reproduction of life, sex posed an even more serious threat than it did to men. While men could devote their lives to creating relatively lasting, eternal objects, many educated women believed they risked creating only perishables, human beings. For educated men, and especially for educated women, therefore, sex was a disturbing, even a tormenting issue, and its problematic quality affected their thinking and writing.[17]

Among social scientists this sexual anxiety marked all of the research about sexual identity, but nowhere was the mark clearer than in writing about sex itself. Whereas scholars achieved a measure of scientific detachment in discussing such issues as sex differences in intelligence and personality formation among boys and girls, they found detachment nearly impossible when they focused on sexual behavior and attitudes. So much depended on defending sexual restraint in their own lives that they rarely opened their minds to the possibility of sexual enthusiasm in others.

Social Control through Sexual Control

Mary Roberts Smith exemplified the turn-of-the-century faith among social scientists that sexual control provided the key to personal fulfillment and social order. When her husband's shifting fortunes took her once again to a new university (this time to Stanford), she tried to arrest her growing sense of domestic ennui by returning to graduate work.

16. Alice B. Stockham, M.D., *Tokology: A Book for Every Woman* (Chicago: Alice B. Stockham and Co., 1889), p. 151; Case nos. 2, 5, 11, 14, 15, 24, 25 [all answered before 1900], and no. 30 [answered in 1920]. For more information on men's anxiety over the economic and intellectual dangers of sexual excess, see G. J. Barker-Benfield, *The Horrors of the Half-Known Life: Male Attitudes toward Women and Sexuality in Nineteenth-Century America* (New York: Harper & Row, 1976), pp. 135– 214; and Charles Rosenberg, "Sexuality, Class and Role in Nineteenth-Century America," *American Quarterly* 25 (May 1973): 131– 53.

17. That this desire to transcend nature is universal and is fundamental to sex-role differentiation is argued in Sherry Ortner, "Is Female to Male as Nature Is to Culture?" in Michelle Rosaldo and Louise Lamphere, eds., *Woman, Culture, and Society* (Stanford: Stanford University Press, 1974), pp. 67– 88. For the centrality of sex functions in nineteenth-century women's lives, see Caroll Smith-Rosenberg, "Puberty to Menopause: The Cycle of Femininity in Nineteenth-Century America," in Hartman and Banner, eds., *Clio's Consciousness Raised,* pp. 23– 37.

Studying with historian George E. Howard and economists E. A. Ross and Amos Warner, she joined the faculty in 1896 as an assistant professor of sociology, teaching courses on the family. Her initial views about the family were typical of progressive, reform-minded social scientists of the 1890s. The American family, she argued, was not disintegrating, as so many popular commentators feared, but was instead evolving toward greater freedom and equality. The higher education of women, far from being a threat to family life, promised to strengthen it by contributing to feminine influence and thereby, as Smith later reflected, enabling women to exact "a higher standard of sex morality for men."[18]

Other Stanford social scientists supported this view of social progress through increased feminine power in their own work. When George Howard finally finished his three-volume study of the history of marriage in 1904, he became the national authority on marriage and the country's most respected advocate of divorce. Greatly influenced by his feminist wife and friends, especially Charlotte Perkins Gilman (a sometime Bay area resident), Howard defended liberalized divorce laws in the name of better marriages, arguing that divorce was necessary to free women who were trapped in a sexually exploitative relationship.

> Girls are trained, or they are forced by poverty, to look upon wedlock as an economic vocation, as a means of getting a living. . . . In the family, therefore, the sex-motive has become excessively pronounced, thrusting into the background higher social and spiritual ideals.

As long as bad legislation and a "low standard of social ethics continue to throw recklessly wide the door which opens to wedlock," Howard argued, "there must of necessity be a broad way out." The family would survive, he assured his readers, but it would be a family "of a higher type," joining "equals whose love is deep enough to embrace a rational regard for the right of posterity."[19]

18. Coolidge, "How I Came to Write *Why Women Are So*," Coolidge Papers, pp. 1– 4; idem, *Why Women Are So,* p. 342. Smith's dissertation was on women committed to the San Francisco Almshouse, Mary Roberts Smith [Coolidge], *Almshouse Women: A Study of 228 Women in the City and County Almshouse of San Francisco* (Stanford: Stanford University Press, 1896). Typical of sociologists in the 1890s, she traced the poverty of many of her subjects to "feeblemindedness," p. 2, but she also noted that most of the older women had never been trained for self-support.

19. George E. Howard, *A History of Matrimonial Institutions: Chiefly in England and the United States, with an Introductory Analysis of the Literature and the Theories of Primitive Marriage and the Family,* 3 vols. (Chicago: University of Chicago Press, 1904), 3:248– 53; *Dictionary of American Biography,* s.v. "George Elliott Howard." See also George Howard, "Divorce and Public Welfare," *McClure's Magazine* 34 (1909): 242. For more information on social scientists' writings on divorce at the turn of the century, see William O'Neill, *Divorce in the Progressive Era,* pp. 168– 97.

To Howard's defense of liberalized divorce laws, E. A. Ross and Amos Warner added that the achievement of a "higher type" of family life would depend on the education of young men to the evils of unregulated sexual energy. Warner often warned young men of the "very great amount of vitality . . . burnt out in the fires of lust," adding that "at the present day, a given amount of such [sexual] preoccupation will diminish a man's efficiency more than ever before, because of the increasing importance of the mental element in all work." Mary Roberts Smith believed that married men should be "unwilling to subordinate their careers to unregulated instinct; preferring few or no children, with a carefree, comely partner and a quiet household."[20]

This academic idealization of sexual restraint carried over to public life, where the campaign against prostitution played an important part in the work of academic reformers. At a time when many scholars believed advocacy to be a natural adjunct of science, and when women were taking an increasingly active part in university life, it was logical that the university should produce some of the most vocal advocates of sexual purity. New discoveries around the turn of the century about venereal disease spurred academics to action. Syphilis had long been known as a dangerous disease, but gonorrhea, an illness fifty times more common, was regarded as hardly more dangerous than a bad cold, inflicted by God to punish sin. In the final decades of the nineteenth century, however, belief in the divine origins of sickness declined and medical study demonstrated the seriousness of gonorrhea—its infectiousness, and its role in causing many women's diseases. The main impulse to reform was the discovery that victims of venereal disease were not just men and prostitutes but wives and children whom men infected. Within a few decades, what had been one of several public-health problems came to be regarded as modern society's most serious menace to health.[21]

In cities across the country reformers founded vice commissions to battle prostitution. Many reformers believed, however, that prostitution represented only the surface manifestation of a more serious problem—male sexual ignorance and irresponsibility. Only sex education, they insisted, could deal effectively with this deeper problem. Mary Roberts Smith spoke often to young men of the importance of sexual

20. Edward A. Ross, "The Significance of Increasing Divorce," *Century* 78 (1909): 150, quoted in O'Neill, *Divorce in the Progressive Era*, p. 181; Amos Warner, speaking in about 1895, as quoted in Mary Roberts Coolidge, "A Man's Job" (about 1912), Coolidge Papers; Coolidge, *Why Women Are So*, pp. 323–24; *Dictionary of American Biography*, s.v. "Amos Griswold Warner."

21. John C. Burnham, "The Progressive Era Revolution in American Attitudes toward Sex," *Journal of American History* 59 (March 1973): 885–908. See also David Pivar, *Purity Crusade: Sexual Morality and Social Control, 1868–1900* (Westport, Conn.: Greenwood Press, 1973), passim.

restraint. "Sex indulgence is not necessary to the health of men," she reassured them. "The time has come when men must learn to restrain themselves if they expect to keep clear of disease and to live happily after they are married."[22]

Conservatives attacked the social scientists and doctors who crusaded for sexual hygiene, arguing "if ever there was a system diabolically devised to injure our youth, and to make them voluptuaries, this is by far the most effective." They were not unrealistic in their fears. In an effort to educate Americans about sexual restraint, social scientists opened the door to a fundamentally different sexual attitude than the one they intended to promulgate.[23]

Forces of Change

Paradoxically, the same educational institutions that produced some of America's most articulate defenders of sexual reserve became, by the early twentieth century, bases for a revolution in sexual attitudes and behavior. In part, this institutional transformation had its roots in the passing of the pioneer phase of women's education. Before 1900, male college students, feeling devalued by the post– Civil War surge in female enrollment, pointedly shunned women students; while women students, trying to prove their academic seriousness, adopted a self-consciously stiff manner in their relations with men. At Cornell, which opened its doors to women in 1872, mutual antagonism segregated the sexes so effectively that sixteen years passed before the administration felt the need to hire a dean of women. By the turn of the century, however, this sexual antipathy was beginning to wane. Mary Roberts Smith, an early Cornell graduate, reported that college women were beginning to dress as well as other women of their social class, and that they were more fully accepted by their male classmates.[24]

As the center of student enrollment shifted from the small-town and the single-sex colleges to the generally more urban, coeducational universities, relations between the sexes gradually relaxed, and administrators found it increasingly difficult to regulate student conduct. The city, with its easy transportation, proliferating dance halls, theaters, and other

22. Mary Roberts Smith, "Facts for Young Men" (n.d.), Dane Coolidge Papers. See also these other speeches given by Smith, "A Man's Job" (n.d.), "The New Attack on the Social Evil" (1914), "Future of the Family" (n.d.), Coolidge Papers.

23. Burnham, "Progressive Era Revolution," pp. 903—04.

24. Charlotte W. Conable, *Women at Cornell: The Myth of Equal Education* (Ithaca, N.Y.: University of Cornell Press, 1977), pp. 101, 116– 17; Mary Roberts Smith [Coolidge], "Statistics of College and Non-College Women," *Publications of the American Statistical Association* 7 (March – June 1900): 1 – 26; Mary Roberts Coolidge, "The Social Value of Coeducation" (n.d.), Coolidge Papers.

centers of entertainment, acted as a solvent on the moral authority of the small-town communities from which most students still came. No longer did the face-to-face contacts of the small town or the omnipresent religious authority of the community church inhibit the young person. Nor did the traditional values of self-denial and austerity have the same power over students that they had had over their parents. The Wisconsin economist Simon Patten characterized the turn of the century as a time of transition from a "pain or deficit" economy to a "pleasure or surplus" economy. Because the cost of a college education was no longer the financial sacrifice it had been for the pioneer generation, students beginning college in the late 1890s were psychologically more prepared to explore the pleasures of their surroundings than earlier scholars had been. As Elsie Clews Parsons observed of the change taking place, "affairs of sex have always been controlled by [the] Elders, i.e. by those who least feel the impulses of sex," but the "modern economy" had created "more leisure in the lives of all younger persons and therefore more opportunity for self-direction in social relations."[25]

When a group of Bryn Mawr alumnae tried to discover how closely colleges and universities regulated the social life of their men and women students in 1900, they found tremendous variation, ranging "all the way from minute and detailed supervision to almost absolute freedom." Absolute freedom tended to preponderate at the urban universities, for in the cities administrators simply threw up their hands in despair over the impossibility of regulating the conduct of those students who did not live in dormitories. At Barnard, where "a majority of the students" lived off-campus, the college assumed "absolutely no responsibility" during the times students were "not actually present in university buildings."[26]

The pell-mell expansion of America's university system in the 1890s outdistanced in virtually every instance the ability of residential construction to keep pace with student enrollment. The University of Chicago was typical in having, as one historian has noted, "too many children for her handsomely made shoe." Every page of the student rosters in the Chicago register was "heavy with residential addresses far from the Quadrangles. Conversely, the paucity of addresses within the Quadrangles [indicated] how impossible it was to think of them as the center of all student life."[27]

The supervisory problems raised by attracting men and women to a large city, where community boardinghouses took up the slack, fell in the

25. Simon Patten, *The New Basis of Civilization* (New York: Macmillan, 1912), quoted in O'Neill, *Divorce in the Progressive Era,* p. 163; Elsie Clews Parsons, *Fear and Conventionality,* p. 206.

26. Louise Saunders, "Government of Women Students in Colleges and Universities," *Educational Review* 20 (December 1900): 475– 98.

27. Ibid.; Richard Storr, *Harper's University,* pp. 173– 74.

laps of the college and university deans. At Chicago, Marion Talbot had to respond to vocal complaints from the public about the loose living of undergraduates who entertained members of the opposite sex in their boardinghouse rooms. After consulting Harper, who deferred to her judgment, Talbot decreed that no rooms be advertised at the university except those "in houses or flats where a reception room is provided." If necessary, she declared, she was prepared to exercise "close scrutiny" over the living arrangements of the students. Talbot walked an ideological tightrope, determined to treat female students as independent women, yet constrained by Victorian conceptions of female virtue in deciding how much independence she was willing to permit.[28]

Student conduct at boardinghouses presented Talbot with only one problem among many. As dance halls proliferated in Chicago at the turn of the century, they drew more and more students searching for entertainment. Not only did the dance halls prove difficult to chaperone, they were widely considered by university officials and social reformers to be dangerous places, frequented by prostitutes and procurers "continually on the lookout for new victims." Official cries of alarm had little impact on student conduct, however, and only seemed to emphasize the growing gulf between the guardians of the old order and the heralders of the new.[29]

Not that greater prosperity and social freedom led directly to increased fornication. In fact, the trend among those entering college between about 1900 and 1910 appears to have been in the other direction. These men and women were less likely to engage in premarital intercourse than were those who had entered college before 1900. This drop in premarital coitus reflects the success of the campaign against venereal disease among educated people and suggests that greater sexual freedom meant, at least initially, greater sexual experimentation short of intercourse. After 1910,

---

28. "One Who Lives among Such Surroundings" to the Dean of Women, U. of C. (1903?), Marion Talbot Papers, University of Chicago Archives, Chicago, Illinois; Marion Talbot to William R. Harper, April 7, 1903, Talbot Papers. Talbot criticized the restrictions that women's colleges imposed on women students. See Marion Talbot, "Present Day Problems in the Education of Women," *Educational Review* 14 (October 1897): 248–58.

29. Talbot discussed difficulties over the dance halls in letters to her mother. See Talbot to Mamma, January 15, 1893, in which she reported recommending that the men and women students go together, dutch treat. See also Talbot to Mamma, November 1893, in which Talbot reported reproving women students for "spooning" [necking] in the dormitory: "I had to tell the girls next day that I was mortified to have Mrs. Palmer see anything so 'country' going on at the Beatrice!" For more on the proliferation of dance halls, see Lewis A. Erenberg, "Everybody's Doing It: The Pre–World War I Dance Craze, the Castles, and the Modern American Girl," *Feminist Studies* 3 (Fall 1975): 155–70; and for their association with vice, see Roy Lubove, "The Progressive and the Prostitute," *The Historian* 24 (May 1962): 323.

however, the rate of premarital intercourse began to climb steadily, especially among engaged couples.[30]

Young people did not need to go to college to escape parental supervision, of course. They could go to work, and increasingly large numbers of
working-class sons and daughters did so. Some historians have suggested
that changes in sexual attitudes and practices came first from the lower
classes. Even as the first generation of students were venturing forth on
the collegiate experiment, young men and women with more modest
financial resources were emigrating from foreign and rural farms to city
boardinghouses in the hope of finding factory, clerical, or sales work. The
moral danger posed by separation from their parents was much discussed
at the time. "No mother should permit her daughter to go to a strange city
unless she can provide the girl with funds to pay for board and room for a
month," wrote one concerned observer of working-class young women.
"The mother who recklessly allows her unskilled daughter to enter a
strange city armed with only a week's board and high hopes is guilty of
criminal neglect as the guardian of her child's future."[31]

The only solid evidence that remains of working-class sexual practices
comes from community studies of illegitimacy rates. These studies suggest that premarital intercourse, as evidenced by illegitimate births, was at
least twice as prevalent in the general population of the late nineteenth
century as it was among the well-educated middle class. Many middle-
class observers reported at the time that working-class men and women
appeared to feel freer about sex than did their more highly educated
contemporaries, and some of these observers even credited the lower
classes with inspiring the middle class to greater sexual enthusiasm.

30. G. V. Hamilton, who conducted a detailed study in the early 1920s of a hundred
married men and a hundred married women born before 1900, reported that of engaged
couples born before 1881, 50 percent were virgins at marriage. Of those born between 1881
and 1885, virginity rose to 62 percent. Of those born between 1886 and 1890, virginity rose
again to 67 percent. But of those after 1891, virginity plummeted to only 30 percent (G. V.
Hamilton, *A Research in Marriage* [New York: Boni, 1929], p. 383). Hamilton's subjects were
far more active sexually than were most of those from that era who have been studied.
Kinsey's figures on virginity, for instance, were over 70 percent for those born before 1900.
Kinsey et al., *Sexual Behavior in the Human Female*, p. 339.

31. Anna S. Richardson, *The Girl Who Earns Her Own Living* (New York, 1909), p. 282,
quoted in Sheila Rothman, *Woman's Proper Place: A History of Changing Ideals and Practices,
1870 to the Present* (New York: Basic Books, 1978), pp. 43 – 44. For work by historians who
argue that the sexual revolution began among the uneducated, see Daniel Scott Smith, "The
Dating of the American Sexual Revolution: Evidence and Interpretation," in Michael
Gordon, ed., *The American Family in Social-Historical Perspective*, pp. 426 – 38; and Edward
Shorter, *The Making of the Modern Family* (New York: Basic Books, 1975), pp. 80 – 119. In
contrast to those who argue that the major shift in sexual behavior in America took place
after 1920, as well as to those who push the revolution back at least to 1910, Smith argues that
it began in the late nineteenth century among the less educated.

Whether the lower class represented a vanguard of the sexual revolution, however, remains uncertain. Rising rates of illegitimacy may say more about the dislocation created by urban growth than about the personal liberation of young workers, especially young female workers. One gynecologist with a practice that included women patients from a variety of social and economic levels reported that, of his patients with premarital sexual experience, working-class women tended to have "brief coitus with disastrous results in pregnancy or venereal disease," while his college-educated patients tended to experiment with sex "for the most part without social obloquy or penalty" and to emphasize the "emotional experience" and "long time connection" they enjoyed with their sexual partners.[32]

Before historians can be confident in their identification of the socioeconomic source of the sexual revolution in the early twentieth century, they must examine not just practice but the meaning that was attached to practice. They must discover whether young women had children out of wedlock as a consequence of their own free choice and determination to gratify their sexual desires, or whether illegitimacy resulted as an unwanted by-product of a sexually exploitative situation. No genuine sexual revolution was possible until sex could be freely chosen by both parties, and few working-class women were in a sufficiently independent position to enjoy freedom of that kind.[33]

In some ways those at school enjoyed greater freedom than those at work simply because of the psychological independence that education fostered. Whereas working-class youths tended to work in sexually segregated occupations, where free and autonomous association between the sexes was often difficult to achieve, the university threw young women together with young men on an unprecedentedly equal footing. In the long run, the jostling in the halls and the easy familiarity among male and female students may have marked a more important change in sexual relations in America than did the rise in the rate of illegitimacy among lower-class youths. The university's celebration of the critical spirit, which encouraged skepticism of old dogma and therefore fostered a greater

32. Robert Latou Dickinson and Lura Beam, *The Single Woman: A Medical Study in Sex Education* (Baltimore: Williams and Wilkins, 1934), p. 425. Daniel Scott Smith provides evidence from community studies that illegitimacy rates ranged from 16 percent to 29 percent. About 30 percent of Kinsey's pre-1900, typically well-educated birth cohort reported premarital coitus. Smith, "The Dating of the American Sexual Revolution," p. 432. For observations of contemporaries, see W. I. Thomas, "The Adventitious Character of Women," p. 43; and Henry Seidel Canby, "Sex in Marriage in the Nineties," *Harper's* 169 (1934): 427–36.

33. For a critique of those who have called the working-class experience liberating for women, see Louise Tilly, Joan Scott, and Miriam Cohen, "Women's Work and European Fertility Patterns," *Journal of Interdisciplinary History* 6 (Winter 1976): 447–76.

frankness between the sexes, further fueled the students' psychological independence. Ironically, at the same time that higher education reinforced sexual repression by encouraging the cultivation of mental faculties and disparaging physical expression as evidence of a less elevated, even a less evolved, character, it was encouraging a critical attitude toward all received wisdom—including, inevitably, the idea that the life of the mind was in conflict with the life of the body.[34]

The tension between these competing academic ideals of self-control and self-expression produced a sometimes disjointed analysis of sexual identity in the work of social scientists whose careers spanned the decades on either side of 1900. Mary Roberts Smith, for instance, was still insisting as late as 1912, in her book *Why Women Are So,* on the need for women to hold men to a higher (that is, more feminine) standard of sexual morality. In the same book, however, she reported that the psychological differences between men and women had all but disappeared through the university's masculinization of women and its feminization of men. The occasional inconsistency in Smith's argument reflected not so much a muddled mind as an incomplete shift in emphasis from the polarized view of sexuality that had characterized her thinking in the early 1890s to a view that emphasized the similarities in sexual capacity between men and women. Whereas she had once believed that the achievement of mutual satisfaction in marriage depended on men's willingness to dampen their passion to correspond to female passionlessness, by 1912 she had come to see mutuality as a more desirable achievement, based on an evener distribution of sexual feeling than she had formerly thought possible.[35]

The shift in Smith's understanding of sex in this twenty-year period derived from the same urban, academic forces affecting all educated people, but experiences peculiar to her own life intensified the power of those forces. First, her training in sociology introduced her to the debates over human evolution that were raging at the turn of the century. While teaching under the direction of E. A. Ross in the 1890s, she began a study of Chinese immigration. Ross, who combined a populist dislike of "rich men and big bugs" with a fervent commitment to racial purity, regarded the Chinese as a lower order of human species and frequently called for an end to coolie immigration in speeches before labor leaders and other political groups. These speeches offended Jane Stanford, widow of founder Leland Stanford and the university's sole trustee. Stanford's fortune had been built on the backs of Oriental labor, and she did not wish to see this diligent labor supply cut short. When Ross refused a di-

34. Rothman, *Woman's Proper Place,* pp. 48–60. For the liberating effect of sexual frankness, see "Sex O'Clock in America," *Current Opinion,* vol. 55 (August 1913); and Agnes Repplier, "The Repeal of Reticence," *Atlantic Monthly* 103 (March 1914): 293–304.
35. Coolidge, *Why Women Are So,* pp. 342, 107, 301, 306–07.

rective in 1900 to temper his remarks, she fired him. The Stanford faculty, especially in the social sciences, rose to Ross's defense, denouncing what they saw as a serious attack upon academic freedom. Professor George Howard, lecturing to his class on the French Revolution, likened the Ross dismissal to the excesses of absolute monarchy, and he resigned in protest when the administration asked him to recant. Only pressure from her husband prevented Mary Roberts Smith from resigning too. Like Howard, Smith defended Ross out of feelings of friendship and a belief in academic freedom. She did not, however, accept his view of Chinese racial inferiority.[36]

The egalitarian roots of Smith's feminism were too deep for her to accept uncritically a charge of group inferiority. Her careful study of San Francisco's Chinese immigrants, together with her wide-ranging reading in the new psychological and sociological literature, made her increasingly suspicious of Ross's teachings. Impressed particularly by the work of John Dewey and W. I. Thomas, she adopted the functionalist belief in the plasticity of human nature and the relativity of cultural practices. *Chinese Immigration* [1909] remains today an important study of Chinese progress and achievement in America and a sensitive account of the cultural transformation that took place as a consequence of Chinese attempts to assimilate to American life. As Smith's feminism affected her understanding of race, so the growing relativism of her approach to race altered her understanding of sex. After completing her study of the Chinese, Smith embarked on her book *Why Women Are So*, in which she openly linked racial to sexual analysis. "Surely, if in so short a time the 'Heathen Chinese' can rise to be a progressive human being in our estimation," she observed, "it is not impossible that women may become social entities, whose acquired 'femininity' may be modifying faster than the carefully digested ideas of scientific observers."[37]

The second experience in Smith's life to affect her understanding of sex was the disintegration of her marriage. After more than a decade of struggling to make a place for herself in the academic world, while at the same time trying to accommodate herself to the expectations of her husband and her own Victorian ideals, she gave up in 1903 and surrendered to a nervous breakdown. Dismissed from Stanford, she was in-

---

36. Mary O. Furner, *Advocacy and Objectivity*, pp. 233–42.

37. Mary Roberts [Smith] Coolidge, *Chinese Immigration* (New York: Holt, 1909), pp. 423–58. Smith commented particularly on the rapidity of change among Chinese women (see pp. 437–40; Coolidge, *Why Women Are So*, p. 301. For the influence of the new work in psychology and sociology, see pp. 306–07.) Havelock Ellis, whose studies of sex influenced many American intellectuals, especially those living in Greenwich Village, does not appear to have shaped Coolidge's thinking. Perhaps his writings on women's periodicity soured her on all his work.

stitutionalized and divorced. Slowly, Smith fought her way back to mental health. Stanford president David Starr Jordan helped her secure funds to finish her study of the Chinese; she busied herself with San Francisco reform clubs; and in 1906 she married Dane Coolidge, a naturalist and writer fifteen years her junior. The change this marriage made in her understanding of conjugality can be seen in remarks she made to Clelia Duel Mosher in 1912. By this date Mosher had completed her medical education at the Johns Hopkins Medical School, had returned to Palo Alto, and had become the physician to the Stanford women students. Around 1910 she returned to the sex survey she had abandoned in the late 1890s and began soliciting answers once again. Mary Roberts Coolidge, who had remained Mosher's closest friend through the years, added an appendix to her original questionnaire, explaining her changed perspective on sex.

> In 1906 I married a second time and have been exceptionally happy and steadily improving in health ever since. My husband is an unusually considerate man; during the earlier months of marriage, intercourse was frequent—two or three times a week and as much desired by me as by him. After that, we formed the habit of about once a week, but if either is too tired or working very hard, it may occur only once or twice a month. My husband is a literary man and when he is doing hard brain work has very little desire for intercourse. Whenever he stops work he at once becomes as passionate as before.[38]

Coolidge had special reasons for revising her attitude toward sex. Her work in sociology had persuaded her of the plasticity of human nature. The warm reception afforded *Chinese Immigration* had given her a new sense of personal autonomy and worth. And a younger and more considerate husband had made her aware that sex could be a happy experience. But she was not alone in her new outlook. Other women who answered Mosher's survey after 1910, especially younger women, demonstrated a noticeably more positive attitude toward sex than had respondents in the 1890s. Something had happened to college-educated American women in general in the intervening years. Though many respondents continued to find greater spiritual fulfillment in sex than they did physical satisfaction, and though some insisted that truly superior people could do without sex entirely, most women answering Mosher's questionnaire after 1910 stressed the value of sex for its own sake. Unlike women in the 1890s, who tended to emphasize the procreative function of sex, these later subjects argued less often that coitus should be restricted to reproduction, and

38. Mosher Survey, case no. 2. David Starr Jordan to Robert S. Woodward [President of the Carnegie Institution], October 11, 1905, Coolidge Papers. Coolidge, "Clelia Duel Mosher," pp. 7–20.

Mary Roberts Smith Coolidge (ca. 1910)

they were more likely to say that sex was "physically necessary to the woman as well as the man for a complete life."[39]

The Sex Lives of 4,200 Women

The shift noted by Clelia Mosher received important confirmation, as well as further impetus, from two major surveys conducted before 1920 on the sexual practices and attitudes of 4,200 women. Katherine Bement Davis embarked on the first survey in 1918, after leaving her prison work to head John D. Rockefeller Jr.'s Bureau of Social Hygiene. Fearing she would have difficulty recruiting a large sample of respectable women for a study of sex, Davis enlisted prominent women in psychology and social work, including Helen Thompson Woolley and Jessie Taft, to legitimize the effort and help guide her. They all agreed on the need for a large-

39. Mosher Survey, case no. 17. See also cases 20, 29–32, 37–38, and 40–47. Of women responding in the 1890s, about 60 percent claimed reproduction to be the primary purpose of intercourse. Of women responding after 1910, only about 25 percent made that claim.

Dane Coolidge (ca. 1910)

scale sex survey, for despite all the literature about sexual attitudes and practices, little solid information existed about normal women. Without such knowledge the social reform movement to which they were all committed, including the abolition of prostitution and the eradication of venereal disease, could not be effectively advanced. They needed to demonstrate, on the one hand, that too much sex could be physically injurious, and, on the other, that women with proper sex education led happier, better-adjusted lives and were less likely to engage in premarital and extramarital sex than those who remained ignorant.[40]

Backed by Rockefeller, Davis and her staff mailed queries to 20,000 married and single women, selected from the membership lists of wom-

40. Katherine Bement Davis, *Factors in the Sex Life of Twenty-two Hundred Women* (New York: Harper and Bros., 1929), pp. vii– xvii. I have searched in vain for the original 2,220 questionnaires used in Davis's survey. Neither the Rockefeller Archive Center, which houses the papers of the Bureau of Social Hygiene, nor the Social Welfare History Archives, which houses the papers of the American Social Health Association, appears to have them.

en's clubs across the country and alumnae registers from women's colleges and coeducational universities. Because the alumnae responded in greater numbers and more promptly than did the noncollege women, and because the final sample was composed of the first 1,000 married and 1,200 unmarried respondents, college women comprised almost 70 percent of the group studied. All the alumnae had been out of college at least five years, and the average had completed their degrees around 1900. With an average age of thirty-seven years, the group as a whole represented women born about 1880 and reared before the turn of the century. Those who agreed to take part in the survey were mailed questionnaires that probed into their educational background, health, happiness, sex education, sexual experience before marriage, frequency of intercourse, tendency to masturbate, and homosexual experiences. Not only did participants in the survey complete the questionnaire, they inserted "additional sheets in order to give a fuller account of their experiences and an expression of their beliefs . . . , [adding] many thousands of pages of manuscript to be digested and treated."[41]

The study bore out a number of the reformers' expectations. Women who had received premarital sex instruction tended to adjust to marriage more easily than those without any. Women who had engaged in premarital intercourse tended to be less happy than those who had not. And though 74 percent of the respondents practiced some form of contraception, they did so to space their children rather than to avoid having them. To the surprise of many, however, other information derived from the survey cast serious doubt on some of the principal assumptions of the purity campaign.[42]

First, the study demonstrated that sex education did not necessarily temper eroticism. Of the 71 women who admitted having engaged in premarital intercourse, 70 percent had had sex education that included information about contraception, compared with about 50 percent of the entire group studied. Additional data collected a few years later suggested even more strongly that sex education could not be counted on to control sexual appetites. As Davis reported of these later results, "the highly erotic group had a much higher percentage of women who had received sex instruction *from responsible sources* before the age of fourteen." Second, contrary to popular belief, frequent intercourse appeared to have no

41. Ibid., p. xiii. Davis's survey was not published until 1929, and it has generally been used as evidence of sex in the 1920s, but since the questionnaires were distributed in 1918 to women who were out of college at least five years, and more typically sixteen years, the women studied clearly represent a pre-1920 population. Though publication was delayed, everyone in the social hygiene movement knew of it, and some of the results were published in journals in the early 1920s, for example, the *Journal of Social Hygiene*, the *Journal of Mental Hygiene*, and the *American Journal of Obstetrics and Gynecology*.

42. Davis, *Factors in the Sex Life of Twenty-two Hundred Women*, pp. 76–77, 58, 13–17.

deleterious effect on either health or reproductive capacity. Of the 81 women who experienced intercourse at least daily, the rate of pregnancy was consistently greater than among the total group. "There is nothing whatever in the material present to suggest in any way a relationship between marked frequency of intercourse and sterility—quite the contrary," admitted Davis. Third, the study showed that masturbation was not only far more widespread than had been generally thought, with rates of 40 percent for married women and 60 percent for unmarried, it did not seem to be inconsistent with good health or marital adjustment. In fact, it even seemed to be conducive to it. Finally, homosexuality proved to be astonishingly widespread. Fifty percent of the unmarried women and 30 percent of the married admitted to having intense emotional relationships with other women. For half of each group the relationship was "accompanied by mutual masturbation, contact of genital organs or other physical expressions recognized as sexual in character." The figures on homosexuality did not surprise Davis as much as some of the others did. Her wide experience in supervising women's prisons and her undergraduate career at Vassar had taught her "that the phenomena described in this study are much more widespread than is generally suspected, or than most administrators are willing to admit."[43]

The Davis study clearly demonstrated that women were more highly sexed than most people thought they could be. When cultural pressure or spiritual ideals blocked heterosexual expression, sexual feeling simply found expression in other ways. Though most people, including many guilt-ridden respondents, frowned on any form of sexual expression outside of marital intercourse as perverse, neither masturbation nor homosexuality appeared to have the serious physical or psychological consequences the public assumed they should have. Ironically, the Davis study, undertaken to serve the sexual hygiene movement, helped undermine it. Despite their moral commitment, investigators like Davis considered themselves scientists first and reformers second. As scientists they could not maintain their belief that people ought to behave in a particular way in the face of overwhelming evidence that well-educated, middle-class women like themselves often behaved very differently.

The Davis survey helped persuade one other investigator to contribute to the nascent field of sex research. Dr. Robert Latou Dickinson, a Brooklyn gynecologist and the country's foremost medical advocate of contraception, had been keeping meticulous records on his patients for over thirty years when Davis sent out her questionnaires in 1918. Throughout his career, Dickinson had worked to maintain family stability by trying to improve his patients' understanding of sexual relations.

43. Ibid., pp. xvii, 19, 26, 147, 247, 298, and 245.

With several thousand case histories behind him, he now believed he was prepared to aid a wider audience.[44]

Like other reform-minded men and women of the early twentieth century, Dickinson wanted to preserve the traditional values of the Anglo-Saxon background from which he came. His professional training and medical experience in an urban setting persuaded him, however, that traditional values could be preserved only if misinformation was corrected and harmful habits altered. To identify misinformation and harmful habits, Dickinson kept careful records of his patients with the help of index cards stamped with anatomical outlines on which he could mark any pathological structures found on examination. Over the years he kept notes on the attitudes, practices, and physical changes of his patients, and by 1918 he had many records that extended back thirty years.[45]

A frank and positive approach to sex, Dickinson believed, provided the key to marital happiness. Though most doctors insisted that the separation of sex from procreation was both unnatural and immoral, Dickinson advised his patients to enjoy sex for its own sake. He argued that children should be spaced several years apart; and even though it was illegal to dispense contraceptive information for birth control in New York, he did his best to provide all of his married patients with the contraceptive means to plan their children. Contraceptive techniques changed little between the 1890s and 1920. Condoms were more often used, but until Margaret Sanger and other birth controllers like Dickinson succeeded in making diaphragms available to women in large numbers after 1920, women continued to depend predominantly on withdrawal and douching for protection.[46]

Dickinson began medical practice with the Victorian view that women were spiritual creatures whose sexual feelings were not typically awakened until marriage. A contrast existed, however, between what conventional wisdom dictated and what he observed in his practice.

44. An excellent sketch of Dickinson and a discussion of Davis's part in interesting him in sex research appears in Reed, *From Private Vice to Public Virtue*, pp. 143– 80.

45. Ibid., pp. 155– 66. Besides writing extensively on gynecological subjects, Dickinson wrote many articles on dress reform, physical exercise, and sex education. For an example of Dickinson's blend of liberalism and moral rectitude, see Robert Latou Dickinson, "Bicycling for Women from the Standpoint of the Gynecologist," *American Journal of Obstetrics* 31 (January 1895): 24– 37, which urged bicycling for women but carefully instructed the reader as to the proper position she should assume on the bicycle seat to avoid masturbation.

46. Reed, *From Private Vice to Public Virtue*, pp. 148, 123– 25. Dickinson's faith in the meliorative potential of science led him not only to play a part in the birth control movement but also to assume a strongly interventionist role as a physician. Few physicians today would induce labor as readily as Dickinson did. See Robert Latou Dickinson and Lura Beam, *A Thousand Marriages: A Medical Study of Sex Adjustment* (Baltimore: Williams and Wilkins, 1931), pp. 459– 60. For a discussion of the federal and state legal restrictions placed on dispensing contraceptives, see David Kennedy, *Birth Control in America*, pp. 218– 71.

Though he firmly believed, for instance, that nice girls did not become pregnant, he reported of one patient early in his practice: "Pregnant, have not asked particulars, I would never have believed it of this girl. My mother often praised her." Nor was this patient unique. In the 1890s about 8 percent of Dickinson's single patients engaged in intercourse, and by 1918 the figure had risen to 18 percent. Perhaps because he practiced in an urban area, Dickinson discovered a higher level of illicit behavior among his patients than the 7 percent rate Davis found in her nationwide sample.[47]

Experience also modified Dickinson's view of masturbation and homosexuality. He began his career believing with Havelock Ellis that "masturbation, when practiced in excess before the age of puberty, has led . . . to an aversion for normal coitus in later life . . . owing to the physical sexual feeling having been trained into a foreign channel." Over the years, however, he found that at least 75 percent of his patients practiced masturbation without seeming to harm their prospects for marital adjustment. Among his single patients, homosexuality, which he at first failed to notice, even among patients who were living together, represented, he gradually realized, a widespread practice. Though Dickinson never abandoned his view that doctors should shape behavior, he developed a much more relaxed attitude toward sex as he grew older and more experienced.[48]

Reviewing his case histories in the 1920s, Dickinson realized, perhaps a little ruefully, that his lifelong commitment to frankness had led in directions he had hardly anticipated. "Our young people . . . regard autoeroticism as natural," he observed. "The removal of taboo on sex writings and sex curiosity has discovered to the young woman that autoeroticism is quite general, and that petting arouses thrills or passion in others besides herself." Though Dickinson continued to urge young, unmarried women to let men "make the advances" and to avoid either heavy petting or intercourse, he sometimes felt that he was whistling in the wind. "In the four cases in which the doctor's opinion about coitus was asked beforehand," he reported of one group of single-women patients, "the doctor advised against it, and two women did not take the contemplated step then, but took it later with some other man. The other two asked

47. Dickinson and Beam, *Single Woman,* pp. 62, 4, 430. Davis, *Factors in the Sex Life of Twenty-two Hundred Women,* p. xviii.

48. Robert Latou Dickinson, "Hypertrophies of the Labia Minora and Their Significance," *American Gynecology* 1 (September 1902): 252–53 (quoting Ellis from *Auto-Erotism* [1901], pp. 171, 186), quoted in Reed, *From Private Vice to Public Virtue,* p. 160. Dickinson and Beam, *Single Woman,* pp. 250, 214. By 1930, Dickinson had lost much of his former certainty about what women were really like. "The burden of history hinders the physiological measurement of woman's native sexual endowment" (Dickinson and Beam, *A Thousand Marriages,* p. 380).

for contraceptive information, which was refused." As with Davis, so with Dickinson, science had a corrosive effect on the very values he sought to defend. In noting the disparity between conventional wisdom and actual behavior, he gave legitimacy to the latter; and in dissociating sex from reproduction within marriage, he opened the possibility for sex outside of marriage.[49]

Sex and the Sex Researchers

Well before the sexual revolution of the 1920s, with its flappers, Fords, and diaphragms, educated American women had fundamentally altered their attitudes toward sex. Women rarely complained any longer that sex made them nervous. Rather, they were beginning to speak openly of their own feelings about sex and of its importance to them apart from its reproductive function. This newfound acceptance stemmed, first, from the frankness made necessary by the campaign for sexual hygiene and, second, from men's and women's changing views of sexual identity.

As Mary Roberts Coolidge explained in *Why Women Are So*, qualities once identified exclusively with one sex were increasingly being claimed by members of the other. Emotionalism, for instance, long regarded as the distinctive mark of femininity, had risen to new heights of psychological prestige among younger researchers. "There is a consensus of opinion among modern psychologists and sociologists," Coolidge wrote, "in placing higher value upon the mental quality [emotion] which was not long ago held to establish women's inferiority." Conversely, reason, traditionally associated with male achievement, no longer held the preeminent position among psychic features it had once enjoyed, both because emotionalism was now vying with it for that position, and because the opening of higher education to women had made rationalism available to both sexes. The blurring of sexual identification that resulted from this cross-fertilization of psychic traits was reflected in the dwindling references to energy conservation in discussions of sex. Feeling less social pressure to achieve a rigidly prescribed set of psychic qualities, men and women could afford to be more relaxed than they formerly had been in the way they behaved sexually. Because society no longer viewed women's sexual functions as their "only really useful contribution," women could accept sexuality more easily. Because society no longer imposed so much pressure on men to dominate their social and economic surroundings, men lost some of their former fascination with the displays of sexual prowess suggested by either sexual abstinence or sexual athleticism.[50]

49. Dickinson and Beam, *Single Woman*, pp. 248, 72–73, 171.
50. Coolidge, *Why Women Are So*, pp. 299, 306–07, 97.

Coolidge predicted that the blurring of gender identification would lead to better marriages. "It would be bold, perhaps, to say that one of the best remedies for domestic infidelity is the feminization of men and the masculinization of women; but if men would be domesticated just a little more, and if women could be persuaded to be a little less feminine in their minds, marriage would be more practicable and the family life somewhat nearer the ideal." In the past century "men were as much too 'masculine' as women were too 'feminine' for the uses of modern life, and the gulf between them made the adjustment of marriage unduly difficult, besides reacting injuriously on the children." Coolidge emphasized that the elimination of the Victorian marital "gulf" depended on a woman's having "an occupational activity of her own choosing" and "a generous attitude toward this on the part of the man." By 1912 Coolidge was secure in her own professional achievements, secure enough to enjoy domestic work when she chose to do it. Marriage therefore no longer seemed so oppressive to her and she was better able to enjoy the physical side of it.[51]

Mary Roberts Coolidge made the achievement of sexual utopia sound easier than it proved to be in the lives of many other social scientists of her generation. The revolution in values that brought her greater personal freedom and happiness produced tremendous personal conflict for many others. However repressive Victorian society may have been, however fervently intellectuals may have fought its dictates, many people found undergoing a mid-life shift of fundamental values to be profoundly disorienting. For women like Jessie Taft, whose closest emotional ties as an adult were with other women, the sexual revolution raised more problems than it solved. Having grown up in a society that sanctioned strong emotional ties between women, and having found greater acceptance and companionship among women than among men, many highly educated women preferred living with other women to marriage. Social scientists' revelation of widespread homosexuality allayed to some degree the guilt produced by the failure of these women to meet society's domestic expectations. But the sexual revolution's tendency toward a more enthusiastic heterosexuality more than canceled out this effect by making the expression of affection between women significantly more difficult than it had been before the age of frankness.[52]

51. Ibid., pp. 347, 345. In urging occupational opportunity, Coolidge was quoting W. I. Thomas, who strongly supported women's working, both for themselves and for their families.

52. The close, affective ties that were possible, and even common, among nineteenth-century women are discussed in Carroll Smith-Rosenberg, "The Female World of Love and Ritual," *Signs* 1 (Autumn 1975): 1 – 29. The dislocating impact of the dissolution of these ties in the twentieth century is discussed in Jessie Bernard, "Homosociality and Female Depression," *Journal of Social Issues* 32 (1976): 213 – 35.

Not only homosexual but heterosexual women suffered under the sexual revolution. Helen Thompson Woolley, reared in the era of Victorian reticence but committed throughout her adult life to the precepts of scientific openness, could never wholly accept the new freedom in sex. She campaigned for birth control, but never discussed sex with her daughters. She applauded frankness in the new woman, but never undressed before her husband. She fought for female autonomy and independence, but suffered a nervous breakdown when her husband left her. Woolley was caught in the middle of a cultural shift that she helped further without being fully able to join.[53]

Clelia Mosher was caught even more painfully than either Taft or Woolley in the dislocation of sexual change. Both intensely romantic and coldly rational, she was a psychological cripple most of her life. Scornful of romantic feeling, Mosher could express passionate feeling only in correspondence with an imaginary friend. Unsure of herself as a scientist, she never finished most of her scientific work. A strong believer in the woman's movement, she never participated actively in it. Apart from Mary Roberts Coolidge she had no friends. No one else would put up with Mosher's difficult, secretive, aloof personality. For Mosher sexual feeling was something to be methodically studied in others but never accepted in herself.[54]

If inhibition often spelled disaster in an age of greater sexual enthusiasm, the loss of inhibition generated its own liabilities. Elsie Clews Parsons, perhaps more than any other social scientist, rejoiced in the openness about sex. She castigated the "Elders" for their suppression of the young; she campaigned for "trial marriage" and birth control; and she insisted that the issue of mating be kept separate from that of parenthood. But more than other sexual enthusiasts she recognized the dangers inherent in the celebration of sex. "Far more will be expected of sex," she predicted, "when it is left free to express itself, than under any repressive system."[55]

53. Eleanor Fowler [Woolley's elder daughter] to the author, July 20, 1976. At a conference on sex problems, sponsored by the National Research Council in 1921, Woolley urged that the NRC sponsor research on birth control, but chairman Robert Yerkes ruled out such research on the grounds that the NRC had decided to "limit ourselves to fundamental research and avoid anything of a controversial nature, as for example, birth control." "Minutes of the Conference on Sex Problems, National Research Council, October 28, 1921," Robert Yerkes Papers, Historical Division, Medical Library, Yale University.

54. For a fuller account of Mosher's personal life and psychological struggles, see Kathryn Allamong Jacob, "Dr. Clelia Mosher: A Victorian Doctor Battles the 'Scientific' Sexual Myths" (paper delivered at the Organization of American Historians, Detroit, Mich., April 3, 1981), pp. 12– 14.

55. Parsons, *Fear and Conventionality*, p. 212. See also Elsie Clews Parsons, "Sex and the Elders," *New Review* 3 (May 1915): 8– 10; idem, "When Mating and Parenthood Are

Charlotte Perkins Gilman worried that sexual expression would bring disappointment of another kind. Society was not ready, she realized two decades after writing *Women and Economics*, to allow women full personal independence. All that had changed since the 1890s, when sex had been woman's only valued social function, was that now sex referred not only to woman's reproductive power but also to her sensual qualities. Women were still being identified and therefore limited by their natural functions. Emphasis on sexual outlet was robbing women of the opportunity, for which the woman's movement had fought so long and hard, for women to realize themselves as free and autonomous human beings, transcending the natural order and shaping it to a more humane vision. Gilman was right. Americans' newfound enthusiasm for sexual openness obscured the fact that women remained a dependent class and that sex was a badge of that dependence. What Gilman did not see, however, was that the revolution in the understanding of male and female sexuality which took place between about 1900 and 1920 gave women something that was essential to their eventual liberation: a broader conception of their own physical needs and a greater confidence in their ability to control their physical destiny.[56]

Theoretically Distinguished," *International Journal of Ethics* 26 (January 1916): 207–16.

56. Charlotte Perkins Gilman, "Sex and Race Progess," in V. F. Calverton and S. D. Schmalhausen, eds., *Sex in Civilization* (New York: MacCaulay, 1929), pp. 109–26.

8 *Beyond Separate Spheres*

Throughout the Progressive era, the Victorian conception of sexual polarity maintained its hold on the popular imagination, while dissident work on sexual identity lay largely unnoticed in dissertations and scholarly journals. Not even feminists found much to recommend in the new view of woman's nature advanced by the young Turks in sociology, psychology, and anthropology. To women active in the settlement houses, suffrage campaigns, temperance unions, and consumer leagues, the traditional ideology of female exceptionalism provided a more satisfying self-portrait than did the skeptical analysis of the new social scientists. The psychologists' study of fatigue, which undermined faith in women's frailty, held no appeal for women battling for protective labor legislation. The sociologists' belief in the plasticity of sex roles did not interest women who were basing the suffrage campaign on women's special aptitude for housekeeping. The anthropologists' criticism of civilization's claim to moral superiority seemed absurd to those women arguing in favor of the female's special claim to that superiority.[1]

Yet the impact of university dissidents on popular thinking about sex steadily broadened, as an ever greater portion of American youth attended college and was introduced to the critical spirit of the new social sciences. Between 1900 and 1930, college and university attendance tripled, growing from 238,000 in 1900 to 1,101,000 in 1930. A few of these students went on to become social scientists and to legitimize in their textbooks, written to service the burgeoning college population, the originally iconoclastic notions of their mentors. However, most of the college students infected by the university's more open attitude toward sexual

---

1. When Josephine Goldmark of the Consumers' League prepared the sociological evidence for Louis Brandeis's famous brief in *Muller* v. *Oregon* (1908), which tested Oregon's ten-hour law for women, she emphasized older medical arguments about the strict limits on energy available to women and made only passing reference to the newer, more skeptical work in psychology, discussed here in chapter 4. See Josephine Goldmark, *Fatigue and Efficiency: A Study in Industry* (New York: Russell Sage Foundation, 1912), pp. 9–42.

identity promoted the new view in less formal ways. In the obscurity of their offices, kitchens, and bedrooms, these anonymous graduates chafed under the constraints of old precepts even as they often tried to fulfill traditional expectations. For no group was the chafing more painful than for the women graduates who abandoned plans for a career in favor of marriage and motherhood. The conflict they felt between the sense of intellectual independence and personal autonomy fostered by their university training, and the dependence and selflessness demanded of them as wives and mothers, made it difficult to adjust to the domestic roles they had chosen. Even those who tried could never hide from their children a certain sense of loss.[2]

Emily Fogg Mead, a classmate of Helen Thompson Woolley at the University of Chicago, was one such conflict-ridden person. Like Helen Thompson, Emily Fogg grew up in Chicago and came to the new university thrilled by its promise of intellectual and personal freedom. After graduation in 1897, she stayed on to do graduate work in sociology, inspired by Thorstein Veblen and W. I. Thomas to study immigrant acculturation. In one of her courses she met economics graduate student Edward Mead, and in 1900, after spending a year as a fellow at Bryn Mawr and another at the University of Pennsylvania, she married him and settled in Philadelphia, where he became a professor at the Wharton School. Though Emily Fogg Mead continued working on her dissertation after her marriage, motherhood and the social reform work of her community gradually supplanted her academic ambitions. Somewhere in the midst of bearing five children and rearing four to maturity, she realized that she could never fully attain her dream of escaping Victorian society's domestic expectations for women. Yet in raising her children, especially her eldest, Margaret, she helped make it a little easier for a later generation to make that escape.[3]

Most historians have argued that World War I and the passage of the Nineteenth Amendment marked the beginning of a long decline in feminist enthusiasm. But to Margaret Mead's generation, those entering college in 1920, the trend toward the achievement of a fuller life for women seemed irreversible. It is true that Mead and many of her contem-

2. Ben Wattenberg, *The Statistical History of the United States* (New York: Basic Books, 1970), p. 383. For a more extended discussion of the rapid growth of student enrollment in colleges and universities between 1900 and 1930 and the effect of that expansion on American life, see Paula Fass, *The Damned and the Beautiful: American Youth in the 1920s* (New York: Oxford, 1977), pp. 127–29.

3. Margaret Mead, *Blackberry Winter: My Early Years* (New York: Simon and Schuster, 1972), pp. 23–79; "Mrs. Emily Mead, A Sociologist," *New York Times,* February 23, 1950, p. 27, col. 2; *General Register of the University of Chicago,* 1892–1902, pp. 139–41.

poraries did not like to be identified as feminists. To them the feminist label represented the strident, sometimes petty, and often divisive anger of their mothers' generation. Taking for granted their mothers' gains, they deplored the sexual antagonism that had so often been the price of those gains. For themselves they sought a greater measure of sexual accommodation. They rejected the public side of feminism, with its ideology of female uniqueness and its organizational focus on female interests; but they never doubted the private side of the feminist impulse— the desire for personal autonomy and self-fulfillment. The principal difference between the feminism of Emily Mead and that of her daughter was that the daughter's struggle was far more self-consciously personal than her mother's ever dared to be. In being personalized, this new struggle sacrificed much of the organizational momentum that the prior generation had so carefully built, but at the same time it opened new avenues never before explored. For Margaret Mead it was possible to consider questions of personal identity that her mother would have considered irrelevant in the face of more pressing issues of family responsibility and social need.[4]

Like her mother, Margaret Mead entered graduate school. Unlike her mother she stayed. By 1920 graduate attendance for women was no longer the novelty it had been in the 1890s, nor was the idea that women should have a career so new a thought. Furthermore, the enthusiasm for reform that had infected students, especially women students, at the turn of the century had largely dissipated by the twenties, leaving women less ambivalent about their scholarly and scientific ambitions than earlier women students had been. Social settlements had failed to eradicate the wretchedness of urban life. The Consumers' League had failed to eliminate child labor. The Women's Trade Union League had made little progress in unionizing women workers. In retrospect, the fervent devotion to charitable societies and reform organizations that had been so important a part of Emily Mead's life struck her daughter as a little

4. Mead, *Blackberry Winter*, p. 54. For evidence of contemporary optimism about women's progress, see Frederick Lewis Allen, *Only Yesterday*, pp. 95– 96; Virginia Collier, *Marriage and Careers: A Study of One Hundred Women Who Are Wives, Mothers, Homemakers, and Professional Workers* (New York: The Bureau of Vocational Information, 1926), pp. 9– 121; Leta Hollingworth, "A New Woman in the Making" (typescript), Hollingworth Papers, University of Nebraska; and Frank Stricker, "Cookbooks and Law Books: The Hidden History of Career Women in Twentieth-Century America," *Journal of Social History* 10 (Fall 1976): 1– 19. For discussions of the decline in feminism after 1920, see William O'Neill, *Everyone Was Brave: A History of Feminism in America* (Chicago: Quadrangle, 1969), pp. 264– 359; William Chafe, *The American Woman*, pp. 3– 22. For a general review of the ways in which women's life in the 1920s has been treated, see Estelle Freedman, "The New Woman: Changing Views of Women in the 1920s," *Journal of American History* 61 (September 1974): 372– 93.

quixotic. The rapid expansion of American universities in the 1920s contributed to the trend among young women away from reform and toward professionalism. The sudden growth of research activity provided women with unprecedented opportunities not only for training in research but also for employment. While faculty appointments for men doubled between 1910 and 1930, appointments for women more than tripled.[5]

Apart from her disenchantment with reform efforts and her attraction to science, Margaret found it easier than her mother had to complete graduate school, because she had a very different attitude toward sexuality. Though Emily Mead fought for women's rights in organizations ranging from the American Association of University Women to the Women's Trade Union League, in her private life she accepted a traditional role. Part of that role prompted her to welcome children as they came, without making any effort to time their appearance. Margaret, a beneficiary of the much more open attitude toward sex that prevailed during the time of her own upbringing, protected her professional ambitions by mastering the literature on the mechanics of sex and contraception well before her marriage. Though, like her mother, she married in graduate school, she had no children for many years.[6]

Institutional, social, and intellectual changes divided those educated at the turn of the century from those educated after World War I, yet the younger generation was still very much the product of the older one, and the insights of social scientists trained after 1920 were firmly and deeply rooted in the ideas and experiences of the preceding generation. It was Margaret Mead's generation that made social science popular in America and persuaded the public to assume a more open attitude toward sexual identity and sex roles, but it was Emily Mead's generation that had laid the foundation for that later achievement.

Coming of Age in Hammonton, New Jersey

From the time Margaret was a year old until she was nine, her family spent each spring and fall in Hammonton, New Jersey. Emily Mead selected Hammonton because of the large number of immigrant Italians living

5. Mead, *Blackberry Winter*, p. 28; William O'Neill, ed., *The Woman Movement: Feminism in the United States and England* (Chicago: Quadrangle, 1971), pp. 89– 97. University expansion and its effect on women is discussed in Jonathan Cole, *Fair Science: Women in the Scientific Community* (New York: Free Press, 1979), pp. 218– 23; A. Caswell Ellis, "Preliminary Report of Committee W, On Status of Women in College and University Faculties," *Bulletin of the American Association of University Professors* 7 (October 1921): 21– 32. Figures for faculty expansion are given in Wattenberg, *Statistical History of the United States*, p. 383.
6. Mead, *Blackberry Winter*, pp. 19, 103, 116– 17.

there, whom she could study for her dissertation. Building on the work she had already done at Chicago, and drawing new inspiration from Franz Boas, with whom she corresponded, she interviewed and tested her immigrant neighbors. If Emily Mead chose Hammonton because of her own interests, she was determined that the experience of living there would be educational for her children as well. When her children complained of the odd behavior of the playmates she found for them, she tried to make them understand why people behave in different ways. Margaret later remembered her mother's telling her that the neighborhood children acted as they did, "not because of differences in the color of [their] skin or the shape of [their] heads," but because of "their life experience and the life experience of their ancestors."[7]

Margaret absorbed her mother's critical spirit, but she sometimes struggled against her strict feminist principles: "I wanted to wear a hat with ribbons and fluffy petticoats instead of the sensible bloomers that very advanced mothers put on their daughters so they could climb trees." In her moments of thwarted femininity Margaret turned to her paternal grandmother, who lived with the Meads when she was growing up and whom she believed to be less filled with "feminist aggrievement" than her mother seemed to be. Premature widowhood had limited Grandmother Mead to only one pregnancy, and Margaret later conceded that "had she borne five children and had [as] little opportunity to see her special gifts and training" as Emily Mead had, she might have been more resentful than she was. Not so frustrated as her daughter-in-law, Grandmother Mead took a less stern view of feminist discipline. But her own personal achievements set a strict limit on how far Margaret could deviate from her mother's ideals. Grandmother Mead, too, had been to college, and she had supported herself and her only child, Edward, after becoming a widow. For Margaret there was not much choice. Within the context set by her grandmother and her mother, she learned that, whether one was happily feminine or resentfully feminine, a girl was expected to develop her mind.[8]

Her father's experience as part of the first generation of professional social scientists reinforced, in a very different way, this impulse toward intellectual fulfillment. Edward Mead, like so many other academic men of his era, often doubted the legitimacy of his social role. In part, his doubt derived from the economic and social uncertainty implicit in being part of a new academic profession at a time when business success still represented the most prestigious attainment in American life. But his doubt had a significant sexual component as well. "It seems to me that in some

7. Ibid., pp. 3, 14, 35, 73, 3; Emily Mead to Franz Boas, August 19, 1905, Boas Papers, American Philosophical Library, Philadelphia, Pennsylvania.
8. Mead, *Blackberry Winter*, pp. 20, 45– 54, 61.

Emily Fogg Mead with her daughter Margaret (1905)

way he thought of purely intellectual endeavor as feminine," Margaret later recalled. Edward Mead's linking of femininity with intellect, together with his wife's feelings of intellectual frustration, persuaded Margaret that the life of the intellectual was legitimately a feminine one, but one which, to be fully realized, must be pursued as a professional, not as an amateur.[9]

Edward Mead encouraged intellectual ambition in his oldest child, but financial reverses on the eve of her departure for college seriously undermined his commitment to her higher education. To the Mead women, being barred from college was equivalent to being barred from becoming completely human; so Margaret went to college. Not, to be sure, to Wellesley, Bryn Mawr, or Chicago, where her mother had studied, but to her father's college, DePauw. She left for Indiana with images of the great openness and freedom that her parents had always taught her the West

9. Ibid., pp. 40–44, 54, 2.

represented. In a year she returned, bitterly denouncing the anti-intellectualism and antidemocratic atmosphere of an institution dominated by sororities and fraternities. Had her mother's conscientious schooling in the evils of prejudice not already penetrated her consciousness in childhood, the rejection she suffered from the sorority of her choice was enough to convince her of bigotry's poison. For her sophomore year she transferred to Barnard College.[10]

Barnard

Barnard had always prided itself on its cosmopolitan character, but never more so than in the 1920s when New York, from Greenwich Village to Harlem, was afire with cultural excitement. Whereas her mother had been absorbed by reform, Margaret, in common with most of the students she met, was absorbed by her own intellectual and artistic growth. She read Freud and Edna St. Vincent Millay; she went constantly to the theater; she worried over her friends' love affairs; and she sought to define herself in the intellectual world. Barnard's avant-garde curriculum helped shape that definition for her. While other women's colleges still clung to the classics as the mark of a college education, Barnard had just decided to make Greek an elective and to require courses in psychology, economics, and sociology instead. Having been introduced to sociology by her mother and to economics by her father, Margaret did particularly well in these courses and decided that her intellectual self-definition would be a social scientific one.[11]

No college in the country, including Columbia, provided better undergraduate training in the social sciences than Barnard did in 1920. As part of its effort to reform its curriculum, Barnard decided to propose a new course of study in the social sciences that would both integrate the courses already offered and add further courses to that core. Students interested in one field would be asked to select some of their classes from a variety of other, related fields. Franz Boas had been trying to persuade Columbia to integrate its work in the social sciences for a number of years, but his efforts had fallen on the deaf ears of Columbia's highly autonomous, and ever more self-consciously specialized, social science disciplines. The autonomy and isolation of Columbia's departments worked to the detriment of small fields like anthropology. "The quality of the Columbia students is on the whole not as good as I would like to see it," Boas complained to

10. Ibid., pp. 34– 37, 86– 88, 100– 01.
11. Ibid., pp. 102– 11; Elaine Kendall, *Peculiar Institutions: An Informal History of the Seven Sister Colleges* (New York: Putnam's Sons, 1975), pp. 161, and 156– 63; Barnard College, *Barnard College Announcement,* 1920– 1921, pp. 54– 55. Barnard required 3 points of psychology and 6 points of economics and social science for graduation. It was also alone among women's colleges in having a department of anthropology. See Barnard College, "Gladys A. Reichard" (1956), pp. 5– 6, Barnard Archives, Barnard College, New York, New York.

President Nicholas Murray Butler. "I think it is largely due to the fact that a large percentage of the Columbia students prepare for professional work, and very few of the better class find time for an isolated subject such as anthropology." Boas much preferred teaching at Barnard, where the interest in preparing for the professional schools was less pronounced and where students were more inclined to take courses out of simple curiosity and interest. In contrast to his Columbia undergraduates, Boas found that "the Barnard students are interested in the subject, intelligent, and take hold of it in a satisfactory way."[12]

World War I contributed to Barnard's influence in the social sciences in unanticipated ways. Henry Hollingworth had taught psychology at Barnard since 1909 and was an important force in making psychology a requirement for graduation, but his importance was augmented still further when Columbia fired his mentor, James McKeen Cattell, for antiwar activities. Cattell's dismissal left psychology on Morningside Heights without the dominating leadership that he had exercised for a generation and thereby heightened the influence of his former students in their respective institutions. In Hollingworth's case, this meant that the environmental and feminist side of psychology no longer operated under Cattell's antienvironmental and antifeminist attitudes.[13]

Sociology at Barnard gained even more than psychology did as a consequence of the war. Sociology had long been an afterthought of the parent department at Columbia, dating back to the 1890s, when Franklin Giddings was given a joint appointment at Columbia and Barnard. For years one of the foremost leaders in sociology, Giddings was an "intellectual casualty" of World War I. Obsessed with anti-Germanism, and, after 1918, with anti-Bolshevism, Giddings gave lectures that became diatribes against his pet hatreds. Gradually he withdrew from teaching at Barnard. When Barnard decided to expand its work in social science, it turned not to Giddings but to Giddings's student, William Ogburn, to head the department of economics and sociology and to build up its sociology curriculum. Ogburn quickly gained a reputation for being a leading and progressive force in sociology.[14]

For very different, war-related reasons, anthropology at Barnard also

12. Barnard College, "Report of the Committee on Instruction to the President and Faculty of Barnard College" (December 1917), Barnard Archives; Franz Boas to Nicholas Murray Butler, November 26, 1917, Columbia University Central Files, Columbia University, New York, New York.

13. On the Cattell case, see Carol S. Gruber, *Mars and Minerva: World War I and the Uses of Higher Learning in America* (Baton Rouge: Louisiana State University Press, 1975), pp. 187–206.

14. Barnes, ed., *Introduction to the History of Sociology*, pp. 199–200; Don Martindale, *The Nature and Types of Sociological Theory*, pp. 324–27. Also teaching in the revamped department of economics and social sciences was Emilie Hutchinson, who conducted a valuable study in the twenties of women Ph.D.'s. See Hutchinson, *Woman and the Ph.D.*, passim.

made major advances during the war. Anthropology, like sociology, had been an afterthought of the Columbia parent department since the 1890s. For most of that time Boas had relegated the teaching of the single introductory course at Barnard to an assistant. Beginning in 1909, he had started teaching one term of the course himself, but the bulk of his teaching time was devoted to Columbia college and graduate school. By 1917, however, relations between Boas and Columbia's President Butler cooled because of Boas's vigorous opposition to the war and his growing support of socialism. More widely liked than Cattell, Boas was never fired. But his antiwar utterances inspired numerous irate letters to Butler from students and trustees who wanted Boas ousted, and they therefore clearly undercut his position at Columbia. First, in 1918, he lost his assistant in anthropology and had to teach both the Columbia and Barnard anthropology courses alone. Then, the following year, he ceased teaching on the undergraduate level at Columbia and confined all his undergraduate teaching to Barnard. The arrangement appears to have been mutually satisfactory. Butler was glad to minimize Boas's contact with Columbia undergraduates, and Boas was glad to focus his under-graduate teaching on students he found more sympathetic to his work and to his independent views.[15]

The attraction of Barnard students to the social sciences in the 1920s had much to do with the politics of World War I and the faculty displace-ment that resulted from it. Columbia under Nicholas Murray Butler had very conservative notions about the kind of faculty to which it was willing to expose its impressionable undergraduates. Barnard, to its great credit, cared more about excellence than it did about patriotic fervor. The training it gave its students in the social sciences reflected that attitude.

Psychology and Mental Capacity

In the three years she spent at Barnard, Margaret Mead dabbled in each of the social sciences, committing herself first to psychology, then to sociology, and only at the end to anthropology. She was "deeply bored" by

15. Columbia University, *Columbia University Catalogue,* 1916–1920; Barnard College, *Announcement,* 1909–20. The Columbia University Central Files include numerous letters from irate students and trustees to Nicholas Murray Butler about Boas's antiwar utterances. (See, for example, John Pine [trustee] to NMB, February 9, 1917, CUCF; and Thomas Sparks to NMB March 9, 1917, CUCF.) Butler was incensed by Boas, but he apparently decided not to try to have him fired because he was a popular figure (as Cattell was not) and was "so close to the time of retirement" (NMB to Willard Kind, December 29, 1919, CUCF). On Boas's frustrating negotiations with Butler on funding and appointments for the an-thropology department, see Boas to NMB, November 26, 1917, CUCF; Boas to NMB, April 12, 1918, CUCF; NMB to Boas, April 13, 1918, CUCF; Boas to NMB, May 3, 1918, CUCF; Boas to NMB, May 4, 1918, CUCF; Boas to NMB, June 6, 1918, CUCF; NMB to Boas, June 7, 1918, CUCF; Boas to NMB, January 9, 1919. During the academic year 1919–20, Boas taught twenty-one hours each week.

her introductory course in psychology but continued to take the necessary courses for a major. Boring or not, psychology was then king of the social sciences, the most developed and the most relevant to contemporary social concerns.[16]

Psychology's prestige derived from events surrounding World War I. The war itself, and the strikes, race riots, and bombings that followed it, generated widespread concern over the country's social stability and exacerbated long-standing anxiety over racial questions and immigration. Mental testers, who up until that time had enjoyed only sporadic success in establishing their discipline, suddenly emerged as potential saviors of the social order, experts capable of identifying who should lead, who should follow, and who should be excluded from society altogether.[17]

In 1916 the National Academy of Sciences created the National Research Council to mobilize America's scientific resources for defense. Robert Yerkes—a Harvard psychologist, the president of the American Psychological Association, and a champion of mental testing—was named chairman of the Psychology Committee. Yerkes recognized that the army's unprecedented conscription of millions of young soldiers provided psychology with a unique testing opportunity. Persuading the military that conventional methods of separating the wheat from the chaff would take too long under wartime conditions, he set to work with Lewis Terman and several other psychologists to devise a test that would measure the native intelligence of those being conscripted into the army. A number of military officials rejected the psychologists' assumption that intelligence should determine one's place in the army, but few questioned their claim that they could measure innate mental ability.[18]

Most people assumed that if professional psychologists said they could measure innate ability, they could. However, the test devised by the Yerkes group, with its arithmetic problems, word analogies, sentence completions, and general knowledge questions, clearly favored those with scholastic skills and an urban background. One of the completion problems, for instance, read:

---

16. Mead, *Blackberry Winter*, p. 109. Frederick Allen wrote that "psychology was king" in *Only Yesterday*, p. 165. On the popular impact of psychology on American society, see John C. Burnham, "The New Psychology: From Narcissism to Social Control," in John Braeman et al., eds., *Change and Continuity in Twentieth-Century America* (Columbus: Ohio State University Press, 1968), pp. 351–98.

17. Hamilton Craven, *The Triumph of Evolution*, pp. 224–27; Loren Baritz, *The Servants of Power: A History of the Use of Social Science in American Industry* (Middletown, Conn.: Wesleyan University Press, 1960), pp. 21–41.

18. Robert M. Yerkes, "Psychology in Relation to War," *Psychological Review* 25 (March 1918): 115; Daniel J. Kevles, "Testing the Army's Intelligence: Psychologists and the Military in World War I," *Journal of American History* 55 (December 1968): 565–71; Cravens, *Triumph of Evolution*, pp. 83–85; Baritz, *Servants of Power*, pp. 45–46.

Margaret Mead sitting in front of Barnard College (1922)

The Knight engine is used in the _____.
Packard   Stearns   Lozier   Pierce Arrow

Because many of those conscripted did not speak English or were illiterate, a separate, chiefly pictorial, test was devised for them. Though the psychologists claimed that this test (called Army Beta) was comparable to the English speakers' test (known as Army Alpha), those tested by it tended to score poorly. The testers believed that the low scores on Army Beta reflected the inferior intelligence of those taking the test, but critics noted that the directions for the test were given in English and that many of the subjects had never before taken a written examination.[19]

19. The question about the Knight engine is quoted in Kevles, "Testing the Army's Intelligence," p. 576. For contemporary criticism of the army tests, see Percy E. Davidson, "The Social Significance of the Army Intelligence Findings," *Scientific Monthly* 16 (February 1923): 185–86.

At the war's end, Robert Yerkes compiled the results of the two million examinations that had been given and noted that the average scores of the various ethnic and racial groups tested varied markedly. Native-born recruits scored highest. Immigrants from English-speaking countries and from northern and western Europe ranked just below. Those from southern and eastern Europe scored still lower; while black recruits scored lowest, southern blacks doing even more poorly than northern blacks. As far as Yerkes was concerned, the army tests settled the nature-nurture controversy in American psychology. Though Leta Hollingworth's work had persuaded most psychologists that sex should be eliminated as a separate category in testing the intelligence of schoolchildren, the army results persuaded them that race remained a reasonable basis of classification. This conclusion was quickly adopted and further popularized by immigration restrictionists.[20]

For Franz Boas, World War I represented a major defeat. His outspoken pacifism barred him from having the influence he should have had on the National Research Council and even led to his temporary ouster from the American Anthropological Association. With the National Research Council under the control of the most conservative figures in the social sciences, it appeared that American research would be directed toward the statistical justification of immigration restriction and other racist endeavors. The leaders of the National Research Council condemned Boas for having seriously neglected the biological aspect of anthropology and for having therefore ignored the significance of the heterogeneous makeup of the contemporary American population. In an effort to rebuild the influence of cultural anthropology and to answer what he considered the faulty research of the wartime mental testers, Boas encouraged his students to study psychology and to bring to it an anthropological perspective. When Margaret Mead, a student in one of his Barnard courses, decided to write a master's thesis in psychology, he encouraged her to conduct her psychological testing among the Italian immigrants where she had spent much of her childhood.[21]

Returning to Hammonton, New Jersey, Margaret tested Italian schoolchildren to evaluate the relationship of fluency in English with performance on standard I.Q. tests. The army testers had assumed that I.Q. measurements of foreign-language speakers were as accurate as

20. Robert M. Yerkes, ed., *Psychological Examining in the United States Army*, Memoirs of the National Academy of Sciences, vol. 15 (Washington, D.C., 1921), passim; Cravens, *Triumph of Evolution*, p. 85.

21. On Boas's ouster from the American Anthropological Association, see "In Re Boas," Columbia University Central Files. On opposition to Boas within the National Research Council, see Stocking, *Race, Culture, and Evolution*, pp. 270–307; Mead, *Blackberry Winter*, p. 122.

those made of subjects fluent in English. Mead's study questioned that assumption. Among the children she examined, she found that the higher the social status of a child's family the higher his or her I.Q. Furthermore, the more English spoken in a child's home, the higher his or her I.Q. was likely to be.

> It is inconceivable that children living in an English speaking environment, hearing, speaking, and reading nothing but English should not have a distinct advantage in tests requiring the findings of opposites, the hunting for an analogy, the filling in of an uncompleted sentence, as compared with children who hear a foreign language at home.

Mead was willing to concede that there was a biological component to intelligence, but she insisited that biology was only one component, and probably a subsidiary one among a complex array of other cultural and environmental factors.[22]

By 1924, when Mead submitted her master's thesis, Boas had recovered most of the ground he had lost during the war. He was by then a principal figure at the National Research Council; he had regained his position in the American Anthropological Association; and psychological work in anthropology, such as that done by Mead, was casting doubt on the work of immigration restrictionists. A steadily growing number of psychologists were convinced that some immigrant groups did better on I.Q. tests than others simply because they had been here longer, and that northern blacks did better than southern blacks because they had access to better educational opportunities. Mead relished having contributed in a small way to this shift in attitude among psychologists, but she decided, upon finishing her thesis, that she did not want to spend her life as a mental tester. The argument over whether women can do as well as men on I.Q. tests had been settled before the war. The argument over whether race affects performance on I.Q. tests was, she believed, all but resolved. Many psychologists were beginning to question the idea that intelligence is a unit factor and were suggesting that mental ability might result from the interplay of a variety of as yet undiscovered factors. But testing alone, Mead concluded, could not do much to illuminate these factors. The way people think and the way people behave depends so heavily on their social and economic situation that to understand the mind she would have to understand the institutional and cultural forces that shape people's lives.[23]

22. Margaret Mead, "Intelligence Tests of Italian and American Children" (Master's thesis, Columbia University, 1924), pp. 35, 64, and passim.

23. Cravens, *Triumph of Evolution*, pp. 224–65; Boring, *History of Experimental Psychology*, pp. 575–77.

Sociology and the Family

Upon graduating from Barnard in 1923, with both B.A. and M.A. degrees, Mead married Luther Cressman, a graduate student in sociology, and began graduate work in anthropology. To help support her graduate study she worked as an assistant to sociologist William Ogburn, whose research then centered on the family. Dissatisfied with what she thought to be the narrowness of psychological research, Mead found Ogburn's work far more relevant to her concern with individual development than the psychometric examinations she had been trained to give in psychology.[24]

The American family became a major focus of sociological research in the 1920s. As industrialization robbed it of its economic and most of its social functions, as the birthrate continued to plummet, the question inevitably arose: Was there any further need for the family? Most sociologists insisted that the answer was yes. As Ogburn put it, "Even if the family doesn't produce thread or cloth and soap and medicine and food, it can still produce happiness, which does not seem such a very bad thing to do after all." In an increasingly alien world, the capacity to provide support and to foster happiness rendered the family a more important institution for human welfare than it had ever been before.[25]

Mixed with this optimism about the family's continuing importance, however, was growing fear—fear that the emergence of the nuclear family, for all of its vaunted democracy and affectional depth, had brought uncontrollable pressures to bear on the family's individual members. Ogburn, while praising the family for being the last institution that could "produce happiness," conceded that the very forces that were making the family the sole source of emotional nurturance were also threatening to pull the family apart through divorce and mental breakdown. Ogburn blamed the strain on the modern family on what he dubbed "cultural lag." Technological change, he argued, proceeds much more smoothly and quickly than cultural change. People cling to old attitudes, especially on such vitally personal subjects as sexual identity, long after technological changes have rendered those attitudes obsolete. Woman's place in the modern nuclear family provided a prime example of cultural lag. Stripped of her traditional economic and social functions, she grew steadily more resentful as she remained tied to the family and the home simply because tradition dictated that she should be there.

24. Mead, *Blackberry Winter*, pp. 111, 115.
25. William Obgurn, "Social Heritage of the Family," in Margaret Rich, ed., *Family Life Today* (Boston: Houghton Mifflin, 1928), p. 39. For a more extended discussion of research on the family in the 1920s, see Fass, *The Damned and the Beautiful*, pp. 53–118; and Christopher Lasch, *Haven in a Heartless World: The Family Besieged* (New York: Basic Books, 1977), pp. 21–43.

Ernest Groves, Ogburn's collaborator on the popular college textbook *American Marriage,* observed that women were beginning to resist this cultural lag.

> The women of our times are less likely to smother or conceal from themselves their genuine desires than has been the habit of women in the past. It is to be expected, therefore, that modern woman will not only, through her industrial experience, decide that like man she desires to be with others as she works; but she will frankly face this and recognize that a marriage that denies her a reasonable quantity of associations is a hardship that risks happiness.[26]

Most sociologists in the 1920s agreed with Groves and Ogburn that economic independence for women was coming and that it was a good thing. But not everyone shared the Ogburn-Groves faith that this independence alone would render the family an untroubled producer of happiness. W. I. Thomas, for instance, argued that the small, modern, isolated family could not deal with the emotional energy generated within it. Whereas once the family had been part of a larger community that had aided in the rearing of children and the mediation of personal differences, now it was isolated from that larger community and was unrestrained in its interpersonal relations. As a result, Thomas wrote, "The family has become introverted, turned upon itself, and has taken a pathological turn in the direction of demanding and conferring response."[27]

Thomas often participated in New York sociological debates on the family. He had been living in New York since 1918, when the University of Chicago had discharged him for being discovered in a downtown Chicago hotel with a woman not his wife. Though the publication of his landmark, *The Polish Peasant in Europe and America* (1918– 1920), distinguished him as the foremost sociologist of his generation, and though his

26. Ogburn, "Social Heritage of the Family," pp. 39, 37– 38; Ernest Groves, *Social Problems of the Family* (Philadelphia: Lippincott, 1927), p. 86. See also William Ogburn, *Social Change: With Respect to Culture and Original Nature* (1922; reprint ed., New York: Viking, 1952), pp. 200– 83.

27. William I. Thomas, "The Configurations of Personality" (1927) in Edmund H. Volkart, ed., *Social Behavior and Personality: Contributions of W. I. Thomas to Theory and Social Research* (New York: Social Science Research Council, 1951), p. 201. Others who criticized the family for focusing too much emotional energy on its various members included: John B. Watson, *Psychological Care of Infant and Child* (New York: W. W. Norton, 1928), p. 127; Samuel Schmalhausen, "Family Life: A Study in Pathology," in V. F. Calverton and Samuel Schmalhausen, eds., *The New Generation* (New York: Macaulay, 1930), pp. 275– 303; Willard Waller, *The Family: A Dynamic Interpretation* (New York: Holt, Rinehart and Winston, 1938), pp. 415– 17; and Willistyne Goodsell, *A History of Marriage and the Family* (New York: Macmillan, 1915), pp. 518– 30. Watson advised parents to discipline themselves against displays of emotion. None of the other authors listed here believed this was possible and urged instead that mothers have careers and that society share in child-rearing.

close friends included such leaders of sociology as Robert Park, Ernest Burgess, and Robert Faris, Thomas never again held a university position. With the support of private benefactors, however, he continued his sociological researches, focusing on the family, childhood development, delinquency, and women's changing roles. Margaret Mead met him in the winter of 1924 when her husband, who was president of Columbia's Graduate Sociology Club, arranged for him to speak and to have dinner with them. Thomas had just finished a study of delinquency among adolescent girls and was about to begin collaborating on a book about child development with one of Mead's friends from Barnard, Dorothy Swaine Thomas. W. I. Thomas's jaundiced view of the emotional hotbox that was the modern family influenced Mead's thinking on family relationships even more strongly than did the work of Ogburn.[28]

Thomas blamed the emotional intensity of the modern family on the breakdown of old community controls. "In the small and spatially isolated communities of the past, where the influences were strong and steady," wrote Thomas, thinking of Polish villages he had studied, "the members became more or less habituated to and reconciled with a life of repressed wishes."

> The repression was demanded of all, the arrangement was equitable, and while certain new experiences were prohibited, and pleasure not countenanced as and end in itself, there remained satisfactions, not the least of which was the suppression of the wishes of others. On the other hand the modern world presents itself as a spectacle in which the observer is never sufficiently participating. . . . All age levels have been affected by the feeling that much, too much, is being missed of life. This unrest is being felt most by those who have heretofore been most excluded from general participation in life, — the mature woman and the young girl.

Women expressed their unrest in various ways. Some ran away, others sought careers, many turned all their restless energy upon their children, overwhelming them in the process. In the isolated family, both parents, but especially the mothers, "tend to use their children for the realization of their own wishes and relief of their own infirmities . . . . Too much love and too much hate are generated in family relations, and it often appears the family is the worst possible place for the child."[29]

28. *New York Times*, April 17, 1918, p. 13, col. 3; Herbert Blumer, *An Appraisal of Thomas and Znaniecki's "The Polish Peasant in Europe and America"* (New York: Social Science Research Council, 1939), pp. 81 – 82; "Biographical Note," in Volkart, ed., *Social Behavior and Personality*, pp. 323 – 24; Mead, *Blackberry Winter*, pp. 102, 118 – 19. Although Thomas left no personal papers, the extensive correspondence he conducted in the 1920s with his principal benefactor, Ethel Sturges Dummer, provides insight into his private life in these years. Ethel Sturges Dummer Papers, The Schlesinger Library, Radcliffe College, Cambridge, Massachusetts.

29. W. I. Thomas, *The Unadjusted Girl*, pp. 71 – 72; Thomas, "The Personality and the

Thomas's interest in the internal workings of the family, and his conviction that the family was so close to collapse, led him to the work of psychiatrists dealing with mental disorders. The case histories of schizophrenic youths, in particular, provided a wealth of evidence for what Thomas called the "pathological turn" taken by the modern nuclear family. Thomas reveled in psychiatry's evidence, but he resisted the newer Freudian currents in its theory. To him, as well as to most American sociologists, the strain in modern family life was not an inevitable part of the human condition, but rather the consequence of historical dislocation which, properly confronted, could be overcome. Once women's "integrity and personality" were not "bound up so closely by tradition with recognition from men," once women were encouraged in "the development of professional interests," and once society found modern alternatives to the community supports that had once aided in the raising of children, mental disorders would diminish. The family, as Americans knew it, might not survive, but that would be just as well.[30]

Anthropology and the Individual

Mead would have become a sociologist had it not been for her friendship with Ruth Benedict. Benedict, a 1909 graduate of Vassar and a married woman, was a latecomer to anthropology. She had tried charity work and secondary school teaching but had disliked them both. She had tried writing about important women in history, but had found it difficult to work in complete isolation. Finally, she had returned to school, taking courses in 1919 at the New School for Social Research. Elsie Clews Parsons taught an anthropology course that year on sex. Benedict took it and discovered her calling. With Parsons's encouragement, she enrolled at

---

Context of the Family" (1926), in Volkart, ed., *Social Behavior and Personality*, p. 193. See also William I. Thomas and Dorothy Swaine Thomas, *The Child in America: Behavior Problems and Programs* (New York: Knopf, 1928), pp. 1–94.

30. W. I. Thomas to E. S. Dummer, Dummer Papers. Thomas worked closely in the twenties with the psychiatrist Harry Stack Sullivan and had a profound influence on Sullivan's work. See Thomas, "Notes from the President [of the American Sociological Association]" (1927), memorandum in Dummer Papers; and Harry Stack Sullivan, "Schizophrenic Individuals as a Source of Data for Comparative Investigation of Personality," in his *Schizophrenia as a Human Process*, ed. Helen S. Perry (New York: Norton, 1962), pp. 221–23. See also Perry, ed. and intro. to Sullivan, *The Fusion of Psychiatry and Social Science*, pp. xiii–xxxv. For the reluctance of sociologists, in general, to accept Freudian theory, see Ernest Groves, "Freud and Sociology," *Psychoanalytic Review* 3 (July 1916): 241–53; Ernest Burgess, "The Influence of Sigmund Freud on Sociology in the United States," *American Journal of Sociology* 45 (November 1939): 356–75; Robert Jones, "Freud and American Sociology, 1909–1949," *Journal of the History of the Behavioral Sciences* 10 (January 1974): 21–39; and John C. Burnham, "The Influence of Psychoanalysis upon American Culture," in Jacques M. Quen and Eric Carlson, eds., *American Psychoanalysis: Origins and Development* (New York: Brunner/Mazel, 1978), pp. 52–72.

Ruth Benedict

Columbia to study with Boas, who quickly appointed her as his assistant at Barnard. It was Benedict who led Boas's introductory classes on field trips to the Museum of Natural History, and whose informal conversation "humanized Boas' formal lectures" for the undergraduates. One day at lunch with Benedict, Mead was agonizing over which field of social science to enter and Benedict responded, "Professor Boas and I have nothing to offer but an opportunity to do what matters." That settled it for Mead. "Anthropology had to be done *now*. Other things could wait." Mead maintained her psychologist's interest in individual differences and her sociologist's interest in the family, but she decided to apply these interests to a field whose subject matter seemed in imminent danger of disappearing.[31]

31. Mead, *Blackberry Winter*, pp. 114 and 111–15; Margaret Mead, ed., *Writings of Ruth Benedict: An Anthropologist at Work* (New York: Avon, 1959), pp. 3–17. Ruth Benedict's papers are at the Vassar College Library, but there is very little in the collection that has not been published in *Writings of Ruth Benedict*.

Mead came to anthropology at a pivotal point in its development, a development that had been almost singlehandedly directed by Boas for over thirty years.

> He had reached one of those watersheds that occur in the lives of statesmen-scientists who are mapping out the whole course of a discipline. He felt that sufficient work had gone into demonstrating that people borrowed from one another, that no society evolved in isolation, but was continually influenced in its development by other peoples, other cultures, and other, differing, levels of technology. He decided that the time had come to tackle the set of problems that linked the development of individuals to what was distinctive in the culture in which they were reared.

Boas believed that the error of his own work had lain "in the overemphasis on historical reconstruction, the importance of which should not be minimized, as against a penetrating study of the individual under stress of the culture in which he lives." He now wanted to focus on particular cultures in greater depth than had been attempted before, to see how the institutions and individuals within them related to each other and to the functioning of society as a whole. Boas's shift to functionalism represented a return, in some ways, to the view of society set forth by Herbert Spencer, a view that stressed the interrelationships and organic growth of social systems. But Boas's approach to functionalism differed in important ways from that of Spencer. He objected to Spencer's thoroughgoing materialism and rejected his tendency to explain social change in terms of natural laws. In common with Dewey in psychology and Thomas in sociology, Boas developed a brand of functionalism that had a distinctively Progressive character.[32]

Dewey, Thomas, and Boas shared two key assumptions. First, they emphasized the importance of scientific method. This emphasis was due, in part, to their belief that the universe was constantly changing and that, as a consequence, knowledge could never be complete. They were, above all else, skeptics, always tentative about their formulations, suspicious of fixed principles, and wary of classificatory schemes. Second, they believed

32. Mead, *Blackberry Winter*, p. 126; Franz Boas, "Some Problems of Methodology in the Social Sciences," in Leonard D. White, ed., *The New Social Science* (Chicago: University of Chicago Press, 1930), p. 98; George Stocking, *Race, Culture, and Evolution*, p. 197; Martindale, *Nature and Types of Sociological Theory*, pp. 441–63; Lowie, *History of Ethnological Theory*, p. 142; Marvin Harris, *The Rise of Anthropological Theory: A History of Theories of Culture* (New York: Crowell, 1968), pp. 519–23. Kingsley Davis has suggested that the term *functionalism* be abandoned because it has come to be synonymous with all modern sociological thinking and therefore can no longer be used to distinguish any one group of social scientists from any other (Davis, "The Myth of Functional Analysis as a Special Method in Sociology and Anthropology," *American Sociological Review* 24 [December 1959]: 757–72). But Davis concedes that at its inception in the early twentieth century functionalism offered a new way of looking at society.

that the social and physical world would respond to human purpose and that the function of science was to guide purposeful human activity. In their analysis, the individual was always as important to social change as was the system of which she or he was a part.[33]

Boas's sudden wave of women students facilitated his shift to the functional examination of the individual's relationship to culture in much the same way that women had facilitated this same shift in psychology and sociology. Elsie Clews Parsons, Ruth Benedict, and Margaret Mead, as well as Ruth Bunzel, Gladys Reichard, Esther Goldfrank, and others, had spent most of their lives trying to find a place for themselves in a culture suspicious of intellectual ambition in women. They were deviants obsessed with the phenomenon of deviancy, and they brought a perspective to the study of the individual's relationship to culture that made them far less ready than many of their male colleagues to identify what is with what ought to be. Ruth Benedict's *Patterns of Culture* was an intensely personal book that examined how a number of different cultures encouraged the development of different personality types, and how those cultures responded to individuals who did not bend to the accepted personality pattern.[34]

South Pacific

Margaret Mead entered anthropology with the intention of working either with immigrant groups in the United States, as her mother had done, or of doing fieldwork among the American Indians, as Elsie Clews Parsons and Ruth Benedict were doing. But a trip to the British Association for the Advancement of Science in Toronto in the summer of 1924 made the prospect of studying the same groups that others had already visited seem unexciting. In Toronto she met professional anthropologists who were working among peoples in Africa and the South Pacific who had never seen an anthropologist before. Everyone talked about "my people," and she felt disadvantaged in having no people of her own to talk about.[35]

For her doctoral thesis Mead tried to determine whether Ogburn's notion of "cultural lag" could be applied to primitive societies. Boas

33. Rucker, *Chicago Pragmatists*, pp. 29–31, 38–40, 77–78. David A. Hollinger, "The Problem of Pragmatism in American History," *Journal of American History* 67 (June 1980): 88–107. I believe that the key assumptions that Hollinger has identified in pragmatism were also essential to functionalism as used by the authors studied here.

34. Ruth Benedict, *Patterns of Culture* (Boston: Houghton Mifflin, 1934), pp. 259–78. For references to Benedict's often unhappy efforts to define herself as a woman and as a scholar, see Mead, ed., *Writings of Ruth Benedict*, pp. 120, 136, 145–46. For the experiences of another Columbia woman anthropologist, see Esther Goldfrank, *Notes on an Undirected Life: As One Anthropologist Tells It* (New York: Queens College Publications in Anthropology, 1977), pp. 26–27.

35. Mead, *Blackberry Winter*, pp. 100, 137, 124; Margaret Mead, *Coming of Age in Samoa: A Psychological Study of Primitive Youth for Western Civilization* (New York: Morrow, 1928), p. 9.

suggested that she compare the relative rates of technical and cultural change among the peoples of a particular area. Mead chose Polynesia simply because it was the one region in which she could get by with only French and German. Having absorbed herself in the literature of Polynesia for her dissertation, and wanting to have a people "on whom I could base my own intellectual life," Mead asked Boas to let her go to the South Pacific.[36]

Boas was appalled. He agreed that the time had come to cast the anthropological net beyond the Americas, but felt the South Pacific was too dangerous, especially for a small, twenty-three-year-old woman. Re-counting "a sort of litany of young men who had died or been killed while they were working outside the United States," he insisted that she venture no farther than the Southwest of the United States. Undaunted, Mead appealed to her mentor's egalitarian ideals. "I knew that there was one thing that mattered more to Boas than the direction taken by an-thropological research. This was that he should behave like a liberal, democratic, modern man, not like a Prussian autocrat." Faced with the charge that he was dealing with a student in an arbitrary manner, Boas not only capitulated but even gave Mead his strong support for a research fellowship from the National Research Council despite the vigorous ob-jections of fellow anthropologists.[37]

For any other woman in 1924, the problems Mead faced in dealing with her advisor and her fellowship committee would have paled before the resistance she would have met from her family. But Mead, unique in so many ways, was especially blessed in her family relations. Trained as social scientists, her parents, as well as her husband, understood the importance of fieldwork and supported her desire to do something original. During the year Mead spent in the South Pacific, her husband studied in Europe.[38]

As part of Boas's plan to shift his students' attention away from the historical analysis of cultural diffusion and toward the examination of the relationship of the individual to his culture, he assigned Mead the task of studying female adolescence among a people who were comparatively

36. Ibid., pp. 124 – 28.
37. Ibid., p. 129. Edward Sapir disapproved of Mead's going to the South Pacific, arguing that she was not strong enough. The National Research Council's decision to support Mead's fieldwork marked a major shift of emphasis away from studies aimed at immigration restriction and toward studies of culture. Mary Van Kleeck, long active in the woman's movement, an official at the Russell Sage Foundation, and Chairman of the NRC Committee on the Scientific Problem of Human Migration, played an important role in this shift. See Mary Van Kleeck to Committee on the Scientific Problems of Human Migration, NRC, March 19, 1923, Robert Yerkes Papers, Historical Division, Medical Library, Yale Univer-sity, New Haven, Conn. See also Cravens, *Triumph of Evolution*, pp. 182 – 84.
38. Mead, *Blackberry Winter*, pp. 124 – 25, 130.

free of Western influence. In particular, Boas wanted to know if adolescence was so stormy everywhere as it was in the modern Western world. Adolescence was not a new topic. Edward Clarke had first generated interest in the issue of female adolescence when he published *Sex in Education* in 1873 and warned that adolescence was such a naturally turbulent period for the growing girl that the trials of education should not be added to its burdens. G. Stanley Hall had developed this theme thirty years later in his massive study of adolescence, in which he had warned anew of adolescence's inevitable difficulties. With the onset of puberty, Hall wrote, "the floodgates of heredity seem opened and we hear from our remoter forebears, and receive our life dower of energy. . . . Passions and desires spring into vigorous life." Boys as well as girls, of course, suffered the storm and stress of adolescence, but Hall, like Clarke, believed that the special demands of the girl's maturing reproductive organs made her particularly subject to the physiological dislocations of puberty.[39]

Most investigators by the 1920s took a dim view of Hall's "hereditary floodgates." No one doubted that the teenage years were difficult ones, but most experimental studies had undermined traditional assumptions about the biological source of adolescent turmoil and pointed instead to social explanations. Helen Thompson Woolley and Leta Hollingworth had found that girls could flourish under the rigors of higher education, both mentally and physically. If girls manifested discontent, they did so not because of organic disturbances but because they were educated to achieve and then were blocked from fulfilling work. W. I. Thomas's studies of delinquent adolescent girls further challenged Hall's assumptions by showing how the specific pressures of poverty and the rapidly shifting demands and expectations of urban life prompted many young women to rebel against traditional constraints. "The beginning of delinquency in girls," Thomas observed, "is usually an impulse to get amusement, adventure, pretty clothes, favorable notice, distinction, freedom in the larger world which presents so many allurements and comparisons." Social pressures, more than biological urges, disturbed modern youth, the social scientists concluded. But because they worked in the same culture, the psychologists and sociologists could only speculate about how much of the rebellion they observed among youths could be avoided. Only by looking at a culture free of Western influence could the issue of the inevitability of adolescent rebelliousness be examined in a fundamentally new way.[40]

39. G. Stanley Hall, *Adolescence*, 1:308.
40. Mead, *Coming of Age in Samoa*, pp. 2–3; W. I. Thomas, *The Unadjusted Girl*, p. 109. See also Leta Hollingworth, *The Psychology of the Adolescent* (New York: Appleton, 1928), pp. 77–82; Helen Thompson Woolley, "A New Scale of Mental and Physical Mea-

Boas suggested the possibilities of a new approach in a letter to Mead at the start of her trip:

We find very often among ourselves during the period of adolescence a strong rebellious spirit that may be expressed in sullenness or in sudden outburst. . . . I am not at all clear in my mind in how far similar conditions may occur in primitive society and in how far the desire for independence may be simply due to our modern conditions and to a more strongly developed individualism.

Mead wanted to visit as primitive and remote a people as she could so that the impact of Western influence would be minimized. Her first choice was the remote Tuamotu Islands, but Boas would not hear of her going there. He insisted that she choose an island to which a ship came regularly at least every three weeks. So she chose American Samoa, a U.S. protectorate in the South Pacific, where the navy had a base and where her way could be eased by the surgeon general of the United States, a friend of her father-in-law.[41]

American Samoa was far from untouched. Congregationalist missionaries from London had been there for over a hundred years, and now missionary schools dotted its islands and a pastor's house graced every village. Despite this missionary influence, however, Samoa remained primitive, and Mead was able to work on one of the most primitive of its islands, the island of Tau, where she lived with the family of the naval officer who ran the dispensary in one of the villages. Each village on Tau was divided into between thirty and forty households whose composition varied from the biological family consisting of parents and children only, to households of fifteen and twenty people who were all related to the head of the household or to his wife by blood, marriage, or adoption. The villagers lived in beehive-shaped houses with floors of coral rubble and walls of perishable woven blinds that were kept rolled up except in bad weather. The villagers were Americanized to the point of wearing cotton cloth rather than the more traditional bark cloth and attending church, but they spoke no English, and in much of their daily life they followed traditional customs, living a mostly self-sufficient existence of fishing and simple agriculture.[42]

Though Mead wanted to study adolescence, she realized that she could

surements for Adolescents," *Journal of Educational Psychology* 6 (November 1915): 521– 50; and W. I. Thomas and D. S. Thomas, *The Child in America,* pp. 330– 576. For a 1920s review of the current social scientific view on Hall and female adolescence, see Willystine Goodsell, *The Education of Women: Its Social Background and Problems* (New York: Macmillan, 1923), pp. 65– 140.

41. Boas's letter is quoted in Mead, ed., *Writings of Ruth Benedict,* p. 289; Mead, *Blackberry Winter,* p. 129.

42. Mead, *Blackberry Winter,* pp. 147– 54; Mead, *Coming of Age in Samoa,* pp. 266– 77.

not understand the adolescent period without understanding its place within the entire female life cycle. Therefore in the nine months available to her for fieldwork, she complemented her intensive study of fifty girls between the ages of ten and twenty with observations of the preadolescent girls and the grown women of the village, in an effort to create a picture of the life cycle of the Samoan female.[43]

The infant girl entered the world without ceremony. Though she slept with her mother as long as she was nursing (two to three years), the principal responsibility for her care rested with an older girl of six or seven, who thereby freed the infant's mother for weaving, gardening, or fishing. Handed carelessly from one person to the next, the infant soon learned not to care "for one person greatly" nor to set "high hopes on any one relationship." At about six the little girl outgrew her guardian and became, in turn, the guardian of some new infant. Baby-tending remained her most important task until puberty, when she was relieved of it to work on the plantation, carry foodstuffs down to the village, and learn the more elaborate household skills.[44]

Of girls at adolescence Mead observed, "It may be said with some justice that the worst period of their lives is over."

> Never again will they be so incessantly at the beck and call of their elders, never again so tyrannized over by two-year-old tyrants. All the irritating, detailed routine of housekeeping, which in our civilization is accused of warping the souls and souring the tempers of grown women, is here performed by children under fourteen years of age.

The adolescent girl was expected to become proficient in the work that would fall to her as an adult—weaving, planting, fishing. But she was in no hurry about this. "Proficiency would mean more work, and earlier marriage, and marriage is the inevitable to be deferred as long as possible."[45]

The greater freedom of adolescence and the casual attitude toward work and preparation for later responsibilities did much to diffuse any tension that might develop between a child and her parents, but perhaps even more important was the fact that every girl had multiple ties to adults in authority. Within her household she could appeal over her father's head to the head of the household. Should she be so unfortunate as to have a father who was also the head of the household, she could run away and live in another household.

> Few children live continuously in one household, but are always testing out other possible residences. . . . The minute that the mildest annoyance grows up

43. Mead, *Coming of Age in Samoa*, pp. 10–11, 131.
44. Ibid., pp. 199, 20, 22, 28.
45. Ibid., pp. 28, 38.

at home, the possibility of flight moderates the discipline and alleviates the child's sense of dependency.[46]

With the onset of puberty came an awakening of interest in the opposite sex, but this new interest constituted no more than a variation on a long-standing sexual awareness. The girl had been masturbating since at least the age of six, had engaged in casual homosexuality, and had frequently witnessed intercourse. While "all expressions of affection are rigorously barred in public," Mead wrote, "The lack of privacy within the houses where mosquito netting marks off purely formal walls about the married couples, and the custom of young lovers of using palm groves for their rendezvous, makes it inevitable that children should see intercourse, often and between many different people." Sex was viewed as natural, and while there was a formal belief that girls should be virgins at marriage, none of them were. With few exceptions, adolescence in Samoa "represented no period of crisis or stress, but was instead an orderly developing of a set of slowly maturing interests and activities."[47]

When Elsie Clews Parsons first used ethnological evidence to criticize American sexual relations, she revealed her lingering Progressive prejudices by concluding that Americans were just as backward as primitive peoples were. Mead revised Parsons's indictment of American society, concluding that Americans had much to learn about sexual relations from at least one primitive society.

First, Americans could greatly minimize the conflicts of adolescence by abolishing the nuclear family, or at least by finding ways of relieving the intense emotional pressure created by the small, tightly knit family. Samoan children could run away if parents became too overbearing; American children could not, without becoming delinquents. Mead thought that everyone would be much better off if parenting were more widely shared in America. Children should not be reared by their mothers alone, but by a variety of other people as well—including, if necessary, social welfare agencies and psychiatrists.

Americans could further diffuse the emotional intensity of adolescence by adopting the Samoans' openness toward sex and their casual attitude toward marriage. Exposed to the sexual relations of others from early childhood, proficient in masturbation, and familiar with many lovers both before marriage and after, Samoan girls did not suffer the intense sexual anxieties so prevalent among American teenagers.

Finally, Mead approved of the Samoan girl's early introduction to work.

46. Ibid., pp. 42, 209, 213.
47. Ibid., pp. 134–35, 157, 136, 147–50. Mead does not discuss contraception, and it is unclear whether young women tend to be pregnant at marriage.

From earliest childhood, girls labored in a purposeful way, working their way into adult activities. American girls, by contrast, suffered from the sharp discontinuities of childhood play, followed by an education that was cut short by maternal drudgery. What children did as children in America, and especially what females did as children, had nothing to do with what they were to do as adults. The advances made by American women in higher education simply exacerbated the sense of discontinuity in their lives by giving women a sense of choice they did not really have. The adolescent girl in America needed to know that she could make choices and that her education was leading toward some purposeful end.[48]

The Cultural Relativity of Sex

On her way back from Samoa, Mead met Reo Fortune, a young New Zealand psychologist, whose work on Freud's and Rivers's theories of dreams had won him a fellowship to study in England. "We talked nonstop for six weeks," Mead later recalled, "fitting all that each of us had learned into a new approach to the study of primitive peoples." By the time Mead rejoined her husband, she found they had grown apart. He wanted a career teaching sociology. She wanted a professional partnership in anthropological fieldwork. More than most women of her time, or later, Mead was willing to pay the personal cost that often accompanies professional growth, and her marriages—first to Luther Cressman, then to Reo Fortune, and finally to Gregory Bateson—were short.[49]

Back in New York, she went to work as an assistant curator for ethnology at the American Museum of Natural History, responsible for the Pacific area. Boas had few academic jobs to distribute to his students, and he assigned those he had on the basis of financial need. Ruth Benedict never had a full-time position at Columbia until she was divorced from her husband, and the jobs at Barnard always went to unmarried women with no other means of support. Because she was married, Mead could not expect Boas's assistance in finding an academic position, but the curatorship offered her by the Museum of Natural History while she was still in Samoa was more attractive in some ways than an academic appointment. In particular, it had the advantage of leaving her time for writing. While many academics were forced to leave their field notes to

48. Ibid., pp. 213– 14, 216, 227. Mead credits Benedict with the idea of discontinuity. See Ruth Benedict, "Continuity and Discontinuity in Cultural Conditioning," *Psychiatry* 1 (May 1938): 161– 67.

49. Margaret Mead, *Letters from the Field, 1925 – 1975* (New York: Harper & Row, 1977), p. 20; Mead, *Blackberry Winter*, p. 164.

gather dust when they returned each fall to their classrooms, Mead made use of her notes immediately.[50]

In writing *Coming of Age in Samoa,* Mead suggested that if the crisis of adolescence with its discontinuities and conflict over goals could be mitigated, woman's lot would be a far happier one. But the more she thought about the problem of women's nature and role, the more she came to believe that adolescence was simply a particularly dramatic episode in a larger pattern. The problem for American women was not so much the crisis of adolescence, but rather the absence of real choice in the matter of personal temperament at any stage in their lives. The West, Mead complained, was so accustomed to a thoroughgoing sexual polarity, that no one seemed able to conceive of sexual relations without extreme sex differentiation. The pervasiveness of this assumption of sexual polarity was amply demonstrated in a widely read feminist work of the 1920s written by Mathilde and Mathis Vaerting, which argued that in early matriarchal societies women had dominated men and had shown all of the qualities of aggression that Western men later came to embody. To Mead this understanding of sex was incredibly narrow and culturally biased. So thoroughly did the Vaertings accept the polarization of the sexes, that they could imagine nothing more radical in sexual relations than simple role reversal. Surely, Mead thought, there were other ways of patterning sexual behavior than either the one condoned by modern civilization or the flip side of that pattern championed by the Vaertings.[51]

In 1931 Mead traveled to New Guinea with Reo Fortune to study sexual differences in primitive cultures. They lived among three different peoples. The first were the Arapesh, a group they visited simply because their carriers did not want to carry their equipment all the way to their original destination and dumped it instead in the Arapesh's mountain village. The steep mountainsides made cultivation extremely difficult, and the possibility of starvation always threatened. Under these harsh conditions, this mountain people had fashioned a simple culture in which the personality and roles of men and women alike were "stylized as parental, cherishing and mildly sexed." For their second group Mead and Fortune journeyed to the cannibalistic region of the Yuat River and studied the Mundugumor, where both the men and the women were fiercely aggressive, highly sexed, and noncherishing toward their children. Finally, they studied the people living on the shore of Tchambuli

50. Mead, *Blackberry Winter,* p. 163; Fred Eggan, "One Hundred Years of Ethnology and Social Anthropology," in J. O. Brew, ed., *One Hundred Years of Anthropology* (Cambridge, Mass.: Harvard University Press, 1968), p. 137.

51. For Mead's critique of Mathilde Vaerting and Mathis Vaerting, *The Dominant Sex: A Study in the Sociology of Sex Differences* (London: Allen and Unwin, 1923), see Margaret Mead, *Sex and Temperament in Three Primitive Societies* (New York: Morrow, 1935), pp. x– xi.

Lake, where Mead found a surprising reversal of conventional Western roles, the women acting in a brisk, businesslike, and cooperative way and the men behaving in a catty, exhibitionist way and preoccupied with decorative and artistic activities. By the time they had finished with the Tchambuli, Mead had the theme she wanted. Sex was not necessarily as important a basis for behavioral differences as Americans, and indeed most Westerners, believed.[52]

"If those temperamental attitudes which we have traditionally regarded as feminine," wrote Mead, "such as passivity, responsiveness and willing-ness to cherish children—can so easily be set up as the masculine pattern in one tribe, and in another be outlawed for the majority of women as well as for the majority of men, we no longer have any basis for regarding such aspects of behavior as sex-linked." The sharply contrasting cultural styles of the Arapesh, Mundugumors, and Tchambuli persuaded Mead that "many, if not all of the personality traits which we have called masculine or feminine are as lightly linked to sex as are clothing, the manners and the form of head-dress that a society at a given period assigns to either sex."[53]

Human nature, she concluded, was "almost unbelievably malleable" and differences among individuals could be "almost entirely explained by "differences in conditioning, especially during early childhood." The form that this conditioning took in any given society was, she emphasized, "culturally determined" and relative to the particular values and needs stressed in that society. Why these sex differences arose in the first place, however, remained a puzzle. Perhaps, she suggested, the origins of these socially standardized differences lay in individual temperament. The idea that the personality of each individual varied from that of all others, given his or her particular endocrine balance or physical structure, gained wide popularity in the 1920s and 1930s, especially with the popularization of work being done in endocrinology. As many social scientists began to doubt that intelligence was a unit factor that could be given a single numerical score, they turned to temperament as an alternative way of understanding human differences.[54]

The notion of innate temperament appealed to Mead, as it did to her friend Ruth Benedict, because they both felt like aliens in American society, and they were therefore sensitive to the fact that some individuals did not respond easily to social expectations. Benedict's work, especially as it was developed in *Patterns of Culture,* suggested that each culture empha-sizes a particular temperament, drawing on the vast range of possibilities within the human pool. "It is, so far as we can see," Benedict wrote, "an

52. Mead, *Letters from the Field,* pp. 101–02.
53. Mead, *Sex and Temperament,* pp. 279–80.
54. Ibid., pp. 280–84. For the growing popularity of the idea of temperament, see W. I. Thomas and D. S. Thomas, *The Child in America,* pp. 370–434.

ultimate fact of human nature that man builds up his culture out of disparate elements, combining and recombining them" until a workable pattern is arranged. Mead adopted this idea in her work on sex and temperament.

> Let us assume that there are definite temperamental differences between human beings which if not entirely hereditary at least are established on a hereditary basis very soon after birth. (Further than this we cannot at present narrow the matter.) These differences finally embodied in the character structure of adults, then, are the clues from which culture works, selecting one temperament, or a combination of related and congruent types, as desireable, and embodying this choice in every thread of the social fabric.

This tendency among cultures to foster particular temperamental types and to denigrate others can be hard on those unfortunate individuals whose own impulses clash with those that have been legitimated in the culture into which they have been cast.

> The Samoans decreed that all young people must show the personality trait of unaggressiveness and punish with opprobrium the aggressive child who displays traits regarded as appropriate only in titled, middle-aged men.

The effort to force members of a society into set temperamental molds violates individual inclinations, at the same time that it robs a culture of the richness it could achieve by recognizing and tapping "the whole gamut of human potentialities." Mead conceded that much of Western culture's richness and many of its contrasting values can be credited to its emphasis on sexual division. But for most purposes, she insisted, sex is an artificial distinction and not a very apt one either—particularly in organizing the work of politics, science, and the arts. To recognize individual differences and to abandon sex as an organizing principle in social relations would permit humanity "to weave a less arbitrary social fabric, one in which each diverse human gift will find a fitting place."[55]

Mead's emphasis on individual temperament served two functions for her: to explain cultural variety and to maintain a link to the idealist belief in individual autonomy and purposefulness that had inspired social thinkers at the turn of the century. Young scientists in 1900 had used their growing awareness of the social forces affecting personality to attack the formalistic, biologically based conceptions of human nature and social behavior that prevailed among Victorian intellectuals. Neither theology nor biology, they had argued, determined how people lived; society did.

---

55. Ruth Benedict, "The Concept of the Guardian Spirit in America," *Memoirs of the American Anthropological Association* 29 (1923): 84–85; Mead, *Sex and Temperament*, pp. 284–85, 322. Both Benedict and Mead credited the Gestalt psychologists, especially Kurt Koffka, with having inspired their idea of pattern in culture.

What society did, they had added bowing to their idealist training, society could undo. Scholars who were trained a generation later took the idea that society shaped the individual even more seriously than their mentors had. If society was really so powerful and individuals really so malleable, how could one person hope to alter the course of social development or even persuade people of the need for alteration? Given the vast complexity and interdependence of modern society, and the speed at which change was taking place, was it not presumptuous of any one person to preach his or her own vision of reform? Who could foresee the consequences? Moralizing Victorian parents had ill prepared their children for the world those children had to face as adults. Part of Mead believed that children should "be taught how to think, not what to think," but part of her also believed that America's family life and its thoroughgoing sexual differentiation were harmful and should be changed. The idea of innate temperament appealed to her because it provided a natural measure of protection, free of moralizing taint, against what might otherwise become an irreversible drift into a materialism and relativity of value as paralyzing as the biological determinism that social science had been fighting against for so long.[56]

That protection, however, proved weak. If human nature was really as malleable as Mead believed, how was anyone to know whether the impulses one felt were truly innate or simply the misunderstood product of social conditioning? The strength of early feminism had been its commitment to an ideal of feminine purpose. The social scientific attack on that ideal left feminism without a unifying vision and both men and women in a vicious circle. They grew up learning to behave toward one another in ways that were often bad for both of them; but lacking a critical perspective on their lives, they found it difficult to question that behavior.

Mead recognized the power of this vicious circle, but she was too much her mother's daughter to submit to it. Returning to an idea first suggested by Jessie Taft, she argued that sexual restrictions would one day be transcended by those caught in the cultural crossfire of rapid social change—by people, like her, whose intellectual tendency made them critical of conventional expectations. If the destructiveness of America's sexual division could only be thus far identified, it would nevertheless be possible to create "a climate of opinion in which others, a little less the product of the dark past because they have been reared with a light in their hand that can shine backwards as well as forwards, may in turn take the next step."[57]

56. Mead, *Coming of Age in Samoa*, p. 246.
57. Margaret Mead, *Male and Female: A Study of the Sexes in a Changing World* (New York: Morrow, 1949), p. 384.

Keeping the Light Burning

Margaret Mead's enduring contribution to the modern understanding of sex differences was her success in giving scholars a light that shone both backward and forward. Her books and articles focused attention on the functionalist arguments first formulated by the social scientists of her parent's generation and presented them in a way that proved inspirational to her daughter's generation. Echoing Dewey and Boas, she emphasized the importance of the scientific habit of mind. Echoing Woolley, Hollingworth, and Parsons, she decried the universal tendency to portray the world in terms of sexual dichotomy. Echoing Thomas and Taft, she emphasized the importance of unconscious forces in motivating human behavior. And echoing Coolidge and Mosher, she illustrated the cultural basis of sexual attitudes.

Like her predecessors she believed that there were no fixed truths, that knowledge could never be complete, and that both society and the individuals within it were constantly changing. Associated with this belief in perpetual change was the idealist conviction that humans could direct that change. Like so many Progressives, Mead was a social engineer, one who insisted that all women and men could come to understand the error of their ways and act to change social institutions. Her books were thinly veiled attacks on modern American society's treatment of women. In discussing the Samoan girls' preparation for adulthood, Mead stressed the absence of conflict within the Samoan system and criticized American society's subjection of girls to contradictory demands; in describing Samoan family life, she attacked the pressures created by modern marriage and family obligations; in analyzing the problem of deviance, she condemned our society's tendency toward rigid classification.

Not all of those on whose work Mead drew would have agreed with everything she said. Taft did not believe in innate temperament and preferred to explain personality differences in terms of social interaction. Parsons objected to Mead's substituting her own classificatory schemes for the sexual ones that they both rejected. But despite these differences, Mead succeeded in capturing the spirit of the first generation's work on sex differences. She popularized the ideas that human nature is remarkably plastic and that society need not be bound by the arbitrary constraints of sexual division which had for so long been assumed to be rooted in the human condition. She kept the light of feminist scholarship burning.[58]

---

58. Elsie Clews Parsons to Robert Lowie, January 25, 1938, Lowie Papers.

Epilogue

Margaret Mead kept the light of feminist scholarship burning, but for a generation after the appearance of *Sex and Temperament* (1935) that light often flickered and at times seemed close to being snuffed out. The skeptical approach to the study of sex differences that had characterized research in the early twentieth century lost momentum in the 1930s and has had to be virtually rekindled in our own time.

Not that feminist scholarship ceased altogether. Throughout the 1930s, 1940s, and 1950s a number of scholars carried on the spirit of early, dissident social scientists. Sociologist Mirra Komarovsky developed ideas first suggested by Jessie Taft in her analysis of role strain among women college students and alumnae. Sociologist Helen Mayer Hacker elaborated on the work of Robert Park in her characterization of women as a minority group. Psychiatrist Clara Thompson echoed Elsie Clews Parsons in describing the cultural roots of female personality formation. Psychologist Anne Anastasi carried on the work of Helen Thompson Woolley in her textbook discussions of the mental differences between the sexes. And psychologists Eleanor Maccoby and Lois Meek Stolz developed the ideas of Leta Hollingworth in questioning whether women are peculiarly suited to child rearing. In the footnotes of this second generation of scholars one can find a thread leading back to those early critics who have been the focus of this study. Despite these continuities in the critical study of sex differences, however, feminist-minded researchers from the thirties through the fifties enjoyed less influence than earlier feminist scholars had. A full explanation of this declining influence must await further research, but among the complex array of institutional, intellectual, and social forces that contributed to it, the following were clearly important.[1]

1. Komarovsky, "Cultural Contradictions and Sex Roles," *American Journal of Sociology* 52 (November 1946): 184–89; idem, "Functional Analysis of Sex Roles," *American Sociological Review* 15 (August 1950): 508–16; idem, *Women in the Modern World: Their Education and Their Dilemmas* (Boston: Little Brown, 1953), pp. 53–86; Helen Mayer Hacker, "Women as a

First, when the university succeeded in establishing itself as a key institution in American society, women found themselves limited to marginal positions within it. Women first gained access to universities in the period of rapid academic expansion and fierce competition that followed the Civil War, and as long as new colleges and universities were struggling for acceptance, women found expanding opportunities there. But as higher education won a recognized place in American political, economic, and intellectual life, women students were quickly overtaken by young men, who recognized the university's usefulness in preparing and certifying them for work in an increasingly professionalized and bureaucratized society. Far from succumbing to the threat of feminization so widely feared at the turn of the century, the university established itself as a distinctively male institution. By the 1920s it was no longer unusual for men to attend graduate school; but it remained unusual for women, for whom graduate education never achieved a corresponding social utility.[2]

As women academics lost momentum in their struggle for institutional acceptance, as they failed to win faculty positions in coeducational schools, and as they relinquished faculty positions in the women's colleges to growing numbers of young men, they understandably grew discouraged. In a study of women Ph.D.'s done in the late 1920s by Barnard sociologist Emilie Hutchinson, social scientists reported that there was opportunity for employment, especially part-time employment, in clinical psychology and social work—but not in the universities. One Ph.D. summed up the attitude of many others when she wrote, "I grow more and more doubtful of the wisdom of urging girls to go on to advanced work unless they have an unappeasable hunger for it, because the scales are so bitterly weighted against women at the present." The impact of the Depression reinforced this malaise among women academics. Museums, which had been an important source of funds in anthropology, found their resources sharply curtailed. In the university, women, always marginal employees, were the first to go. Women continued to attend graduate school, but the sense of promise there once had been among them was gone.[3]

Minority Group," *Social Forces* 30 (October 1951): 60–69; Clara Thompson, *On Women* (New York: Mentor, 1964), pp. 111–41. Anne Anastasi, *Differential Psychology* (New York: Macmillan, 1937), pp. 381–450, 2d ed. (1949), pp. 612–88, 3d ed. (1958), pp. 452–504; Eleanor Maccoby, "Effects upon Children of Their Mothers' Outside Employment," in National Manpower Council, *Work in the Lives of Married Women* (New York: Columbia University Press, 1958), pp. 150–72; Lois Stolz, "Effects of Maternal Employment on Children: Evidence from Research," *Child Development* 31 (December 1960): 749–82; not to mention the important work done outside America by Alva Myrdal, Viola Klein, and Simone de Beauvoir.

2. Graham, "Expansion and Exclusion," pp. 759–73.

3. Emilie Hutchinson, *Woman and the Ph.D.*, p. 203; Fred Eggan, "One Hundred Years of Ethnology and Social Anthropology," p. 137.

The first generation of women scholars had hoped that academics would prove to be an open avenue of opportunity. The second generation knew better, and their discouragement affected work in the social sciences. Without women acting as a vanguard of social change, as they had done in the universities' early years, social scientists no longer saw evidence of women's ability to make dramatic changes in their social roles, and, increasingly, researchers doubted that women could do so. Furthermore, the very success of the university in establishing a place for itself in American society made it a less attractive setting than it had been for dissident thinkers, whether male or female. As long as social scientists fancied themselves social critics, the men and women described here felt at home among them; but that feeling changed once social scientists became consultants to those in power.[4]

While the success of the university served to render women marginal figures, intellectual trends made it more difficult to raise questions about feminine potential. Social scientists of the Progressive generation frequently condemned their predecessors for their tendency to hasty generalization, their formalistic thinking, their idealism, and their moral certitude. They called instead for greater scientific rigor, greater skepticism, and a greater appreciation of the indeterminancy of the human condition. But for all their criticism of formalism, they retained a healthy dose of it in their own work. John Dewey, for instance, managed to keep a lingering attachment to idealism at the same time that he was urging the importance of scientific skepticism and suspicion of all ideals. Few of Dewey's contemporaries, and fewer of his intellectual descendents, could sustain this delicate balancing act. The next generation, tending to do as Dewey said rather than as he did, tried to follow his methodological exhortations instead of his reformist vision. Younger scholars seemed to have less faith in individual creativity and a greater sensitivity to human frailty. They were more sensitive to the limits society set on individual adaptation. They were less sure of the possibility of social reconstruction and less clear about the direction reformers should take. Finally, they were more impressed by how little social scientists knew about society.[5]

Gradually, concern for scientific method overwhelmed reformist ambition. The scholars discussed here were trained broadly in philosophy, history, ethnology, and literature; the next generation deplored the lack of precision in this generalist approach and favored more specialized training. For example, Jessie Taft became a psychiatric social worker only after taking a degree in philosophy and working in a variety of feminist

---

4. Anthony Oberschall, ed., *The Establishment of Empirical Sociology: Studies in Continuity, Discontinuity, and Institutionalization* (New York: Harper and Row, 1972), pp. 240–44.

5. Fred H. Matthews, *Quest for an American Sociology,* pp. 179–93.

reform efforts; psychiatric social workers of the next generation tended to receive more specific training for their work and were therefore less accustomed than Taft to seeing women's psychiatric problems within a broad social context. The tendency to specialize also further segregated women into "women's" fields, thus undermining the possibilities for iconoclasm inherent in the situation of men and women working together in new fields. Women became social workers; men became sociologists. Women specialized in practice; men specialized in theory.[6]

Hand in hand with specialization went a trend toward greater quantification. Especially in sociology, younger researchers reacted against George Herbert Mead's impressionistic approach to social problems, although they were faintly aware of what was being lost in abandoning Mead's approach and often lamented that "it is a shame that no one has made George Herbert Mead (or Cooley or Thomas, etc.) researchable." The desire to quantify tended to narrow the topics studied to those susceptible to statistical analysis; it also led to further sexual segregation. In 1900, Helen Thompson was as well equipped to study the mental traits of men and women as anyone else: she could study all of her subjects personally; she had mastered all of the relevant techniques; her research required no special financial outlay; and her work became the instant authoritative source in the area, for there was no other study that could compete with it. The research of the next generation, however, differed from hers in a number of important respects. It covered thousands of subjects rather than a few dozen, and therefore required teams of workers and considerable financial support. Such research was typified by Lewis Terman's 1936 study of *Sex and Personality*, carried out with the help of a large grant from the National Research Council and the efforts of a large team of psychologists. As soon as research teams took over, women found themselves playing subordinate roles within them; for, as all of the women discussed here found, it was hard to win foundation support for themselves.[7]

Political and economic events intensified this trend away from the Progressive era's concern with the possibility for change in the concepts of women's nature and social role. As the Depression, labor conflicts, and the rise of European fascism came to dominate national and international concerns in the 1930s, the issue of women's potential seemed at best irrelevant and at worst subversive of social order. In the field of sociology, concern with social class and stratification supplanted interest in the creative possibilities inherent in sexual conflict and in personal adaptation

6. Margaret Rossiter, " 'Women's Work' in Science," pp. 381– 98.
7. Don Martindale, *The Nature and Types of Sociological Theory,* p. 442. Rossiter, " 'Women's Work' in Science," pp. 381– 98.

to new social problems. Progressive era theorists had discussed the social basis of individual behavior, but they had always believed that the individual is a creative agent in social activity. By the 1930s, sociologists tended to regard the social system as primary and the individual within it as distinctly secondary to the functioning of that system. Functionalism lost the dynamic element that Progressive theorists had thought essential to it and seemed at times to be returning to the organicism of the late nineteenth century against which the Progressives had revolted. The same tendency can be seen in anthropology, in which A. L. Radcliffe-Brown and Bronislaw Malinowski relied on organic analogies in discussing cultures and sex roles within them, prompting Ruth Benedict to complain that until anthropologists could abandon "the superstition that [culture] is an organism functionally interrelated, we shall be unable to see our cultural life objectively, or to control its manifestations."[8]

World War II even further undermined the work of the first generation of social scientists. The rise of totalitarianism generated widespread pessimism about human nature. Suddenly, Dewey's faith in the perfectibility of humanity gave way to a belief in man's natural aggressiveness. And with the return of the awareness of aggression in man came a new enthusiasm for woman's nurturant qualities as a protection against his aggressive excesses. The massive work that had been done in endocrinology and ethnology since the 1920s was a fertile new source of evidence for this old-fashioned view. In the twenties and thirties, references to work in these fields were almost always accompanied by the qualification that the results were as yet inconclusive. The memories of the eugenic craze of the World War I era were still too fresh to encourage much in the way of genetic reductionism. By the end of World War II that memory had faded. Ethnologists and endocrinologists showed an enthusiasm for social pronouncements that had been out of fashion among them for two decades, and social scientists showed a new interest in the biological sciences. The immigration of European psychoanalysts in the late 1930s and early 1940s contributed to this trend back to nature, and psychiatry, which in America had shown the heavy influence of the environmentalist social sciences throughout the twenties and into the thirties, began to

8. Ruth Benedict, "The Concept of the Guardian Spirit in America," p. 85. For a general discussion of functionalism in these years, see Robert Lowie, *History of Ethnological Theory*, pp. 230–91; Martindale, *Nature and Types of Sociological Theory*, pp. 441–521. The social sciences' continuing fascination with the organic analogy, especially in discussing sex differences, is treated in Donna Haraway, "Animal Sociology and the Natural Economy of the Body Politic, Parts I and II," *Signs* 4 (Autumn 1978): 21–60; and Robert M. Young, "The Human Limits of Nature," in Jonathan Benthall, ed., *The Limits of Human Nature* (New York: Dutton, 1974), pp. 235–76.

incorporate the views of orthodox analysis and to push the social sciences, in turn, in a more conservative direction.[9]

Evidence of these intellectual shifts can be seen with particular clarity in the social scientific response to *Sex and Temperament* (1935). Mead enjoyed an enthusiastic popular response to her book, and her work inspired many other social scientists, especially women, to follow in her foosteps; but the mainstream of social scientific research flowed in a more cautious direction. Where Mead claimed to see almost infinite psychological plasticity, most others claimed to see the repetition, in varying guises, of basic feminine and masculine types.

Criticism coalesced around two points. First, reviewers charged Mead with methodological laxity. Lewis Terman complained that she had studied only a small number of people and could offer no objective measurement of the temperament she purported to study. Terman freely granted a "growing tendency" among social scientists "to concede equality or near equality with respect to general intelligence and the majority of special talents," but he insisted that the personality tests he had developed proved that the sexes differ fundamentally in "their instinctive and emotional equipment." He therefore took strong exception to Mead's suggestion that human nature is almost infinitely malleable, and he questioned whether any anthropologist could hope to achieve the accuracy in assessing personality in the field which he believed the experimental psychologist could achieve under carefully controlled testing conditions.[10]

Second, critics found fault with Mead for her sweeping ethnological generalizations about temperament. The most vigorous critique came from within anthropology and started with Reo Fortune. Strained by personal conflicts as well as theoretical battles, the Mead-Fortune marriage failed to survive the fieldwork of New Guinea. In 1939, Fortune attacked Mead publicly in his article, "Arapesh Warfare," which denied Mead's claim that the "entire Arapesh social culture" had "selected a maternal temperament, placid and domestic in its implications, both for men and for women." Arapesh men were, in fact, Fortune claimed, essentially warlike. That they did not display this characteristic was simply a matter of very recent historical accident. German colonizers had prevented them from engaging in war for the last fifteen years. Convinced that the placid behavior of the Arapesh males was not "real," Fortune

9. Haraway, "Animal Sociology," pp. 27– 36; Morton White, *Social Thought in America: The Revolt against Formalism,* 2d ed. (Boston: Beacon, 1957), pp. 247– 80; Marianne Horney-Eckhardt, M.D., "Organizational Schisms in American Psychoanalysis," in Jacques Quen and Eric Carlson, eds., *American Psychoanalysis: Origins and Development,* pp. 141– 67.

10. Lewis M. Terman, *Sex and Personality: Studies in Masculinity and Femininity* (New York: McGraw-Hill, 1936), p. 461.

accused Mead of having imposed her own vision of sexlessness on a culture with clearly differentiated expectations for male and female temperaments. Sociologist Jessie Bernard agreed. "Margaret Mead can be proved wrong by her own data," Bernard observed. "Strangely enough, among the gentle, effeminate Arapesh, 'brawls and clashes between villages do occur, mainly over women' (Mead, p. 23)." Why is it always the Arapesh men, Bernard wondered, "who engage in the wars and the brawls," if the Arapesh do not differentiate the sexes temperamentally?[11]

Methodologically and theoretically, Mead had gone too far for most of her peers, and as anthropologist Marvin Harris has observed, "among anthropologists, a second generation of culture and personality studies have been approached with a more modest and sober if considerably less exciting regard for methodological complexities." Even Mead tended to be more cautious in her later work, employing cameras and tape recorders in her fieldwork, and taking greater account of the social significance of women's childbearing function.[12]

While the success of the university limited the role of women within it, and intellectual trends made it more difficult for women to assert reformist claims, the decline of organized feminism after 1920 added to the problems of those who clung to the intellectual heritage of an earlier day. Women academics often disagreed with feminist activists and even undermined some of the assumptions that lay at the core of suffrage ideology with their research, but the woman's movement of the early twentieth century was important to female scholars in providing a sense of shared oppression and open possibilities. As organized feminism declined, this sense was lost. Women academics came to identify more fully with their professional than with their sexual status, and, as a consequence, women like Mead found it increasingly more difficult to raise doubts about the inevitability of conventional sexual arrangements.

Mead's early work was clearly marred by both methodological and theoretical failures, but the most serious impediment to her making her case for human plasticity was the fact that, with feminism in decline, the burden of proof rested with her. The early twentieth-century woman's movement had given women scholars the perspective to question Victorian conceptions of women's nature and social role and the power to make themselves heard. That perspective and power not only altered thinking

11. Reo Fortune, "Arapesh Warfare," *American Anthropologist* 41 (January 1939): 36 and passim; Gwendolyn Safier, "Jessie Bernard: Sociologist" (Ph.D. diss., University of Kansas, 1972), p. 85; Jessie Bernard, "Observation and Generalization in Cultural Anthropology," *American Journal of Sociology* 50 (January 1945): 288, 284–91.

12. Marvin Harris, *The Rise of Anthropological Theory*, p. 415; Margaret Mead, *Male and Female*, pp. 78–104.

about the inevitability of female inferiority but also contributed in critical ways to the work of scholars who were beginning to question the biological determination of human behavior in general. Significantly, the dissident work of the first generation of social scientists had a greater impact, from the 1930s through the 1950s, on the study of race than on the study of sex—in part because blacks were better organized than women during those years and were therefore better able to keep alive the challenge to conventional wisdom about racial differences. Though dissident work in the field of sex differences never ceased, by the 1930s women like Mead were on the defensive in their efforts to raise doubts about the inevitability of sexual polarity. When feminism began once again to gather political strength in the 1960s, its theorists drew heavily on the social scientific work that had been done to combat racism—work which, ironically, had been nurtured in its infancy by the early dissident work on sex.[13]

As women have begun once again to work in an organized way to change their lives, the burden of proof has gradually shifted to those who insist that women are biologically impeded from making significant changes in sexual relations. Social scientists are more willing than Mead was to concede that the sexual differentiation of social roles may be universal, but most accept her belief that differentiation is fundamentally a product of society. Today there is a greater appreciation of men's and women's potential for change than there was after Mead wrote *Sex and Temperament*.[14]

And yet, the story told here should serve as a cautionary tale. Intellectual revolutions have always been limited by the social settings in which they have taken place, and the social transformation that is sparking the current debate over woman's nature and role has fallen well short of a unified challenge to traditional sexual arrangements. The difficulties faced by the women of this study in realizing greater personal freedom for themselves and articulating the basis for that freedom for others are likely, therefore, to persist for some time.

Foremost among the difficulties women still face is the fact that belief in the inevitability of separate sexual spheres endures and has even intensified in recent years as a consequence of the writings of sociobiologists. Elsie Clews Parsons's observation that "to be declassified is very painful to most persons" is still true today, especially with respect to sexual classification, which continues to provide the most important basis ever created for insuring social stability. The fact that motherhood remains an important occurrence in most women's lives makes declassification in the absence of

13. William Chafe, *Women and Equality: Changing Patterns in American Culture* (New York: Oxford, 1977), pp. 81–113.
14. Michelle Zimbalist Rosaldo, "The Use and Abuse of Anthropology: Reflections on Feminism and Cross-cultural Understanding," *Signs* 5 (Spring 1980): 389–417.

fundamental social reform particularly frightening to women. Since women continue to take private responsibility for most childcare and, more generally, for social welfare, alternative ways of satisfying these social needs must be found if most women are to be both willing and able to claim greater personal freedom.[15]

In important ways, access to professional careers, which enabled the women studied here to claim much greater personal freedom than had previously been possible, has made the creation of social alternatives to traditional female roles more difficult, not easier. Professions were constructed principally by men, with the traditional needs and aspirations of men in mind. All of the women in this study who found careers as social scientists did so at great personal cost. Furthermore, the professions, in emphasizing the primacy of expertise over political conflict as a means of insuring social progress, set strict limits on the personal freedom that could be created for women. Access to the professions, as presently constituted, is not enough for women. Both the professions and society must change if personal fulfillment for women is ever to be realized.

Most early women social scientists thought that, once the arbitrariness of sexual classification was recognized, separate sexual spheres would fade away. Only a few understood that this recognition would have to be accompanied by a social revolution that would make separate spheres unnecessary. Early feminists may have erred in their insistence that women are innately nurturant, supportive, community-minded beings, and yet it is true that women, more often than men, have accepted the responsibility of fostering these values. Only when men are willing to endorse the social vision that has long been the particular concern of women will we finally be able to move, as the scholars studied here long ago hoped we could, beyond separate spheres.

15. Alice S. Rossi, "A Biosocial Perspective on Parenting," *Daedalus* 106 (Spring 1977): 1–31; Parsons, *Social Rule,* p. 55.

Bibliography

The history of the American social sciences and of women's place within them is only beginning to be written. Fortunately, there are a number of valuable archival sources and a growing body of specialized secondary literature with which to work. For this study the Presidents' Papers at the University of Chicago provided important information on the development of the social sciences at a key university. The papers of Marion Talbot and of Mary Roberts Coolidge enabled me to study the relationship of the social sciences to feminism and reform at the turn of the century. The papers of the philanthropist Ethel Sturges Dummer proved a useful aid in continuing that study into the 1920s. Among the many social scientists with whom Dummer corresponded was William Isaac (W. I.) Thomas, whose research she financed in the early 1920s. Thomas's letters to Dummer provide a rare glimpse of his personal life and thoughts during the period after his dismissal from the University of Chicago. The Franz Boas Papers are an essential source for the history of anthropology, as are the James McKeen Cattell Papers and the George Herbert Mead Papers in psychology. Unfortunately, I was unable to find much manuscript material for either Helen Thompson Woolley, Jessie Taft, or Leta Hollingworth. Furthermore, the pre-1918 papers of Elsie Clews Parsons and the Margaret Mead Papers were not available for use at the time of this study.

Scholarly journals provided an important guide to the development of the ideas discussed here, and I made systematic use of the *American Journal of Sociology,* the *American Journal of Psychology,* the *Psychological Review,* the *Psychological Bulletin,* and the *American Anthropologist.* The *Woman's Journal,* the *Journal of Social Science,* and *Popular Science Monthly* were important sources for the late nineteenth century.

Of the secondary works cited in the footnotes, the following stood out as especially valuable in helping me understand the social, intellectual, and institutional background against which the modern view of woman's nature developed. Laurence Veysey's history of the emergence of the modern research university after the Civil War is the best introduction to late nineteenth-century higher education. For the origins of American social science in the American reform tradition, start with Thomas L. Haskell and Mary O. Furner. For an overview of the intellectual revolution that occurred in America at the turn of the century, one should still begin with Morton White, but also read the work of John Higham, Edward A. Purcell, and Hamilton Cravens. To understand the interaction of biological theory and social thought in the late nineteenth century, read Charles Rosenberg, *No Other Gods*; Robert C. Bannister, *Social Darwinism*; John and Robin Haller, *Eugenics*; Stephen Jay Gould, *Ever Since Darwin*; and Robert M. Young, "The Human Limits of Nature." On the origins and development of psychology, Neil Coughlin, *Young John Dewey,* and Dorothy Ross, *G. Stanley Hall,* are excellent introductions to the new psychology and two of its founders. Darnell Rucker gives the best introduction to the early years of social science at Chicago. John C. Burnham's many articles on the development of psychology and psychiatry in America are important guides, as is Nathan Hale's work on Freud's reception in America. The standard history of experimental psychology remains Edwin G. Boring's. Carl Murchison's *History of Psychology in Autobiography* includes personal information on many of psychology's early leaders. On sociology, Don Martindale provides a good guide to the various schools of sociological theory, and Harry Elmer Barnes includes much useful information on the lives of important sociologists. For the history of sociology in America, see the work of William F. Fine, Fred H. Matthews, Henrika Kuklick, and Anthony Oberschall. The best introduction to the development of the anthropological theories discussed here is George W. Stocking, Jr.; but see also Marvin Harris and Robert Lowie.

On women's entry into higher education, Thomas Woody remains the standard work, but much new research is now being done on this subject by Barbara Solomon and others. On feminism's importance in the early years of social science, see William Leach. American women's later role in American social science is discussed by Jessie Bernard, Jonathan Cole, and Margaret Rossiter. The classic treatment of the changing ideology of woman's nature is Viola Klein, *Feminine Character,* a book on which this study attempts to build.

Manuscript Collections

Berkeley. University of California. Bancroft Library. Dane Coolidge Papers.
———. Alfred L. Kroeber Papers.
———. Robert H. Lowie Papers.
Boston. Countway Medical Library. Robert Latou Dickinson Papers.
Cambridge. Radcliffe College. The Arthur and Elizabeth Schlesinger Library on the History of Women in America. Blackwell Family Papers.
———. Ethel Sturges Dummer Papers.
———. Charlotte Perkins Gilman Papers.
Chicago. University of Chicago. Joseph Regenstein Library. William Rainey Harper Papers.
———. George Herbert Mead Papers.
———. Presidents' Papers.
———. Marion Talbot Papers.
Lincoln. University of Nebraska Library. Leta Stetter Hollingworth Papers.
New Haven. Yale University. Sterling Memorial Library. James R. Angell Papers.
———. Robert M. Yerkes Papers.

New York. Barnard College Library. Archives.
New York. Columbia University Library. Franklin Giddings Papers.
New York. Columbia University. Low Library. Columbia University Central Files.
Philadelphia. American Philosophical Society Library. Franz Boas Papers.
————. Elsie Clews Parsons Papers.
Poughkeepsie. Vassar College Library. Ruth Benedict Papers.
Stanford. Stanford University Library. Clelia Duel Mosher Papers.
————. Lewis Terman Papers.
Washington, D.C. Library of Congress. Manuscript Division. James McKeen Cattell Papers.

Other Unpublished Sources

Albrecht, Frank M. "The New Psychology in America, 1880– 1895." Ph.D. dissertation, Johns Hopkins University, 1960.
Anastasi, Anne. "Sex Differences: Historical Perspectives and Theoretical Implications." 1979. American Psychological Association. Manuscript 1999.
Antler, Joyce. "The Educated Woman and Professionalization: The Struggle for a New Feminine Identity, 1890– 1920." Ph.D. dissertation, State University of New York at Stony Brook, 1977.
Boas, Franziska. "The Reminiscences of Franziska Boas." Oral History Collection, Columbia University.
Borell, Merriley Elaine. "Origins of the Hormone Concept: Internal Secretions and Physiological Research, 1889– 1905." Ph.D. dissertation, Yale University, 1976.
Brand, Barbara Elizabeth. "The Influence of Higher Education on Sex-Typing in Three Professions, 1870– 1920: Librarianship, Social Work, and Public Health." Ph.D. dissertation, University of Washington, 1978.
Capelle, Elizabeth. "Elsie Clews Parsons: A New Woman." Master's thesis, Columbia University, 1977.
Church, Robert. "The Development of Social Sciences as Academic Disciplines at Harvard University, 1869 – 1900." 2 vols. Ph.D. dissertation, Harvard University, 1965.
Cowan, Ruth Schwartz. "Sir Francis Galton and the Study of Heredity in the Nineteenth Century." Ph.D. dissertation, Johns Hopkins University, 1969.
Fee, Elizabeth. "Science and the 'Woman Question,' 1860– 1920: A Study of English Scientific Periodicals." Ph.D. dissertation, Princeton University, 1978.
Herman, Debra. "College and After: The Vassar Experiment in Women's Education, 1861– 1924," Ph.D. dissertation, Stanford University, 1979.
Jacob, Kathryn Allamong. "Dr. Clelia Mosher: A Victorian Doctor Battles the 'Scientific' Sexual Myths." Paper delivered at the Organization of American Historians, Detroit, Mich., April 3, 1981.
Kennedy, Elsie Parsons. "The Reminiscences of Mrs. John D. Kennedy, 1966." Oral History Collection, Columbia University.
Kern, Stephen. "Freud and the Emergence of Child Psychology, 1880– 1910." Ph.D. dissertation, Columbia University, 1970.

Leach, Eugene Edward. "Concepts of Human Sociality in American Social Philosophy, 1890– 1915." Ph.D. dissertation, Yale University, 1977.

McCaughey, Robert. "A Statistical Profile of the Barnard College Faculty, 1900– 1974." Mimeographed. New York: Barnard College, Department of History, 1975.

Mead, Margaret. "Intelligence Tests of Italian and American Children." Master's thesis, Columbia University, 1924.

Napoli, Donald S. "The Architects of Adjustment: The Practice and Professionalization of American Psychology, 1920– 1945." Ph.D. dissertation, University of California, Davis, 1975.

O'Donnell, John M. "The Origins of Behaviorism: American Psychology, 1870– 1920." Ph.D. dissertation, University of Pennsylvania, 1979.

Rosenberg, Rosalind. "The Dissent from Darwin, 1890– 1930: The New View of Woman among American Social Scientists." Ph.D. dissertation, Stanford University, 1974.

Safier, Gwendolyn. "Jessie Bernard: Sociologist." Ph.D. dissertation, University of Kansas, 1972.

Sahli, Nancy. "Changing Patterns of Sexuality and Female Interaction in Late Nineteenth-Century America." Paper delivered at the Third Berkshire Conference on Women's History, Bryn Mawr, Pa., June 11, 1976.

Sicherman, Barbara. "The Quest for Mental Health in America, 1880– 1917." Ph.D. dissertation, Columbia University, 1967.

Sokal, Michael Mark. "The Education and Psychological Career of James McKeen Cattell, 1860–1904." Ph.D. dissertation, Case Western Reserve University, 1972.

Tedesco, Marie. "Science and Feminism: Conceptions of Female Intelligence and Their Effect on American Feminism, 1859– 1920." Ph.D. dissertation, Georgia State University, 1978.

Books and Articles

Aberle, Sophie, and Corner, George. *Twenty-five Years of Sex Research: History of the National Research Council Committee for Research in Problems of Sex, 1922 – 1947.* Philadelphia: Saunders, 1953.

Addams, Jane. *Democracy and Social Ethics.* New York: Macmillan Co., 1902.

Alaya, Flavia. "Victorian Science and the 'Genius' of Woman," *Journal of the History of Ideas* 38 (April– June 1977): 261– 80.

Albrecht, Frank M. "A Reappraisal of Faculty Psychology." *Journal of the History of the Behavioral Sciences* 6 (January 1970): 36– 40.

Allen, C. N. "Studies in Sex Differences." *Psychological Bulletin* 24 (April 1927): 294– 304.

Allen, Frederick Lewis. *Only Yesterday: An Informal History of the Nineteen-Twenties.* New York: Harper and Bros., 1931.

Allen, Garland. "Thomas Hunt Morgan and the Problem of Sex Determination, 1903– 1910." *Proceedings of the American Philosophical Society* 110 (February 1966): 48– 57.

————. *Thomas Hunt Morgan: The Man and His Science.* Princeton: Princeton University Press, 1980.

Allen, Grant. "Woman's Place in Nature." *Forum* 7 (May 1889): 258–63.

Allport, Gordon. "The Historical Background of Modern Social Psychology." In Gardner Lindzey, ed., *Handbook of Social Psychology,* 1: 3–56. 2 vols. Cambridge, Mass.: Addison Wesley, 1954.

American Social Science Association. "Constitution, List of Officers, and Members, 1884–5. " *Journal of Social Science* 20 (December 1885): 181–86.

Ames, Van Meter. "George Herbert Mead: An Appreciation." *University of Chicago Magazine* 23 (June 1931): 370–73.

Anastasi, Anne. *Differential Psychology.* New York: Macmillan, 1937; 2d ed., 1949; 3d ed., 1958.

Angell, James B. "Coeducation at Michigan University." *Pennsylvania School Journal* 29 (January 1881): 281.

————. "Coeducation in Relation to Other Types of College Education for Women." *Proceedings of the National Education Association,* 1904, pp. 548–49.

————. "Our Young Women." *Woman's Journal,* August 23, 1873, p. 267.

Angell, James R. "The Influence of Darwin on Psychology." *Psychological Review* 16 (May 1909): 152–69.

————. "James R. Angell." In Carl Murchison, ed., *A History of Psychology in Autobiography,* 3: 1–38. 3 vols. Worcester, Mass.: Clark University Press, 1936.

————. "The Province of Functional Psychology." *Psychological Review* 14 (March 1907): 61–91.

————. "Some Reflections upon the Reaction from Coeducation." *Popular Science Monthly* 62 (November 1902): 5–26.

————, and Thompson, Helen B. "A Study of the Relations between Certain Organic Processes and Consciousness." *Psychological Review* 6 (January 1899): 32–69.

Astin, Helen S. *The Woman Doctorate in America: Origins, Career and Family.* New York: Russell Sage Foundation, 1969.

Bain, Alexander. *Mind and Body: The Theories of Their Relation.* London: King and Co., 1873.

Bakan, David. "Behaviorism and American Urbanization." *Journal of the History of the Behavioral Sciences* 2 (January 1966): 5–28.

Bannister, Robert C. *Social Darwinism: Science and Myth in Anglo-American Social Thought.* Philadelphia: Temple University Press, 1979.

Baritz, Loren. *The Servants of Power: A History of the Use of Social Science in American Industry.* Middletown, Conn.: Wesleyan University Press, 1960.

Barker-Benfield, G. J. *The Horrors of the Half-Known Life: Male Attitudes toward Women and Sexuality in Nineteenth-Century America.* New York: Harper & Row, 1976.

Barnard College. *Barnard College Announcement,* 1909–21.

————. *Dean's Annual Report,* 1896.

Barnes, Harry Elmer, ed. *An Introduction to the History of Sociology.* Chicago: University of Chicago Press, 1948. Abridged ed. Chicago: Phoenix Books, 1966.

————. "The Place of Albion Woodbury Small in Modern Sociology." *American Journal of Sociology* 32 (July 1926): 15–44.

Baumgardner, Steve R. "Critical Studies in the History of Social Psychology." *Personality and Social Psychology Bulletin* 3 (Fall 1977): 681–87.

Beard, George. *Eating and Drinking, A Popular Manual of Food and Diet in Health and Disease.* New York: G. P. Putnam, 1871.

Benedict, Ruth. "The Concept of the Guardian Spirit in America." *Memoirs of the American Anthropological Association* 29 (1923): 1–97.

———. "Continuity and Discontinuity in Cultural Conditioning." *Psychiatry* 1 (May 1938): 161–67.

———. *Patterns of Culture.* Boston: Houghton Mifflin, 1934.

Berg, Barbara. *The Remembered Gate. Origins of American Feminism: The Woman and the City, 1800–1860.* New York: Oxford University Press, 1978.

Bernard, Jessie. *Academic Women.* University Park: Pennsylvania State University Press, 1964.

———. *American Family Behavior.* New York: Harper and Bros., 1942.

———. "Homosociality and Female Depression." *Journal of Social Issues* 32 (1976): 213–35.

———. "My Four Revolutions, An Autobiographical History of the American Sociological Assocation." In Joan Huber, ed. *Changing Women in a Changing Society*, pp. 11–29. Chicago: University of Chicago Press, 1973.

———. "Observation and Generalization in Cultural Anthropology." *American Journal of Sociology* 50 (January 1945): 284–91.

Bernard, Luther Lee. "The Objective Viewpoint in Sociology." *American Journal of Sociology* 25 (November 1919): 298–325.

———. "The Teaching of Sociology in the United States." *American Journal of Sociology* 15 (September 1909): 164–213.

———, and Bernard, Jessie. *Origins of American Sociology: The Social Science Movement in the United States.* New York: Thomas Crowell, 1943.

Bernard, Richard, and Vinovskis, Maris. "The Female School Teacher in Ante-Bellum Massachusetts." *Journal of Social History* 10 (June 1977): 332–45.

Bissell, Dr. Mary T., M.D. "Emotions vs. Health in Women." *Popular Science Monthly* 32 (February 1888): 504–10.

Blackwell, Antoinette Brown. "Sex and Work." *Woman's Journal*, April 18, 1874.

———. *The Sexes throughout Nature.* New York: Putnam, 1875.

Blumer, Herbert. *An Appraisal of Thomas and Znaniecki's "The Polish Peasant in Europe and America."* New York: Social Science Research Council, 1939.

Boas, Franz. *Anthropology and Modern Life.* New York: W. W. Norton, 1928.

———. *Changes in the Bodily Form of Descendents of Immigrants.* U.S., Congress, Senate Document no. 208, 61st Cong., 2d sess. 1910.

———. "Elsie Clews Parsons, Late President of the American Anthropological Association." *Scientific Monthly* 54 (May 1942): 480–82.

———. "Human Faculty as Determined by Race." *Proceedings of the American Association for the Advancement of Science* 43 (1894): 301–27.

———. "Psychological Problems in Anthropology." *American Journal of Psychology* 21 (July 1910): 371–84.

———. Review of Cesare Lombroso, *The Female Offender.* In *Psychological Review* 4 (March 1897): 212–13.

———. "Some Problems of Methodology in the Social Sciences." In Leonard D.

White, ed., *The New Social Science,* pp. 84–98. Chicago: University of Chicago Press, 1930.

Bogardus, Emory. "The Sociology of W. I. Thomas." *Sociology and Social Research* 34 (September–October 1949): 34–48.

Boring, Edwin G. *A History of Experimental Psychology.* 2d ed. New York: Appleton-Century-Crofts, 1950.

Boydston, Jo Ann, ed. *The Early Works of John Dewey, 1882–1898.* 5 vols. Carbondale: Southern Illinois University Press, 1967–72.

Brackett, Anna C. *The Education of American Girls.* New York: n.p., 1874.

Brew, J. O., ed. *One Hundred Years of Anthropology.* Cambridge, Mass.: Harvard University Press, 1968.

Briscoe, Anne, and Pfafflin, Sheila, eds. *Expanding the Role of Women in the Sciences.* Annals of the New York Academy of Sciences, vol. 323. New York: New York Academy of Sciences, 1979.

Bronner, Augusta. "Attitude as It Affects Performance of Tests." *Psychological Review* 23 (July 1916): 303–31.

———. "The Clinical Psychologist." In Catherine Filene, ed., *Careers for Women,* pp. 471–74. Boston: Houghton Mifflin Co., 1920.

Brooks, William K. "The Condition of Women from a Zoological Point of View." *Popular Science Monthly* 15 (June 1879): 145–55, 347–56.

———. "Woman from the Standpoint of a Naturalist." *Forum* 22 (November 1896): 286–96.

Bryan, Alice, and Boring, Edwin. "Women in American Psychology: Factors Affecting Their Professional Careers." *American Psychologist* 2 (January 1947): 3–20.

———. "Women in American Psychology: Prolegomenon." *Psychological Bulletin* 41 (July 1944): 447–56.

———. "Women in American Psychology: Statistics from the OPP Questionnaire." *American Psychologist* 1 (March 1946): 71–79.

Bullough, Vern, and Vought, Martha. "Women, Menstruation, and Nineteenth-Century Medicine." *Bulletin of the History of Medicine* 47 (January–February 1973): 66–82.

Bunkle, Phillida. "Sentimental Womanhood and Domestic Education, 1830–1870." *History of Education Quarterly* 14 (Spring 1974): 13–48.

Burgess, Ernest. "The Influence of Sigmund Freud on Sociology in the United States." *American Journal of Sociology* 45 (November 1939): 356–75.

———. "William I. Thomas as a Teacher." *Sociology and Social Research* 32 (March–April 1948): 760–64.

Burnham, John C. "The Influence of Psychoanalysis upon American Culture." In Jacques M. Quen and Eric Carlson, eds., *American Psychoanalysis: Origins and Development.* New York: Brunner/Mazel, 1978.

———. *Lester Frank Ward in American Thought.* Washington, D.C.: Public Affairs Press, 1956.

———. "The New Psychology: From Narcissism to Social Control." In John Braeman et al., eds., *Change and Continuity in Twentieth-Century America,* pp. 351–98. Columbus: Ohio State University Press, 1968.

————. "On the Origins of Behaviorism." *Journal of the History of the Behavioral Sciences* 4 (April 1968): 143– 51.

————. "The Progressive Era Revolution in American Attitudes toward Sex." *Journal of American History* 59 (March 1973): 885– 908.

Buss, Allan, ed. *Psychology in Social Context.* New York: Irvington Publishers, 1979.

Calkins, Mary W. "Association." *Psychological Review* 1 (September 1894): 476– 83.

————. "Community of Ideas of Men and Women." *Psychological Review* 3 (July 1896): 427– 30.

Calverton, V. F., and Schmalhausen, Samuel, eds. *The New Generation.* New York: Macaulay, 1930.

Campbell, Barbara Kuhn. *The "Liberated" Woman of 1914: Prominent Women of the Progressive Era.* Ann Arbor: UMI Research Press, 1979.

Canby, Henry Seidel. "Sex in Marriage in the Nineties." *Harper's* 169 (June– November 1934): 427– 36.

Castle, Mary, ed. *Henry Northrup Castle: Letters.* London: Sands and Co., 1902.

Castle, W. E. "The Beginnings of Mendelism in America." In Leslie Dunn, ed., *Genetics in the Twentieth Century,* pp. 59– 76. New York: Macmillan, 1952.

Cattell, James McKeen, ed. *American Men of Science.* New York: Science Press, 1906.

————, ed. *Leaders in Education: A Biographical Dictionary.* New York: Science Press, 1932.

————. "Mental Tests and Measurements." *Mind* 15 (July 1890): 373– 81.

————. "The School and the Family." *Popular Science Monthly* 74 (January 1909): 84– 95.

————. "A Statistical Study of Eminent Men." *Popular Science Monthly* 62 (February 1903): 359– 77.

————, and Farrand, Livingston. "Physical and Mental Measurements of the Students of Columbia University," *Psychological Review* 3 (November 1896): 618– 48.

Chadwick, F. E. "The Woman Peril in American Education." *Educational Review* 47 (February 1914): 109– 19.

Chafe, William. *The American Woman: Her Changing Social, Economic and Political Role, 1920– 1970.* New York: Oxford, 1972

————. *Women and Equality: Changing Patterns in American Culture.* New York: Oxford, 1977.

Chamberlain, Isabel Cushman, "Contributions toward a Bibliography of Folklore Relating to Women." *Journal of American Folklore* 12 (January– March 1899): 32– 37.

Chodorow, Nancy. *The Reproduction of Mothering: Psychoanalysis and the Sociology of Gender.* Berkeley: University of California Press, 1979.

Christakes, George. *Albion Small.* Boston: Twayne, 1978.

Clarke, Edward. *The Building of a Brain.* Boston: Osgood and Co., 1874.

————. *Sex in Education; Or, A Fair Chance for the Girls.* Boston: Osgood and Co., 1873.

Clews, Henry. *Financial, Economic, and Miscellaneous Speeches and Essays.* New York: Irving, 1910.

Clouston, T. S. "Women from a Medical Point of View." *Popular Science Monthly* 24 (December 1883): 214– 28, 319– 34.

Coben, Stanley. "The Assault on Victorianism in the Twentieth Century." *American Quarterly* 27 (December 1975): 604– 25.

Cole, Jonathan. *Fair Science: Women in the Scientific Community.* New York: Free Press, 1979.

Collier, Virginia. *Marriage and Careers: A Study of One Hundred Women Who Are Wives, Mothers, Homemakers, and Professional Workers.* New York: The Bureau of Vocational Information, 1926.

Columbia University. *Bulletin of Information: Faculties of Political Science, Philosophy and Pure Science.* Announcement 1901– 02.

———. *Bulletin of Information: List of Theses Submitted by Candidates for the Degree of Doctor of Philosophy in Columbia University, 1872 – 1910,* July 10, 1910.

———. *Columbia University Catalogue, 1916– 20.*

———. *Eleventh Annual Report of President Low to the Trustees,* October 1, 1900.

———. *Minutes of the Trustees,* December 7, 1981.

———. Teachers College, *President's Report,* 1898.

Cominos, Peter T. "Innocent Femina Sensualis in Unconscious Conflict." In Martha Vicinus, ed., *Suffer and Be Still: Women in the Victorian Age,* pp. 155– 72. Bloomington: Indiana University Press, 1972.

Conable, Charlotte W. *Women at Cornell: The Myth of Equal Education.* Ithaca N.Y.: University of Cornell Press, 1977.

Conway, Jill. "Stereotypes of Femininity in a Theory of Sexual Evolution." In Martha Vicinus, ed., *Suffer and Be Still: Women in the Victorian Age.* Bloomington: Indiana University Press, 1972.

Cooley, Charles Horton. *Human Nature and the Social Order.* New York: Scribner's, 1902.

———. *Organization: A Study of the Larger Mind.* New York: Scribner's, 1909.

[Coolidge], Mary Roberts Smith. *Almshouse Women: A Study of 228 Women in the City and County Almshouse of San Francisco.* Stanford: Stanford University Press, 1896.

Coolidge, Mary Roberts. *Chinese Immigration.* New York: Holt, 1909.

———. "Clelia Duel Mosher, The Scientific Feminist." In *Pioneer Women in Physical Education,* supplement to the *Research Quarterly of the American Physical Education Association* 12 (October 1941): 633– 45.

[Coolidge], Mary Roberts Smith. "Education for Domestic Life." *Popular Science Monthly* 53 (August 1898): 521– 25.

———. "Statistics of College and Non-College Women." *Publications of the American Statistical Association* 7 (March– June 1900): 1– 26.

Coolidge, Mary Roberts. *Why Women Are So.* New York: Holt, 1912.

Cott, Nancy F. *The Bonds of Womanhood: "Woman's Sphere" in New England, 1780 – 1835.* New Haven: Yale University Press, 1977.

———. "Passionlessness: An Interpretation of Victorian Sexual Ideology, 1790– 1850." *Signs* 4 (Winter 1978): 219– 36.

Coughlan, Neil. *Young John Dewey.* Chicago: University of Chicago Press, 1975.

Cravens, Hamilton. *The Triumph of Evolution: American Scientists and the Heredity-Environment Controversy, 1900 – 1941.* Philadelphia: University of Pennsylvania Press, 1978.

————, and Burnham, John C. "Psychology and Evolutionary Naturalism in American Thought, 1890– 1940." *American Quarterly* 23 (December 1971): 634– 57.

Cremin, Lawrence et al. *A History of Teachers College, Columbia University.* New York: Columbia University Press, 1954.

————. *The Transformation of the School: Progressivism in American Education 1876– 1957.* New York: Knopf, 1961.

Curti, Merle. *Human Nature in American Thought: A History.* Madison: University of Wisconsin Press, 1980.

Darwin, Charles. *The Descent of Man and Selection in Relation to Sex.* 2 vols. London: John Murray, 1871.

————. "Inheritance." *Popular Science Monthly* 19 (September 1881): 663– 65.

————. *On the Origin of Species by Means of Natural Selection; or, The Preservation of Favoured Races in the Struggle for Life.* London: John Murray, 1859.

Davenport, Frederick Morgan, Review of Elsie Clews Parsons, *The Family.* In *Political Science Quarterly* 22 (December 1907): 744– 47.

Davids, Leo. "Franklin Henry Giddings: Overview of a Forgotten Pioneer." *Journal of the History of the Behavioral Sciences* 4 (January 1968): 62– 73.

Davidson, Percy E. "The Social Significance of the Army Intelligence Findings." *Scientific Monthly* 16 (February 1923): 185– 86.

Davis, Allen, *American Heroine: The Legend and Life of Jane Addams.* New York: Oxford, 1973.

————. *Spearheads for Reform: The Social Settlements and the Progressive Movement, 1890– 1914.* New York: Oxford, 1967.

Davis, Katherine Bement. *Factors in the Sex Life of Twenty-two Hundred Women.* New York: Harper and Bros., 1929.

————. "A Study of Prostitutes Committed from New York City to the State Reformatory for Women at Bedford Hills." In George Kneeland, *Commercialized Prostitution in New York City* (1913). Rev. ed. New York: Century, 1917.

————. "Why They Failed to Marry." *Harper's* 156 (March 1928): 460– 69.

Davis, Kingsley. "The Myth of Functional Analysis as a Special Method in Sociology and Anthropology." *American Sociological Review* 24 (December 1959): 757– 72.

Deegan, Mary Jo, and Burger, John S. "George Herbert Mead and Social Reform: His Work and Writings." *Journal of the History of the Behavioral Sciences* 14 (October 1978): 362– 73.

Degler, Carl. *At Odds: Women and the Family in America from the Revolution to the Present.* New York: Oxford, 1980.

————. "What Ought To Be and What Was." *American Historical Review* 79 (December 1974): 1467– 90.

Desmonde, Willam H. "G. H. Mead and Freud: American Social Psychology and Psychoanalysis." *Psychoanalysis* 4– 5 (1957): 31– 50.

Dewey, Jane M., ed. "Biography of John Dewey." In Paul A. Schilpp, ed., *The Philosophy of John Dewey.* Evanston, Ill.: Northwestern University Press, 1939.

Dewey, John. "From Absolutism to Experimentalism." In George P. Adams and William P. Montague, eds., *Contemporary American Philosophy*, 2: 13– 27. 2 vols. New York: Macmillan, 1930.

————. "Health and Sex in Higher Education." *Popular Science Monthly* 28 (March 1886): 606– 14.

————. *Human Nature and Conduct.* New York: Random House, 1957.

————. *The Influence of Darwin on Philosophy.* New York: Henry Holt, 1910

————. "The Interpretation of Savage Mind." *Psychological Review* 9 (May 1902): 217– 30.

————. "The New Psychology." *Andover Review* 2 (1884): 278– 89.

————. "Psychology and Social Practice." *Psychological Review* 7 (March 1900): 105– 24.

————. "The Reflex-Arc Concept in Psychology." *Psychological Review* 3 (July 1896): 357– 70.

————. "The Theory of Emotion." *Psychological Review* 1 (November 1894): 553– 69, and 2 (January 1895): 13– 32.

Dibble, Vernon K. *The Legacy of Albion Small.* Chicago: University of Chicago Press, 1975.

Dickinson, Robert Latou. "Bicycling for Women from the Standpoint of the Gynecologist." *American Journal of Obstetrics* 31 (January 1895): 24– 37.

————, and Beam, Lura. *The Single Woman: A Medical Study in Sex Education.* Baltimore: Williams and Wilkins, 1934.

————. *A Thousand Marriages: A Medical Study of Sex Adjustment.* Baltimore: Williams and Wilkins, 1931.

Diner, Steven J. *A City and Its Universities: Public Policy in Chicago, 1892 – 1919.* Chapel Hill: University of North Carolina Press, 1980.

————. "George Herbert Mead's Ideas on Women and Careers: A Letter to His Daughter-in-Law, 1920." *Signs* 4 (Winter 1978): 407– 09.

Dinnerstein, Dorothy. *The Mermaid and the Minotaur: Sexual Arrangements and Human Social Malaise.* New York: Harper & Row, 1976.

Dorr, Rheta Childe. *A Woman of Fifty.* 2d ed. New York: Funk and Wagnalls, 1924.

————. "Is Woman Biologically Barred from Success?" *New York Times Magazine,* September 19, 1915, p. 119.

[Douglas], Ann Douglas Wood. " 'The Fashionable Diseases': Woman's Complaints and Their Treatment in Nineteenth-Century America." In Mary Hartman and Lois Banner, eds., *Clio's Consciousness Raised: New Perspectives in the History of Women,* pp. 1– 22. New York: Harper & Row, 1974.

Douglas, Ann. *The Feminization of American Culture.* New York: Knopf, 1977.

DuBois, Ellen Carol. *Feminism and Suffrage: The Emergence of an Independent Women's Movement in America, 1848 – 1869.* Ithaca, N.Y.: Cornell University Press, 1978.

Duffey, Eliza Bisbee. *No Sex in Education: Or, An Equal Chance for Both Girls and Boys.* Philadelphia: Stoddart and Co., 1874.

————. *The Relations of the Sexes.* New York: Wood and Holbrook, 1876.

Dunn, L.C. *Genetics in the Twentieth Century.* New York: Macmillan Co., 1951.

Dykhuizen, George. *The Life and Mind of John Dewey.* Carbondale: Southern Illinois Press, 1973.

Eastman, Mary F. "The Education of Women in the Eastern States." In Annie Nathan Meyer, ed., *Woman's Work In America,* pp. 3– 53. New York: Holt, 1891.

Eggan, Fred. "One Hundred Years of Ethnology and Social Anthropology." In

J. O. Brew, ed., *One Hundred Years of Anthropology,* pp. 119– 49. Cambridge, Mass: Harvard University Press, 1968.

Eiseley, Loren. *Darwin's Century: Evolution and the Men Who Discovered It.* 1958. New York: Doubleday, Anchor, 1961.

Elliot, C. W. *Stanford University: The First Twenty-five Years.* Stanford: Stanford University Press, 1937.

Ellis, A. Caswell. "Preliminary Report of Committee W, On Status of Women in College and University Faculties." *Bulletin of the American Association of University Professors.* 7 (October 1921): 21– 32.

Ellis, Havelock. "The Evolution of Modesty." *Psychological Review* 6 (March 1899): 134– 45.

———. *Man and Woman: A Study of Human Secondary Characteristics.* London: Walter Scott, 1895.

———. "Variation in Man and Woman." *Popular Science Monthly* 62 (January 1903): 237– 53.

Emmet, Thomas. *Principles and Practices of Gynaecology.* Philadelphia: Lea, 1879.

Epstein, Cynthia Fuchs. *Woman's Place: Options and Limits in Professional Careers.* Berkeley: University of California Press, 1970.

Erenberg, Lewis A. "Everybody's Doing It: The Pre– World War I Dance Craze, the Castles, and the Modern American Girl." *Feminist Studies* 3 (Fall 1975): 155– 70.

Faris, Ellsworth. "W. I. Thomas (1863– 1947)." *Sociology and Social Research* 34 (March– April 1948): 755– 59.

Faris, Robert. *Chicago Sociology, 1920– 1932.* Heritage of Sociology Series. Chicago: University of Chicago Press, 1967.

Fass, Paula. *The Damned and the Beautiful: American Youth in the 1920s.* New York: Oxford, 1977.

Fee, Elizabeth. "Science and the Woman Problem: Historical Perspectives." In Michael Teitelbaum, ed., *Sex Differences: Social and Biological Perspectives.* New York: Anchor Press, 1976.

———. "The Sexual Politics of Victorian Anthropology." In Mary Hartman and Lois Banner, eds., *Clio's Consciousness Raised: New Perspectives on the History of Women,* pp. 86– 102. New York: Harper & Row, 1974.

Fernberger, Samuel. "The American Psychological Association." *Psychological Review* 50 (January 1943): 33– 60.

Feuer, Lewis. "John Dewey's Reading at College." *Journal of the History of Ideas* 19 (June 1958): 415– 21.

Filene, Catherine, ed. *Careers for Women.* Boston: Houghton Mifflin Co., 1920.

Filene, Peter Gabriel. *Him/Her/Self: Sex Roles in Modern America.* New York: Harcourt Brace Jovanovich, 1974.

Fine, William F. *Progressive Evolutionism and American Sociology, 1890– 1920.* Ann Arbor: UMI Research Press, 1979.

Fleming, Donald. "Attitude: The History of a Concept." *Perspectives in American History* 1 (1967): 287– 365.

Fortune, Reo. "Arapesh Warfare." *American Anthropologist* 41 (January 1939): 22– 41.

Frankfurt, Roberta. *Collegiate Women: Domesticity and Career in Turn-of-the-Century America.* New York: New York University Press, 1977.

Freedman, Estelle. "The New Woman: Changing Views of Women in the 1920s." *Journal of American History* 61 (September 1974): 372– 93.

———. "Separatism as Strategy: Female Institution Building and American Feminism, 1870– 1930." *Feminist Studies* 5 (Fall 1979) 512– 29.

———. *Their Sisters' Keepers: Women's Prison Reform in America 1830– 1930.* Ann Arbor: University of Michigan Press, 1981.

Freeman, Frank. *Mental Tests: Their History, Principles and Applications.* Boston: Houghton Mifflin, 1926.

Friedan, Betty. *The Feminine Mystique.* New York: Norton, Dell, 1963.

Fuhrman, Ellsworth R. *The Sociology of Knowledge in America, 1883– 1915.* Charlottesville: The University Press of Virginia, 1980.

Furner, Mary O. *Advocacy and Objectivity: A Crisis in the Professionalization of American Social Science, 1865– 1905.* Lexington: The University Press of Kentucky, 1975.

Furumoto, Laurel. "Mary Whiton Calkins (1863– 1930): Fourteenth President of the American Psychological Association." *Journal of the History of the Behavioral Sciences* 15 (October 1979): 346– 56.

Galton, Francis. *Hereditary Genius.* London: Macmillan, 1869.

Geddes, Patrick, and Thomson, J. Arthur. *The Evolution of Sex.* London: Scott, 1889.

Geertz, Clifford. *The Interpretation of Cultures.* New York: Basic Books, 1973.

Gesell, Arnold. "Accuracy in Handwriting, As Related to School Intelligence and Sex." *American Journal of Psychology* 17 (July 1906): 294– 305.

Giddings, Franklin Henry. "The Concepts and Methods of Sociology." *American Journal of Sociology* 10 (September 1904): 161– 76.

———. *Democracy and Empire.* New York: Macmillan, 1901.

———. *Principles of Sociology: An Analysis of the Phenomena of Association and of Social Organization.* New York: Macmillan, 1905.

———. "The Relation of Sociology to Other Scientific Studies." *Journal of Social Science* 32 (November 1894): 144– 50.

———. "A Theory of Social Causation." *Publications of the American Economic Association* 5 (1904): 139– 74.

Gillin, John L. "Franklin Henry Giddings." In Howard Odum, ed., *American Masters of Social Science,* pp. 190– 230. New York: Holt, 1927.

Gilman, Charlotte Perkins. "Herland." *Forerunner* 6 (1915): 12– 17, 38– 44, 65– 72, 94– 100, 123– 29, 150– 55, 181– 87, 207– 13, 237– 43, 265– 70, 287– 93, and 219– 325.

———. *The Living of Charlotte Perkins Gilman.* New York: Appleton-Century, 1935.

———. *The Man-Made World; Or, Our Androcentric Culture.* New York: Charlton Co., 1911.

———. "Sex and Race Progress." In V. F. Calverton and S. D. Schmalhausen, eds., *Sex in Civilization,* pp. 109– 26. New York: Macaulay, 1929.

———. *Women and Economics: The Economic Factor between Men and Women as a Factor in Social Evolution.* Edited by Carl Degler. Reprint. New York: Harper & Row, 1966.

Ginger, Ray. *Altgeld's America: The Lincoln Ideal versus Changing Realities.* New York: Funk and Wagnalls, 1958.

Goddard, Henry. "Two Thousand Normal Children Measured by the Binet Measuring Scale of Intelligence." *The Pedagogical Seminary* 18 (June 1911): 232–59.

Goldenweiser, Alexander. "Four Phases of Anthropological Thought: An Outline." In *Factors in Social Evolution.* Publications of the American Sociological Society, vol. 16 (1922), pp. 50–69.

Goldfrank, Esther. *Notes on an Undirected Life: As One Anthropologist Tells It.* New York: Queens College Publications in Anthropology, 1977.

Goldmark, Josephine. *Fatigue and Efficiency: A Study in Industry.* New York: Russell Sage Foundation, 1912.

Goodenough, Florence. "The Consistency of Sex Differences in Mental Traits at Various Ages." *Psychological Review* 34 (November 1927): 440–62.

Goodsell, Willystine. *The Education of Women: Its Social Background and Problems.* New York: Macmillan, 1923.

———. *A History of Marriage and the Family.* New York: Macmillan, 1915.

Gordon, Linda. *Woman's Body, Woman's Right: A Social History of Birth Control in America.* New York: Grossman, 1976.

Gordon, Michael. "From Unfortunate Necessity to a Cult of Mutual Orgasm: Sex in Marital Education Literature, 1830–1940." In James Henslin, ed., *Studies in the Sociology of Sex,* pp. 53–77. New York: Appleton-Century-Crofts, 1971.

———, ed. *The American Family in Social-Historical Perspective.* 2d ed. New York: St. Martin's Press, 1978.

Gould, Meredith. "The New Sociology." *Signs* 5 (Spring 1980): 459–67.

Gould, Stephen Jay. *Ever Since Darwin: Reflections in Natural History.* New York: Norton, 1977.

Grabhill, William H., et al. "A Long View." In Michael Gordon, ed., *The American Family in Social-Historical Perspective,* pp. 267–80. New York: St. Martin's Press, 1973.

Graham, Patricia Albjerg. "Expansion and Exclusion: A History of Women in American Higher Education." *Signs* 3 (Summer 1978): 759–73.

Grand, Sarah. "The New Aspect of the Woman Question." *North American Review* 158 (March 1894): 270–76.

Groves, Ernest. "Freud and Sociology." *Psychoanalytic Review* 3 (July 1916): 241–53.

———. *Social Problems of the Family.* Philadelphia: Lippincott, 1927.

Gruber, Carol. *Mars and Minerva: World War I and the Uses of Higher Learning in America.* Baton Rouge: Louisiana State University Press, 1975.

Hacker, Helen Mayer. "Woman as a Minority Group." *Social Forces* 30 (October 1951): 60–69.

Hadley, Arthur T. "Admission of Women as Graduate Students at Yale." *Educational Review* 3 (May 1892): 486–89.

Hale, Nathan. *Freud and the Americans: The Beginnings of Psychoanalysis in the United States, 1876–1917.* New York: Oxford, 1971.

Hall, G. Stanley. *Adolescence: Its Psychology and Its Relations to Physiology, Anthropology, Sociology, Sex, Crime, Religion, and Education.* 2 vols. New York: Appleton, 1904.

————. "The Awkward Age." *Appleton's Magazine* 12 (August 1908): 248–54.

————. "The Budding Girl." *Appleton's Magazine* 13 (January 1909): 47–54.

————. "Coeducation in the High School." *Proceedings of the National Educational Association,* 1903, pp. 446–60.

————. "Feminization in School and Home." *World's Work* 16 (May 1908): 10237–44.

————. "The Feminist in Science." *New York Independent,* March 22, 1906, pp. 661–62.

Hall, Lucy M. "Higher Education of Women and the Family." *Popular Science Monthly* 30 (March 1887): 614–18.

Haller, John and Haller, Robin. *The Physician and Sexuality in Victorian America.* Urbana: University of Illinois Press, 1974.

Haller, Mark. *Eugenics: Hereditarian Attitudes in American Thought.* New Brunswick, N. J.: Rutgers University Press, 1963.

Hamilton, G. V. *A Research in Marriage.* New York: Boni, 1929.

Haraway, Donna. "Animal Sociology and the Natural Economy of the Body Politic. Parts I and II." *Signs* 4 (Autumn 1978): 21–60.

Harper, Robert. "Tables of American Doctorates in Psychology." *American Journal of Psychology* 62 (October 1949): 579—87.

Harris, Marvin. *The Rise of Anthropological Theory: A History of Theories of Culture.* New York: Crowell, 1968.

Hartman, Mary, and Banner, Lois, eds. *Clio's Consciousness Raised: New Perspectives on the History of Women.* New York: Harper & Row, 1974.

Haskell, Thomas L. *The Emergence of Professional Social Science: The American Social Science Association and the Nineteenth-Century Crisis of Authority.* Urbana: University of Illinois Press, 1977.

Hawkins, Hugh. *Between Harvard and America: The Educational Leadership of Charles W. Eliot.* New York: Oxford, 1972.

————. *Pioneer: A History of The Johns Hopkins University, 1874–1889.* Ithaca, N. Y.: Cornell University Press, 1960.

Hayes, James R., and Petras, John W. "Images of Persons in Early American Sociology. Part III: The Social Group." *Journal of the History of the Behavioral Sciences* 10 (October 1974): 391–96.

Henslin, James., ed. *Studies in the Sociology of Sex.* New York: Appleton-Century-Crofts, 1971.

Herskovits, Melville. *Cultural Anthropology.* New York: Knopf, 1955.

————. *Franz Boas: The Science of Man in the Making.* New York: Scribner's, 1953.

Higginson, Thomas W. *Women and the Alphabet.* Boston: Houghton Mifflin, 1861.

Higham, John. *From Boundlessness to Consolidation: The Transformation of American Culture, 1848–1860.* Ann Arbor, Mich.: William Clements Library, 1969.

————. "The Reorientation of American Culture in the 1890s." In John Higham, *Writing American History: Essays in Modern Scholarship.* Bloomington: Indiana University Press, 1970.

————. *Strangers in the Land: Patterns of American Nativism, 1860–1925.* New Brunswick, N.J.: Rutgers University Press, 1963.

————, and Conkin, Paul K., eds. *New Directions in American Intellectual History.* Baltimore: The Johns Hopkins University Press, 1979.

Hill, Mary. *Charlotte Perkins Gilman: The Making of a Radical Feminist, 1860–1896.* Philadelphia: Temple University Press, 1980.

Hitchcock, Dr. Edward. "Athletic Education." *Journal of Social Science* 20 (June 1885): 27–44.

Hofstadter, Richard. *Social Darwinism in American Thought.* 1944. Reprint. New York: Beacon Press, 1955.

————, and Metzger, Walter. *The Development of Academic Freedom in the United States.* New York: Columbia University Press, 1955.

Hollinger, David A. "Ethnic Diversity, Cosmopolitanism and the Emergence of the American Liberal Intelligence." *American Quarterly* 27 (May 1975): 133–51.

————. "The Problem of Pragmatism in American History." *Journal of American History* 67 (June 1980): 88–107.

————. "T. S. Kuhn's Theory of Science and Its Implications for History." *American Historical Review* 78 (April 1973): 370–93.

Hollingworth, Henry L. "Judgments of Persuasiveness." *Psychological Review* 18 (July 1911): 234–56.

————. *Leta Stetter Hollingworth.* Lincoln: University of Nebraska Press, 1943.

————. *Vocational Psychology.* New York: Appleton, 1916.

Hollingworth, Leta. "Comparison of the Sexes in Mental Traits." *Psychological Bulletin* 25 (December 1918): 427–32.

————. "Differential Action upon the Sexes of Forces Which Tend to Segregate the Feebleminded." *Journal of Abnormal Psychology and Social Psychology* 17 (April–June 1922): 35–57.

————. "The Frequency of Amentia as Related to Sex." *Medical Record,* October 25, 1914, pp. 1–14.

————. *Functional Periodicity: An Experimental Study of the Mental and Motor Abilities of Women during Menstruation.* New York: Teachers College, 1914.

————. "The New Woman in the Making." *Current History* 27 (October 1927): 15–20.

————. *The Psychology of the Adolescent.* New York: Appleton, 1928.

————. "Sex Differences in Mental Traits." *Psychological Bulletin* 13 (October 1916): 377–85.

————. "Science and Feminism." *Scientific Monthly,* September 1916, pp. 277–84.

————. "Social Devices for Impelling Women to Bear and Rear Children." *American Journal of Sociology* 22 (July 1916): 19–29.

————. "Variability as Related to Sex Differences in Achievement." *American Journal of Sociology* 19 (January 1914): 510–30.

————. "The Vocational Aptitudes of Women." In Henry L. Hollingworth, *Vocational Psychology,* pp. 222–43. New York: Appleton, 1916.

————, and Montague, Helen. "The Comparative Variability of the Sexes at Birth." *American Journal of Sociology* 20 (November 1914): 335–70.

————, and Schlapp, Max. "An Economic and Social Study of Feeble-minded Women." *Medical Record,* June 6, 1914, pp. 1–15.

Horney, Karen. "The Flight from Womanhood: The Masculinity-Complex in

Women as Viewed by Men and Women" (1926). Reprinted in Jean Strouse, ed., *Women and Analysis: Dialogues on Psychoanalytic Views of Femininity,* pp. 199– 215. New York: Dell, 1974.

Horney-Eckhardt, Marianne. "Organizational Schisms in American Psychoanalysis." In Jacques Quen and Eric Carlson, eds., *American Psychoanalysis: Origins and Development,* pp. 141– 67. New York: Brunner/Mazel, 1978.

Houghton, Walter. *The Victorian Frame of Mind.* New Haven: Yale University Press, 1957.

Howard, George E. "Divorce and Public Welfare." *McClure's Magazine* 34 (December 1909): 232– 42.

———. *A History of Matrimonial Institutions: Chiefly in England and the United States, with an Introductory Analysis of the Literature and the Theories of Primitive Marriage and the Family.* 3 vols. Chicago: University of Chicago Press, 1904.

Howe, Julia Ward, ed. *Sex and Education: A Reply to Dr. Clarke's "Sex in Education."* Cambridge, Mass.: Roberts Bros., 1874.

Howes, Annie. *Health Statistics of Women College Graduates: Report of a Special Committee of the Association of Collegiate Alumnae.* Boston: Massachusetts Bureau of Statistics of Labor, 1885.

Hoxie, R. Gordon, et al. *A History of the Faculty of Political Science: Columbia University.* New York: Columbia University Press, 1957.

Huber, Joan. "Sociology." *Signs* 1 (Spring 1976): 685– 97.

Hughes, Helen MacGill. "Maid of All Work or Departmental Sister-in-Law? The Faculty Wife Employed on Campus." In Joan Huber, ed., *Changing Women in a Changing Society,* pp. 5– 10. Chicago: University of Chicago Press, 1973.

Hume, David. *An Inquiry concerning Human Understanding.* 1748. Reprint. New York: Library of Liberal Arts, 1955.

Hummer, Patricia. *The Decade of Elusive Promise: Professional Women in the United States, 1920 – 1930.* Ann Arbor: UMI Research Press, 1979.

Hutchinson, Emilie. *Woman and the Ph.D.: Facts from the Experiences of 1,025 Women Who Have Taken the Degree of Doctor of Philosophy since 1877.* Greensboro: North Carolina College for Women, 1929.

Institute of Educational Research, Division of Psychology, Teachers College, Columbia University. "Sex Differences in Status and Gain in Intelligence Scores from Thirteen to Eighteen." *Pedagogical Seminary and Journal of Genetic Psychology* 33 (1926): 167– 81.

Jackson, John Huglings. "The Evolution and Dissolution of the Nervous System." *Popular Science Monthly* 25 (June 1884): 171– 80.

Jacobi, Mary Putnam. *The Question of Rest during Menstruation.* New York: Putnam, 1876.

———. "Women in Medicine." In Annie Nathan Meyer, ed., *Woman's Work in America,* pp. 139– 205. New York: Holt, 1891.

James, Edward T., ed. *Notable American Women, 1607 – 1950.* 3 vols. Cambridge, Mass.: Harvard University Press, 1971.

James, William. "The Chicago School." *Psychological Bulletin* 1 (January 1904): 1– 5.

———. "The Powers of Man." *American Magazine* 65 (November 1907): 56– 65.

———. *The Principles of Psychology.* 2 vols. New York: Holt, 1890.

Jastrow, Joseph. "Community and Association of Ideas: A Statistical Study." *Psychological Review* 1 (March 1894): 152– 58.

———. "Community of Ideas of Men and Women." *Psychological Review* 3 (January 1896): 68– 71.

———. "Community of Ideas of Men and Women." *Psychological Review* 3 (September 1896): 548– 50.

Jensen, Richard. "Family, Career, and Reform: Women Leaders of the Progressive Era." In Michael Gordon, ed., *The American Family in Social-Historical Perspective,* pp. 374– 96. New York: St. Martin's Press, 1973.

Johnson, Allen, ed. *Dictionary of American Biography.* 20 vols. New York: Scribner's, 1928.

Joncich, Geraldine. *The Sane Positivist: A Biography of Edward L. Thorndike.* Middletown, Conn.: Wesleyan University Press, 1968.

Jones, Edward. "The Army Tests and Oberlin College Freshmen." *School and Society* 11 (March 1920): 389– 90.

Jones, Robert. "Freud and American Sociology, 1909– 1949." *Journal of the History of the Behavioral Sciences* 10 (January 1974): 21– 39.

Kellor, Frances. "A Psychological and Environmental Study of Women Criminals." *American Journal of Sociology* 5 (July 1899– May 1900): 527– 43, 671– 82.

Kelly, Howard A. *A Cyclopedia of American Medical Biography: Comprising the Lives of Eminent Deceased Physicians and Surgeons from 1610 – 1910.* 2 vols. Philadelphia: Saunders, 1912.

———, and Burrage, Walter L., eds. *Dictionary of American Medical Biography.* Boston: Milford House, 1928.

Kendall, Elaine. *Peculiar Institutions: An Informal History of the Seven Sister Colleges.* New York: Putnam, 1975.

Kennedy, David. *Birth Control in America: The Career of Margaret Sanger.* New Haven: Yale University Press, 1970.

Kett, Joseph. *The Formation of the American Medical Profession: The Role of Institutions, 1780 – 1860.* New Haven: Yale University Press, 1968.

Kevles, Daniel J. "Testing the Army's Intelligence: Psychologists and the Military in World War I. " *Journal of American History* 55 (December 1968): 565– 81.

Kinsey, Alfred et al. *Sexual Behavior in the Human Female.* Philadelphia: Saunders, 1953.

Klein, Viola. *The Feminine Character: History of an Ideology,* London: Routledge and Kegan Paul, 1946.

Kohn, Melvin, and Schoaler, Carmi. "Occupational Experience and Psychological Functioning: An Assessment of Reciprocal Effects." *American Sociological Review* 38 (February 1973): 97– 118.

Komarovsky, Mirra. "Cultural Contradictions and Sex Roles." *American Journal of Sociology* 52 (November 1946): 184– 89.

———. "Functional Analysis of Sex Roles." *American Sociological Review* 15 (August 1950): 508– 16.

———. "Presidential Address: Some Problems in Role Analysis." *American Sociological Review* 38 (December 1973): 649– 62.

————. *Women in the Modern World: Their Education and Their Dilemmas*. Boston: Little, Brown, 1953.

Kraditor, Aileen. *The Ideas of the Woman Suffrage Movement, 1890–1920*. New York: Columbia University Press, 1965.

Krantz, David, and Allen, David. "The Rise and Fall of McDougall's Instinct Doctrine." *Journal of the History to the Behavioral Sciences* 3 (October 1967): 326–38.

Kroeber, A. L. "Elsie Clews Parsons." *American Anthropologist* 45 (April–June 1943): 252–55.

Kuhn, Thomas. *The Stucture of Scientific Revolutions*. 2d ed. enlarged. Chicago: University of Chicago Press, 1970.

Kuklick, Bruce. "Harry Stack Sullivan and American Intellectual Life." *Contemporary Psychoanalysis* 16 (July 1980): 307–19.

————. *The Rise of American Philosophy: Cambridge Massachusetts, 1860–1930*. New Haven: Yale University Press, 1977.

Kuklick, Henrika. "Boundary Maintenance in American Sociology: Limitations to Academic 'Professionalization.' " *Journal of the History of the Behavioral Sciences* 16 (July 1980): 201–19.

Ladd-Franklin, Christine. "Sophie Germain, An Unknown Mathematician." *Century* 48 (October 1894): 946–49.

Lamphere, Louise. "Anthropology." *Signs* 2 (Spring 1977): 612–27.

Lasch, Christopher. *Haven in a Heartless World: The Family Besieged*. New York: Basic Books, 1977.

————. *The New Radicalism in America, 1889–1963: The New Intellectual as a Social Type*. New York: Knopf, 1965.

Leach, William. *True Love and Perfect Union: The Feminist Reform of Sex and Society*. New York: Basic Books, 1980.

Lee, Alice. "A Study of the Human Skull." *Science* 12 (December 1900): 946–49.

Lincourt, John M., and Hare, Peter H. "Neglected American Philosophers in the History of Symbolic Interactionism." *Journal of the History of the Behavioral Sciences* 9 (October 1973): 333–38.

Lippmann, Walter. *Drift and Mastery*. New York: Kinnerly, 1914.

Lombroso, Cesare. *The Female Offender*. 1895. Reprint. New York: Appleton, 1900.

Lopata, Helene Z. "Review Essay: Sociology." *Signs* 2 (Autumn 1976): 165–76.

Lowie, Robert. *The History of Ethnological Theory*. New York: Farrar and Rinehart, 1937.

————, and Hollingworth, Leta. "Science and Feminism." *Scientific Monthly* 4 (September 1916): 277–84.

Lowry, Richard. "The Reflex Model in Psychology: Origins and Evolution." *Journal of the History of the Behavioral Sciences* 6 (January 1970): 64–69.

Lubove, Roy. *The Professional Altruist: The Emergence of Social Work as a Career, 1880–1930*. Cambridge. Mass.: Harvard University Press, 1965.

————. "The Progressive and the Prostitute." *The Historian* 24 (May 1962): 308–30.

Maccoby, Eleanor. "Effects upon Children of Their Mothers' Outside Employment." In National Manpower Council, *Work in the Lives of Married Women,* pp. 150– 72. New York: Columbia University Press. 1958.

————, and Jacklin, Carol Nagy. *The Psychology of Sex Differences.* Stanford: Stanford University Press, 1974.

McGovern, James R. "The American Woman's Pre– World War I Freedom in Manners and Morals." *Journal of American History* 55 (September 1968): 315– 33.

McGuigan, Dorothy Gies. *A Dangerous Experiment: One Hundred Years of Women at the University of Michigan.* Ann Arbor: University of Michigan Press, 1970.

McNemar, Quinn. *The Revision of the Stanford-Binet Scale: An Analysis of the Standardization Data.* Boston: Houghton Mifflin, 1942.

Malinowski, Bronislaw. "The Group and the Individual in Functional Analysis." *American Journal of Sociology* 44 (May 1939): 938– 64.

Mall, Franklin. "On Several Anatomical Characters of the Human Brain Said to Vary according to Race and Sex, with Especial Reference to the Weight of the Frontal Lobe." *American Journal of Anatomy* 9 (1909): 1– 32.

Maudsley, Henry. "Sex in Mind and in Education." *Popular Science Monthly* 5 (June 1874): 198– 215.

Martindale, Don. *The Nature and Types of Sociological Theory.* Boston: Houghton Mifflin, 1960.

Marvel, Louis. "How Does College Life Affect the Health of Women?" *Education* 3 (May 1883): 501– 12.

Matthews, Fred H. *Quest for an American Sociology: Robert E. Park and the Chicago School.* Montreal: McGill-Queens University Press, 1977.

May, Elaine Tyler. "The Pressure to Provide: Class, Consumerism, and Divorce in Urban America, 1880– 1920." *Journal of Social History* 12 (Winter 1978): 180– 93.

May, Henry. *The End of American Innocence: A Study of the First Years of Our Own Time, 1912– 1917.* 1959. Reprint. New York: Quadrangle, 1964.

Mead, George Herbert. "Cooley's Contribution to American Social Thought." *American Journal of Sociology* 35 (March 1930): 693– 706.

————. *George Herbert Mead on Social Psychology.* Edited by Anselm Strauss. Heritage of Sociology Series. Chicago : University of Chicago Press, 1964.

————. "The Mechanism of Social Consciousness." *Journal of Philosophy* 9 (July 1912): 401– 06.

————. *Mind, Self, and Society: From the Standpoint of a Social Behaviorist.* Edited by Charles W. Morris. Chicago: University of Chicago Press, 1934.

————. *Movements of Thought in the Nineteenth Century.* Edited by Charles W. Morris. Chicago: University of Chicago Press, 1936.

————. *The Philosophy of the Act.* Edited by Charles W. Morris. Chicago: University of Chicago Press, 1938.

————. Review of Jane Addams, *The Newer Ideals of Peace.* In *American Journal of Sociology* 13 (July 1907): 121– 28.

————. "Social Consciousness and the Consciousness of Meaning." *Psychological Bulletin* 7 (December 1910): 397– 405.

———. "Social Psychology as a Counterpart to Physiological Psychology." *Psychological Bulletin* 6 (December 1909): 401– 08.

———. "The Social Self." *Journal of Philosophy* 10 (July 1913): 374– 80.

———. "What Social Objects Must Psychology Presuppose?" *Journal of Philosophy, Psychology and Scientific Methods* 7 (March 1910): 174– 80.

———. "The Working Hypothesis in Social Reform." *American Journal of Sociology* 5 (November 1899): 367– 71.

Mead, Margaret. *Blackberry Winter: My Early Years.* New York: Simon and Schuster, Touchstone, 1972.

———. *Coming of Age in Samoa: A Psychological Study of Primitive Youth for Western Civilization.* New York: Morrow, 1928.

———. "An Ethnologist's Footnote to Totem and Taboo." *Psychoanalytic Review* 17 (July 1930): 297– 304.

———. *Letters from the Field, 1925 – 1975.* New York: Harper & Row, 1977.

———. *Male and Female: A Study of the Sexes in a Changing World.* New York: Morrow, 1949.

———. "Sex and Achievement." *Forum* 94 (November 1935): 301– 03.

———. *Sex and Temperament in Three Primitive Societies.* New York: Morrow, 1935.

———, ed. *Writings of Ruth Benedict: An Anthropologist at Work.* New York: Avon, 1959.

Meigs, Charles D. *Lecture on Some of the Distinctive Characteristics of the Female. Delivered before the Class of the Jefferson Medical College, January 5, 1847.* Philadelphia: Collins, 1847.

Meyer, Annie Nathan, ed. *Women's Work in America.* New York: Holt, 1891.

Miles, Catherine Cox. "Sex in Social Psychology." In Carl Murchison, ed., *Handbook of Social Psychology,* pp. 683– 797. Worcester, Mass.: Clark University Press, 1935.

Miller, David L. *George Herbert Mead: Self, Language, and the World.* Austin: University of Texas Press, 1973.

Mitchell, S. Weir. *Lectures on Diseases of the Nervous System.* London: Churchill, 1881.

Morantz, Regina Markell. "The Lady and Her Physician." In Mary Hartman and Lois Banner, eds., *Clio's Consciousness Raised: New Perspectives on the History of Women,* pp. 38– 53. New York: Harper & Row, 1974.

———. "The Scientist as Sex Crusader: Alfred Kinsey and American Culture." *American Quarterly* 29 (Winter 1977): 519– 46.

———, with Zschoche, Sue. "Professionalism, Feminism, and Gender Roles: A Comparative Study of Nineteenth-Century Medical Therapeutics." *Journal of American History* 67 (December 1980): 568– 88.

Morgan, Thomas H. *Heredity and Sex.* New York: Columbia University Press, 1913.

Mosher, Clelia Duel. "Functional Periodicity in Women and Some Modifying Factors." *California Journal of Medicine,* January– February, 1911, pp. 1– 21.

———. "Some of the Causal Factors in the Increased Height of College Women." *Journal of the American Medical Association* 81 (August 1923): 528– 35.

Munsterberg, Hugo. "The American Woman." *International Monthly* 3 (June 1901): 607– 33.

Murchison, Carl, ed. *A History of Psychology in Autobiography*. 3 vols. Worcester, Mass.: Clark University Press, 1936.

Murphy, Gardner, and Kovach, Joseph. *Historical Introduction to Modern Psychology*. 1949. Reprint. New York: Harcourt Brace Jovanovich, 1972.

Murphy, Robert F. *Robert H. Lowie*. Leaders of Modern Anthropology Series. New York: Columbia University Press, 1972.

National Cyclopedia of American Biography, vol. 8. New York: White, 1924.

National Research Council. *A History of the National Research Council, 1919 – 1933*. Washington, D.C.: National Research Council, 1933.

Nevers, Cordelia C. "Wellesley College Psychological Studies, Directed by Mary Whiton Calkins: Dr. Jastrow on Community of Ideas of Men and Women." *Psychological Review* 2 (July 1895): 363 – 67.

Newcomer, Mabel. *A Century of Higher Education for Women*. New York: Harper, 1959.

Noble, David. *America by Design: Science, Technology, and the Rise of Corporate Capitalism*. New York: Knopf, 1977.

Noble, Ellis L., and Arps, George F. "University Students' Intelligence Ratings according to the Army Alpha Test." *School and Society* 11 (March 1920): 233 – 37.

Northcott, Clarence. "The Sociological Theories of Franklin Henry Giddings: Consciousness of Kind, Pluralistic Behavior and Statistical Method." In Henry Barnes, ed., *An Introduction to the History of Sociology*, pp. 180 – 204. Chicago: University of Chicago Press, 1948.

Oates, Mary J., and Williamson, Susan. "Women's Colleges and Women Achievers." *Signs* 3 (Summer 1978): 795 – 806.

Oberschall, Anthony. "The Institutionalization of American Sociology." In Anthony Oberschall, ed., *The Establishment of Empirical Sociology: Studies in Continuity, Discontinuity, and Institutionalization*, pp. 187 – 215. New York: Harper & Row, 1972.

O'Donnell, John M. "The Crisis of Experimentalism in the 1920s: E. G. Boring and His Uses of History." *American Psychologist* 34 (April 1979): 289 – 95.

Odum, Howard, ed. *American Masters of Social Science*. New York: Holt, 1927.

———. *American Sociology: The Story of Sociology in the United States through 1950*. New York: Longmans, Green and Co., 1951.

Ogburn, William. *Social Change: With Respect to Culture and Original Nature*. 1922. Reprint. New York: Viking, 1952.

———. "Social Heritage of the Family." In Margaret Rich, ed., *Family Life Today*, pp. 24 – 39. Boston: Houghton Mifflin, 1928.

Oleson, Alexandra, and Voss, John, eds. *The Organization of Knowledge in Modern America, 1860 – 1920*. Baltimore: The Johns Hopkins University Press, 1979.

Olin, Helen M. *Women of the State University*. New York: Putnam, 1909.

O'Neill, William. *Divorce in the Progressive Era*. New Haven: Yale University Press, 1967.

———. *Everyone Was Brave: A History of Feminism in America*. Chicago: Quadrangle, 1969.

———, ed. *The Woman Movement: Feminism in the United States and England*. Chicago: Quadrangle, 1971.

Ortner, Sherry. "Is Female to Male as Nature Is to Culture?" In Michelle Rosaldo and Louise Lamphere, eds., *Woman, Culture, and Society*, pp. 67– 88. Stanford: Stanford University Press, 1974.

Palmer, Alice Freeman, and Palmer, George Herbert. *An Academic Courtship. Letters of Alice Freeman and George Herbert Palmer, 1886–1887*. Cambridge, Mass.: Harvard University Press, 1940.

Park, Robert E. "Introduction." In Everett V. Stonequist, *The Marginal Man: A Study in Personality and Culture Conflict*, pp. xvii– xviii. New York: Scribner's, 1937.

———. "Human Migration and the Marginal Man." *American Journal of Sociology* 33 (May 1928): 881– 93.

Parlee, Mary Brown. "Psychology and Women." *Signs* 5 (Autumn 1979): 121– 33.

Parsons, Elsie Clews. "The Aim of Productive Efficiency in Education." *Educational Review* 30 (December 1905): 500– 06.

———. "American Society," pts. 1-2. *New Republic* 9 (December 1916): 184– 86, 214– 16.

———. "The Aversion to Anomalies." *Journal of Philosophy, Psychology, and Scientific Methods* 12 (April 1915): 212– 19.

———. "Avoidance." *American Journal of Sociology* 19 (January 1914): 480– 84.

———. "The Ceremonial of Growing Up." *School and Society* 2 (September 1915): 408– 11.

———. "Circumventing Darwin." *Journal of Philosophy, Psychology, and Scientific Methods* 12 (October 1915): 610– 12.

———. "Discomfiture and Evil Spirits." *Psychoanalytic Review* 3 (July 1916): 288– 91.

———. *Educational Legislation and Administration of the Colonial Govenment*. New York: Columbia University Press, 1899.

———. "Ethnology in Education." *New Review* 2 (April 1914): 228– 29.

———. "Facing Race Suicide." *Masses* 6 (June 1915): 15.

———. "The Family." In Harold Stearns, ed., *America Now: An Inquiry into Civilization in the United States*, pp. 404– 10. New York: Scribner's, 1938.

———. *The Family: An Ethnological and Historical Outline*. New York: Putnam, 1906.

———. *Fear and Conventionality*. New York: Putnam 1914.

———. "Feminism and Sex Ethics." *International Journal of Ethics* 26 (July 1916): 462– 65.

———. "Field Work in Teaching Sociology." *Educational Review* 20 (September 1900): 159– 69.

———. "Gregariousness and the Impulse of Classify." *Journal of Philosophy, Psychology, and Scientific Methods* 12 (September 1915): 551– 53.

———. "Higher Education of Women and the Family." *American Journal of Sociology* 14 (May 1909): 758– 63.

———. "Ideal-Less Pacificism." *New Review* 4 (April 1916): 115– 16.

———. "Marriage and Parenthood—A Distinction." *International Journal of Ethics* 25 (July 1915): 514– 17.

———. "Marriage and the Will to Power." *Psychoanalytic Review* 2 (October 1915): 447– 78.

———. *The Old-Fashioned Woman: Primitive Fancies about the Sex*. New York: Putnam 1913.

———. "A Pacifist Patriot." *Dial* 68 (March 1920): 367–70.

———. "Penalizing Marriage and Childbearing." *Independent* 60 (January 1906): 146–47.

———. "Privacy in Love Affairs." *Masses* 6 (July 1915): 12.

———. "A Progressive God." *New Review* 4 (June 1916): 181–82.

———. "The Religious Dedication of Women." *American Journal of Sociology* 11 (March 1906): 610–22.

———. Review of Arthur Calhoun, *A Social History of the American Family from Colonial Times to the Present.* In *Dial* 65 (September 1918): 160.

———. Review of J. A. Todd, *The Primitive Family as an Educational Agency.* In *Science* 39 (May 1914): 655.

———. "The School Child, the School Nurse, and the Local School Board." *Charities* 14 (1905): 1102.

———. "Seniority in the Nursery." *School and Society* 3 (January 1916): 14–17.

———. "Sex and the Elders." *New Review* 3 (May 1915): 8–10.

———. "Sex and Morality and the Taboo of Direct Reference." *Independent* 61 (August 1906): 391–92.

———. *Social Freedom: A Study of the Conflicts between Social Classifications and Personality.* New York: Putnam, 1915.

———. *Social Rule: A Study of the Will to Power.* New York: Putnam, 1916.

———. "Teknonymy." *American Journal of Sociology* 19 (March 1914): 649–50.

———. "The Teleological Delusion." *Journal of Philosophy, Psychology, and Scientific Methods* 14 (August 1917): 463–68.

———. "A Warning to the Middle Aged." *New Review* 3 (June 1915): 62–63.

———. "When Mating and Parenthood are Theoretically Distinguished." *International Journal of Ethics* 26 (January 1916): 207–16.

———. "Wives and Birth Control." *New Republic* 6 (March 1916): 187–88.

[Parsons, Elsie Clews], Main, John. *Religious Chastity: An Ethnological Study.* New York: n.p., 1912.

Parsons, Talcott. "Age and Sex in the Social Structure of the United States." *American Sociological Review* 7 (October 1942): 604–16.

Pastore, Nicholas. *The Nature-Nurture Controversy.* New York: King's Crown Press, 1949.

Patrick, G. T. W. "The Psychology of Woman." *Popular Science Monthly* 47 (June 1895): 209–25.

Pearson, Karl. "Variation In Man and Woman." In his *Chances of Death*, pp. 234–56. London: E. Arnold, 1897.

Peck, M. W., and Wells, F. L. "On the Psycho-Sexuality of College Graduate Men." *Mental Hygiene* 7 (October 1923): 697–714.

Perry, Edward. "Philosophy." In Columbia University, *Annual Reports of the President and Treasurer to the Trustees*, 1906.

Person, Ethel Spector. "Sexuality as the Mainstay of Identity: Psychoanalytic Perspectives." *Signs* 5 (Summer 1980): 605–30.

Petras, John W. "Changes of Emphasis in the Sociology of W. I. Thomas." *Journal of the History of the Behavioral Sciences* 6 (January 1970): 70–79.

———. "John Dewey and the Rise of Interactionism in American Social Theory." *Journal of the History of the Behavioral Sciences* 4 (January 1968): 18–27.

————. "Psychological Antecedents of Sociological Theory in America: William James and James Mark Baldwin." *Journal of the History of the Behavioral Sciences* 4 (April 1968): 132– 42.

Pivar, David. *Purity Crusade: Sexual Morality and Social Control, 1868–1900.* Westport, Conn.: Greenwood Press, 1973.

Potter, David. "American Women and the American Character." In Don E. Fehrenbacher, ed., *History and American Society: Essays of David M. Potter.* New York: Oxford, 1973, pp. 227– 304.

Purcell, Edward A. *The Crisis of Democratic Theory: Scientific Naturalism and the Problem of Value.* Lexington: University of Kentucky Press, 1973.

Raphelson, Alfred. "The Pre-Chicago Association of the Early Functionalists." *Journal of the History of the Behavioral Sciences* 9 (April 1973): 115– 22.

Rapp, Reyna. "Anthropology." *Signs* 4 (Spring 1979): 497– 513.

Redfield, J. W. "Measures of Mental Capacity." *Popular Science Monthly* 5 (May 1874): 72– 76.

Reed, James. *From Private Vice to Public Virtue: The Birth Control Movement and American Society since 1830.* New York: Basic Books, 1978.

Reichard, Gladys F. "Elsie Clews Parsons." *Journal of American Folklore* 56 (January– March 1943): 45– 56.

Repplier, Agnes. "The Repeal of Reticence." *Atlantic Monthly* 103 (March 1914): 293– 304.

Robinson, Paul. *The Modernization of Sex: Havelock Ellis, Alfred Kinsey, William Masters and Virginia Johnson.* New York: Harper & Row, 1976.

Robinson, Virginia, ed. *Jessie Taft: Therapist and Social Worker.* Philadelphia: University of Pennsylvania Press, 1962.

Rosa, F. B. "The Human Body as a Machine." *Popular Science Monthly* 57 (September 1900): 491 – 99.

Rosaldo, Michelle Zimbalist. "The Use and Abuse of Anthropology: Reflections on Feminism and Cross-cultural Understanding." *Signs* 5 (Spring 1980): 389– 417.

————. "Woman, Culture, and Society: A Theoretical Overview." In Michelle Rosaldo and Louise Lamphere, eds., *Woman, Culture, and Society,* pp. 17– 42. Stanford: Stanford University Press, 1974.

Rosaldo, Michelle, and Lamphere, Louise, eds. *Woman, Culture, and Society.* Stanford: Stanford University Press, 1974.

Rosenberg, Charles. *No Other Gods: On Science and American Social Thought.* Baltimore: The Johns Hopkins University Press, 1976.

————. "Sexuality, Class and Role in Nineteenth-Century America." *American Quarterly* 25 (May 1973): 131– 53.

Rosenberg, Rosalind. "In Search of Woman's Nature, 1850– 1920." *Feminist Studies* 3 (Fall 1975): 141– 54.

Ross, Dorothy. "The Development of the Social Sciences." In Alexandra Oleson and John Voss, eds., *The Organization of Knowledge in Modern America, 1860– 1920.* Baltimore: Johns Hopkins University Press, 1979.

————. *G. Stanley Hall: The Psychologist as Prophet.* Chicago: University of Chicago Presss, 1972.

Ross, Edward A. "The Significance of Increasing Divorce." *Century* 78 (May 1909): 149– 52.

Rossi, Alice S. "A Biosocial Perspective on Parenting." *Daedalus* 106 (Spring 1977): 1– 31.

———. "Equality between the Sexes: An Immodest Proposal." *Daedalus* 93 (Spring 1964): 607– 52.

Rossiter, Margaret. "Sexual Segregation in the Sciences: Some Data and a Model." *Signs* 4 (Autumn 1978): 146– 51.

———. *Women Scientists in America.* Baltimore: The Johns Hopkins University Press, forthcoming.

———. "Women Scientists in America before 1920." *American Scientist* 62 (May– June 1974): 312– 23.

———. " 'Women's Work' in Science, 1880– 1910." *ISIS* 71 (September 1980): 381– 98.

Rothman, Sheila. *Woman's Proper Place: A History of Changing Ideals and Practices, 1870 to the Present.* New York: Basic Books, 1978.

Rothstein, William G. *American Physicians in the Nineteenth Century: From Sects to Science.* Baltimore: The Johns Hopkins University Press, 1972.

Rucker, Darnell. *The Chicago Pragmatists.* Minneapolis: University of Minnesota Press, 1969.

Russett, Cynthia. *The Concept of Equilibrium in American Social Thought.* New Haven: Yale University Press, 1966.

Saunders, Louise. "Government of Women Students in Colleges and Universities." *Educational Review* 20 (December 1900): 475– 98.

Schilpp, Paul A., ed. *The Philosophy of John Dewey.* Evanston, Ill.: Northwestern University Press, 1939.

Schmalhausen, Samuel. "Family Life: A Study in Pathology." In V. F. Calverton and Samuel Schmalhausen, eds., *The New Generation,* pp. 275– 303. New York: Macaulay, 1930.

Schwendinger, Herman, and Schwendinger, Julia. *The Sociologists of the Chair: A Radical Analysis of the Formative Years of North American Sociology, 1883 – 1922.* New York: Basic Books, 1974.

Schwendinger, Julia, and Schwendinger, Herman. "Sociology's Founding Fathers: Sexists to a Man." *Journal of Marriage and the Family* 33 (November 1971): 783– 99.

"Sex O'Clock in America." *Current Opinion* 55 (August 1913): 113– 14.

Shade, William G. "A Mental Passion: Female Sexuality in Victorian America." *International Journal of Women's Studies* 1 (January– February 1978): 13– 29.

Sharp, Stella. "Individual Psychology: A Study in Psychological Method." *American Journal of Psychology* 10 (April 1899): 329– 91.

Shields, Stephanie. "Functionalism, Darwinism, and the Psychology of Women: A Study in Social Myth." *American Psychologist* 30 (August 1975): 852– 57.

———. "Ms. Pilgrim's Progress: The Contributions of Leta Stetter Hollingworth to the Psychology of Women." *American Psychologist* 30 (July 1975): 739– 54.

Shorter, Edward. *The Making of the Modern Family.* New York: Basic Books, 1975.

Sklar, Kathryn Kish. *Catherine Beecher. A Study in American Domesticity.* New Haven: Yale University Press, 1973.

Small, Albion. "Fifty Years of Sociology in the United States." *American Journal of Sociology* 21 (May 1916): 721– 864.

———. *The Meaning of Sociology.* Chicago: University of Chicago Press, 1910.

———. Review of Franklin Giddings, *Principles of Sociology.* In the *American Journal of Sociology* 2 (September 1896): 288– 305.

———. "Scholarship and Social Agitation." *American Journal of Sociology* 1 (March 1896): 581– 82.

Smith, Daniel Scott. "The Dating of the American Sexual Revolution: Evidence and Interpretation." In Michael Gordon, ed., *The American Family in Social-Historical Perpsective*, pp. 426– 38. 2d ed. New York: St. Martin's Press, 1978.

———. "Family Limitation, Sexual Control, and Domestic Feminism in Victorian America." In Mary Hartman and Lois Banner, eds., *Clio's Consciousness Raised: New Perspectives on the History of Women*, pp. 119– 36. New York: Harper & Row, 1974.

Smith, Mary Roberts. *See* [Coolidge] Mary Roberts Smith.

Smith, T. V. "The Social Philosophy of George Herbert Mead." *American Journal of Sociology* 37 (November 1931): 368– 85.

Smith-Rosenberg, Carroll. "The Female World of Love and Ritual." *Signs* 1 (Autumn 1975): 1– 29.

———. "Puberty to Menopause: The Cycle of Femininity in Nineteenth-Century America." In Mary Hartman and Lois Banner, eds., *Clio's Consciousness Raised: New Perspectives on the History of Women*, pp. 23– 37. New York: Harper & Row, 1974.

———, and Rosenberg, Charles. "The Female Animal: Medical and Biological Views of Women." In Charles Rosenberg, *No Other Gods: On Science and American Social Thought*, pp. 54– 70. Baltimore: The Johns Hopkins University Press, 1976.

Smuts, Robert. *Women and Work in America.* New York: Columbia University Press, 1959.

Sommer, Barbara. "The Effect of Menstruation on Cognitive and Perceptual-Motor Behavior: A Review." *Psychosomatic Medicine* 35 (November– December 1973): 515– 34.

Spencer, Herbert. *The Study of Sociology.* New York: Appleton, 1874.

Spier, Leslie. "Elsie Clews Parsons." *The American Anthropologist* 45 (April– June 1943): 244– 51.

Stern, Bernhard. "Franz Boas as Scientist and Citizen." In Stern, *Historical Sociology: The Selected Papers of Bernhard J. Stern*, pp. 208– 41. New York: Citadel, 1959.

Stockham, Alice B., M.D. *Tokology: A Book for Every Woman.* Chicago: Alice B. Stockham and Co., 1889.

Stocking, George W., Jr. *Race, Culture, and Evolution: Essays in the History of Anthropology.* New York: Macmillan, Free Press, 1968.

Stolz, Lois. "Effects of Maternal Employment on Children: Evidence from Research." *Child Development* 31 (December 1960): 749– 82.

Stonequist, Everett V. *The Marginal Man: A Study in Personality and Culture Conflict.* New York: Scribner's, 1937.

Storr, Richard J. *Harper's University: The Beginnings.* Chicago: University of Chicago Press, 1966.

Stricker, Frank. "Cookbooks and Law Books: The Hidden History of Career Women in Twentieth-Century America." *Journal of Social History* 10 (Fall 1976): 1–19.

Strouse, Jean, ed. *Women and Analysis: Dialogues on Psychoanalytic Views of Femininity.* New York: Dell, 1974.

Sullivan, Harry Stack. *The Fusion of Psychiatry and the Social Sciences.* 1964. Edited by Helen Swick Perry. New York: W. W. Norton, 1971.

———. *Schizophrenia as a Human Process.* Edited by Helen S. Perry. New York: Norton, 1962.

Swinburne, R. G. "Galton's Law—Formulation and Development." *Annals of Science* 21 (March 1965): 15–31.

Taft, Jessie. "Analysis and Treatment of Behavior Problems in Children." In Catherine Filene, ed., *Careers for Women,* pp. 461–65. Boston: Houghton Mifflin Co., 1920.

———. "Mental Hygiene Problems of Normal Adolescence." *Annals of the American Academy of Political and Social Science* 98 (November 1921): 61–67.

———. "Some Problems in Delinquency—Where Do They Belong?" *Publications of the American Sociological Society* 16 (1922): 186–96.

———. "Supervision of the Feeble-minded in the Community." *Mental Hygiene* 2 (July 1918): 434–42.

———. "The Woman Movement and the Larger Social Situation." *International Journal of Ethics* 25 (April 1915): 328–45.

———. *The Woman's Movement from the Point of View of Social Consciousness.* Chicago: University of Chicago Press, 1916.

Talbot, Emily. "Methodical Education in the Social Sciences." *Journal of Social Science* 21 (September 1886): 13–21.

———. "Social Science Instruction in Colleges, 1886." *Journal of Social Science* 21 (September 1886): 34–49.

Talbot, Marion. "The Challenge of a Retrospect." *University Record* (Chicago) 11 (April 1925): 87–101.

———. "On the Determination of Organic Matter in Air." *Technology Quarterly* (September 1887): 29–34.

———. "Domestic Science in the Colleges." *Table Talk* 10 (September 1895): 289–92.

———. *History of the Association of Collegiate Alumnae.* Chicago: n.p., 1920.

———. *More Than Lore.* Chicago: University of Chicago Press, 1936.

———. "Present Day Problems in the Education of Women." *Educational Review* 14 (October 1897): 248–58.

———. "Sanitation and Sociology." *American Journal of Sociology* 2 (July 1896): 74–81.

———. "The Women of the University." In *President's Report* (Chicago), 1892–1925.

———, and Rosenberry, Lois. *The History of the American Association of University Women.* Boston: Houghton Mifflin Co., 1931.

Tanner, Amy. "The Community of Ideas of Men and Women." *Psychological Review* 3 (September 1896): 548–50.

Tarde, Gabriel, *The Laws of Imitation*. Translated by Elsie Clews Parsons. 1890. 2d ed., New York: Holt, 1903.

Terman, Lewis M. "Lewis M. Terman." In Carl Murchison, ed., *History of Psychology in Autobiography*, 2: 297–331. 3 vols. Worcester, Mass.: Clark University Press, 1936.

———. *Sex and Personality: Studies in Masculinity and Femininity*. New York: McGraw-Hill, 1936.

———. *The Stanford Revision and Extension of the Binet-Simon Scale for Measuring Intelligence*. Baltimore: Warwick and York, 1917.

———. "A Study of Precocity and Prematuration." *American Journal of Psychology* 16 (April 1905): 145–83.

Thomas, M. Carey. "The ACA in Its Relation to Women's Education." *Publications of the Association of Collegiate Alumnae* 1 (December 1898): 40–46.

Thomas, William I. "The Adventitious Character of Women." *American Journal of Sociology* 12 (January 1906): 32–44.

———. "On a Difference in the Metabolism of the Sexes." *American Journal of Sociology* 3 (July 1897): 31–63.

———. "Eugenics: The Science of Breeding Men." *American Magazine* 68 (June 1909): 190–97.

———. "Is the Human Brain Stationary?" *Forum* 36 (October 1904): 305–20.

———. "The Mind of Woman and the Lower Races." *American Journal of Sociology* 12 (January 1907): 435–69.

———. "The Psychology of Modesty and Clothing." *American Journal of Sociology* 5 (September 1899): 246–62.

———. "The Psychology of Race Prejudice." *American Journal of Sociology* 9 (March 1904): 593–611.

———. "The Scope and Method of Folk-Psychology." *American Journal of Sociology* 1 (January 1896): 434–45.

———. *Sex and Society: Studies in the Social Psychology of Sex*. Chicago: University of Chicago Press, 1907.

———. "Sex in Primitive Morality." *American Journal of Sociology* 4 (May 1899): 774–87.

———. "The Sexual Element in Sensibility." *Psychological Review* 11 (January 1904):61–67.

———. *Source Book for Social Origins*. Boston: Richard G. Badger, The Gorham Press, 1909.

———. *The Unadjusted Girl: With Cases and Standpoint for Behavior Analysis*. Criminal Science Monograph no. 4. Boston, 1923. Supplement to the *Journal of the American Institute of Criminal Law and Criminology*. Reprint. New York: Harper & Row, 1967.

———. *W. I. Thomas on Social Organization and Social Personality*. Edited by Morris Janowitz. Heritage of Sociology Series. Chicago: University of Chicago Press, 1966.

———, and Thomas, Dorothy Swaine. *The Child in America: Behavior Problems and Programs*. New York: Knopf, 1928.

———, and Znaniecki, Florian. *The Polish Peasant in Europe and America*. 5 vols. Boston: Richard Badger, 1918–20.

Thompson, Clara. *On Women.* Edited by Maurice Green. New York: Mentor, 1964.

Thompson, Helen Bradford. *See* [Woolley], Helen Bradford Thompson.

Thorndike, Edward L. "Animal Intelligence: An Experimental Study of the Associative Processes in Animals." *Psychological Review,* Monograph Supplement, no. 8 (June 1898).

———. *Educational Psychology.* Vol. 1, *The Original Nature of Man.* New York: Teachers College, 1913.

———. *Educational Psychology.* Vol. 3, *Mental Work and Fatigue, and Individual Differences and Their Causes.* New York: Teachers College, 1914.

———. *Educational Psychology: Briefer Course.* New York: Teachers College, 1914.

———. *Heredity, Correlation, and Sex Differences in School Abilities.* Columbia University Contributions to Philosophy, Psychology and Education, vol. 11, no. 2, 1903.

———. "Mental Fatigue." *Psychological Review* 7, no. 1 (September 1900): 466–82, no. 2 (November 1900): 547–79.

———. "Professor Cattell's Relation to the Study of Individual Differences." In Robert S. Woodworth, ed., *The Psychological Researches of James McKeen Cattell.* Archives of Psychology, no. 13 (April 1914), pp. 92–101.

———. "Sex in Education." *Bookman* 23 (April 1906): 211–14.

——— et al. "The Relation of Accuracy in Sensory Discrimination to General Intelligence." *American Journal of Psychology* 20 (July 1909): 364–69.

Ticknor, Caroline. "The Steel Engraving Lady and the Gibson Girl." *Atlantic Monthly* 88 (July 1901): 105–08.

Tilly, Louise; Scott, Joan; and Cohen, Miriam. "Woman's Work and European Fertility Patterns." *Journal of Interdisciplinary History* 6 (Winter 1976): 447–76.

Toksvig, Signe. "Elsie Clews Parsons." *New Republic* 2 (November 1919): 17–20.

Tolman, Frank. "The Teaching of Sociology in Institutions of Learning in the United States." *American Journal of Sociology* 7 (May 1902): 797–838.

Trall, R. T., M.D. *Sexual Physiology and Hygiene.* New York: Fowler and Wells, 1866.

Trecker, Janice. "Sex, Science, and Education." *American Quarterly* 26 (October 1974): 352–66.

Tufts, James. "On the Psychology of the Family." *Psychological Bulletin* 4 (December 1907): 371–74.

———. "The Senior Colleges," pp. 83–84. *President's Report* (Chicago), 1892–1902.

———, and Thompson, Helen B. *The Individual and His Relation to Society.* Chicago: University of Chicago Press, 1898.

University of Chicago. *General Register of the University of Chicago,* 1892–1902.

———. Joseph Regenstein Library. *One in Spirit.* Chicago: University of Chicago, 1973.

Vaerting, Mathilde, and Vaerting, Mathis. *The Dominant Sex: A Study in the Sociology of Sex Differences.* London: Allen and Unwin, 1923.

Van de Warker, Ely. "The Genesis of Woman." *Popular Science Monthly* 5 (July 1874): 269–81.

Van Kleeck, Mary. "A Census of College Women." *Journal of the Association of Collegiate Alumnae* 11 (May 1918): 557–87.

Veblen, Thorstein. "The Barbarian Status of Women." *American Journal of Sociology* 4 (January 1899): 503–14.

Veysey, Laurence. *The Emergence of the American University.* Chicago: University of Chicago Press, 1965.

Vicinus, Martha, ed. *Suffer and Be Still: Women in the Victorian Age.* Bloomington: Indiana University Press, 1972.

Volkart, Edmund H., ed. *Social Behavior and Personality: Contributions of W. I. Thomas to Theory and Social Research.* New York: Social Science Research Council, 1951.

Wallace, David. "Reflections on the Education of George Herbert Mead." *American Journal of Sociology* 72 (January 1967): 396–408.

Waller, Willard. *The Family: A Dynamic Interpretation.* New York: Holt, Rinehart and Winston, 1938.

Walsh, Mary Roth. *"Doctors Wanted: No Women Need Apply": Sexual Barriers in the Medical Profession, 1835–1975.* New Haven: Yale University Press, 1977.

Ward, Lester. "Genius and Woman's Intuition." *Forum* 9 (June 1890): 401–08.

———. "Individual Telesis." *American Journal of Sociology* 2 (March 1897): 699–717.

———. "Our Better Halves." *Forum* 6 (November 1888): 266–75.

———. "The Past and Future of the Sexes." *New York Independent,* March 8, 1906, pp. 541–45.

———. *Pure Sociology.* New York: Macmillan, 1903.

Wasserstrom, William. *Heiress of All the Ages: Sex and Sentiment in the Genteel Tradition.* Minneapolis: University of Minnesota Press, 1959.

Watson, John B. *Psychological Care of Infant and Child.* New York: W. W. Norton, 1928.

———. "Psychology as the Behaviorist Views It." *Psychological Review* 20 (March 1913): 158–77.

Wattenberg, Ben. *The Statistical History of the United States.* New York: Basic Books, 1970.

Weidensall, Jean. *The Mentality of Criminal Women.* Baltimore: Warwick and York, 1916.

Whipple, Guy. "Sex Differences in Army Scores in the Secondary Schools." *Journal of Educational Research* 15 (April 1927): 269–75.

White, Frances Emily. "Woman's Place in Nature." *Popular Science Monthly* 6 (January 1875): 292–301.

White, Marian Churchill. *A History of Barnard College.* New York: Columbia University Press, 1954.

White, Martha S. "Pedagogical and Social Barriers to Women in Science." *Science* 170 (October 1970): 413–16.

White, Morton. *Social Thought in America: The Revolt against Formalism.* 2d ed. Boston: Beacon, 1957.

Wilson, Edmund B. "The Origin of Sex." *New York Independent,* March 22, 1906, pp. 662–63.

Wilson, Jackson R. *In Quest of Community: Social Philosophy in the United States, 1860–1920.* New York: Oxford, 1968.

Winchester, A. M. *Heredity: An Introduction to Genetics.* 2d ed. New York: Barnes and Noble, 1966.

Wissler, Clark. "The Correlation of Mental and Physical Tests." *Monograph Supplement to the Psychological Review* 3, no. 16 (June 1901): 1–60.

———. "Professor Ward and Ethnology." *New York Independent,* March 22, 1906, pp. 663–65.

Woodworth, Robert. *Contemporary Schools of Psychology.* New York: Ronald Press, 1942.

———. "Psychiatry and Experimental Psychology" (1906). In *Psychological Issues: Selected Papers of Robert S. Woodworth,* pp. 166–76. New York: Columbia University Press, 1939.

Woody, Thomas. *A History of Women's Education in the United States.* 2 vols. New York: Science Press, 1929.

Woolley, Helen Thompson. *An Experimental Study of Children at Work and in School between the Ages of Fourteen and Eighteen Years.* New York: Macmillan, 1926.

[Woolley], Helen Bradford Thompson. *The Mental Traits of Sex: An Experimental Investigation of the Normal Mind in Men and Women.* Chicago: University of Chicago Press, 1903.

Woolley, Helen Thompson. "A New Scale of Mental and Physical Measurements for Adolescents, and Some of Its Uses." *Journal of Educational Psychology* 6 (November 1915): 521–50.

Woolley, Helen T. "The Psychologist." In Catherine Filene, ed., *Careers for Women,* pp. 439–43. Boston: Houghton Mifflin and Co., 1920.

———. "The Psychology of Sex ." *Psychological Bulletin* 11 (October 1914): 353–79.

———. "A Review of Recent Literature on the Psychology of Sex." *Psychological Bulletin* 7 (October 1910): 335–42.

———. "Sensory Affection and Emotion." *Psychological Review* 14 (November 1907): 329–44.

Yerkes, Robert M. *Chimpanzees: A Laboratory Colony.* New Haven: Yale University Press, 1943.

———. "Psychology in Relation to War." *Psychological Review* 25 (March 1918): 85–115.

———, ed. *Psychological Examining in the United States Army.* Memoirs of the National Academy of Sciences, vol. 15. Washington, D. C., 1921.

———; Bridges, James W.; and Hardwick, Rose S. *A Point Scale for Measuring Mental Ability.* Baltimore: Warwick and York, 1915.

Young, Robert M. *Mind, Brain and Adaptation in the Nineteenth Century: Cerebral Localization and Its Biological Context from Gall to Ferrier.* Oxford: Clarendon Press, 1970.

———. "The Human Limits of Nature." In Jonathan Benthall, ed., *The Limits of Human Nature,* pp. 235–76. New York: Dutton, 1974.

Zirkle, Conway. "The Knowledge of Heredity before 1900." In L. C. Dunn, ed., *Genetics in the Twentieth Century.* New York: Macmillan, 1951.

Index

Abbott, Edith, 34, 50

Abbott, Grace, 34

Adaptation, personal, 241–42

Addams, Jane, 33, 34, 43, 53, 65; *Democracy and Social Ethics,* 41

Adolescence, 42; female, 227–28, 229–30, 233

Altruism, 161–62

American Anthropological Association, 218, 219

American Association of University Women, 210. *See also* Association of Collegiate Alumnae

American Journal of Sociology, The, 30, 34, 35, 37, 38

American Museum of Natural History, 232

American Samoa, 229–32, 235

American Social Science Association (ASSA), 19, 20, 25, 36, 151

Anabolism, 40–41, 46, 70

Anastasi, Anne, 238

Angell, James B., 62–63

Angell, James R., 68, 76, 81, 115, 116, 123, 126, 140; and equal opportunity for women, 64; New Psychology, 56, 57–58, 61; and Thompson, "A Study of the Relations between Certain Organic Processes and Consciousness," 66

Angell, Marion Watrous, 64

Anthropology (discipline), 163–64, 165–66, 169, 242; at Columbia University, 177, 213, 215; study of individual in, 223–26

Anthropometry, 9, 13, 94, 102, 118

Arapesh, 233–34, 243–44

Association, theory of, 73–74

Association of Collegiate Alumnae (ACA), 18–27, 34, 65, 81; "Health Statistics of College Women," 22, 45; health survey of women graduates, 19–22, 178. *See also* American Association of University Women

Attitude, 93, 105

Bain, Alexander, 6; *Mind and Body,* 8

Barnard College, 86, 148–49, 154, 166, 232; control of social life at, 190; social sciences at, 213–15

Barnes, Harry Elmer, 121n15, 248

Bateson, Gregory, 232

Beard, Charles, 8

Bedford Hills Reformatory, 34, 117–18, 120, 144–45

Behavior (human), 114, 115, 131, 170, 173; biological determination of, 245; criminal, 118–19, 126–27; instinctive, 91; unconscious, 237

Behaviorism, 80; of George Herbert Mead, 135

Bella Coolas, 164

Bemis, Edward, 50–51

Benedict, Ruth, 223–24, 232, 235n55, 242; *Patterns of Culture,* 226, 234

Bernard, Jessie, 244, 248

Binet, Alfred, 76

Biological determinism, 5–12, 107, 163, 245

Biology, 6, 7, 61; theory of sex differences in, 51, 70, 79, 194

Birth control, 161, 168, 180, 181–83, 199, 205; methods of, 182, 201

Blackwell, Antoinette Brown, 16, 53

Boas, Franz, 105, 125n23, 147, 169, 219, 237; at Barnard and Columbia, 213–14, 215, 232; empiricism in anthropology of,

279